AF413807

When Michael Saltz invited me to appear on the *MacNeil/Lehrer NewsHour* many years ago, I hesitated. I thought: As a writer, I best existed on the page and had no business as a talking head on TV. My face, my voice—all wrong for the screen, I thought. And the attention span required for a televised essay was too short to invite complexity. In the end, we agreed to experiment. He became truly my producer; I played the "talent" in front of the camera. In fact, the man you meet in this book is a man who was full of ideas about America and animated with an optimism about the intelligence of a mass audience. He understood how and why one could communicate to millions of people with a good sentence or an apt image. With pride, I introduce Michael Saltz to you now—my teacher for nearly twenty years.

Richard Rodriguez
Author:
Hunger of Memory: The Education of Richard Rodriguez
Days of Obligation: An Argument with My Mexican Father
Brown: The Last Discovery of America

◆

When a creative person finds their unique art form, something no one has ever done in the same way, it is a cause for wonder and celebration. It does not often happen that someone steps out of the box, especially if that box is television, moreover a television news program. But out stepped Michael Saltz and put his hungry, humane talents to work crafting hundreds of beautiful, layered, questioning essays for the *MacNeil/Lehrer NewsHour*. I know because I was one of his essayists, and he took the words I wrote —be they about a remarkable artist or museum or the death of my beloved dog — and turned them into visual tone poems, small polished gems. He taught me the deep pleasures of creative collaboration as he did the rest of his stable of writers, we usually solitary souls, and made forever friends of us along the way. Now, in his captivating memoir, he is looking back at his life, the winding road that led him out of his childhood among noisy, creative people and into television and the joys — and duress; yes, some of that too — of being true to your talent and finding a place for it to flourish. A moving American story in which, lucky me, I play a small grateful part.

Anne Taylor Fleming
Associate Director of the Sun Valley Writers' Conference
Author:
Marriage: A Duet
As If Love Were Enough

On the *MacNeil/Lehrer NewsHour*, which became the *PBS NewsHour*, Mike Saltz helped to produce what many understandably call the smartest daily news show on television. He produced the essayists, a tight little group of commentators who fortunately included me. When we were out on video shoots, I often thought that his stories about 1950s New York and early television could make a good memoir. I'm just happy that he wrote it. He has learned a lot in his life's journey in and out of media—from the rise of television to the rise of Twitter and beyond. I hope the lessons he learned can help prepare the rest of us for whatever comes next.

Clarence Page
Pulitzer Prize-winning columnist
Editorial board member at the *Chicago Tribune*

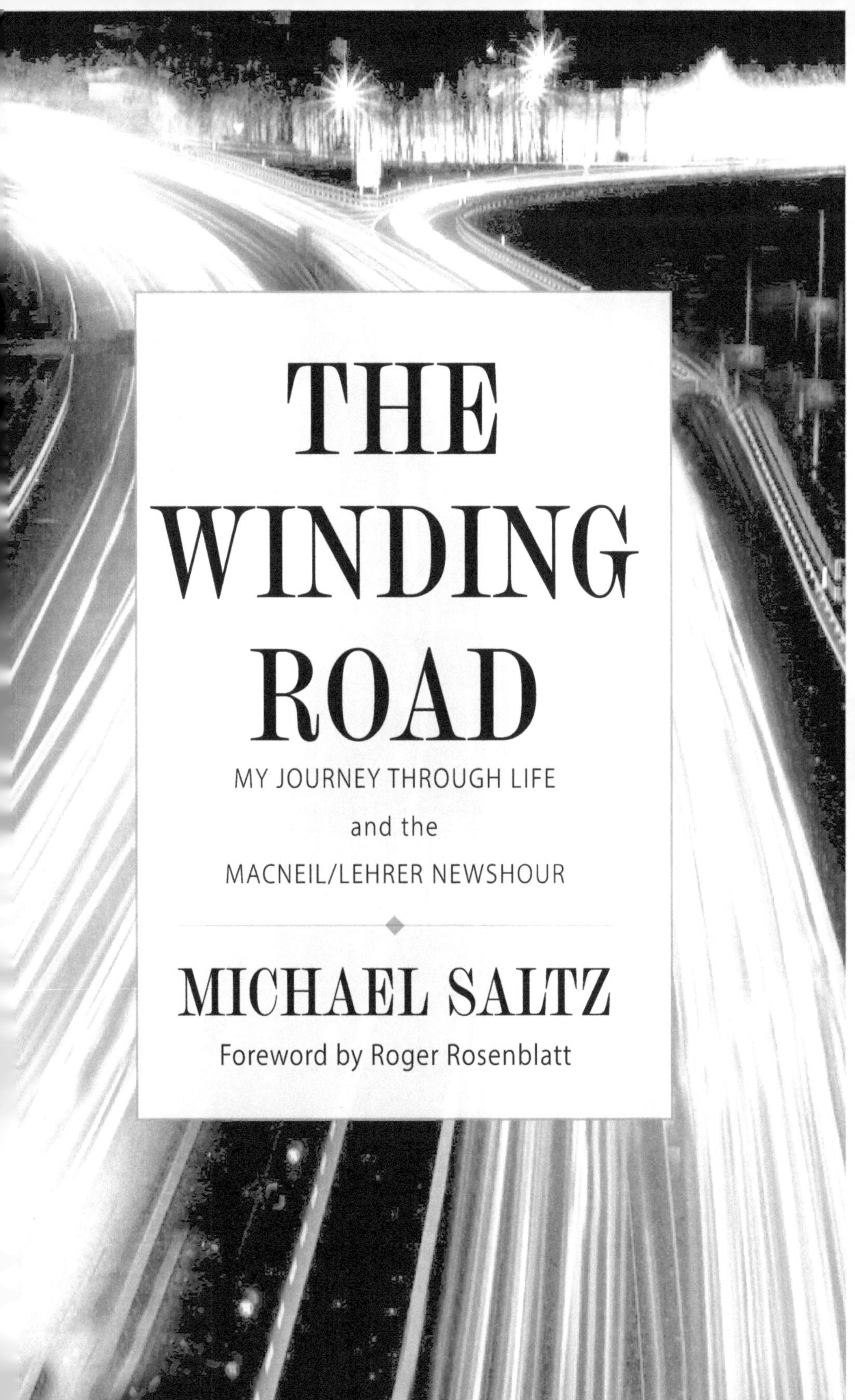

THE WINDING ROAD

MY JOURNEY THROUGH LIFE

and the

MACNEIL/LEHRER NEWSHOUR

MICHAEL SALTZ

Foreword by Roger Rosenblatt

*This book is dedicated to my grandchildren
Karas, Jane, Cleo, and Jax*

CONTENTS

The pure serene of memory in one man,
—A ripple widening from a single stone
Winding around the waters of the world.
The Far Field
—THEODORE ROETHKE

A NOTE

A word about dates, times, and places: I have never consistently made notes, kept diaries, or written journals. There are calendars from most of my years with *MacNeil/Lehrer*, which, though helpful, are both incomplete and not always informative. There are also accounts of some events that I wrote during or shortly after their occurrence. Generally, though, the dates and events I relate are the best guesses that I've been able to make based on whatever files I kept and what I remember about those and surrounding events.

Memory, as you know, is not always precisely accurate as to fact, but I hope it is more so regarding substance. Therefore, the obvious statement is that mistakes, etc., are my own and no one else's. Mostly, though, it is simply to say that this is the past as I remember it. As they say, any resemblance to actual people and events is purely coincidental. Well, *almost*.

FOREWORD

◆

by Roger Rosenblatt

Customarily, the foreword to a book tries to establish some distance between its author and the book's in an attempt to offer an objective appraisal. I shall try to give you an objective appraisal, but I cannot establish the distance. As an essayist on the *MacNeil/ Lehrer NewsHour,* I had the great good luck to work with Michael Saltz for 23 years. As the first of the many essayists to follow, I also had the luck to have a partner in foraging for the right form and content for something brand new to television and to television news. Intellectually and artistically, Mike Saltz was a gift to me and to all the remarkable writers he selected and worked with. As every writer knows, it is nice to be appreciated. But it's rare to be appreciated by a colleague who so shares your general sense of things, can correct your course when it wanders, play to your strengths, spot your weaknesses, and who can make use of your doubts and satisfactions.

What set Mike apart from most people in television was that while he was good at TV, he wasn't enthralled by the medium. He thought much more like an old-fashioned liberal humanist. As a result, the substance of the essays was far more important to him than cuteness or colloquial appeal — the sort of criteria that seems to be driving TV essays today. More important still was intellectual kindness — the feeling that the world ought to be treated well when it deserved to be. In his elegy to Yeats, W.H. Auden wrote of teaching the "free man how to praise." We did many essays in praise of, or in plain wonder at life for the *NewsHour*, and they were at least as powerful as our critical and angry pieces.

A quiet essay I did about speculating as to what Rosa Parks was looking at from her famous, hard-earned seat on the bus gave me unusual pleasure. And it could only have been done on *MacNeil/Lehrer*. (I speculated that Ms. Parks was looking at a white man or woman, whose lives she had monumentally improved.) That was largely because neither Jim Lehrer nor Robin MacNeil were TV newsmen at heart. They were artists at heart, as both proved with their writing. And kind, generous men.

So was Mike. As this beautiful memoir tells us, Mike grew up worrying about history, steeped in poetry, and attached to music. As good as Robin, Jim and Mike were at discerning what was indispensable in world events — and were they ever — each was detached enough from the demands of his job to see life "steadily and whole," as Matthew Arnold advised.

One must remember that the *NewsHour* was an original undertaking, like a work of art. Before it, no news program thought to probe and reach an understanding of what was happening in the world. The *NewsHour* was basically Robin's inspiration, but it never could have been created without his partner Jim and colleagues like Mike, Judy Woodruff, Charlayne Hunter-Gault, Linda Winslow, Les Crystal, and so many other thoughtful, talented people. Jim was a perfect partner for Robin, both men serving as different voices of the same scrupulous mind. Judy, who now heads the program, has enhanced it tremendously by her own gifts and by creating a special prominence for women reporters and analysts of all colors, who shine in and elevate their roles. The *NewsHour*, an establishment today, was a pioneer 40 some years ago. In many ways, it still is. And all its success may be traced to a shared sensibility.

One of the many fascinating things about *The Winding Road* is that it shows how the development of an extraordinary intelligence contributed to the development of an extraordinary place. The book is an elegant memory of both a child growing up and the institution he grew into. As such, it might feel like two separate books, but it does not, which makes it as original an undertaking as the *NewsHour* itself. We see a life growing toward the job it was born for. The accumulation of the family stories, the songs, the politics, and poems that constituted Mike's self-developed education somehow wound up in a TV producer of essays. The mysteries of winding roads — his education included the loves of his life. And the love. Had Mike not met his beautiful, good-hearted, down-to-earth wife Lee, it is doubtful that he would have understood how much of life is worth cherishing.

So, here is the story of a whole person, arrived now in his final years, and asking himself, what was that all about. From his childhood, he was always asking a version of that question. Here he writes of seeking purpose, validation — the sort of quest that usually only occurs to great men. Mike doesn't think of himself as a great man. It's one of his few poor evaluations. He thinks of himself as a worker in the vineyard. But it was he who created the vineyard. No matter how good I or Richard Rodriguez, Phyllis Theroux, Molly Ivins, Jim Fisher, Anne Taylor Fleming, Clarence Page, and the other writers in Mike's ensemble were, it was he who assembled the ensemble. Each one of us had a particular tone and bent of mind. But when anyone stood back and looked at the whole enterprise, as in a praising newspaper article or other laudatory assessment, whether they knew it or not, they were seeing the man who put us together.

I said at the outset that I was lucky to have been in Mike's hands at the *NewsHour*. I'm luckier to have been his friend for 42 years and counting. There are moments in a long friendship that serve to justify and illuminate it. When our daughter Amy, a physician and mother of three small children, died at age 38 in December 2007, Mike went to a lot of trouble to find an essay I did celebrating Amy's graduation from high school so that my wife Ginny and I could see our daughter as a girl again, at a happy time. He did this without any fanfare, or overt suggestion that he knew what seeing the essay again would mean to Ginny and me. He simply handed it to me without ceremony or comment.

By such gestures does one know a person. Now, in *The Winding Road*, you will know him too. It is an enriching experience.

INTRODUCTION

On Monday, November 25th, 1974, I started my first day as a production manager at WNET-TV, Channel 13, the PBS affiliate in New York City. On Tuesday, March 17th, 2009, I retired from *The NewsHour with Jim Lehrer* as a senior producer.

It's a span of time that began just three months after Richard Nixon resigned in disgrace and ended during Barack Obama's first term. (That's seven presidencies, in case you were wondering.) Between those years, the Soviet Union collapsed, and the Cold War ended. There was 9/11. New hot wars came and went (or never left at all). There were oil embargos and general turmoil in the Middle East, as there was in Asia and the whole of Latin America. The European Union was formed. Nuclear weapons proliferated. There were recessions and recoveries at home, along with the ebb and flow of the never-ending struggles for civil rights, women's rights, and gay rights. There was the rise of conservative and the decline of moderate Republicans, alongside the growth of identity politics on the Democratic side. But, above all, there was an America that was constantly and restlessly in search of itself, an America that was and still is a winding road with no end in sight.

Accompanying the twists and turns in our public life were dramatic changes in journalism through which those twists and turns were communicated. There was, in particular, the end of the Fairness Doctrine and Equal Time requirements for TV during the Reagan years. This spurred the rise of cable news networks, the decline of the major network news broadcasts, and the explosive growth of conservative talk radio, which was no longer required to voice other viewpoints. Then, too, the increasingly centralized ownership of newspapers resulted in control by owners living in distant cities. And local TV stations were allowed to buy newspapers within their own communities. Finally, the introduction of the internet and the proliferation of personal computers and other digital instruments like cell phones and tablets gave rise to the growth of digital news outlets (that didn't have the costs of printing and distribution) and social media as a primary source of news and information. With it all came the decline in readership of newspapers and magazines, both in large cities and small communities.

Among the changes in journalism was the coming of *MacNeil/Lehrer* in all its iterations. Beginning with the ½ hour show, it quickly established itself as one of America's most highly regarded and trusted sources of news and information, one that held steady in its idea of what TV journalism should be amidst all the surrounding turmoil.

What follows is my life's journey through the turmoil, a life filled with its own twists and turns, with successes and failures. But, above all, it was a search for purpose, validation, and self-actualization. It was a search for understanding myself and all of the America and world in which we all live. It was a search aided and abetted by the things I experienced while working for both PBS and the *NewsHour*, a show that I began working on before its first iteration, *The Robert MacNeil Report,* even existed.

Because this is my story, my journey — what I did and what I learned along the way, what I brought to *MacNeil/Lehrer,* and what it gave to me — this story neatly divides itself into two parts. Part One is about the beginning of my life — my family, education, interests, and the first fumbling fits and starts — up until 1974. Part Two is what happened next, meaning PBS and the *NewsHour* — what I did and made of it all.

Though the two parts might seem separate, nothing in my professional career could have unfolded as it did without the things that happened to me before it began. Yet, at the same time, nothing that happened in my early life guaranteed whatever success I may have had in my professional life, much less the direction it took. Except, that is, for this: At the end of the road — of all our roads *if* we can only travel far enough — we are who we always were.

PART ONE
THE WINDING ROAD

Chapter 1
THE POND

◆

1940

My desk is surrounded by old-fashioned date books and file folders filled with notes and letters from earlier times; a computer stores digital records from more recent ones.

The wide bay window in front of me overlooks a lawn that sweeps down to a pond stretching long and wide from east to west, the sun's shadows moving in harmony as it traverses the water. Daylight comes, followed by night, followed by day again. In the summer, the pond is covered by lily pads in bloom; the deer walk across the ice in the winter. The seasons pass from winter to spring to summer to fall and winter, endlessly repeating. The leaves on the trees in the surrounding hills turn from green to their fall colors, drop to the ground, and are then reborn. Geese and ducks splash in the water in the spring, only to disappear in the summer only to reappear in the spring.

As time goes by, the date books and files gradually return to the basement as I sit at my desk, looking at the pond and the world it contains. I sit and I think. I ruminate and I remember.

I was born on May 23rd, 1940, in New York City.

The New York Times predicted a day of wind and rain, with temperatures in the mid-60s. Reports indicated the war was not going well for the French and British trying to break out of the closing trap focused on Dunkirk. Meanwhile, the Nazis continued their attack by flanking their opponents to the south. The United States was not yet in the war. The previous day, the Senate unanimously passed an increased budget for the Army. The Nazis were moving German government deposits out of American banks to Sweden. Soviet/British trade talks failed because the Soviets were unwilling to discuss the Nazi/Soviet non-aggression pact. Senator Byrnes argued that Charles Lindbergh's speeches gave aid and comfort to the Nazis. Also, on the previous day, all three NY baseball teams (the Yankees, Dodgers, and Giants) won their respective games.

I was aware of none of this.

But I do remember something of World War II. One thing, really. On a Saturday afternoon in the late fall or early winter of 1944 or 45, my grandfather and I were in his apartment on West 75th Street in Manhattan, the building with a white limestone facade and the crosshatched red brick sidewalk at its entrance. We were in his study listening to the radio news about the war. Thumbtacked up on one wall was a *National Geographic* map of Europe. We put pins in it to mark the positions of the advancing Allied forces following D-Day and the increasingly desperate retreat of the Nazis. Green pins for the Allies; red for the Nazis.

Amidst the sketchy lines etched on a field of gray, some memories stand out like colorful enameled *bas reliefs*. They are as real to me as real can be.

A summer day in 1943: My grandparents live in Ardsley, a suburb of New York, although I don't know if this is a full or part-time residence.

We are in the living room, Grandma and me. The room is dark, shaded from the summer sun, save for the beams of light that pierce the filigreed white lace curtains, dust motes dancing in the light. Grandma sits in a chair, a dark, almost black wooden chair with wide wooden arms, off-white cushions on the seat and back. I am sitting in her lap; the curtains behind us glow. She wears a brown dress spotted with large white polka dots. Her body is thick, her face round with round, steel wire-rimmed spectacles over her nose, her very long, floor-length salt and pepper hair, which I would watch, and sometimes help

her to brush out every morning, wound round and round her head. Her lap is comfortable, and I lean against her ample, soft bosom, her arms around me. There is no place as calm, as serene, in the world. There is no place I'd rather be. There is no place as safe.

Off to our left is a grand piano that she sometimes plays, its keys still white but yellowing, facing us. Across the room, there is a couch and a rattan coffee table; it has an ashtray on it. Next to the couch is a Victrola, a platter spinning at 78 rpm, a Bach fugue's many threads dancing scratchily amidst the dust motes.

"What does this make you think of?" Grandma asks.

"… God knitting."

Where did that answer come from? I know of no reason then or now why I should have said that, thought that, certainly not as a 3-year-old. What did I know of knitting? What did I know of God, think of God, as either a reality or a metaphor? Neither my grandparents nor my parents were religious. God was not a part of our lives, of our conversation except, perhaps, during the annual Seder when it was hard to read the Haggadah without mentioning His name (though my father tried to do exactly that on one hilarious occasion).

That this scene remains such a vibrant memory for over 75 years must mean something, don't you think? "God knitting." It can certainly be used as a metaphor for life, for a life, the many roles we play, the many threads of a life — family, school, love, work, spirit — being gradually woven together into a single tapestry, yet the threads able to be untangled, pulled apart, each visible on its own. In truth, I've often thought of my life that way. But not today. Not for this book. Not while I am looking out at the pond. Not while I'm thinking of Roethke's line. "A ripple widening from a single stone winding around the waters of the world." A winding road indeed.

Besides, what has always struck me as being most important in this scene, what matters as much to me now as it did then, was sitting in Grandma's lap, being held warm, safe, and utterly at peace. There are times in life, in my life, when there was nothing more important.

So, instead of "God knitting," I'm thinking of — dreaming of — the pond, the sun glittering through the fluttering green tree leaves, the sounds of birds softly trilling in the warm, late spring air. The still water, smooth and unruffled as glass, as a mirror. A stone — a tiny pebble, really — drops into the water. The splash is small, but the ripples widen out in circles, ever-widening out over time, as far as the eye can see.

On May 23rd, 1940, I dropped from my mother's womb and emerged into the world.

Chapter 2
THE TIES THAT BIND

◆

1940 — 1945

The world I first emerged into was clearly defined, limited, and filled with family. And ghosts. The present and the past. My mother, father, and younger sister, mainly, but there were others as well, particularly Mom's brother and sister, their children, and her parents, along with the many cousins, aunts, and uncles. Before them, though, invisible but always looming large in the background, were the ghosts — my mother's grandparents, my great grandparents.

There was Eliakum Zunser, the revered patriarch of the Zunser clan, the father of my mother's father, my grandfather, Charles Zunser. Eliakum was born into poverty in Vilna, Lithuania in 1840, a time when it was an integral part of the Russian Empire, so integral that Grandpa always thought of himself as having been born in Russia. Yet, Eliakum became a poet and songwriter despite all odds and expectations. He was a *badchen*, a wedding singer, an entertainer, traveling from town to town, from wedding to wedding, bringing with him his songs about the lives of ordinary people and news of the world beyond the community in which he was performing. Over time, he wrote some 600 songs, most published in some 50 booklets. There was hardly a Jew in Lithuania or northern Russia who hadn't heard of him or wasn't familiar with his poems and songs.

Famous though he was, Eliakum's life was not easy, as was the case for anyone who lived in Russia, particularly for Jews. He married and had seven children. All the children died in one year of cholera, and his wife died the following year. Eventually, still in Russia, he remarried and had five more children, including Grandpa.

Anti-Semitism was rife in Russia (as it was in all of Europe), its intensity rising or falling at the whim of the Tsars. Pogroms were always to be feared, always to be expected. One year, Jews might be permitted to go to universities. Another year, it might be forbidden. Eliakum, like everyone else, lived through these peaks and valleys. Finally, he became a Zionist, thinking it would be best if Jews left Russia and settled in Palestine. Being famous and having become a respected intellectual, he warned his fellow Jews about the dangers of assimilation. He thought that anti-Semitic attitudes would inevitably reassert themselves; Jews shouldn't get too comfortable thinking that they had been accepted into the larger society and that assimilation was genuinely possible. In time, he was sadly proved right when, following the assassination of Alexander II, there were more pogroms, and prohibitions against Jews participating in economic and intellectual life were reinstated. Eliakum, fearing arrest by the Tsarist police, thinking he must do everything to preserve his new family, decided to leave Russia. But, Zionist though he was, he felt he was too old to go to Palestine, that it was a country for the young, and so, in 1889, he emigrated to New York with his family.

Settling in New York's Lower East Side amongst all the other recent immigrants, his life was never easy. His fame may have accompanied him, but his popularity waned, as did his output of songs. He worked as a printer and publisher but was so financially pressed that a benefit was held for him in 1905 to raise money to live. That year, an article in the *New York Times* called him "the father of Yiddish poetry." Eliakum died in 1913.

Sol Liptzin's biography of Eliakum, "Eliakum Zunser: Poet of his People," was published in 1950. My mother thought it was one of the dullest books she'd ever read. I took advantage of her opinion and have never read it. However, I have read his autobiographical memoir, "*A Jewish Bard,*" published by the Zunser Jubilee Committee in 1905. There was nothing dull about that.

As for Grandma's father, my mother's mother's father, my other great grandfather, he was as well known as Eliakum. Nahum Meir Schaikewitz, far better known by his pen name, Shomer, was a giant in the history of Yiddish literature. He was born in 1849 in Nexvizh, within the Minsk Governate, which is now the capital of Belarus, and spent time in Vilna and Bucharest. Throughout his life, he wrote several novels in Hebrew but, more importantly, over 200 novels in Yiddish. Many consider Shomer to be the first Yiddish novelist, more significant in that regard than his critics were ever willing to acknowledge. In addition, he wrote over 30 plays, many produced in Russia but also in New York after he emigrated with his family in 1889, the same year as Eliakum. He died in 1905, the year of Eliakum's Jubilee celebration.

Shomer's books, which dealt with the problems encountered by ordinary Jews in their daily lives, particularly women, were enormously popular. Unfortunately, his very popularity encouraged Sholem Aleichem to severely criticize him. Early in his career, Aleichem, who eventually became one of the most popular and esteemed writers of Yiddish literature, publicly declared that Shomer was unworthy of adulation and his large following — a following that Aleichem apparently thought should be his. Aleichem accused Shomer of merely being a "pulp" writer, a writer of trash, thereby trying to boost his own popularity and standing among the intelligentsia by denigrating Shomer. Despite Shomer's counter-arguments, Aleichem's campaign prevailed, and Shomer virtually disappeared from view for many decades.

Perhaps it is not so unusual for so-called intellectuals to denigrate popular artists. High art versus low art. Classical music versus pop music. These are arguments that have gone on for centuries. For me, those arguments are specious. James Joyce's *Ulysses* and Melville's *Moby Dick* may be wonderful (if you can manage to actually read them to the very end and still find them pleasurable). Still, I don't know that they are intrinsically "better" books than Sinclair Lewis's *Elmer Gantry* or James Lee Burke's *A Morning for Flamingos*. I'm a big fan of Burke with his flawed heroes, and his apocalyptic view of America contrasted with the transcendent and indifferent beauty of the natural world. And could any American novelist in the Trump and post-Trump years be any more pertinent than Lewis? Maybe Lewis wrote the Great American Novel and not Melville, Fitzgerald, or anyone else. These discussions of the distinctions between high and low art (if such distinctions are meaningful) often came up around my parents' dinner table. They even came up once at *MacNeil/Lehrer* when MacNeil wondered if anyone cared enough about Elvis to waste airtime on him.

In the United States, at least, once popular artists like Eliakum and Shomer virtually disappeared from recognition within the Jewish community. Years ago, I looked for their names in a cultural history of Jews in America and couldn't find them. More recently, though, they have been somewhat "rediscovered." I would not argue that either were great artists. But they mattered in at least two ways. First, by helping legitimize Yiddish as a language and not simply a bastardized version of German and Hebrew. Second, they recognized ordinary people's social and economic problems regardless of whether they lived in big cities or small towns. Women, whose concerns tended to be dismissed or ignored by most Jewish writers (all men), intellectuals (all men), and orthodox rabbis (all men), were championed by Shomer. In telling stories about these people's lives, Shomer and Eliakum provided a kind of recognition and validation that more "elevated" writers like Aleichem never achieved or rarely (if ever) attempted. Those concerns, passed on to their children, grandchildren, and beyond, had a lasting impact. Their ghosts, friendly ones, peer over all our shoulders.

Memory is so strange. It can be hard to distinguish between what we remember and what we have been told by others and adopted as our own memories, particularly regarding our early years. It is like a gray canvas, a gray wall, blank with hints of life waiting to be uncovered, waiting for us to paint pictures or unearth shards of bones beneath layers of paint that remind us of something real even if it isn't real at all, as if we've just made it up to fit whatever our need might be.

In April 1945, almost five years old but not quite, I was in Brooklyn Jewish Hospital, a place where I spent too much time during my early years. I had polio.

> **I don't know how I got here. I don't know why I'm here.**
> **I have been quarantined (although I'm unaware of it) in a**
> **narrow room by myself, lying on a small bed, more crib than**

bed, the guard rails pulled up. A nurse is standing next to me. She is pulling hot steaming towels from a steam table of some sort, wrapping them around my body, and then wrapping some kind of plastic or rubber sheeting around the towels.

For a month, I lie, sometimes stand, peering into the darkened corridor beyond, in a quarantined hospital area, hot towels being applied, being taken off, applied again, day after day. The so-called Sister Kenny treatment was named after an Australian nurse who, in 1911, thought up this method of covering the muscles of the newly crippled with hot, damp rags so they wouldn't waste away. Despite initial resistance from doctors (she was only a nurse, after all), the treatment seemed helpful often enough that it spread throughout the world.

Through those long, lonely days, my only companion is Benny, my dark brown teddy bear. No one other than the nurse is allowed in the room, the door open with a burgundy velvet rope barring entrance to all others. Visitors sit in the dim hallway. There is Grandma; there is my mother. I can barely see them, but they are a hovering, almost ghostly presence through the silent days.

When the time comes to leave the hospital, I am told that I can't take Benny with me. He might carry germs with him. I refuse to leave without him. Mom and the nurse huddle together. They go off with him and boil him in water. When Benny returns, he is pale and bedraggled, a dirty gray. But he did return, and we go home.

I never played with Benny again, but he sat across the bedroom from me for many years, his black button eyes looking at me while I slept, always looking after me while I was awake and alone in the empty room during all my illnesses.

Illness, doctors, and hospitals played a significant role in my life until I was ten. For a time, I made almost weekly visits to the doctor. I had what he called a floating spleen that he was constantly trying to locate. Before resorting to surgery, he suggested that I put on weight (I was a skinny kid back then), and so my diet became mashed and baked potatoes with lots of butter, broiled or pan-fried steak, lamb chops, and pork chops, and a bit later, collard greens or kale boiled with fatback, and key lime pie. The diet had the intended effect: I put on weight. The spleen became findable. My eating habits were changed forever, along with my weight. To this day, I'd rather eat a rare rib-eye steak with a baked potato slathered in butter and sour cream than anything else. They were (and still are) more than comfort food; they are lifesaving. Maybe that's the same thing.

I had most of the typical childhood diseases in those pre-vaccine days: measles, German measles, mumps, tonsillitis, chickenpox, and impetigo, among others. In addition, there were a couple of eye operations and a tonsillectomy. Some other illness kept me in bed for two or three weeks.

And then, the final illness of my childhood in the summer of 1950. I was 10. There was a cut, a scrape on my elbow (my right, I think), and after a day at the beach at Jacob Riis Park, splashing in the surf, making castles in the sand, it became infected. The infection would not be controlled, and I was taken to the hospital and given a spinal tap. It is/was the single most physically painful experience of my life. I remember screaming bloody murder, though I do not know whether I screamed out loud. But I remember being wheeled into that room on a gurney, being rolled over onto my stomach or side. I can still remember the hot, intense shaft of light burning on my back, the needle, it being shoved into my back. To this day, I can recall the screams, the screams, over and over and over again.

Then came the subsequent long days, the even longer nights, being awakened every two hours to take more pills. I remember being delirious. I remember staring out the window in the dark children's ward faintly lit only by the shaded light at the nurse's station at the far end of the room, listening to the elevated subway train, the wheels clacketing on the tracks, the brakes screeching as the subway came out of its subterranean tunnel. But above all, the long, long silence that seemed endless and forever. Finally, after a couple of weeks or so, I was sent home. Blood poisoning was the diagnosis. I was lucky, I'm told, that they hadn't amputated my arm though they considered it.

And then my six-year run of illness, from polio to blood poisoning, was over, and I was hardly ever sick again, not until my heart attack when I was 59.

It would be surprising if these incidents from the first 10 years of my life didn't find corresponding echoes throughout my life. Spending that much time in the hospital, particularly the time with polio, reinforced my sense of aloneness, forced me to accept that I had to somehow learn how to live and survive while being alone, even while wanting more than anything not to be alone, to be in Grandma's lap, wanting nothing more than to be safe in her arms, in my mother's arms, in someone's arms even as I, too often, insisted on being alone. The yin and yang of life. The push and pull, the to and fro, the twixt and tween of living, of my life. A bit reductive, don't you think? Well, yes, I do think, but it'll do until something better comes along.

Speaking of Grandma, let me return to Eliakum and Shomer and the way their presence in life and memory permeated the family. Shomer's concern about the state of women who, in both Jewish and Russian tradition, had little in the way of rights, who might hope for love but more frequently had to settle for unhappy arranged marriages, who might want to be treated well but whose husbands had the license to beat them, who might want to have children but might not want to be baby factories no matter what their rabbis told them, whose husbands felt free to desert them either literally or by spending all their time studying the Torah, all these concerns were passed on to his daughter, Miriam, my mother's mother, my grandma.

Grandma (called Minnie by her friends and family) was born on November 25, 1882, in Odessa to Shomer and his wife, Dinneh. The family, which aside from Grandma included her two sisters and a brother, emigrated to America in 1889, the same year as Eliakum and his family. Both settled in New York's Lower East Side.

Grandma went to public school in America, learned to speak English, and took drawing lessons at the Educational Alliance on the Lower East Side, where I think I did volunteer work while in high school. She frequently wrote for various Jewish publications, usually on women's issues, and was an ardent and vocal suffragette. Later, she wrote plays in Yiddish, often collaborating with her sister, Rose. Some of the most famous female Jewish actors of their time, like Bertha Kalich and Molly Picon, starred in their work. Grandma also wrote several plays in English, at least one of which appeared on

Broadway. But she wasn't only a writer. She also sculpted and played the piano. She was an active Zionist, founded a chapter of Hadassah in Brooklyn, and was a delegate to the first American Jewish Congress, convened by her brother. And she founded an organization designed to promote Jewish music in Palestine and the United States. That organization became the Jewish Music Forum, of which she was the treasurer and the only non-professional musician member. To top it all off, *Yesterday: A Memoir of a Russian Jewish Family,* her memoir about her family, was published in 1939. Although it is out of print, you can still find it online either in its original form or, more likely, in the edition edited by Emily Wortis Leider, a poet and biographer aside from being Minnie's granddaughter, the daughter of my mother's sister.

1905 was clearly a big year in the family history. There was the Jubilee celebration of Eliakum and the publication of his autobiography. Then, there was the death of Shomer. In that year, too, Grandma and Grandpa were wed. It was the joining of two of the most prominent families of the Lower East Side's Jewish intelligentsia. The "Prince and Princess" had married, the Jewish press declared in front-page headlines.

I don't have many memories of Grandma. Aside from the episode I've already related, there are two others. In the summer of 1944 or 45, my parents and grandparents rented a bungalow together on a beach in Shelter Island, an island situated between Gardiners and Little Peconic Bays, lying in the jaws of the North and South Forks of Long Island. Our days were filled with sun, sand, water, and jellyfish. Helen, my mother's sister, and her family had a house just a couple of miles away, and we were frequent visitors. I'd play with Avi, their youngest son, who was two years older than me and my best childhood friend. We went for rides in his father's sailboat, clammed, fished for blowfish, watched the scuttling crabs on the sand, hunkered down over the busy life in the shallow tidal pools, popped the pod-like sacks on the seaweed with seagulls wheeling overhead. We watched storms march across the bay, watched the setting sun. Those summers were the happiest days of my childhood.

The house was next to a summer retreat for the Passionate Fathers, a Catholic monastic order. It sat wide and broad, a couple of stories tall, at the top of a sand and scrub hill. A long wooden pier stretched from near the top of the hill and down into the bay. Father Joseph(?), the abbot, and Grandma somehow became friends. He would take Grandma and me out in his boat, a sort of skiff/rowboat with a small outboard motor. Grandma would sit in the prow with Father Joseph in the back handling the outboard motor and me in the middle seat as we putt-putted over the chilly, white-capped waves, the bright sunlight bouncing hard off the blue water, and they would discuss religion. Now that must have been a sight, don't you think? There was Grandma in her polka dot dress, large and round, her eyes intent behind her round spectacles, an old-style Russian secular Jewish suffragette discussing God and religion with the Roman collared Jesuit priest who drank too much. What I remember most about these encounters is their mutual good humor; they teased each other and laughed at each other's jokes. They clearly disagreed about almost everything. Yet they listened to each other, neither insisting on their rightness, neither giving an inch, yet both looking forward to their next encounter. I wish I had been old enough to know what they were talking about and enjoy it as much as Grandma obviously did.

Those summers ended because Grandma was sick, something I didn't learn until years later. She had breast cancer that would prove fatal. The only evidence of her illness was her right arm, which had become enormously swollen as a byproduct of whatever treatment she was undergoing, radiation or, perhaps, the surgical removal of lymph glands.

In 1951 when I was 11, I was in the bedroom of Grandma and Grandpa's Manhattan apartment. The shades were drawn, the light dim. Grandma was lying in bed as I sat next to her, her hand — her right hand, the one with the swollen arm — her hand holding on to mine as we said goodbye. I thought I was saying goodbye for just that visit, never realizing it was a goodbye for all time. I never saw her again. My parents thought me too young to go to her funeral.

Grandpa, Charles Zunser, my mother's father, my grandfather, was influenced just as much by his father, Eliakum, as Grandma had been by Shomer. Born in Russia in 1881, Grandpa arrived in New York in 1889 with the rest of his family. As a young man, he dabbled in poetry, strolling around the Lower East Side in a swirling black cape. I think his poems were published in the Jewish press from time to time, but he decided on a more traditional, more stable life, becoming a lawyer. Even so, his career reflected the kinds of concerns that both Eliakum and Shomer wrote about.

During the great wave of Eastern European and Russian Jewish immigration at the end of the 19th century, particularly among the poor living in the tenements of the lower East Side, desertion of families by men was a severe and largely unrecognized problem. As strong as the tradition of the cohesiveness of the Jewish family was, the dislocation of families through migration, the difficulties of adjusting to a new world, and poverty caused far too many men to desert their families, not only physically but in all the other ways women and their children can be abandoned, particularly financially. If many wanted to turn their eyes away from the problem, perhaps thinking it didn't reflect well on the reputation of Jews, Grandpa would not. In 1905, at the age of 24, he became head of the Committee for the Protection of Deserted Women and Children. Grandpa went on to become Co-founder of the National Desertion Bureau and its Secretary and General Counsel from 1922 to 1948. He was instrumental in creating New York's Family Court and, I was told, drafted the law establishing it. He was also a member of the Board of Directors of YIVO Institute for Jewish Research, an organization "dedicated to the preservation and study of the history and culture of East European Jewry worldwide."

Important though Grandpa's work was, it isn't what mattered to me. The same summer that I spent listening to Bach while sitting on Grandma's lap, I spent mornings with Grandpa weeding or picking vegetables in his garden. Eliakum had urged his fellow Jews not to forget their agricultural roots, and Grandpa took him at his word. So most mornings, we'd go off to the garden, Grandpa in his white tank-style undershirt and denim overalls, sweat already streaming down his unshaven face, with me trudging behind dragging a pitchfork or a hoe.

You already know about listening to the news of the war on the radio and putting pins into the European Theater of Operations map, but you don't know about Grandpa and Mickey Spillane. Not too long after Grandma died, Grandpa needed a hernia operation. He spent the weeks of his recovery at our apartment. He slept in my bedroom, and I slept on a daybed placed in the dining room. After I went to bed, I would read Mickey Spillane under the covers with the help of a flashlight. Was it *I, the Jury* or *Vengeance is Mine?* The one with the girl at the end with the scarred stomach that Mike Hammer kills. And the voluptuous Velma, of course. So, thanks for that, Grandpa.

Did I mention that Grandpa liked to draw? Like Grandma, he had taken drawing classes at the Educational Alliance when he was young, and throughout his life, he liked to doodle. His doodles were always of people, sometimes serious, sometimes wicked caricatures. I'd often see him in his idle time, doodling with his fountain pen and paper. Then, in his later years, he tried his hand at drawing with pastels more seriously. Hanging on my wall is a portrait he made of an old, very somber, Jewish man, perhaps a rabbi, perhaps not. It's wonderful.

One more incident involving Grandpa and me was significant for me, but I'm going to save it for the next chapter.

Grandpa died in 1976 at the ripe old age of 94. By then, I was working for *MacNeil/Lehrer* and was traveling much of the time and missed his funeral.

Grandma and Grandpa had three children. The oldest, Helen Zunser Wortis, was born in 1906. She and Joe, her husband, lived about a block from us in Brooklyn Heights. She and my mother were close for as long as Helen lived. She died in 1976. Cancer again.

Their son, Shomer, named after his grandfather, was a watercolorist but worked as a draftsman for Dupont for much of his life. He died at the age of 57 due to Parkinson's Disease.

And then came the baby of the family, my mother, Florence Zunser Saltz. Born in 1910, she lived until the day after Thanksgiving 1993, a victim of a yearlong struggle with lung and brain cancer.

The three children were all artists of one sort or another at one time or another in their lives. The passion that drove Eliakum and Shomer to be artists passed down through the generations into their children, grandchildren, great-grandchildren, and great-great-grandchildren, most of whom also found their careers or passions in the arts. Within their collective midst, you can find artists of all kinds. Writers, painters, poets, and musicians.

As for my mother, she might be the most interesting character in my life, someone who I know a great deal about and yet feel I barely knew, perhaps because I both loved her so much and resisted her so fiercely.

Her portrait hangs in my country home in New York's upper Hudson Valley, painted by her brother. In the painting, she is in her late teens or early twenties. She wears a reddish sweater over a white blouse. Her head is tilted slightly, her brown wavy hair falling to her shoulders, her eyes closed demurely.

But there was nothing demure about Flossie Zunser. She didn't go to college, either by choice or economic necessity, but that never stopped her from doing anything. Instead, she became a nightclub reporter writing for Playbill magazine, still given to every Broadway theatergoer. Her main hangout was the Cotton Club with its white-only patrons composed of Manhattan's upper crust, and celebrities, along with assorted gangsters and wannabes. The club's musicians and entertainers were, of course, all Black. Duke Ellington, Cab Calloway. Artists like that. Not surprisingly, she dated men she met there. She was even willing to name one or two, like Kermit Bloomgarten, who became a well-known Broadway producer.

In later years I would sometimes wonder who else she dated or knew. Whenever there was a gangland killing, she wanted to know if the suspected killer was Jewish. I don't think this was simply because Jews are often understandably concerned about other Jews who might reflect poorly on the reputation of all Jews. Instead, I wondered if it wasn't something closer to home: The organized crime group based in Brooklyn — Murder Incorporated — was composed of Jewish-American and Italian-American killers who performed contract work for other mob families. Some of their names have become part of American mythology: Louis "Lepke" Buchalter, Albert Anastasia, Harry "Philadelphia Phil" Strauss, Mendy Weiss, Abe Reles, and others. Who among them frequented the Cotton Club? If they did, I'm sure Mom knew them or certainly knew who they were. But did she date any of them? I hesitated too long to ask her. She is now long past being able to answer, which I'm sure is the way she'd prefer it. But, come to think of it, if I did ask, I'm sure she would imitate her pose in that painting, her eyes looking down, eyelids closed, with perhaps a bit of a smile. Or she would laugh.

For a time, she was the Inquiring Photographer for the *New York Evening Graphic*, a one-time tabloid paper in the city that was noticeably inventive, shall we say, with facts. The newspaper was published from 1924 until 1932 and was considered so trashy that the New York Public Library declined to save any copies, so none still exist. The publisher was Bernarr Macfadden, a man who once had Republican presidential ambitions. Mom recalled that he liked to have meetings in his hotel suite, engaging visiting employees dressed in his pajamas. The paper was enormously popular for its sheer trashiness and fabricated stories. It was also wildly profligate with its spending, the cause of its ultimate demise. One of its critics called it "one of the low points in American journalism," with sample headlines like "Aged Romeo Wooed Stage Love with a Used Ring" and "Rudy Vallee Not So Hot in Love's Arms." That said, the *Graphic* produced some notable journalists (the word "notable" not referring to their excellence as journalists), Walter Winchell and Ed Sullivan in particular. And, of course, my mother.

One thing that Mom perhaps took from the *Graphic* was her enjoyment of telling stories. Not merely telling them but knowing that no story was so good that it couldn't be improved upon. On the other hand, storytelling clearly runs in the family, evidenced by everyone from Eliakum and Shomer on down.

Just think of my mother: She wasn't simply a nightclub reporter and girl about town. She wrote plays, wrote articles for the slicks (as women's magazines were called), became the administrator of the largest family service agency in New York, had a marriage that lasted over fifty years, and raised two children, one of whom became a multi-award-winning TV producer (uh, that's me) and the other a life-long award-winning theater director and teacher (uh, that's Amy). Despite Mom's lack of formal education, she was widely read. She read every book I was ever assigned from grade school to high school (including those that I refused to read) and loved making dioramas and displays on big sheets of oak tag when I was in grade school (when I couldn't or wouldn't). She played a more than respectable game of chess, loved to draw and create costumes with her grandchildren, went to Broadway plays and to evenings at the Philharmonic, had a thirst for gardening that she inherited from her father (not to mention her grandfather), loved to entertain, and wanted everyone to be everything they could be.

Her love of entertaining was inherited from her parents. Grandma and Grandpa had salons on Friday nights (a clear reflection, by the way, of the secular nature of their Jewishness), where guests would be whatever actors, writers, opera singers, and others among the secular Jewish intelligentsia who happened to be in town and not performing that night. From New Year's Eve gatherings in full formal dress to casual sit-down Thanksgiving dinners, her parties were composed of family and close friends. She would think nothing of having 20 for dinner. In 1952 after they bought a summer house on Lake Copake in New York's Columbia County, about 110 miles north of the city, the house was always full of guests on weekends. For several years friends bought or rented houses next to ours, and they'd have guests too, and everyone would gather on Saturday nights for barbecues and martinis.

You'll notice that I haven't said much about Jerome (Jerry) Laurence Saltz, my father, and yet he was a constant presence. Though Mom shone brighter than he did, he was the glue that held everything together, the solid, often silent but steady presence in all our lives.

His family was uninteresting, certainly in comparison to Mom's. He was a late, accidental child, born in 1907, to Issac and Helen Saltz, with an older brother and sister, the youngest of whom was 15 years older than him. I don't know if his parents liked him or not, but he certainly didn't think they did, nor did they ever understand him. They never made him feel that he could depend on them for anything. At an early age, they refused to take him to a dentist to treat an infection that resulted in a permanent scar on his right cheek that he liked to pretend was the result of a duel. At 16, they insisted that he pay rent for his bedroom.

Issac was a businessman. After he came to America, he became a furrier and later owned a couple of apartment houses in the Bronx. Helen, as far as I know, was always a housewife. I think their other two children each had small shops, millinery, and lingerie. In all the times I visited them, something that happened only at my mother's insistence, I never saw so much as a book in their house. Maybe there might be a *Reader's Digest*, perhaps a *Daily News*. They couldn't have been more different than the Zunser clan. Dad always said that if he and Mom had a fight, he'd go home to be with her parents. The Zunsers, for their part, welcomed him with open arms.

Dad, too, never went to college. He taught himself to read by going to the library, trying to read everything, starting in the A section, and going on from there. Despite his ambition to be a writer, he decided he wasn't good enough. I never saw anything he wrote, so I don't know if it's true, and Mom never said a word about the quality of his writing. Before the 1932 stock market crash, he somehow became a railroad bond analyst on Wall Street. He hated it and never trusted Wall Street. Perhaps after meeting my mother and her parents, he went to work for the Federation of Jewish Philanthropies, an umbrella organization with 125 social service agencies, everything from hospitals to family service organizations, community centers, etc., under its aegis. For many decades he was its Budget Director, the primary staff executive responsible for allocating the money Federation raised to the other agencies. The Distribution Committee, which he chaired, was composed of the wealthiest Jews in NY. Despite his familiarity with them, he never felt comfortable around rich people and rejected most opportunities to socialize with them. He thought that they had distorted social and economic values, and their proximity could seduce you to want things that were beyond your means. That, and his Wall Street experience, led him to be very conservative when it came to family economic matters. My parents never took a mortgage. When they bought the country house, they paid cash for it. He never took out a car loan, paying cash for a new car every two years. They lived in a large, pre-war rent-controlled apartment building in Brooklyn for most of their married life. Although my mother wanted to live in Manhattan, in particular as they grew older and their children left home, he resisted, primarily for economic reasons, and they stayed where they were for the rest of their lives.

Dad, as well as Mom, loved music, mainly classical romantic composers. He loved Beethoven, in particular. Gustav Mahler was as modern as he got. But his favorite works were the Berlioz and Verdi Requiems. I remember many Sunday afternoons when Dad would sit in his leather chair, his eyes closed, with one or the other playing in the background. He and Mom had season tickets to the Philharmonic. The summer house was always closed the week after Labor Day so they could go to the theater or concerts. It wasn't reopened until April 15th, when Mom would start planting or weeding in her garden while Dad would build a cabinet or a dock or make sour pickles with a recipe he got from a Polish farmer a few miles away. Many Saturday mornings were spent on the lawn at Tanglewood listening to the rehearsals of the Boston Symphony. After their retirement, there would be trips to Chautauqua for The Great Books Society and to Stratford, Ontario, for the Shakespeare Festival.

Their initial courtship was conducted by mail while Mom lived in Ardsley and Dad in the Bronx. They started off as pen pals, introduced (by mail) by a mutual friend. Gradually those letters turned into a courtship and romance. Their first date at the height of people jumping out of Wall Street windows (which Dad witnessed) was at a free concert in a Greenwich Village church. After that, he would join Mom at the Cotton Club (Jellyroll Morton was his favorite) and with her friends in Manhattan (including George Gray Barnard, the renowned sculptor who designed The Cloisters in New York City). Once they married, they lived in an apartment on 8th Street in Greenwich Village, buying the occasional painting from artists who displayed their work around Washington Square Park. After that, they moved to Brooklyn Heights, in part to be near Mom's sister. At the time, I think their combined income was around $35 a week, and though it wasn't much, it was enough to help feed their friends in the neighborhood who were out of work during the Depression. And then, of course, I came along, followed by Amy three years later.

Dad died in 1995, about 10 months after Mom. The end of his life wasn't happy. In the 1970's he had an aneurysm, and he was never the same after that. His remaining years were spent in a long slow physical decline. Eventually, everything he loved in his life, his music and reading, became increasingly impossible as he gradually lost his hearing and sight. Watching his decline wasn't easy for any of us, particularly Mom, of course. She hung on as long as possible after she got cancer, not so much for herself but for him. She didn't know how he would manage to survive without her, but eventually, the choice was taken away from her as her death became inescapable. And, in truth, those last 10 months for him were awful, and it was almost a relief that he finally died.

At his funeral, one of the eulogies was given by a cousin, Sheila Zunser Rogoff, a painter, a watercolorist like Shomer, Mom's brother, but quite different. If Shomer's paintings were heavy and dark, Sheila's were light and airy. On my living room wall in our Manhattan apartment, there's a portrait she painted of me, all skinny and wide-eyed.

I think I'll end this chapter with her eulogy at Dad's funeral, her description of a summer spent with the Zunser clan before I was born.

> I'd like to recall Jerry to you as a young man. Of course, that means recalling Flossie too, and my parents Mary and Jesse Zunser (Dad was Flossie's cousin) and Minnie and Charles, and all the rest of our great extended family.
>
> When Jerry joined the Zunser clan, I must have been 7 or 8 years old. So he was fifteen or more years older than me – a handsome young man with what I imagined to be a dueling scar on his cheek. He worked in Wall Street ... which hinted at future great wealth. Flossie said he had a mysterious past. All of these assumptions proved to be incorrect. But I always saw Flossie and Jerry as a romantic couple—a sort of "roaring twenties" couple, although it was, by now, the early thirties.
>
> They lived on 8th Street in the Village in a flat filled with posters, divans with throw pillows, lots of guitar music – in an atmosphere of what we now call chez chic. They had lots of friends who were in journalism, the arts - really every kind of life in the city. I knew all this because I would often be dragged along to their parties. In the thirties, babysitters were not a viable option.

Well, time passed. Jerry advanced in his career. My father found employment on Cue Magazine. He started it, actually. Flossie worked at the Agency; my mother continued to sell her stories. The four of them (and me too) became better and better friends. And then mother and Flossie began to write plays together. And that is how it came about that the five of us spent many of the summers of my childhood together.

This would be the scenario: all fall and winter Mother and Flossie would write their new play a few evenings a week. (My father and I and often Jerry would scrounge about in the kitchen looking for some dinner on these evenings). By spring they had a play and their agent looked for a producer. Finally, one would be found. He'd take an option, conditional on their rewriting the second act. Mother and Flossie would declare they had to get away to someplace quiet in the country so they could concentrate, free of all household responsibilities.

They'd find someplace cheap, and off we'd go—Jerry driving the roadster, Flossie beside him. My little mother in the very cramped small space behind the front seat and my father and me in the rumble seat with an umbrella for protection.

I had wonderful adventures this way. We lived as boarders on various farms, once in a lakeside hotel. Daddy and Jerry spent their vacation and weekends with us. Jerry taught me to swim, dive, row a boat, paddle a canoe. My most persistent memory is of Jerry, on the lake, trying hard to turn me into an athlete.

...Jerry... Jerry was usually a quiet guy, except when he was arguing politics. But he was the lynchpin of our group. He was the one cool head that kept all this artistic expression from running amok.

The final summer we spent together was 1939, the summer before World War II, when I was sixteen. By then, we all were a little richer, so we had rented a big house that year on Lake Secor. Minnie and Charles shared it with us. Shomer and Frances were frequent guests. Helen and Joe lived nearby. The Viennese pianist and the refugee dentist, and assorted others came often. My friends came on bicycles with sleeping bags.

It was a great big house with a huge central room and an interior balcony with the bedrooms off them and a deck overlooking Lake Secor. It looked like a stage set. Mother and Flossie and the ever-present typewriter would be out on the deck finishing, I think, the second act of "Women at Work" – (a place about the problems of working women set in – would you guess – a social work agency). It was produced later by the WPA [*the Works Progress Administration* - ms]. Minnie was sculpting a portrait bust of Charles. Charles passed the time doodling wicked caricatures of everybody. I was painting, already committed to my lifetime passion of painting. Shomer was giving me his input. Jerry, always the practical man, was out there barbecuing a big steak.

At night, after dinner, and after we'd tired of arguing politics, we'd read plays for amusement (no TV back then, remember?): Shaw, Ibsen—each of us reading a part. (Amy, you never had a chance. You were predestined).

About that time, there was a great smash hit play on Broadway called *You Can't Take It With You*. It was about a crazy joyful family with many talents and volatile tempers sharing a large house. We were so smug. We were the ones who set style! We are the ones who knew how to live!

Well, it all changed forever on Labor Day 1939 – 55 years ago. That morning the 8 AM news on WQXR greeted us. During the night, Hitler had marched into Poland. It was the end of an era. It was also the last day of our summer rental. And the last of our summers spent together.

But the news that day wasn't all bad. Flossie and Jerry announced they were going to start a family. Flossie thought she was pregnant. Jerry loaded us into the car, and we headed back to the city.

Chapter 3

LESSONS FOR LIFE

◆

1945 — 1953

Of course, nothing ever comes to a complete end. Family certainly doesn't. All of them, even the ghosts of those who are no longer here, they will all still be with me hovering somewhere at the edge of my memory for as long as I'm alive, for as long as anyone remembers any of them.

And as lovely an end as Sheila's reminiscence provided, it also was a beginning and not just of me. My parents and Mom's sister had a big fight over her sister's pro-Soviet view of Hitler's invasion during that last weekend in Lake Secor. It was as bad a fight as many that happened between friends and family members during the Trump era. In the case of the two sisters, they agreed that if they were ever to have a relationship, politics had to be left out of any conversation. And so it was. I don't recall them ever discussing politics in all the years thereafter.

On the other hand, I was, in fact, born and spent five years within the general warmth, safety, and acceptance of the family circle. But, inevitably, there would come a time to step outside it. So a year in nursery school was followed by PS 8, a public K-8 school where I was for all of it, except for when my whole class skipped the third grade for some unknown and unwise (for me) reason.

I was a lousy student, at least most of the time. Maybe that wasn't apparent to everybody in those early days, but it was obvious enough to me if I had thought of it, and I doubt if it escaped Mom's attention since little ever escaped her. What may have been less apparent to others, not to mention myself, was why. It certainly

27

wasn't because I wasn't smart enough, but there were walls that I kept crashing into.

In those early years, Mom always gave me a bath at night. One that I've always remembered was when I was in the 1st or 2nd grade:

> I'm in the bathtub. Mom is sitting on its rim with a yellow-lined pad in her lap and is talking to me. "Let's write a story," she says. "A bunny is hopping down the road. What does he see?"
> "I don't know."
> "Well, does he see a tree?" I nod.
> "How about a flower?" I nod again.
> "Is there anything else?"
> I cannot think of anything.
> "Where is he going?"

My mind was completely blank, nothing there. It was like staring at a flat gray wall rising before me, stretching to the sky as wide as the horizon. I could not climb it; I could not break through it. I was frozen. I could say nothing.

It was not the last time that my mind seemed to simply freeze. When I was in the fourth and fifth grades, there were similar occasions, and my mother would simply do my homework, maybe hoping that watching what she was doing would help or encourage me to do it myself the next time. Even later, when I was in high school and college, there were two subject areas I felt absolutely hopeless in. One was grammar. I never understood it and still don't. I never passed a grammar test, whether in the 5th grade, high school, or college. I can no more diagram a sentence now than when I was 10. So, too, with French. If English grammar was a mystery, so were things like conjugating verbs in the pluperfect and every other tense in French. To this day, I cannot tell you what the pluperfect tense is. It took my entire college career to pass sophomore French. Even then, the passing grade came through the generosity of my professor. After the French final exam in my last semester at NYU, the professor pulled me aside. "Mr. Saltz," he said, "I understand that you're not planning on going on for an advanced degree in an academic subject." "Yes, sir." "Well, then, you'll graduate without a problem." He gave me a "D."

During the immediate aftermath of Hurricane Katrina in 2005, I had a dream:

> We are in a helicopter, my camera crew and I flying towards New Orleans. I am sitting next to the pilot in the clear bubble of the chopper. We are flying toward a wall of mud. The pilot starts climbing higher and higher, trying to get above the wall. No matter how high we rise, we can't go as high as the top; it grows higher and higher as we climb up and up.

I woke up and immediately thought of those other walls, the French, the 4th grade homework assignment about the Aztecs and Cortez, failing to parse sentences correctly in the 5th grade, failing to understand calculus as a college freshman, all the times I flailed and crashed and gave up because the barrier seemed impenetrable.

You would think that I was a complete academic failure, yet this was not so. Grammar aside, elementary school was mainly successful academically. The highlight was a 99+ in science from Mr. Malinkowski, my 8th grade teacher. He said it was the highest grade he could give because no one knew everything about science. It was the same grade that my cousins had received before me, so I was "carrying on the family tradition," he said. I was proud of the achievement, even if I had no idea what I had done to merit it.

In the long run, whatever I did or didn't learn in the classroom may not have been as important as what I learned outside. But having just passed through a year of pandemic watching my grandkids struggle or not with the advent of online learning, part-time school attendance, or even no attendance, and the lack of social contact with their peers, I've thought a lot about my own out of schoolroom learning and realized again how meaningful those experiences were.

In those first few years, at least through the 5th grade, Philip Santos, Joe Louis Stewart, and I were good friends. Philip lived in the slums in the shadow of the Manhattan Bridge, in what is now, in a more gentrified era, called Dumbo. Joe was probably my best school friend at the time. He was one of eight children, somewhere in the middle of the pack. His father was a milkman; his mother lived at home in an apartment on the second floor of a dilapidated building with a green door just down the block from school, all the kids sleeping in one room.

Joe was a short, skinny kid who was particularly fond of his middle name. Joe Louis, the great American heavyweight boxing champ, was his hero, and he liked to stage imaginary fights between Joe Louis and Max Schmeling, with himself being the original Joe Louis and, of course, always winning the fight. Joe would have been happy to drop the Stewart part of his name and just be known as Joe Louis, which was how most of us thought of him. He certainly tried to live up to his idea of the champ, meaning that he was always getting into fights (and usually winning). I visited both Philip and Joe's houses (rarely), and they visited mine (more often). We mostly played together, roaming the streets of Brooklyn Heights after school.

Did I mention that Joe was Black? Maybe it's just an indication that his race was no factor in our relationship in the early days anymore than Philip being Puerto Rican was. Regardless, Joe was just Joe to me then and still is today in my memory.

In the 4th grade, two new students came into the class, Ruth Nagashima and Frank Fenza. Though Ruth and I were never close, we were in school together until we graduated from high school. Ruth had spent the war years in an internment camp, her family having been uprooted from San Francisco. She lived on Hicks Street in a brownstone somewhere between Pierrepont Street and Atlantic Avenue. Frank, as it happened, lived on Atlantic Avenue where his father either owned or tended the bar at a saloon. The three of us were just about the only ones in the school who lived in the same direction at that time, and we would often walk home together.

One afternoon early in the school year, Frank started teasing Ruth for some reason that I don't remember. It may have been her ethnicity since she was the only Japanese person in the school, but it could have been anything. You know the way kids can be — unmerciful. For some reason, I objected, and before I knew it, Frank and I were in a fight. He kept knocking me down, and I kept getting up, going after him again. Four, five, six times, he knocked me down, finally sitting on my chest, his fist raised to strike again. "Uncle?" he said. I just nodded. And from that time, he, too, became a friend. Well, maybe not exactly a friend but certainly an ally, which is sometimes more important.

Not surprisingly, there were other fights over slights, real or imagined. More important than those, perhaps, were the non-fights, the fights that didn't happen.

My friendship with Joe Louis Stewart and Philip Santos came to an end towards the end of 1949. It was after they had come to my house one afternoon. Philip accidentally put his elbow through the hall window on their way out the door (we were boys, after all, not exactly given to walking calmly from place to place or overly decorous behavior). Regardless, the friendship just stopped. They never played with me again, and we barely talked until we graduated.

I've often wondered what happened between us. Maybe they thought that my parents were angry about the window (they were, but not very). Maybe they were simply embarrassed at having done something they knew they shouldn't have. What I've really wondered is if they had, by that time, the time we were all nine, come to think that the differences between us mattered more than the similarities. Had they become uncomfortable in the presence of what might have seemed to them as wealth compared to the poverty in which they both lived. Maybe in time, had we remained friends, it would have been me who created the separation, particularly after we left elementary school. Probably so, since I left everyone behind except a couple of kids who went on to the same high school that I did. But at least in this instance, our friendship ended at their insistence.

Did either of them ever think about that incident? Was it anywhere near as important to them as it was to me? I'll never know, just as I'll never know if they know why they abandoned our friendship. Did they even think of us as friends? Did they think of us at the time as Black, brown, and white? In fact, did Philip or anyone else have "brown" as a label? In New York at the time, more accurate labels would have been "Negro, Puerto Rican, and white." And, aside from embarrassment, did they insist on the separation based on those differences? Maybe, yes.

Here's a question for you: How do I write about this event at this point in my life (over 80) and in our nation's story (it's 2022 at the moment I'm writing this)? Would I think differently about it if I were writing this during the Obama years or even earlier, at age 40 or 20? I suppose every autobiographical writer faces the same problem when looking for meaning from events. I might have thought differently about it at any one of those times, and so might you. Or not.

More to the point, was I aware of color differences between the three of us when we were, say, 9 years old? I'm sure the answer is yes for me as well as them. Did our differences in color matter to me then? No. Did it matter to them? I have no idea. But there came a time when those differences did matter.

Speaking generally of that era, around 1949/50, it was a time, and we were of an age when ethnic differences seemed to become more exacerbated. Our school was primarily populated by Puerto Ricans, Negroes (as Blacks were called then), and a smattering of white Italians. There weren't many other whites and even fewer Jews, and the school was beginning to break down along ethnic lines. Moreover, the whole city seemed to be breaking down.

Among young people, something new was happening, the beginning of the organized, so-called "bopping" gangs. Bopping gangs were simply gangs, usually organized along racial or ethnic lines, fighting each other over whatever excuse seemed necessary — girls, insults, turf, whatever. The camaraderie and social cohesion that resulted from mutually shared conflict seemed to be their primary purpose. Maybe it was more the other way around, that kids who wanted — needed — camaraderie and cohesion and allies — surrogate extended families, if you will — found that it was enhanced if they fought together, faced danger together, as a group. It's possible that a kind of social cohesion, or truce, at any rate, had developed in the city during the almost universal desperation and misery of the Depression, followed by the collective urgency of the war against the Nazis and Japan. Now, less than five years after that great victory, maybe things were starting to fall apart along the great, ever-present American fault lines of race, class, and ethnicity.

Regardless of the reason, by the time the 6th grade came along, there were three gangs in the school, each based on ethnicity: Negro, Puerto Rican, and Italian. This was exacerbated by the influx of new students in the 7th and 8th grades. Unlike ours, another elementary school in the general area ended in the 6th grade. The kids who came into our school were, for the most part, considerably older than we were, being fifteen and sixteen years old. These were kids, again Negro and Puerto Rican like Robert Long and Eddie Ramirez. They had been left back for behavioral and/or academic issues and were serving their time until they could no longer be legally forced to attend school. If rumors that I heard much later were correct, both ended up in jail, Robert going away for a very long time in Sing Sing or Dannemora for murder. It was Eddie from whom I bought a switchblade knife when I was in the 7th grade that was confiscated from me one morning when the teachers inspected us as we entered school (obviously with good reason). And it was these kids who taught Joe Louis, Philip, and Frank (among others) how to make zip guns in shop class.

I've often wondered what particular brand of insanity would make the Board of Education think that putting a bunch of 15 and 16-year-old illiterate gang members in with a group of 11 and 12-year-olds was a good idea.

But getting back to the 6th grade: For some reason, something that I presume had to do with the shifting social turmoil that we all were part of, whether we wanted to be or not, or whether we were even conscious of it, Joe decided that I was a victim to be targeted. He was making money by running what, in effect, was a protection racket in the schoolyard. It was simple. He'd ask you for the money in your pocket, and if you didn't hand it over, he'd beat you up. It was my turn on a Tuesday in the spring at recess in the schoolyard. He asked me for my money, and I said, "No." It's a reaction I have, one that pops up from time to time, when, although agreement might seem to be the wisest course, I will get my back up and decide to stand fast based on some sort of principle no matter what the cost, just as happened with Ruth Nagashima and Frank Fenza two years earlier. Joe wasn't interested in my principle (and I doubt that I could have articulated one at the time) and simply said that I'd be sorry if I didn't do what he wanted. I shrugged. He said he'd meet me right after school on Thursday in front of the garden of the Plymouth Church where, when we were even younger, our class was taken to see the two tablets on which were written the Ten Commandments mounted on a wall in the stairwell just inside the entrance, and the statue of Frederick Douglass in the garden that was open to view from the street. And I'd better show up, or there was no telling what would happen.

Why the two-day delay? Joe wanted to arrange for an audience. Wednesday afternoon? That was reserved for going to church. In those days, students were allowed to take the last period on Wednesdays to attend a church of their choice to receive "religious instruction." I have no idea how long the practice survived in New York, and, for all I know, it still exists. What I do know is that it did little to improve the moral character of some of the kids with whom I went to school.

On our way home that afternoon, I told Frank Fenza about the threat and that I didn't know what to do about it. Frank told me not to worry about it. "Just show up," he said, and there wouldn't be any trouble. So, with considerable trepidation at three o'clock on Thursday afternoon, I made my way for the two and a half blocks to the appointed place at the garden fence with Fredrick Douglas lurking in the background. And Joe Louis was waiting for me as he said he would be. He hadn't forgotten about it as I'd hoped. Not only that, but he wasn't alone. He was with his gang of ten or fifteen Negro kids waiting for me. But also, to my amazement, there was Frank and his entire gang of white Italians, most of whom didn't go to our school and thus were complete strangers to me. Now I had no idea what was going on. Had Frank changed his mind and decided to support Joe in the thrashing I was about to get?

I walked up to Frank, and he put me behind him and walked up to Joe. "Leave him alone," Frank said. "Don't bother him again." They whispered to each other for a few moments, and then Joe said, "OK," and that was that. He never bothered me again. Joe and his gang disbanded, heading back towards the school and their turf. Frank's gang disbanded, heading in the opposite direction, back towards *their* turf, and Frank walked me home, never telling me what he and Joe whispered to each other. And all of this happened because I had decided to defend Ruth Nagashima's honor or something two years earlier and because I wouldn't stop getting up no matter how many times Frank hit me. As I said, maybe having allies is better than having friends.

I'm not done with being ten and the 6th grade yet. Would that I was.

> It is about 3:30 in the afternoon of a wintry January day. The wind is blowing, the air really cold, and I'm bundled in a coat, a scarf around my neck, gloves on (though no hat – I refused to wear one then and rarely do to this day – a totally pointless bit of macho inanity). I carry my schoolbooks in my arms as I trudge my way home.
>
> Walking along the east side of Hicks between Pineapple and Clark Streets, there is a wall. It is virtually featureless except for

the tan brickwork that stretches up for three or four stories before the first windows of the St. George Hotel appear. Behind the wall is the main ballroom of what was, before the war, a somewhat ritzy hotel with a large swimming pool in the basement under the ballroom. Aside from the brickwork, the only detail in the wall is the brass exhaust flue from the swimming pool. As I approach it, the damp smell of chlorine permeates the air.

Walking towards me from the opposite direction is a big kid, a much bigger kid. He must be at least 16, maybe older, wearing a leather jacket, maybe a bomber jacket. He deliberately stands in front of me, refusing to let me go past him. We're directly in front of the swimming pool exhaust, mist from the heated moisture swirling around us as it condenses in the frigid air, the chlorine smell almost choking me.

"Hey, kid," he says, "you Jewish?"

I nod.

He sneers, snarls, "Fucking Christ killer."

We stand still for a moment, me barely daring to breathe, not knowing what comes next. Then, suddenly, he reaches for me, pushes me aside, and keeps walking down the block.

And that's all, but not really. Just down the block from PS 8 was the Catholic parochial school, which ran through the 12th grade and generated problems for me until I graduated. Several of the kids, all of whom were white, would congregate on the front stoop of a building that I had to pass on my usual route home. They would yell out to me as I neared, "Hey, kike," or "Hey, Christ killer."

I was terrified that I couldn't avoid a fight with these kids, all of whom were older and much bigger than I was. So if I walked in their direction, I'd carry a ruler with its sharp metal edge in my hand or, maybe, a compass with its pointed end. Most afternoons for those two years after I got home, I'd practice throwing it into the dresser in my bedroom or try to improve the speed with which I could whip my garrison belt from around my waist and wrap it around my fist, the heavy buckle dangling loose. Most often, though, I'd avoid them altogether by taking a roundabout way home. Believe me, it wasn't fun.

Looking back at these school years, I'm struck by how important the events of 1949/51 were, the years when I was 9 and 10 years old.

In particular, there was the final illness, the various fights, the collapse of friendships, the climactic non-fight, the first personal experience of anti-Semitism. It's a lot, and most of it wasn't pleasant. On the other hand, I don't know if it was more or less than what other kids typically experience around that time. I suspect not all that different, yet I'm sure it all left a mark on me, although I'm not entirely sure what it was.

While I was just 18 and a sophomore at the University of Maryland, five years later, I was the Associate Editor of the school's literary magazine, *The Old Line*. We needed a story for the upcoming issue, so I wrote one. I include it, not because of its literary merit (of which I'm entirely unsure), but because it's the most evident reflection of what I took away from those early years in Brooklyn and the people I knew, excluding family and their friends. And maybe it says something about how I saw myself in my life.

DOORS ONLY OPEN TO LET YOU IN
A short story by Michael Saltz

Saturday morning's sunlight filtered through the grimy second-floor window of a three-story cold-water flat. The room it barely illuminated was equally bare. Two beds, a table with a guitar on it (the body's veneer scratched and worn after long, hard use), and a floor lamp were the only furnishings. Water-stained, once-blue wallpaper hung raggedly from the walls. Motionless in the shadows, a naked light bulb hung on a long cord from the cracked, yellowing ceiling. Bright sunshine sneaked through a clean patch in the window, framing the body of a sleeping seventeen-year-old boy on one of the beds.

His eyes opened, fluttered as he tried to blink away the nighttime fog. His nose unconsciously wrinkled at the stench of rotting garbage that permeated the room, indeed, the whole building. Pulling on an old, worn pair of Levi's, a faded blue muscle t-shirt, and dirty white sneakers, he stumbled into the only other room of the flat - a tiny kitchen - put his head under the faucet, let the cold water stream over his head, dried himself with the greasy towel that hung on a hook over the sink, combed his hair, looked at the lukewarm pot of coffee on the stove that his father had left before going to work, glanced into the refrigerator (almost empty except for the bottles of beer), muttered in disgust, walked out the door leading to the hall, opened the bathroom door at the end of the hall, peed, went down the stairs, out the front door, saw a rat scurry from a pile of somebody's garbage as he ran down the stoop's stairs into the street ...

The sky was burned white by the noon sun, making it and the sky almost indistinguishable from one another. Shimmering waves of heat rose from the concrete pavement. Black, all shades of brown, and a few white children ran yelling and laughing through the streets. Mothers sat on the buildings' stoops holding sometimes-crying babies; their out-of-work boyfriends or husbands standing in small groups, drinking from beer cans, talking about the races, last night's ballgame, and the latest murder which glared luridly from the front page of the Daily News. A rainbow of new brightly colored easy-credit, no-money-down cars crowded the curbs, interrupted by old heaps miraculously resurrected from the auto graveyards that dotted some Brooklyn neighborhoods.

... walked quickly, stopped. Across the street, a garish purple and white sign said, "RED'S." A boom box was blaring with a heavy, thumping sound. Red stood behind the counter, a broad, sneering smirk splitting his face. The store was the only local source of such delicacies as candy, sodas, ice cream, cigarettes (in front), pot, and various other pills, powders, and crystals (in back). It was also the hangout of the Barons, one of the less appreciated of the gangs in the Greater New York area, one whose only claim to virtue was that its membership was not restricted by race, color, or religion.

Nick was a Baron.

He turned around and walked even faster in the direction from which he had come, walking towards the river. They were all there: Dirk, Jose, Spider, Frank, Pablo, Carlos. He didn't want to see them. Not today. Maybe not ever. He was tired, so tired of it all. Living like an animal in the jungle. All of his life, he had lived in the jungle, a place in which there were no children. You were an infant, a baby, and then you were on your own in the jungle, where everyone grows up fast or else they don't grow. Survival of the fittest was the only law that they observed or knew. Survival meant learning to feel trouble, to smell trouble, learning to kick for the balls first and think later, if you had time. Survival meant living on instinct - living like an animal. Survival meant being a Baron. Why?

Why was it that if he wasn't a Baron, he might be walking home alone one night and never walk home again? It didn't help to think about it; it only led to despair, confusion. "Think about something else," he told himself. "Think about the sun, the blue sky, think about walking on the Promenade and the skyline of the city just across the river." But he couldn't help himself, couldn't keep other thoughts at bay. "So, we got kicked out of that club last night. So what. We've been kicked out of places before. That keyboard guy was pretty good. And the sax dude could really wail. I'd love to try to sit in with them. Would they let me? Am I good enough? Why did Dirk and Spider, that skinny little kid he calls his War Lord, say we had to stay away from there?"

The cool breeze wafting in from the bay cooled the sweat on his brow as he sat on one of the benches on the Brooklyn Promenade. This wide walkway, stretching for several blocks, filled with strollers and children, was as far from where he lived as he ever went, as he had ever been. It felt like an oasis, a place in between, a place where he felt free to dream, to long for he didn't know what but long for it anyway. Behind him, the rear window of the mansions of the neighborhood's wealthy seemed blank, empty, impenetrable; the gardens behind the houses, fenced in by stout iron bars. Before him, Manhattan rose like a fairyland from the river, the soaring buildings like hands trying to reach for something, to grab ahold of something. If only he could reach out and touch it, but it always felt just out of reach, too far to go.

In the harbor, the sun was setting behind the Statue of Liberty, casting an orange glow over the city, the Promenade gradually emptying as families headed home for a dinner they would share together. Nick's footsteps echoed on the almost-deserted streets, lit windows watching balefully as he walked. "Red's" was empty, Red standing in the same place he had been earlier, the same smirk splitting his face.

The flat was dark, his father having already found himself a convenient bar stool. Nick turned on the floor lamp, walked to the refrigerator, opened the door, took out some cold meat that his father had left, put it between two pieces of bread, ate it. Dinner. He went into the other room, picked up the guitar, and sat on the bed. He played a chord, a riff, shimmering notes finding their way into nooks and crannies through the shadows. A knock. Holding the guitar tightly, he walked to the hall door, opened it. Spider.

"hey, nick." *... he is flying ... his eyes dilated, gazing at some invisible object in the distance ... he glides into the room on a cloud ... nodding ... his speech is slow and slurred and soft ...*

"What do you want, Spider?"

... a shrug ... "what you doin' tonight?"

"What difference is it to you?"

"we been kinda worried 'bout you, dirk en me. thought you might be doin' somethin' you shouldn't."

"What're you talking about?"

"come off it, man. you know what i mean.

"Yeah."

"you can't do it. you can't go to that club tonight.

"Sure, I can."

a long pause...a really long pause. "no, you can't."

"Why not? There's nothing else going on."

Spider sighs, shakes his head. "it don't matter, man. you're a baron. you don't got a choice."

"Why not?"

"'cause dirk said so."

"Dirk can go to hell!"

"ooooh, man, you don't know what you're sayin'."

...Nick shakes his head, backing away from Spider ...

"you show up at Red's."

"What for?!"

"it don't matter. 'cause dirk said so. that's all you need to know."

"No."

"you're just askin' for it. you'd better be there."

"What d'you mean I better be there?"

"dirk said to be there, so you better be there."

...angrily... "What right has he got to tell me what to do?"

"you're a baron; you wanted to be a baron. you're either in or out. If you're out ... well..."

... pleadingly ... "But why can't I do what I want? Isn't my life my own to live?"

... nodding ... "to lose too."

... softly ... fearfully ... "You can't mean that.

a giggle ... "yeah." *... a click ... a knife blade ... a murmur as he glides out the door.*

Nick stood stiffly, taut in the middle of the room, his head shaking, one fist clenched, the other still clutching the neck of his guitar, murmuring "no, no, no, no..." He felt walls closing in on him, trapped ... like an animal. His eyes darted wildly about, not understanding, not seeing anything but the door. He ran to it and pushed. It wouldn't open. He hit it. Again! AGAIN! But cage doors only open to let you in.

He slowly collapsed to the floor. Exhausted, thoughts flitting rapidly, almost incoherently, skidding, bouncing around the corners of his mind. "Why can't they leave me alone? How can they get away with it? Demand that I give up *me*? No one has the right to tell me what I can and can't do. This is a free country. Right? A load of crap. What kind of freedom do I have? The freedom to obey? To say yes? To act, live, talk, dress like Dirk tells me to? What if I say, 'I won't do what you want?' What happens? I can't be the only one. What happens to them? I don't know anything. Only this dump. And the Barons. What other family do I have? A dad who spends his life in bars? Mom ... I don't even remember what she looks like. That teacher I had? A real ass. 'Yours not to reason why; yours but to do or die.' Right. No different than what Spider just said to me. Maybe what they tell everyone like me. What can I do about it? Not like there's a bunch of other guys who don't do whatever. It's only me. The other teacher, the one who said, 'To thine own self be true.' What does he know? How to do that when there are 50 guys making sure you don't? How do I stop thinking, empty my brain 'til there's nothing left? It's got to stop somewhere, sometime. I've got to start living my life before it's too late. Tonight? But I'm afraid. So what?"

Slowly, hesitantly, he reached for the doorknob and pulled on it. The door opened.

Midnight found Nick slowly walking home. He hadn't really enjoyed the club. Too nervous. For better or for worse, he had committed himself. It was done. There was no turning back. He wondered if he would miss the Barons – the companionship, no matter how little it was. They were as close to real family as he had, but it really wasn't much when you came down to it. It didn't matter anymore. He had chosen to be alone, to be one of the night people, people who wander alone until they find something worthwhile to hold onto. Well, it sure would be different, a new and strange ...

a footstep somewhere behind him

...experience to see people he knew and grown up with but who he didn't really know and who never really knew him, people who he would never say hello to again. It was worse, maybe, to know that he would be hated and maybe feared because he had left, had chosen not to be with them. But what could they do? Maybe beat him up. But that'd just be once. It's not that big a price to pay.

He heard the footsteps behind him. He stopped. They stopped. Started again. The block stretched out long before him. At the corner, a solitary streetlamp glowed with light. The windows on either side were black, eyelids closed, turning inward, hiding from the night. More footsteps. Stop. They came faster. Barons! Nick ran. Almost home!

They seemingly rose before him from the street into the light: Dirk, Spider, and all the rest. A bicycle chain. A piece of rebar. Brass knuckles. A knife ...

Sunday was a monotonous, dull, sad gray. Streams of rain fell from the heavy clouds and splashed into the streets. A purple sign leered with lascivious indifference at the cold, wet, empty streets. Black, brown, and a few white children nervously played in their flats. Mothers sat in their sweating kitchens holding sometimes-crying babies; husbands and boyfriends sitting in overstuffed, rotting chairs, drinking from beer cans, dreaming of lottery prizes that they never won, and reading about last night's teenage gang killing that glared sensationally from the front page of the Daily News.

The fact that Nick played the guitar in the story was hardly coincidental. So did I, if not as well as I imagined Nick did. In 1950 I had spent the first of several summers at sleep-away camp. I hated it. On the other hand, I started to learn how to play the guitar, something I would do for the rest of my life.

Once I got home from summer camp, I began to take guitar lessons from Margot Mayo, my guitar counselor in camp. Once a week, I'd take the IRT subway from Brooklyn Heights all the way up to 125th Street in Manhattan north of Columbia University and walk up the hill on Tieman Place to Margot's apartment building. There Margot would be, with her salt and pepper hair that she wore in a long single braid down her back and a green and black-checked unbuttoned flannel shirt that she always wore over whatever else she was wearing and her blue jeans. I would learn chords, and we would sing folk songs, mostly English ballads, and songs from the Appalachians. If we used a songbook, it would be *The Fireside Book of Folk Songs.* Those songs, most of which emanated from the British Isles, perhaps account (in part) for my love of the Irish and Scottish influenced music that still inhabits the Southern Appalachians.

Margot wasn't the first to introduce me to folk music. My parents took us to see plays and musical concerts throughout my childhood, usually at Manhattan's 92nd Street Y. I remember seeing Richard Dyer-Bennet, Burl Ives, and Susan Reed, who played zither to accompany herself. In the late 1940's we went to what I understood was the first post-war hootenanny (officially, an impromptu gathering of folksingers, and though hardly spontaneous, it was undeniably a gathering). I remember that Cisco Houston was there and Ramblin' Jack Eliot. Do I remember Brownie McGhee and Sonny Terry, too? I know Earl Robinson was there, and I remember he sang two of his own songs, "The Free and Equal Blues" and "The House I Live In."

Earl was married to Mom's brother-in-law's sister and by 1952 had moved to a brownstone in Brooklyn Heights. He was a composer of considerable talent. One of his songs, "The House I Live

In," was a big hit for Frank Sinatra. It still is a wonderful song, filled with the highest ideals of America, the America of neighbors and neighborhoods, the America of Lincoln, Jefferson, Paine, Washington, and Roosevelt, of the dream and promise of America.

> **What is America to me,**
> **a name, a map, the flag I see,**
> **a certain word, "Democracy."**
> **That is America to me.**

Earl had been accused of being a Communist (with justification), and he was blacklisted in the 1950s. Despite this, he wrote these extraordinarily patriotic songs. The cantatas, *The Ballad for Americans,* and *The Lonesome Train* are among the most patriotic works I know. That irony, the simultaneous devotion to the ideals of America and the loyalty to the Soviet Union and its promotion of violent revolution and murderous, even genocidal domestic social policies are conundrums to me still, the contradictions between ideological fantasy and practical reality too enormous to ignore.

Ironically, on the 100th Anniversary of the Statue of Liberty in 1986, the song Sinatra chose to sing to Ronald Reagan, the great anti-Communist leader of America and the Free World, was "The House I Live In." The song was written by a man accused of being a Communist and blacklisted along with his family members. Moreover, it was being sung by a man who had been severely criticized for hiring screenwriter Albert Maltz, who, too, had been accused of being a Communist and was one of the infamous Hollywood Ten.

Every once in a while, I blink in amazement at the unintended interrelatedness of people and events. In January 2008, the Library of Congress named a film of *The House I Live In* as one of 25 "important" films to be preserved that year in the library. The script was written by Albert Maltz, whose anti-Nazi novel, *The Cross and the Arrow,* was a favorite of mine as a teenager. He also wrote the script of another film named to be preserved that year, *The Naked City.* One of the movie's stars was Don Taylor, who went on to direct many of the episodes of the TV series based on the film. Don's daughter, Anne Taylor Fleming, later became one of my essayists at the *NewsHour* and among my closest and best friends. Mere coincidence? Synchronicity?

What did the symbolism of the 1986 anniversary event really mean, with President Ronald Reagan sitting in Battery Park with Frank Sinatra and his song between him and the Statue of Liberty, the great symbol of American promise all lit up in the background? Was it simply that all was forgiven? That the past extremes were temporary aberrations that time had erased? That we were in a forgiving mood? That Communists, too, could be patriotic Americans? That the conservative Republican president felt nostalgic about his once liberal past? That someone who was thought of as a covert enemy was really a patriot? That there was a time in the President's union past that Earl, a onetime composer of Hollywood film scores, had been a more familiar and sympathetic figure to the onetime union leader? Or was it simply that the President's memory only stretched back as far as a 3"x5" file card in his hand. Or was it simply that Sinatra liked the song, the President's PR people didn't see anything wrong with it, and the past was long past, or it never existed, ignored, or wiped out from our collective memory as are so many things in our past? Were the Soviets the only ones to airbrush history?

During the summer of 1952, Earl scratched up enough money to make a movie of a short cantata, *The Children's Cantata*, although we knew it by the song's name, "When We Grow Up." His son (who became an eminent *avant-garde* jazz clarinetist) was in it along with a saxophone-playing friend and a friend of mine who wound up dating Ruth Nagashima throughout high school. We filmed on weekends in an audio recording studio above the Paramount Theater on Flatbush Avenue where, not too many years later, Alan Freed, the famous Rock 'n Roll disc jockey, held his concerts with their lines of hysterical bobbysoxers stretching around the block.

> **When we grow up,**
> **wh-e-e-en we grow up,**
> **oh, what'll we be wh-e-en we grow up?**
> **I want to be a farmer!**
> **A farmer?!**

… I'd sing in my still-soprano voice. During breaks or after we were done for the day, we would walk around the block smoking Kents.

That wasn't the first time I'd smoked. I had started the year before on a dare. I was walking with Philip Santos, Joe Louis, and Moses

Pedro on the northern end of the Brooklyn Promenade that overlooked a playground. I think Moses challenged me to smoke, so I did. I smoked from then on until I quit in the fall of 1977. That playground, by the way, was the inspiration for the playground in *West Side Story.*

I also sang in a choir sometime in 1951 or 52 as a second soprano, but I don't remember more about it than that. Except I still remember singing "*Dona nobis pacem, pacem,*" the prayer for peace from the Latin mass. All these years later, I think I could still sing it — all three parts. Between the guitar lessons, the folk songs, *When We Grow Up,* and the chorus, my participation in making music became a significant part of my life for many years. Maybe Benny, my ragamuffin teddy bear, was replaced by my guitar; my guitar and music could temporarily fill the empty space around me. They provided a safe and comforting space from which I could emerge to face the world.

> **It is an early Spring afternoon, a cool wind blowing, and I am wearing a gray windbreaker when on my way home from school (walking down Henry Street to avoid the parochial schoolboys waiting for me on Hicks Street). I stop in the stationary store in the St. George Hotel as I often did. In the back of the store, there is a rack of paperbacks. Walking over to it, I look at the titles, picking up this one, then that, and then another. Finally, I pick up a western by Max Brand and slip it into my partially open jacket. After picking up a couple of other books and putting them back, I saunter out the door, saying goodbye to the owner.**

That began a period lasting several years when I compulsively stole books. I had no explanation for why I did it then. I have none for why I did it now. All I know is that I did it until I was caught stealing a math textbook from the NYU bookstore and was suspended for a semester. And then I stopped, never to steal again.

Also in 1952, when I had just turned 12 and was about to graduate from the 8th grade, Grandpa decided to take a direct hand in my education. This time, instead of teaching me to plant, weed, and pick the fruits of our labor in the garden, instead of sticking pins into a wartime map of Europe, he decided to teach me something about America, the land he had come to as a boy, the land he had come to love. So, he took me on a week-long trip to Washington, DC.

Many years later, in 2018, I had been invited to contribute op-ed pieces to the *Hudson Register-Star,* the local paper near my home in upstate New York. As we neared July 4th, I decided to write about that trip.

BECOMING AN AMERICAN
Michael Saltz

Grandpa took me on my first trip to Washington, D.C.

It was the spring of 1952, and I had just turned 12. The Korean War was ongoing, Truman was still president, anti-Semitism was not uncommon in America, and Jim Crow laws still ruled the South. Grandpa, with whom I had shoved push pins into a map of Europe hanging on the wall in his office/bedroom to mark the progress of the war in 1944, had decided that he wouldn't simply leave parents, much less school, to introduce me to his notion of America.

He had come here as a young boy from Russia in 1890 along with his family from Vilna in what is now a free Lithuania. He grew up in Manhattan's Lower East Side, where his father started a small publishing company while living the life of a poet, singer, and a leading light of the Jewish immigrant community. Not for nothing did his biography call him the "Poet of his People."

As a young man, Grandpa, too, tried his hand at poetry before exchanging his romantic flowing cape for a life in the law and social service. In 1905 he co-founded the National Desertion Bureau, an organization assisting immigrant women who had been deserted by their husbands and helped write the law creating New York's Family Court. His wife, the immigrant daughter of another famous Jewish writer and intellect, was a pianist, sculptor, playwright, and social activist. She died in 1951, a victim of breast cancer, the year before our trip.

So there we were, Grandpa and me, he a widower of one year, and me, a young boy taking his first tentative steps beyond the confines and safety of home and family into the wide, wide world.

We left on the Pennsylvania Railroad from Pennsylvania Station (yes, Virginia, there really was a real Pennsylvania Station and railroad) rolling along the tracks, making our way down the map I had studied in Geography class: Trenton, Philadelphia, Wilmington, Baltimore, and all the cities and towns in between and then, finally, Washington, D.C., and the majestic Union Station.

Nights we would have dinner with Grandpa's sister and husband, a Washington builder who kept his revolver, holster, and chaps from his days in the Oklahoma oil fields in a trunk, before repairing to the Shoreham Hotel to sleep.

Days, however, belonged to Grandpa's agenda, and we did the tourist thing. We visited the White House and the Capitol; we went to see the Supreme Court, and the FBI building, and Arlington Cemetery; we visited the Smithsonian, the National Gallery, and the Washington Monument (we didn't climb the stairs).

There were three places, though, that were special to Grandpa and the real purpose of the trip: the Jefferson Memorial, the Lincoln Memorial, and the National Archives with its display of America's founding documents. He read aloud to me the words inscribed on the walls of those memorials, wanting to make sure I *heard* the words, all of them.

"We hold these truths to be self-evident: that all men are created equal, that they are endowed by their Creator with certain inalienable rights, among these are life, liberty, and the pursuit of happiness, that to secure these rights governments are instituted among men," and

"No man shall be compelled to frequent or support any religious worship or ministry or shall otherwise suffer on account of his religious opinions belief, but all men shall be free to profess and by argument to maintain, their opinions in matters of religion." From the Jefferson Memorial.

For Grandpa, though, nothing was more important than the Lincoln Memorial and his 2nd Inaugural address more than the Gettysburg address. Lincoln clearly stated that slavery was the root cause of the war. *"One eighth of the whole population were colored slaves, not distributed generally over the Union, but localized in the Southern part of it. These slaves constituted a peculiar and powerful interest. All knew that this interest was, somehow, the cause of the war."* And he noted the terrible irony of the war: *"Both read the same Bible and pray to the same God; and each invokes His aid against the other. It may seem strange that any men should dare to ask a just God's assistance in wringing their bread from the sweat of other men's faces; but let us judge not that we be not judged. The prayers of both could not be answered; that of neither has been answered fully. The Almighty has his own purposes."*

So we talked about the Civil War, and the freeing of the slaves, and the founding of America, and the idea that all men are created equal, and that no idea, no religion was automatically superior to any other, that America was unique in the world because it was founded on the basis of those ideas.

His lesson must have taken root because not only do I still remember our trip, but in all the scores of times I've driven past those monuments in the past 66 years, I cannot do so without a quickening of my heart.

Did that visit play a role in the eventual course of my life? So much of who and what we are, what we believe in, what we are prepared to believe in, comes from the accretion of scores, hundreds, thousands of incidents that it's hard to pinpoint the one time, the Aha! moment. But there was this visit along with dinner table conversations, and the pushing of pins into the map, and the history classes, and the Seders and Thanksgivings, and the books I've read, the places I've been, the things I've experienced, and I don't know what else, and in the end, through it all, I became an American, a patriot.

If I sometimes get furious at America and find it incomprehensible and willfully blind and sometimes stupid, I also find it majestic and bountiful, always holding out the hope that change for the better is possible if we are willing to make it happen, that it is always we, the people, who ultimately hold the power and responsibility to create our present and our future.

Life, the life one lives, the life I've led, is not, of course, all high drama. A trip to the Lincoln Memorial and playing the guitar, sickness and health, fights and bigotry, kisses and angels (yes, there were those too, although you'll find them barely mentioned them in this book), criminality even, are merely the high points, signposts in the topography of a road well-traveled, of ripples in a pond, the contours of which I've just begun to explore as my world continued to expand.

Chapter 4
TO YOU EI HIGH

◆

1953 — 1957

In September 1953, having turned 13 the previous May, I left the world of my childhood, a world dominated by family and Brooklyn Heights, and stepped forever into a wider world. I took the subway from Brooklyn to Manhattan's Greenwich Village and stepped into Elisabeth Irwin High School, my formal introduction into the world of ideas, imagination, and the past.

> **To you EI High our faith we'll not deny,**
> **And e'er shall hold your red and gold**
> **Aloft to a shining sky....**
> **—Elisabeth Irwin School Song**

Yes, we, too, had a school song that I sang with considerable embarrassment, not liking to be too rah, rah about anything.

If the purpose of elementary school was to give me some basic tools with which to apprehend the world (however imperfectly I learned them), the result of going to EI, intended or not, was to provide me with the most basic part of my education about that world, at least that part that can be learned by going to school. Not that I hadn't learned other things at PS 8, things about friendship and alliances, about race and class, about anger and fear, about violence and religious bigotry, and about what was supposed to be my place in the world. But I doubt PS 8 knew it played any role in what I learned about those things, just as I don't know that I was aware of what I had learned.

It is hard to underestimate the educational role that EI played. I see its fingerprints everywhere in my life. This is not to say that I was a good student. I had no more success with grammar than I'd had in elementary school. I discovered my inability to learn foreign languages. If I was able to focus on some things sufficiently long to accomplish something real, I also came up against that impenetrable wall over and over again. My best grades were in the 9ᵗʰ grade, and they deteriorated throughout my four years there. Despite that, I got an education.

EI was a small school with approximately 200 students from the 7ᵗʰ through the 12ᵗʰ grade. There also was an elementary school, the Little Red Schoolhouse, a few blocks away on Bleeker Street. It used to be said of Little Red and EI (and maybe still is, for all I know) that they were where all the little Reds went. It was not inaccurate. The student body was filled with the children of what some would have called West Side liberals, not to mention those who could fairly be labeled "red diaper babies." And several of the teachers (or all, for all I know) had been blacklisted in the anti-Red hysteria of the early Cold War years. For all that, I never thought that they sought to create baby Communists. Though there was often a Marxist slant on specific issues, it wasn't insisted on; there wasn't a political line to which you had to adhere to pass a course or graduate. If there were students who became notable leftists among its graduates, like Angela Davis, who ran for vice president as a Communist, there were also kids who became well-known conservatives, like Eliot Abrams, who prominently served in the Reagan, Bush 43, and Trump administrations. Sometimes there were brothers and sisters who became one of each, like Kathy and Michael Boudin, who couldn't have wound up with more different political views and lives no matter how hard they tried. Kathy was a member of the Weather Underground and served 22 years in prison for murder. Michael was the conservative chief judge of the First Circuit of Appeals in Boston, appointed to the federal bench by Bush 41. And there were some, like historian Ronald Radosh, who started at the extreme left in the '50s and ended at the extreme right in the '80s (though he never evolved into a Trumpist). As for me, I've wound up sort of all over the map, at least in my own mind.

All that said, on that first day of school, I entered a class of somewhere between 30 and 35 students, all except one of whom were a year older than I was, many of whom had gone to school together for many years at Little Red before moving on to EI. Not everyone was a stranger to me. Ruth Nagashima, who I had so ferociously defended in the 4th grade, had moved on to EI with me, as had Judy Flynn, who had entered PS 8 in the 7th grade. And there were a few others, particularly my cousin, Avi, who was in the 11th grade.

My homeroom teacher was Bob Leicester, a ruddy-faced man with a ready laugh and a dynamic personality. He also taught two classes, among the most impactful courses I've ever had.

The first was Civics. Yes, there was the traditional course work, the reading about the structure of American government, city, state, and federal. The way bicameral legislatures work, the three branches of government, how they interact, etc. What made the class special was the requirement to cover that year's election. We had to go to rallies, we had to interview campaign workers, we had to find out what the candidates' positions were on various issues, we had to put together scrapbooks and make reports. That year there were the candidates for mayor, for the city council, for the borough presidencies, for judges, and there were the Democratic and Republican Parties, of course, along with minor parties, like the Liberal Party and the American Labor Party, and probably others that I no longer remember. It all happened in that short, intense two-month period between Labor Day and Election Day. It was a wonderful introduction to the process of our democracy, another step that helped fuel my life-long interest in electoral politics.

Can we please make that a part of everyone's education? You know, one can actually do that without making it ideological or political. Then again, maybe the point of today's partisanship is that seemingly nothing is allowed to be non-ideological or non-partisan. It does not bode well for our future.

The second area of importance was a part of our English class. Whatever else we were doing for that class, we also had to read three short stories by the same writer each week so that by the end of the school year, if it had lasted for, say, forty weeks, we would have read three stories by forty different writers. I read Hemingway and Faulkner, Turgenev and Chekhov, Stephan Crane and Ambrose Bierce, Edgar Allan Poe and Walter van Tilburg Clark, Ray Bradbury and Robert Heinlein for the first time. We weren't required to write formal reports but had to make a 3" x 5" note card for each story on which we wrote a brief description of the plot and a statement of the theme. Do you know how many people cannot tell you the difference between plot and theme no matter how many years of schooling they've had? It's something that has proved invaluable my entire life. That, and the exposure to so many different writers. I was reading quite a bit on my own before EI, but doing this exercise expanded my reading breadth and interests enormously and far more quickly and efficiently than I think would have happened otherwise.

Those weren't the only things we had to read, and I wasn't too diligent when it came to some of them. Samuel Butler's novel, *The Way of All Flesh*, was one required book. Almost 70 years later, I can only say that I've never read more than the first 10 pages if that. Next, I think in the spring, we read *Macbeth*. I actually read that, though without enthusiasm, unlike my mother. She enjoyed reading it as she did most everything I was ever assigned (though I'm not sure that even she managed to read all of Samuel Butler). Another confession: I've never actually enjoyed reading Shakespeare. Years later, when I was at NYU, I was required to take a Shakespeare course to fulfill my major. Professor Harrier was a popular lecturer, and his classes were always well populated. The course I took had a couple of hundred students in it, all apparently happily reading play after play and listening to Harrier's no doubt brilliant lectures. As for me, I was bored silly and napped in the back of the class. I was somewhat interested in the plays as plays but not as literature. I can still be amazed at how an actor can make a speech reasonably comprehensible, even compelling, when I couldn't have cared less about it on the page.

On a winter's night in 1961, Avi and I went to see a production of *Hamlet*, with Donald Madden, at the Phoenix Theater in NY. The one thing I still remember about the production was its use of a thrust stage. Madden's soliloquies would find him on the lip at the front of the almost tongue-like thrust portion of the stage, a spotlight on his face, the rest of the stage behind him dimmed, almost feeling like he was in the middle of the audience, more a part of the audience than of the play. It was a wonderfully dramatic and engaging effect. On a less dramatic note, we were sitting on the stage right side of the thrust so that Madden was virtually in a profile, and we could see his spittle arcing out over the first few rows of seats.

There are two other memorable productions of Shakespeare's plays that I've seen. One was James Earl Jones's Obie-winning performance as Othello in 1964. The other was the 1967 production of *Titus Andronicus*, Shakespeare's bloodiest, if not his most successful play, presented by The New York Shakespeare Festival and director Gerry Freedman, a longtime friend and mentor of my sister, Amy. Gerry found a way to transform both the ideas of the play and some of the action into a mesmerizing concept simultaneously abstract and entirely physical. I remember a red banner some four or five feet high that unfurled itself around the entire stage while everybody was busy killing everybody else, encircling the actors in a rippling river of blood. Stunning.

As Shakespeare himself said, "the *play's* the thing."

Unlike say, *Moby Dick*, which I liked much of when I was assigned to read it, but found the *Classics Illustrated* comic version far more enjoyable (and easier to get through) than the actual novel. On the other hand, I loved all of *The Scarlet Letter*. And the less said about *The Iliad,* the better. What a Philistine I am. Well, not entirely.

In the 10th grade Ed Stillman, our English teacher from the 10th through the 12th grades, made me a lover of poetry or, perhaps more accurately, of some poems and poets. Passionate about poetry, his enthusiasm carried itself over to me and, I think, most kids in my class. How could one not fall in love with Dylan Thomas, particularly after hearing that extraordinary Welsh rolling, dynamic voice filled with rhythm and rhyme and passion and ... well, *poetry*. I can hear it still...

> Now I was young and easy under the apple boughs
>> About the lilting house and happy as the grass was
>> green,
> The night above the dingle starry,
>> Time let me hail and climb

> Golden in the heydays of his eyes,
> And honored among wagons I was prince of the apple
>   towns
> And once below a time I lordly had the trees and leaves
>   Trail with daisies and barley
>   Down the rivers of the windfall light.

"Down the rivers of the windfall light." What a line.

And Ed's great passion, William Butler Yeats. He helped me to love *The Second Coming* and *Sailing to Byzantium*, *Leda and the Swan*, the pale lady poems, and all the others. And there was Carl Sandburg, Richard Wilbur, Hart Crane, William Carlos Williams, Wallace Stevens, and W. H. Auden.

> I'll love you, dear, I'll love you
>   Till China and Africa meet,
> And the river jumps over the mountains
>   And the salmon sing in the street.

And there was T. S. Eliot and *The Love Songs of J. Alfred Prufrock*.

> Let us go then you and I,
> When the evening is spread out against the sky
> Like a patient etherized upon a table...

Without Ed, would I have been interested enough in Eliot in future years to think that Eliot (a notorious anti-Semite, something never mentioned by Ed) actually had something to say to me? I don't think so.

One more book, or, more correctly, an essay in a book, had surprising repercussions for me in later years. While we were reading *Moby Dick* in Ed's class, he had us read D. H. Lawrence's *Studies in Classic American Literature* and, in particular, his essay on the great white whale. What I took from it was not anything Lawrence said about Moby Dick and America but a sense of how he used words, even in non-fiction. It was their rhythm, their music, the way they bobbed and weaved, the way they stopped and started, the way he constructed sentences, the conscious attempt to affect the reader, to envelope — capture, even — the reader in a web and carry him where Lawrence wanted him to go. I remember being thrilled by the first few sentences when I first read them. I was so caught in them at the time that I couldn't go on. (I'm sure that's not what Lawrence had in mind — my not going on — and I'm not sure I ever read the entire essay.) And I remembered that moment while standing in an editing room cutting a short film about genocide for the Simon Wiesenthal Center's Museum of Tolerance forty years later.

I'm sure Ed would be surprised to hear me heap all this praise on him and thank him so publicly and Bob, too. But there it is.

As long as I'm thanking teachers (and there are few enough of them through my educational sojourn that I think are worth thanking), here's a backhanded sort of thanks to Harold Kirshner, the history teacher from the 10th through the 12th grades. If there was one place where the Marxist influence was particularly felt, it was in Mr. Kirshner's classes. For Harold, there was no fault too minor in America's conduct in the world that was not worth mentioning, no fault too major in the Soviet Union's conduct in the world that was not worth ignoring. My memories of those classes are primarily of arguments he and I had. In fact, they were memorable enough to the editors of our school yearbook that their wish for me was that I would eventually win an argument with Harold. And yet, for all that arguing and disagreeing, my grades never suffered because of it. On the contrary, any suffering they did was well deserved by me. But without him, I might never have read Charles Beard's *The Rise of American Civilization* and learned of the notion of the prism that economics can afford in looking at the past and present.

And without his concurrence, I might never have delved into what, to my mind at that time, was one of the great historical mysteries: How the Germans allowed the Nazis to come to power and allowed the Holocaust to happen. In the 10th grade, when we were asked to write a paper on some subject or other, I asked if I could do it on the Nazis, and he agreed. So I started reading, at my mother's suggestion, William Shirer's *Berlin Diary*, and moved on to Howard K. Smith's *Last Train from Berlin*, and then Konrad Heiden's *Der*

Fuhrer, and Albert Maltz's novel, *The Cross and the Arrow*, and Erich Maria Remarque's novel about life in a concentration camp, *Spark of Life*, and on and on. I read everything I could find in secondhand bookstores and in libraries. Finally, I wrote the paper and found that it still made no sense to me, no matter how much I read. I knew what had happened but still could not fathom why it had been allowed to occur by the Germans most of all, but also by everyone else. Some 70 odd years after these events, having lived through the 21st century's "War on Terror" and the Trump years, I understand it better. We've personally witnessed how, in the presence of fear and a barrage of misinformation and lies, people can, quietly, voluntarily, and without being aware of it, surrender their rights. But understanding it better doesn't make me feel better. It only makes me mourn how foolish, how blind and self-deluding even the best of us can be. It makes me understand why Jews have said, "never again," and yet they must know, as I know, as *you* know, that it *has* happened again and will always happen again because of all that we humans are and are not. Or, as one friend later put it, "The only trouble with earth is earth people."

There isn't much to say about the other teachers. Blanche Schindelman, cordially disliked by most of us, taught biology. Her favorite biologist was Lysenko, the "great" Soviet biologist, Joe Stalin's favorite, most of whose experiments were failures. Fortunately, she could fall back on Mendel, whose experiments had been more successful and who, happily for him, died long before the Bolshevik Revolution and, thus, never found himself in Siberia or worse.

As for the French teacher, an attractive woman with *café* au lait skin who spoke French with a soft Southern accent, whose name I remember as well as I do the conjugation of any number of French verbs, all I can say is that it wasn't her fault that I was such a miserable student. The constant D's (I don't know that I ever got as much as a C) didn't make me any more excited at the prospect of taking yet another French class. My most frequent memory of doing French homework was to spend a half-hour fruitlessly banging my head against a stone wall, a brick wall, an impregnable fortress of a wall, and then giving up and surrendering to the allure of Robert Heinlein, Ray Bradbury, or A. E. van Vogt.

It was Mr. Kirshner who, in the 10th grade, first spoke to me about my "potential," something that I apparently wasn't living up to. It wasn't the last time I would hear that. It gradually spread to every teacher I had except for the French teacher who, I'm sure, didn't think it was worth the effort and who, perhaps, disagreed with the premise.

I wonder what we actually mean by "education." Certainly, I was a poor student for much of my academic life, from elementary school through graduate school. I could do well — very well — in those things that I was intensely interested in. As for the rest, my performance was mediocre to poor at best. Forgetting about language, particularly the formal structure of language where I obviously had some difficulties that might better have been defined and even somewhat resolved in a later time when there came to be a better understanding of "learning disabilities," there were other problem areas, and maybe they were all related. I was no great shakes as a math student. The notion of science education which required the brute memory of fact upon fact, of formula after formula, made me literally dizzy. If I remembered enough, after studying all night, to pass an exam, it would slip from my memory within a day or two. It all seemed pointless. When all was said and done, what did I gain from my high school science classes? Not much. What a waste.

So my high school education continued outside the classroom. My interest in the Nazis led me to read Churchill's six volumes on World War II and Robert E. Sherwood's *Roosevelt and Hopkins*. I read Bruce Catton's *A Stillness at Appomattox*, which led me to the first two volumes of his great Civil War trilogy. I became fascinated with the physicist George Gamow and devoured *One, Two, Three...Infinity* and *The Birth and Death of the Sun*, along with the astronomer Fred Hoyle's *Frontiers of Astronomy*. Reading Hemingway's, *A Clean Well-Lighted Place* for Bob Leicester led me to read all of his short stories and novels. So, too, with Fitzgerald and on and on. Then there was science fiction, which I also gobbled up: Ray Bradbury's *The Martian Chronicles*, A.E. van Vogt's *The World of Null-A*, Isaac Asimov's *I, Robot*, Robert Heinlein's *Methuselah's Children*, and *Stranger in a Strange Land*. And last but not least, there was Mickey Spillane's *I, the Jury, My Gun is Quick*, and *Vengeance is Mine,* all of which I carefully read either with the door to my room closed or in bed under the covers at night with a flashlight.

I came across *Der Fuhrer* in a used bookstore in Brooklyn Heights. It was owned by Sam Colton, and that's what we called the store – Sam's. Sam had been a long-time labor organizer, and when he retired, he opened the shop. He'd sit in a broken-down office chair, its brown leather cracked and the stuffing oozing out, his gray hair thinning and uncombed, face unshaven, crooked teeth yellowed and stained from the pipe clenched in his teeth, peering through thick-lensed tortoise-shell glasses, and we'd talk. He led me to places I might never have found, to adventures I might never have had. He led me to books about labor, love, and sex. And books about the Soviet Union, where I first began to get my own sense of the true nature of the Soviet state. It was probably Sam more than anyone else who led me to the information I used to argue with Mr. Kirshner. But what he did most of all was to treat this 12, 13, 14-year-old boy seriously, and I remained a loyal customer until I left Brooklyn Heights as an adult. I may have stolen books from other bookstores and never returned some books to the library, but I never stole from Sam.

Each year, our class would go on a trip. One was a day trip to FDR's home in Hyde Park, NY. After that visit, I started reading about the New Deal and FDR's administration, beginning with Robert Sherwood's *Roosevelt and Hopkins,* which somehow prompted me to read all of Upton Sinclair's eleven Lanny Budd historical novels about the period between 1913 to 1947.

More memorable were a few days spent with dairy farm families near New Paltz, NY. We each stayed for a night or two with a different family. I learned how to milk a cow and remember drinking the still warm, raw milk for breakfast and eating pancakes with warm maple syrup and butter that I had helped churn the day before. I remember being awakened in the early morning hours to help a calf be born, grabbing onto an emerging hoof, and helping to pull her out, then watching from outside the stall as the calf struggled to her feet. We also visited a tannery on that trip, seeing one possible future of that calf. There cannot be many worse smells than that of various acids eating away at flesh.

On the other hand, is there anything louder than the thunderous roaring and shaking of the giant coal sorter that we saw on our visit to the anthracite coal mines in Jim Thorpe, PA? The massive sorter shook tons of coal through various sized sieves so that it could be divided into different sizes before being loaded onto the long trains waiting on the side spur to begin their trip to the power plants and homes of America.

I remember putting on helmets and going down and down the long, deep, underground coal shafts, seeing the coal-dust covered miners, the whites of their eyes in stark contrast to their blackened faces. And then the evening we spent in the miners' union hall, the old, retired miners, and the still working but aging miners who lived such hard lives. They told stories of mine explosions and cave-ins, of death and survival. They sang songs.

> **Come all you young miners,**
> **So young and so fair,**
> **And seek not your fortune**
> **Way down in the mine.**
> **It'll form as a habit**
> **And seep in your soul**
> **'Till the stream of your blood**
> **Flows as black as the coal**

After visiting the coal mines, Sam, the retired labor organizer and bookstore owner, suggested reading Samuel Yellen's *American Labor Struggles*. It was the first book I'd read about the American labor movement. Though out of print, it's still a useful book with its depiction of ten attempts by workers to organize and the often bloody lengths to which management and government went to break the back of the individual strikes and the labor movement as a whole. Big business and the government usually united against workers. Nothing new about that. Whose interests is the government supposed to represent?

I was still in EI when Jewish Family Service (JFS), my mother's organization, had its first strike. She had begun her career there as a caseworker in Brooklyn. She had no formal training for it, no MSW, no master's in psychology, no PhD, no BA. But what she did have was intelligence, good sense, and a willingness to be forthright in saying what she saw. Too bad those still aren't primary requirements. Over the years, she had worked her way up through the ranks. As the organization itself grew, she moved into management, eventually responsible for the agency's day-to-day operations. JFS was one of the pioneers in the concept of family therapy along with individual counseling; they helped families in need by providing childcare workers and home workers. They were a non-profit philanthropic organization and had a sliding pay scale for their clients. She was the number three person in a city-wide organization employing hundreds of workers in several branch offices serving thousands of clients.

The first job I had after I got my working papers when I was 14 was in the JFS mail room. I worked for a woman who had worked with my mother for years, as had most everyone else in the organization. What I remember most about that summer was the evident affection and respect that everyone who had worked there for more than a year or two had for Mom, including my boss, and how fair they thought she was, and how much they thought she tried to keep their interests in mind. I no longer remember why there was a strike or what the issues were. But I remember my impression that the parent union urged the local's workers to strike.

Things must get acrimonious before strikes happen, and the acrimony needn't emanate locally. If there are reasonably good relations between labor and management, the union leadership must find a way to make management the devil incarnate. It's sort of like a president trying to take a country to war. So, the strike began. Where a month or two previously, all was smiles, and "good morning," and "how are you," all now was angry stares and picket signs. My mother went to work one of these mornings and stepped into the elevator. A clerical worker she had known for many years leaned through the elevator door and spat in her face. The strike ended a few days later, and my mother said that this same woman smiled at her the following day and said "good morning" as though nothing had happened. Mother never forgave her, never forgot her own shock at the enmity, and never felt the same about the union movement.

I wonder now how much my mother's experience with her union affected my own attitudes in the mid-80s. Shortly after *MacNeil/Lehrer* changed to the hour-long format with many new employees, a couple of the new hires from a major TV network led a movement to unionize the staff. However sympathetic I was to the labor movement (and still am), I vigorously and publicly opposed it, notably in a lengthy open letter that I sent to the whole staff wherever they were based across the country. The union lost the election.

Not surprisingly, I learned about the JFS strike at the dinner table. Dinner table conversations between Mom and Dad mainly were about their jobs, which meant they were about social policy, politics, and finances, especially as they related to New York's Jewish community. I remember Dad, for example, talking about a meeting at City Hall (during Mayor Lindsay's administration) during which city officials expressed astonishment that there were *actually* poor Jewish people. Didn't all Jewish people have money? Why couldn't wealthy Jews provide whatever resources would be necessary to help what must be the very few poor Jews (who couldn't really be *that* poor since they were Jewish)? Why did they need the city's support? The city finally agreed to help the philanthropic endeavors of the 125 social service agencies and hospitals under the Federation umbrella, provided the services would be provided on a non-sectarian basis. Do you suppose such a discussion happened with Catholic Charities? Maybe they did, but I don't know.

What do you suppose today's religious liberty advocates would make of such a discussion? Suppose one thinks of religious liberty as meaning that a Catholic adoption agency can refuse to allow the adoption of a child by LBTGQ individuals or couples. How far does that kind of permitted discrimination go? If, for example, my wife and I wanted to adopt a child and raise them as a Jew, can they deny me the adoption based solely on the fact that I'm not a Catholic or that I plan to raise the child as a Jew? Or *vice versa,* for that matter. And what about my religious liberty rights? Do those same rights apply to me as an atheist or agnostic? If not, why not? If not, is the state granting officially sanctioned religions rights that I as an individual don't have even if I have no religion? And isn't that simply a back door evasion of the notion of state-sanctioned and promoted religion? In other words, where is the wall between church and state? Unfortunately, some believe there should be no such wall and are constantly trying to erode it. (And if you think that edges into beliefs held by Muslim extremists, well …)

Those meal-time conversations were an important part of my education. They are how I first learned about Eliakum and Shomer and all their children and grandchildren and about my father's family, not to mention all their various friends. They were the first place I heard about anti-Semitism and civil rights, about Israel and Germany, about city, state, and national politics, and about the economy. Not to be forgotten, of course, were the constant discussions of the various social service agencies with which they were connected. In particular, my mother had discussions about the pros and cons of different kinds of psychiatric or psychological therapy, adoption, and health care workers. My father's concerns were more wide-ranging as they included the needs of my mother's agency as well as those of hospitals, community centers, senior centers, nursing homes, etc.

Those conversations could turn rancorous, not between my parents but between my father and me as I got older. Dad felt he had to counter whatever he thought was left-wing propaganda, particularly in my high school history classes. I, of course, would argue the opposite even if I agreed with him. It somehow was incumbent on both of us to argue these positions passionately, much to the distress of everybody, particularly my sister.

Dad could be cantankerous, particularly during the spring months when he would often work late into the night, not coming home until 10 or 11, his dinner awaiting him in the oven to keep warm. It was budget time, time to allocate all the money available to be distributed to the various Federation institutions. In those pre-computer days, he would usually be the only one in the office, fingers dancing on his Freiden calculator, trying to make the numbers dance to his tune, laying them all out on the paper spreadsheets spread before him. His decisions were pressure-filled because most budgetary requests were understandable and even necessary. Yet, he could not fulfill everyone's wish list, no matter how worthy their projects were. So, at home, he could be short-tempered.

I, of course, could be short-tempered too. I was a teenager, after all. And I could be stubborn and obstinate, often unreasonably so. It was a characteristic that would crop up from time to time as an adult (and not always to my benefit), including during my years at the *NewsHour*.

Meanwhile, I wasn't done with playing the guitar or singing. At EI, I moved from singing English ballads to more or less American folk songs, songs of the labor movement and Black spirituals. We may have sung *Judas Maccabeus* for Bob DeCormier, our music director when I was in the 9th grade, but he had a great love of folk music, as did much of the school. He spent many years as a conductor and arranger for Harry Belafonte. For something like 20 years or more, he was the musical director for Peter, Paul, and Mary, about as successful and enduring a folk music group as there has been. Mary Travers, in fact, a neighbor of Bob's, had also gone to EI, dropping out after the 10th grade for some reason, just before I got there. She had been in Avi's class and at the time was in love (I know that's a word with which she would still agree if she were alive since we discussed it) with Avi's older brother, Henry. I thought it was that tie, her memory of Henry, which gave us room to become friends when we met some 25 years later.

EI was filled with singing groups, formal and informal, in just about every grade and, in a more formal way, in choral groups under Bob's direction when I was in the 9th grade and then with his successor, Earl Robinson (yes, that same Earl from earlier on). I moved from *The Fireside Book of Folk Songs* to Alan Lomax's *Folk Song, U.S.A.*, to *The People's Song Book*, from Burl Ives and "On Top of Old Smokey" to Woody Guthrie and "Pastures of Plenty," and most of all, to Pete Seeger and The Weavers.

There was no more influential folk music group than The Weavers. They were blacklisted in the early '50s, despite their enormous popularity in 1949 with Leadbelly's "Goodnight, Irene," as non-political a song as there ever was. Not that they didn't sing political songs. Their origin probably was with The Almanac Singers, a group in the '40s that included Woody Guthrie (whom Seeger had met in 1940), Seeger, and Lee Hays. They found their audiences primarily in union halls. After the war, Seeger and Hays formed The

Weavers with Ronnie Gilbert and Fred Hellerman. Peter, Paul and Mary, The Kingston Trio, The Tarriers, Three Dog Night, all the folkie groups of the '50s and '60s would not/could not have existed without The Weavers before them. The Weavers taught them all how to sing and what to sing. Even more important, they created a national audience for folk music.

Their 1955 Christmas Eve concert was one of the most memorable concerts I've ever attended. After The Weavers had been blacklisted, they thought they might never sing again. But they, and their manager, Harold Leventhal, thought there was still an audience for their music, if only it could be mobilized. They rented out Carnegie Hall that Christmas Eve and sold it out. Do I remember this correctly? From that first song: Pete singing out in his high tenor voice, his skinny body all angles, his banjo sticking way up into the air as he leaned into the microphone ...

> **Wake up, wake up, darling Corey,**
> **what makes you sleep so sound.**
> **The revenue man is a-comin',**
> **he's going to tear your still house down"**

... they had me and everyone else in their hands. I think every concert of theirs after that opened with that song. Folk songs, political songs, labor songs, Christmas songs, Jewish songs, songs from the Spanish Civil War, they sang them all. It was a wonderful night, maybe even better in retrospect than it was at the time. We could never thereafter, no one could thereafter, sing their songs without hearing the arrangements of The Weavers in the back of our heads. So in 1959 or '60, when a friend and I sang at Goucher College, it was my memory of The Weavers that taught me how to arrange the songs, even if most of them weren't songs that The Weavers had sung.

In 1956, I again took guitar lessons for a few months with Guy Carawan, from whom I learned a lot; new strums, new runs, new songs. Later on, Guy sang with The Weavers for a bit after Pete left the group, and he became the musical director of The Highlander Folk School in Tennessee. It is said that he introduced "We Shall

Overcome" to the civil rights movement. At the Highlander School, many civil rights workers, black and white, including Rosa Parks before the Birmingham bus boycott, got their training in non-violent civil disobedience before moving on to work in the south. In 1961 the school was closed by the state for violating segregation laws. It reopened as The Highlander Research and Education Center and continued doing just what it was doing before.

Here's the thing: it seemed to me that for many years, the only people that I knew of, at least the only white people, who were doing anything to oppose segregation were either Jews or leftists, including those who were accused of belonging to the Communist Party or of being "fellow travelers." It seems to me that way still. To argue that because the Old Left, from my aunt and uncle to the Weavers, were vehemently opposed to Jim Crow, to the notion that Black people were inherently inferior to whites and weren't entitled to be treated as fellow human beings, and that therefore, there was nothing sincere in their opposition, that it was all a Commie plot, is to do them a great disservice. Most of them, I think, became Communists out of their disillusionment with America and *laissez-faire* capitalism (particularly during the Depression) and out of the disinclination of the major political parties of the United States to do anything or enough about the real social and economic ills of America. The wonder is not that some people became Communists during the Depression; the wonder is that more did not (thankfully). If I sometimes felt furious with Pete Seeger and all the others for following the twists and turns of the Soviet Comintern like automatons, for ignoring or justifying the incalculable evil done by the Soviet Union both internally and wherever in the world it insinuated itself (and the Chinese Communists, as well), I do not believe that it was all a charade when it came to America. More than that, we are better as a people and nation in no small measure because of them.

The Civil Rights Movement was a revolution, a revolution in the best tradition of the Constitution as I had learned it from Grandpa. Like all revolutions that I've witnessed in my lifetime, domestic or foreign, peaceful or violent, it only succeeded when two things occurred simultaneously: First, that those who were most directly affected by repression, in this case, the Blacks of America, decided that enough was enough and second, that the white middle-class decided in large numbers that it, too, had had enough. Jews in America (even those who weren't Communists) had long been involved in the civil rights movement, in fact long before it became a widespread movement, through their support of and participation in the NAACP from early in the 20th century, if nothing else. But the Left, more than any other group of whites (at least from my perspective at the time), was responsible for making sure that the rest of us didn't forget about the inherent injustice and immorality of Jim Crow, particularly in the aftermath of a World War in which bigotry, religious and political hatred, and the Holocaust were so central.

There was one more group that was responsible: The Bull Connor's and George Wallace's and Orville Faubus's and Strom Thurman's, and all the ministers who asserted the moral and religious Godliness and righteousness of segregation and white superiority, and the people who bombed churches, burned crosses, and all the rest. As my friend and former colleague, Roger Rosenblatt said, to the mystification of many of the viewers of the *NewsHour*, Rosa Parks didn't free only Blacks; she also freed you (my fellow whites) and me. And so did Pete Seeger, and so did EI, despite their other political flaws.

If today we achieve some meaningful, measurable, lasting change in race relations, it, too, will be due to the joining of all races insisting on that change. And it will be a direct result of the revival of that old group of bigots, the Trumpists and primarily Southern Baptist pastors and politicians, who are so reminiscent of those who fought so hard against the dismantling of Jim Crow, against the end of legalized segregation, and against the right of every American to vote.

Amen.

End of sermon.

End of high school.

Chapter 5

A STRANGER IN A STRANGE LAND

1957 — 1959

It is a drizzly, gray early fall afternoon, the air heavy and leaden.

No, that's not right.

It's an early fall afternoon. The air is light and crisp in the waning rays of the sun.

That's not right either.

I'm standing in a small, narrow room. A narrow bed, an open suitcase lying on the thin, unmade mattress, a small, dark brown wood desk with a red gooseneck lamp on it, a small dresser with a gray clock radio on top.

Well, at least I got that part right.

Where am I? How did I get here?

Where I am, at least physically, is easy enough to answer: I'm in one of a suite of three bedrooms on the third floor of a dormitory on the campus of the University of Maryland in College Park, MD. Outside the purely physical location, where I am is anybody's guess, but it's certainly not here.

As for how I got here? I guess that's simple enough, too. I am here because I filled out an application and sent it in. It wasn't the only school I applied to. There were others favored by one member of my family or another, not to mention the guidance counselor at EI. I wasn't particularly interested in any of them, and I wasn't disinterested in them either. It just didn't seem to make any difference to me.

I could hardly have picked a stranger place in which to plop myself down. A New Yorker, a wanderer of Greenwich Village, a singer of folk songs, a lover of poetry, a mediocre athlete, a graduate of a progressive high school — a school, moreover, with a total population of two hundred and a graduating class of something like thirty-two kids, I found myself in the middle of a state university with thousands of students. Not only was it a state university, but it was almost like a local school, the locality being Baltimore, MD, and its suburbs and the Maryland suburbs of Washington, DC. With few exceptions, every student I met was from Baltimore. Even more, most of the kids I met were from the Forest Park section of Baltimore, a Jewish neighborhood, and most of them had gone to the same high school, Forest Park High School. For the record, the two who became my best friends went to another high school. But why spoil a good generalization? For them all, no matter how far from home they had come, they had scarcely moved an inch. In the seventeen years since I was born, I had moved into an ever-widening world only to have landed on an alien planet.

If the campus looked huge that first day — buildings you could have fit scores of EI's into, red bricks and white columns, the grassy distances between buildings cut by asphalt pathways, the fraternities and sororities along a U shaped drive on Fraternity Row across Baltimore Avenue, otherwise known as U.S. Route 1, the main road between Baltimore and Washington in the days before the Baltimore-Washington Expressway and the Interstate — then imagine my shock upon entering the gymnasium to register for classes. Thousands – *thousands* – of kids snaking in long lines to meet with harried registrars. It took forever. Hours. Yes, I'd take English. I had done well enough on the SATs to take something beyond introductory Algebra. Calculus? Sure. How about English History, a survey course? Why not? Physical Ed? Swimming sounded like fun. ROTC. Sorry, no choice about that. *Jesus Christ.* French. Did I hold my head in agony at the prospect?

English class was actually sort of fun, though it met at 8 am, a truly ungodly hour. The instructor was a young guy, probably still in graduate school. Mr. Something, all crew cut, and a suit. I hadn't seen a crew cut since I was ten. I enjoyed talking to him, though the class was kind of silly. I had read more in the first month of the ninth grade in EI than the rest of them had in their entire lives. There wasn't any book or writer that Mr. Something ever mentioned that I hadn't read.

As for calculus, that was a horse of a different color. I tried. I really did try. But I didn't understand a word of it and dropped out of the class before I flunked it.

English History was one of those classes that was all lecture and dates. Date after date after date, King after King after King, the Battle of This and That, Prince Him and Princess Her, not to mention the Queens. A thousand years in sixty seconds. Who could care? Why should I care? Is that really what History is? I always managed to find myself at the back of the lecture hall where I couldn't hear a thing and could nap peacefully. The hours I might have spent trying to memorize all those names and dates, I instead spent reading Max Lerner's *America as a Civilization* and William Appleman Williams' *The Contours of American History*. The final was like the rest of the course, gray and drab to match the drizzly weather outside. When was this or when was that, pick one from A to D, and so on. I had extensive crib notes written all over my hands and arms. I flunked anyway. How many ways are there to fail a class? Let me count the ways.

Swimming, ah, swimming, now that should be a cakewalk, don't you think?

It is around two o'clock on a chilly November afternoon. We are in the swimming pool. This is a "men only" class (there are no co-educational swimming classes, more's the pity), and we are all naked, all fifteen or so guys, except for the instructor. Why are we naked? Beats me. I'm sure there's a good reason for it. We shouldn't get swimming trunks wet? No, that couldn't be it.

Today we're going to have a real treat. We're going off the high board, a little three-meter affair. No, you don't have to

dive. You can jump if you'd prefer. I await my turn and then climb slowly to the top and stand at the edge of the platform. I remember how scared I was when I dove off a ten-foot platform in Camp Kokosing. I look down at the water. It seems very far away, the pool tiny. "Come on, Saltz," a voice calls, "Jump." I just stand there. This is ridiculous. "Come on." I slowly turn around and, with as much dignity as a nude, slightly pudgy, seventeen-year-old can muster, climb back down the stairs, and walk the length of the pool and out the door. "Saltz, where are you going?!" Away, far away from here. I never return.

I flunked that course, too.

You might have thought that I would be opposed, in principle, to ROTC, but you would be wrong. I didn't like war; who in their right mind would? But I knew we were right to fight World War II. I even thought I understood why we fought in Korea. Israel couldn't survive without having to fight wars, it seemed. Yes, I thought (in these pre-Vietnam years), there are actually things worth fighting for, that you have to be willing to fight for. Even a few months later, in the spring when I turned eighteen, I willingly, though reluctantly, registered for the draft. I thought then, as later, that if drafted, I would go; that there were obligations to being a citizen of the country, and in a democracy, one wasn't always going to be in the majority. I must admit, though, that the thought of basic training scared me to death, more so than the thought of bullets. Maybe I was just naive. I was classified 1-Y, eligible to be drafted in a national emergency but not otherwise. The classification was because of my hearing. I've been deaf in my left ear since birth. Can't say I was sorry to hear that, though.

Although I had no intrinsic objection to the ROTC, I objected to three things: spit polishing shoes, hair kept trimmed above the ears, and the Atomic Bomb. I can think of no sillier pastime in the world than spit polishing shoes. But unit discipline, unit cohesion, everybody looking spiffy and identical on the parade ground, everybody *being* identical on the parade ground, whatever the justification? I wasn't buying any of it. Besides, it was too much trouble. Oh, I'd give my shoes a wipe every once in a while before trotting out to the parade grounds, but I couldn't/wouldn't take it seriously.

As for short and frequently trimmed hair, well, I had given that up as soon as my mother stopped forcing me to get a haircut on some predetermined schedule. I don't know that I thought of myself as Samson and, so far as I was concerned, the length of my hair was hardly a matter of social or political principle as it became for so many later on, or at least I didn't think so. Maybe I underestimate my penchant for silent, grudging protest in small things as well as large. Yes, I'm sure I do. Haircuts were like going to the dentist without the pain. Something you have to do but as rarely as can be managed. I certainly was not about to manage it for the ROTC. My sergeant, or whoever, was not too happy with me. I wasn't too happy with him either. All these years later, I still feel the same way about haircuts. And polished shoes.

Then there was the Bomb — that is, the atomic bomb. This was not a parade ground issue but one argued in the classroom. I knew all the arguments and had made my decision about them before I ever got to Maryland, and just because some guy in a uniform thought the more bombs we had the better, and that maybe we should have used them a little more often (like in Korea), and maybe we should have taught the Chinese a lesson for butting in, well, that didn't mean I was about to agree with him, regardless of what it meant for my grade.

The instructor decided to resolve our impasse by getting it out of the classroom, where it tended to come up in every class at my instigation. He sent me to the school's Catholic chaplain to talk about it. It didn't occur to me then how absurd it was to send me to a Catholic priest to resolve my moral objections to the bomb. Why on earth did he think a Jew should go to a Catholic for instruction in morality? Maybe it never occurred to him that I was Jewish. Perhaps he knew the priest would be on his side and that the rabbi at the local Hillel Society wasn't.

So, here I am talking about peace and the Brotherhood of Man and that the Japanese were going to give up anyway, and the immorality of killing one or two hundred thousand civilians at a time with barely a second thought, and a priest is justifying the barbarity of the Bomb and the inhumanity of war. Every Wednesday afternoon, the same afternoon that my one-time PS 8 classmates would go off for religious instruction, I'd go off to the chapel to engage in the same conversation, the same kind of conversation, that Grandma had in the motorboat of a priest on Coecles Inlet off the shoreline of Shelter Island 12 years before. And, like Grandma, I was having a wonderful time doing it. Those conversations were the most fun, maybe the only real fun, I had that first year at Maryland.

Unlike haircuts and spit-polished shoes, I've long since changed my mind about the Bomb. Of course, war is inhumane (though too obviously very human) and barbaric, unpredictable, and incalculable in its awfulness and results. But I don't think that dropping the Bomb on Hiroshima and Nagasaki was any different in its morality than the London Blitz, the firebombing of Dresden or Tokyo and the other Japanese cities, or, even more, the attack on Pearl Harbor. And, yes, I am sure it brought the war to an end faster than if it hadn't been dropped, even if "faster" meant a week or two. In those now long-ago days, I was fond of saying that if you sow the wind, you will reap the whirlwind. I had just forgotten the fact that it was the Germans and the Japanese who had done the sowing and that they each fully deserved to reap whatever whirlwind came their way. So, no, it doesn't bother me very much anymore.

That is not to say that I think of the use of atomic bombs in a cavalier way. They are obviously horrible weapons, weapons whose sole purpose is to maximize the efficacy of destroying large amounts of property while inevitably killing of lots and lots of people with minimal cost in human life to those doing the bombing. In fact, if my understanding is correct, they were the antithesis of American war doctrine during the first years of World War II. The initial goal of the American bombing campaign in Europe was to destroy the industrial manufacturing capacity of Germany rather than kill civilians. The hope was that by reducing the ability of the German Army to re-equip itself, we would render them ineffective. Unfortunately, the campaign was largely ineffective, with one particular exception, the destruction of the fighter plane manufacturing capacity of the Luftwaffe. By the time of the invasion of Normandy, German dominance of the air fighting space was a thing of the past. On the other hand, the British didn't believe that they could effectively engage in "pinpoint" bombing. Nor did they want to expose themselves to the risks necessary for pinpoint targeting (meaning daytime bombing raids) and so engaged in "area" targeting, meaning that they inevitably killed lots of people without too many (if any) qualms while mostly missing whatever industrial targets they were aiming at.

In Japan, America eventually gave up on the notion of only bombing industrial manufacturing capacity and turned to the massive bombing of civilian populations. Thus the firebombing of Japanese cities during which many thousands of civilians were killed. I believe that in Tokyo alone, 100,000 people died, more than were killed by the dropping of the Atomic Bomb on Nagasaki. In the documentary film, *The Fog of War*, Robert McNamara said that he thought using the bomb in Hiroshima and Nagasaki had been wrong. McNamara, who had brought his expertise in statistical data analysis to both the European and then the Japanese bombing campaigns, contradicted his own logic. During the war, he was constantly trying to define how to get the biggest bang for the buck, or to put it another way, how to best balance the effectiveness of the dropping of bombs versus the cost to America in both material (meaning airplanes, etc.) and personnel (meaning pilots and their crews). The atomic bomb proved the most cost-effective solution America had yet found. One plane and one crew successfully killed some 150,000 people in Hiroshima, an event far less costly than the firebombing of Tokyo, which utilized and lost far more American assets and thus had been far less efficient. The post-war capacity to employ ICBMs to deliver nuclear warheads made it seem still more efficient.

Of course, the risks involved in using nuclear weapons were practically non-existent when no one else had them. However, once the Soviets had their own bombs, all the calculations changed. The question now became how many millions of Soviets killed were worth the risk to millions of Americans and *vice versa*. Thus, the apparent insanity or logic of MAD, the doctrine of Mutually Assured Destruction.

Did insanity produce sanity? Not really. It only produced fear, fear on the part of both civilians and militaries on all sides. Fortunately — so far — it has scared everyone, but no one can guarantee that fear will always trump the impulse of some towards nihilism.

In fact, the lack of that guarantee lay behind the success of the Bush campaign to win the support of the American people for the invasion of Iraq. I do not think most Americans would have backed the idea of the war without the invoked threat of "mushroom clouds." And I think he won reelection based on the assumption that individuals will use a nuclear weapon regardless of who dies. Fear. It's a hell of a way to live, don't you think?

But I digress.

Did I flunk out of Maryland that first semester? Was it the second? The third? It could have been any of them, though I think it was the third. So let me assume that and recount the only two episodes of my second semester that seem to matter.

When I returned home during the Christmas break in the winter of 1957, I asked my parents if they'd agree to my trying to join a fraternity. The campus emptied out on the weekends. My roommates went home, and the school, aside from sports events, had no organized activities on the weekends, and neither did the dormitories, at least none that I knew of. Oh, yes, I went to one football game. I guess it was fun if you can call 60,000 screaming, banner-waving, heavily drinking fans who seemed to care deeply, or at least passionately, about what was going on while I sat, a mildly interested observer, having … fun. But there was the strange and otherworldly experience of the halftime show. All marching bands and "I wish I were in the land of Dixie" and waving Confederate flags, as I sat, the lyrics and music of "Lift Every Voice and Sing," the so-called "Negro National Anthem," running through my mind. Were we on the same planet?

Football and basketball weekends aside, the campus was dead on weekends. Except, that is, in the fraternity and sorority houses. To be sure, those kids went home from them too, but it was far less common. So, I "rushed" the fraternities with my parents' agreement.

I know of no one who's ever known me that I've told about joining a fraternity who hasn't said (in disbelief), "You belonged to a fraternity?" Believe me that I only exaggerate slightly. I, myself, could hardly believe that I wanted to be in a fraternity, and I'm still not entirely comfortable with the idea of telling anyone. I joined the Maryland chapter of Zeta Beta Tau, ZBT, a well-known Jewish fraternity.

As for why ZBT actually accepted me into their fold, you'll have to ask someone who knows. What did this bunch of well-pressed Forest Park High graduates want with a scruffy New Yorker who knew from sitting in coffee houses and strumming a guitar playing something other than "Blueberry Hill" (not there was anything wrong with "Blueberry Hill;" I loved Fats Domino) but wouldn't have known what a prom was if it smacked me in the face. I wasn't even the only New Yorker. The chapter president, Hank Goldberg, was a New Yorker too … sort of. Hank was from Long Island, which is definitely not the same thing. The only reason I've ever been able to come up with is that a bunch of us would-be pledges were taken to the local beer place called, I think, the Rathskeller (what else?), where we were put to the true fraternity test: how fast and how much of a pitcher of beer could we chug-a-lug. I dropped the whole pitcher down my throat in a flash and won by a mile. Cheers and wild applause. *This* New Yorker, at least, was good for something!

Now, there were the occasional parties on weekends, with their kegs of beer and people wandering around in various states of inebriation and, sometimes, undress. And that's how I discovered the strange mating practices among fraternity "men" and sorority "girls." Suppose someone from ZBT wanted to go out with a girl and, hopefully, get laid with no thought of the possibility of eventual marriage or the pretense, even, of such a possibility. In that case, he'd go out with a girl from a non-Jewish sorority. The same was true, supposedly, of guys in non-Jewish fraternities; they'd go out with Jewish sorority girls to get laid but not married. This resulted in the rather odd situation of everyone pretending that the girl who you were or might be hoping to marry wasn't having sex since she if she was having it, she wasn't having it with you but with someone else who wasn't of your (or her) religion, which, therefore, in the magical way of these things, kept her hymen intact. I'm not sure if this should be classified as simply an odd form of religious bigotry or something more fundamentally akin to insanity. I vote for the latter. On the other hand, maybe they're the same thing.

Let it be said that Hank Goldberg was dating Margie Aronstein, an absolutely delightful girl, and so it could be presumed that there was hope that marriage would be in their future. Margie, lively and sparkling as she was, was also intelligent (why, then, was she with Hank?), and I loved talking to her. She was pursuing a degree in education. Her future plans were to get married after graduation, teach in elementary school for two years, and retire to become a housewife and raise her yet-to-be-born two children. She was a complete mystery to me. Every girl I knew, all the girls I went to high school with, all wanted to be doctors, lawyers, novelists, actors, poets, singers, and, yes, teachers. They wanted to change the world. I think they would have found Margie as strange a creature as I did.

That summer, the summer of '58, I returned to New York dispirited. At Maryland, things were not going well academically, and I wasn't doing all that well personally. Partly out of necessity, partly out of boredom, I needed to get a job. Burt Hanft, the husband of my mother's one-time secretary, Bernice, who had all become good friends, offered to help. He was a lawyer, a man with bright eyes, a ready smile, who liked to drink, to smoke cigars and, I think, could be tough as nails. Burt was now in the entertainment business, vice president of Screen Gems, a subsidiary of Columbia Pictures, and one of the largest producers of TV programs. *The Adventures of Rin Tin Tin* was its most successful program. They also had the extensive library of Columbia movies and others licensed for airing on local stations around the country. My job was to survey programming schedules of stations around the country to see what movies were being aired compared with what the stations were reporting. Not exciting, to be sure, but I did it diligently.

ZBT wasn't wholly absent that summer. There was a national conference of ZBT members in Montreal over one weekend. I decided to go and got there somehow. We were all staying at the Queen Elizabeth Hotel, and the first night we were there, all the guys from Maryland decided to go to a whorehouse. I felt highly uncomfortable at the prospect of frat house group sex, and I didn't go with them. I wondered what on earth I was doing there, what I was doing with these people with whom I seemed to have so little in common, most of whom I didn't even like. The next day I went back to New York.

I returned to Maryland in the fall with considerable hesitancy. I didn't really want to be there or with these people, but there wasn't any other place I wanted to be either. At least I no longer had to live in the dorms, and I moved into the ZBT house. I didn't have enough seniority (or money?) to live in a private or shared room, so I slept in their dorm on the bottom of a bunk bed. Sometime that September, or maybe it was early October, there was a party. I got drunk. Massively, stupendously, drunk. So drunk that I blacked out. I woke up the next morning curled up on the floor, reeking of vomit. The downstairs bathroom floor was covered with my vomit, and I had to clean it up. After managing to do that and showering, I dragged myself up to my bunk and didn't get up for the next three days. I barely got out of bed for the rest of the semester. I would sleep until noon or one o'clock, get up in time to have lunch, play basketball with the rest of the guys on the court behind the house (I wasn't any better than I had been in high school), eat dinner, and watch TV until 10 or 11 when I'd go down to the deli on Baltimore Avenue and get a steak sub and then watch TV some more until three or four in the morning and start the cycle all over again. I barely, if ever, went to classes.

Despite all, I managed to make two friends. Why Marty Miller and Bill Levy were in a fraternity is almost as much of a mystery as why I was in one. Both of them had gone to City College (the two exceptions to my earlier generalization about Forest Park High School), though neither of them knew each other well. They both had been in fraternities there, whatever fraternities in high school meant, so I guess it's not a surprise that they wound up in one at College Park. They were both a year ahead of me. A short, not particularly handsome guy (think Dustin Hoffman), Marty was a diligent pre-med student, and my impression was that he worked hard at it even if he wasn't sure that he really wanted to be a doctor. On the other hand, Bill wasn't an especially serious student, or so it seemed to me. He was okay-looking but not much more than that. I somehow have an image of him twirling a waxed mustache with a devilish gleam in his eye. It never happened (well, maybe the gleam was real), but that's how I think of him. His interests were poetry and literature (the more radical, the better) and drugs. I don't know who started talking to whom first, but we gradually became friends.

No event bonded us more than a poetry reading that we went to in Baltimore that fall. Allen Ginsberg, Peter Orlovsky, and Gregory

Corso (I'm sure there was a fourth, though I don't remember who) were touring the country giving readings. It was my first exposure to them. Ginsberg read "Howl." It was thrilling in its imagery, intensity, energy, and rhythms. It attacked, engaged, the senses; one couldn't just hear it; one smelled it, touched it, tasted it. Nothing else that evening was anywhere near as good, but that was enough. Indeed, it spurred a fair amount of my reading over the next couple of years. Bill was also, I think, excited, and he was soon writing poetry (including parodies) that took after Ginsberg.

Truth be told, I don't really remember Marty's reaction. But my impression is that Marty felt like he was lapping around the edges of some exotic culture. Many years later, after we'd not talked to each other in decades, Marty said that I'd changed his life. It was news to me. I didn't see how I could have changed anyone's life in those years. He explained it by talking about what I had introduced him to, that is, all the things that made me such an alien in Maryland and ZBT. He said, in fact, that I'd dropped into Maryland like a Martian from another planet. Now that he's said it, I'm pleased to think that I had some responsibility for what happened to him in the long run; he became a Professor of History and Slavic Languages at Duke. Something good, at least, came out of that awful semester.

Need I tell you that I flunked out of school?

Is there any question that I was depressed? No, but I had no idea how to try to get myself out of it. I asked to return to Maryland for the next semeste, and the university agreed, putting me on probation. Maybe if I switched to some easy major, I could manage the required 2.0-grade average.

So, I returned to Maryland for the spring semester of 1959, this time as Bill Levy's roommate and as a business major. Unfortunately, I discovered that changing my major was no solution to anything. I was even more bored and distracted than I had been in the various English and history classes I had taken. At least I managed to pull myself together enough to muster up the requisite 2.0-grade average. I knew, though, that I couldn't keep it up and decided to switch back to the liberal arts school come the fall.

The other thing that I did that semester was to join the staff of the Maryland literary magazine. In short order, I found that I was doing much of the work, editing stories and poems, and doing paste-ups. I even wrote the story, "Doors Only Open to Let You In," which you've already read. Do you suppose it was a metaphor for my life, not only my life at PS 8 but my current life as well? It never occurred to me when I wrote it. Today, I'm less sure. I certainly wanted out of the life I was in, but I couldn't think how to do that, much less what kind of life I'd rather be in.

Meanwhile, Bill, Marty, and I were still friends. We'd hang out and go places together, often joined by another friend of theirs, Chuck Hollander, who wasn't at Maryland but at another school in Baltimore, and his girlfriend. We'd often go to a bar on the docks in Baltimore to hear bluegrass music, particularly Earl Taylor and the Stony Mountain Boys.

As often as not, we'd wind up the evening at the Pimlico Diner. If you're interested in knowing what the diner was like, watch Barry Levinson's excellent 1982 movie, *Diner*. The film is set in roughly the same era that I was in Maryland (maybe a couple of years later), and the characters are like some of the people at ZBT at their best, particularly in their obsession with the Baltimore Colts. It would not have been too great a stretch to imagine certain of my fraternity brothers requiring their girlfriends to pass a test about the Colts before asking them to marry, just as Steve Gutenberg did in the movie. But that was my brothers at their best. At their worst, some of them were, I thought, dreadful human beings.

One night during the week, a high school girl from Baltimore had come out to the fraternity house. Anybody who wanted to fuck her in her car could do so for $3.00. The guys gleefully lined up, awaiting their turn. Once again, as in Montreal, I couldn't bring myself to join in and walked back to my apartment. I can't say that I left out of any great sense of moral outrage or because the girl was in high school. But, whatever else it was, because of the way it was being done, because of the way my fraternity brothers were behaving, it seemed ... dirty somehow, and I didn't want any part of it. I wanted to be better than that. I wanted my fraternity brothers to be better than that. I wanted sex to be more meaningful than that. But most of all, I wanted girls, all girls, to be better than that. I still do.

When I returned to New York that summer, I went to summer school at NYU. I needed to make up some ground, and I thought that might be a way to do it, so I took a course in Hemingway and Faulkner. It was perfect for me, combining the short stories and novels of two of my favorite writers, and, even better, it met daily and only lasted six weeks. It seemed that I didn't have the endurance for the months of spread-out and disjointed work, but this kind of totally immersive concentration, at least in something I was interested in, worked very well. It was the first A I had gotten since high school. I might be lost, but my mind wasn't completely gone.

My success at NYU didn't mean that I returned to Maryland for the fall semester with anything less than dread. I was now an English major, but I remember none of my courses, with one exception. I enrolled in Professor Thelma Levine's class in Philosophy and Literature for some reason. Maybe Marty suggested it since I know he took the course and loved it so much that he later found a way to acknowledge Levine in his book, *Freud and the Bolsheviks: Psychoanalysis in Imperial Russia and the Soviet Union.*

Regardless, it was a popular class and deservedly so. Levine, as I recall, was a flame-haired *zaftig* woman with intellectual sparkle, verve, and acuity. Her reading list was the first one at Maryland that I enjoyed: Freud's *Interpretation of Dreams*, Thomas Mann's *The Magic Mountain*, Arthur Koestler's *Darkness at Noon*, Shakespeare's *Hamlet*, Kafka's *Metamorphosis. The Magic Mountain* was a particularly wonderful surprise since I'd never read Mann before. Over the next year, I'd work my way through most of his remaining work, from *Joseph and his Brothers* (which had been in my parents' bookcase for as long as I remembered) to *Stories of Three Decades.*

In one of her early lectures, Levine said something about Edith Hamilton saying, in *The Greek Way,* that "the ancient Egyptians worshiped death." I had never read a word of the book. When it came time to write a major paper for the course, I decided to question the truth of the line, no matter what Hamilton had actually said. It seemed to me that a civilization could not survive and thrive for thousands of years and "worship death." Whatever time I spent academically that semester was devoted to reading and writing about ancient Egypt. I had a good time trying to demonstrate my thesis (if I remember correctly) that life and death were virtually the same for the Egyptians. For example, if one read Egyptian poetry, it was enormously earthy, full of life, of the pleasures to be found in life, etc. In death, one could only hope to improve on things; it was like life, only better. I don't know if Levine agreed with my conclusions or not, but that didn't matter. Another A.

Meantime, there were Bill and Marty and Chuck. Marty had a girlfriend who took me that fall to my first synagogue service, a Yom Kippur service in Baltimore. It was the first time I'd set foot inside a synagogue since my *bar mitzvah* when I was thirteen, which I never thought of as anything more than a monumentally inconsequential event, although I supposed it pleased my mother and, I presume, my grandparents. However, the experience didn't cause me to be more interested in becoming more religiously involved personally.

The University of Maryland in 1959 was not a big drug campus. In fact, I don't think that any campus was, although that would change very soon. But one could always trust Bill to find the unusual and exotic. Bill was happy to get high. He wanted to try everything there was to try and did. In fact, the last moments that we spent together were spent in a new experiment for him. He had never tried peyote and had gotten a button from somewhere. Hearing of its awful taste, he wanted to mask it. So he chopped it up and made a sandwich filled with whatever was in the refrigerator — plenty of ketchup and mustard, anything to disguise the flavor. After turning down an offer to join him, he ate the sandwich up and waited to see what happened.

Bill was fond of saying that he felt like a character in someone else's novel. I'm not sure how or why he thought that getting high and/or having hallucinations would help him find his way into his own life. But, if you look him up in Wikipedia, I think you'll see that his life after Maryland followed the straightest ... well, the most direct and consistent path of the three of us.

As for me, drugs scared me to death. I felt that I was in such fragile condition that drugs could provide my own door that, once opened, would shut behind me forever, would send me on a downward spiral that I could never recover from, that I would be lost forever. So I stayed away from them.

Marty and I had started singing folk songs together, and Chuck was singing along with us. I wrote arrangements for various songs, things sung by The Weavers or others. I don't remember how it happened, but we were invited to sing at some sort of event at Goucher, a college for women in Baltimore. Chuck dropped out at the last minute, and Marty and I did the gig ourselves. I have absolutely no idea how it went, whether we were good or bad or indifferent. We performed and were paid our money, which was the end of our professional folk singing career, though not my singing.

The semester was all but formally over, and so was my career at Maryland. While Marty was trying to decide what to do about medicine, I, too, was trying to decide what to do with my life. I returned home for the Christmas vacation filled with trepidation. I was depressed. I didn't know what I was doing. I didn't know why I was doing anything. I didn't know what I wanted to do. I didn't even know why I was alive. But, I knew I had to do something, and the only thing I could think of doing was to leave school. I needed time to figure out my life, though I had no idea how to go about doing that.

Most of all, I didn't know how my mother would react. I wasn't worried about Dad; he'd support whatever decision I made. Mom, though, was something else. I don't know if I've adequately conveyed what a formidable person she could be. It wasn't simply that she was astute and articulate; it was more her apparently enormous self-assurance and confidence. She understood, sometimes, more than I would have liked. For her, understanding a situation meant that she would think of a solution and urge that solution on you with the considerable intellectual force she could muster. It didn't matter if I was four or 18 (and that's all I was at this point). She was sure of her prescriptions and delivered them with equal vigor. I don't think it was so much a matter of wanting to control things (though if she could, she would) but of simply wanting me to be doing better than I was. If either Amy or I made her angry, her punishment could be fearsome. She'd either become very icy, and her entire voice would change into what Amy and I would call her office voice, or, even worse, she might stop talking to us. She could go for a week without saying a word directly to us, something that was far worse than the one spanking I'd had as a child. It's not that her concerns were unwarranted. On the contrary, it was obvious that my life was not going well, and there would come other times in the future when it teetered. But sooner or later, I would have to find my own solutions, and they couldn't be hers, and they wouldn't ever be hers.

Over the years, I've learned how much children can underestimate their parents' capacity to allow their children to do what they truly need to do while praying or hoping they won't crash and burn. So it was with Mom. As fearful as I was of telling her of my decision when I returned home, sure that she wouldn't hear of it and would insist that I return to school and buckle down and push myself to do better, she surprised me.

> It is Tuesday, December 29, 1959. I have been home for a few days now, still unsure how to tell Mom about my decision, wondering, almost, if I hoped she would convince me that I was wrong, that this was not the way to do things, that there was a better way. I've been sitting in my room all afternoon, the sky getting darker and darker as night creeps across the sky, the sun gradually lowering behind the Statue of Liberty just barely visible out the window. She'll be home soon.
>
> At 6:30, I hear the door slam. "Michael," she calls out, "are you home?"
>
> I don't say anything. Mom finds her way to my room, the room Amy used to have when she was a baby, the room she had until I left home. "Why is the light out? Are you okay"
>
> "I don't know."
>
> She turns on a table lamp and sits on a chair while I sit on the bed with its white, red, and yellow Navajo-like designed wool blanket on top of it. She looks very grave. "Is there something you want to tell me?"
>
> I'm not sure I actually want to say the words. I look out the window, at the lamp, at the books on the shelves, at the desk.
>
> She remains silent, waiting, barely breathing, I think.
>
> "I think I want to leave school. I need time to figure things out. I can't keep doing this."

"Are you saying you want to leave school forever?"

"I don't know. I don't think so. But I can't go back without knowing why I'm there."

"Are you sure?" she asks.

"…Yes."

"Okay, then."

I feel like crying, but I don't. I don't know why not, but I don't. I have been so afraid of this moment. But I gradually feel a sense of relief, an unburdening. After a time, we both stand and hug each other.

"Well," she says, "let's have dinner."

Did she know all along? Was she just waiting for me to make up my mind? Had I completely, totally underestimated her, her capacity to see into the very heart of my confusion? I don't know the answers, and I'll never know. But sitting here now writing this, I understand, once again, why I was so afraid of her and why I loved her so much.

There is one more event to relate from that Christmas, an event that happened the very next day, an event that was as surprising and as shocking as any that has ever occurred to me, an event that would forever change the course of my life.

Is it too much to think that the convergence of these two events is related? That the decision to leave the University of Maryland somehow allowed the other to happen? It is not the only time that seemingly unrelated events would happen in close proximity so that one might think that they were tied together with bands of steel.

As long as I've known Amy, at least since she was more than a very little girl, she wanted a life in the theater. Now fifteen, she had become involved in a community theater group, the Brooklyn Heights Players, and was stage managing a production of John Osborn's *Epitaph for George Dillon*. Earlier in the week, she had asked if I'd like to see a rehearsal, and I had agreed to go the day after I told Mom of my decision to quit school.

The play was rehearsing in the top floor ballroom of the Hotel Bossert on Montague Street. The stage was a makeshift affair, a group of platforms on the floor resting against the back wall, between four pillars. The lights were amateurish, PARs, ordinary floodlights lodged in tin cans, colored gels covering them. An over-stuffed chair sat mid-stage left. I remember an ironing board down-stage right.

> **A slight girl sits in the chair, chewing gum, her brown hair in curlers. She is wearing a thin robe that she barely bothers to keep closed, a bra, panties. She is reading a magazine, flipping through the pages nervously.**
>
> **"Fancy writing up and asking that!" She continues flipping through the pages, tosses the magazine on the floor. "Soppy cow," she mutters as she gets up and crosses downstage to the ironing board.**

I sat through the rehearsal of John Osborne's play mesmerized. The director, Herman Shonbrun, talked to the actors. Why are they doing this? Why that? What are they thinking, what is their motivation? Why move this way rather than that? What's the actual meaning of this line? What is Josie really saying? What is George? How about if you tried this? How to express ideas through action? The dialog between the actors and the director flows back and forth, the intensity with which each of them listens, the attempt to understand each other, to manifest the result of the conversation in the play's action, in the *beingness* of the characters.

I had seen plays, lots of them, children's plays, Broadway and off-Broadway plays, musicals, comedies, and dramas, all through my life. I had even done my own tiny bit of acting, from the grocery clerk in the 1st grade to a minor role in the EI senior class production of Arthur Miller's *The Crucible*. Why had I never understood or felt any of this? Perhaps it was because, at this very moment, I was looking for a way to understand human emotions and actions, to think about them, my own included, and this was a way to do it, to experiment with them, but with and through characters who were not real but whose life on stage had to seem genuine and under-standable to those of us in the audience while at the same time being outside looking in. Maybe it was Herman, a word magician, a born storyteller filled with southern charm and intelligence and passion. Or perhaps I had just stepped out of one world and was poised to enter another, and this is the one that came along. Were Eliakum and Shomer whispering in my ear? Was it fate, a karmic wind blowing through the universe? Who knows? Not me. It didn't matter; it doesn't matter. The earth had moved as clearly for me as it had for Hemingway on a Spanish hillside, and I could actually hear, feel the pieces clicking into place, a place that, though I didn't know it then, would form the rock on which the rest of my life would be built.

Looking back, it seems that as I moved into an increasingly widening world, I was, at the same time, increasingly losing myself within it. I don't want to stretch the metaphor too far, but somehow from that time when I sat in Grandma's lap listening to Bach busily knitting, I was continually dropping a stitch — me. Or, maybe, sinking like a stone in the pond. To be sure, I discovered things of enormous importance along the way, more than I was aware of finding. Sometimes it takes time to discover what one has discovered. And there was this one newly discovered thing without which I might not have survived. But I was going to have to retrace my steps, to go back to where I had begun to try to find myself again. It would take 14 more years of wandering in my own wilderness before I started to get my bearings.

Chapter 6
SAY SOMETHING REAL, TRUE, HEARTFELT

◆

1960 — 1963

Happy New Year!

I was back in New York. It was a new year, a new beginning, yet I was a man (I use that word loosely, *bar mitzvah* aside) without a plan. After trudging around employment agencies, I got a job, a bit of drudgery as a clerk in a pipe and cigar store. They advertised in the back of various men's magazines, magazines for hunters and fishermen, magazines for outdoorsmen, and their ads were for corn cob pipes. Send in 50 cents (coins only), and you'd get a corn cob pipe. I was surprised at how many people actually sent in money for these things. My job was to collect the money and put the addresses in a pile so other clerks could type out address labels and still others could mail out the pipes. I quit after two months.

Amy had a friend, Dorothy Rudo, who she babysat for. They had become very close, Dorothy providing the sympathetic adult counselor Amy felt she needed in her life. I, too, would appear at her door every once in a while to talk about things with an adult who was not my parents. When I told her I was looking for another job, she helped find one for me at the company she worked for as a copy editor. Every night I'd go into the office and proofread column after mind-numbing column of numbers. I left this job, too, after only a couple of months.

Marty Miller and Bill Levy were still a part of my life. They came up to New York at least a couple of times during these months. Bill was looking to score. He reported that he found one place on East

14th Street in Alphabet City, as Avenues A, B, and C were called, named The Monkey's Paw. Amusingly appropriate, don't you think? It was a Potemkin Village of a coffee shop. I don't know that they actually sold coffee. What they did sell was in a dusty display case. In it were all their wares: pills of various sorts and mushrooms. On the wall was a price list that I'm sure Bill studied carefully. And Marty? He was happy with his philosophy courses and planned to go to Europe that summer. It was the last time we were really in touch for many years.

I frequently found myself wandering alone in the Village at night. I spent most of my time at Gerdy's Folk City or at the Village Gate, places I would regularly visit over the next few years. I saw all sorts of singers at Gerdy's, many more than once. Smooth-voiced Leon Bibb, who had released an album of folk music in 1959 that I liked very much, was a frequent act. I had first seen him in 1954 when he was in Earl Robinson's musical, *Sandhog*, about the digging of the subway tunnels under the North River, as the Hudson River was called then. Bob DeCormier, Earl's predecessor as the music director of EI, was also in it as was David Hooks who, as I later found out, was an old friend of Herman Shonbrun's from Florida and who, like Herman, was among the first actors in the Circle in the Square theater company.

I saw many others there or at the Gate: Brother John Sellers, Odetta (who made a recording of Earl's *Ballad for Americans*), Ian and Sylvia, and The Staple Singers among them. There were jazz musicians, too, either at the Gate or the Village Vanguard, like Cannonball Adderly and Olatunji.

I saw no one more often than the great blues singer and guitarist, Josh White. I don't think there was anyone I would have liked to have been more like, at least as a musician. I was nowhere close. White was shunned by most of the folk world because his politics didn't mesh with theirs, a phenomenon that was also true of Burl Ives and a few others like Katie Lee, who I would meet later on during my *MacNeil/Lehrer* career. That didn't mean that White was a conservative. He simply refused to go along with anyone's politics. A friend of Franklin and Eleanor Roosevelt, he was a popular artist both in America and abroad. His sole political interest was civil and human rights. He was a fierce public advocate even as he refused to align himself with any political party or faction. His advocacy resulted in being accused of being a Communist and blacklisted during the McCarthyite years. Volunteering to testify before Congress, he hoped to clear his name, but it made no difference. The political right wouldn't have him, and the political left, including most of those in the folk music world, wouldn't have him either. In effect, he was blacklisted by one and blackballed by the other. By the time I saw him in 1960, his exile from the performing world was waning, but his rejection by the left seemed permanent and may have been the reason that he appeared at the Gate rather than Gerdy's.

And no, I never saw Bob Dylan at Gerdy's, however often I was there. Maybe he was off sitting by himself, just as I was. And yes, I was mildly upset at the introduction of electric guitars into folk music. But, even if I wasn't a Dylan fan, I got over it. How could I object? I loved the electric guitar. I loved Les Paul and Mary Ford and all the early rock 'n rollers I had heard on the radio. Eventually, I had more than one electrified acoustic guitar and even a solid body one.

Amidst all this, I spent time with Herman and his wife, Peggy, who, as a poet and playwright, used her maiden name, Margaret Thompson. Herman was 32 at the time, though I assumed he was much older because he seemed wise and knowledgeable. He had been born in Tampa, his father a cigar maker, his mother a housewife. He had graduated from the University of Florida in Gainesville, had taught theater there, had been in the Army as World War 2 ended, and had come to New York with Peggy in 1951. Once here, he was one of the earliest members of the Circle in the Square theater company, among the finest off-Broadway theater companies of the '50s, '60s, and '70s, under the direction of Jose Quintero and Ted Mann. Herman always thought of himself as one of the founders, but Mann told me it was untrue and that there were originally only five board members. But Herman, he said, was one of the first members of the company. It has always struck me as ironic and uniquely American that Quintero, a Panamanian by birth, the aristocratic son of a former vice-president of that country, was the foremost interpreter and director of Eugene O'Neil, one of America's greatest playwrights. When I met Quintero at a cocktail party with Herman, he was wearing jodhpurs and riding boots, and we all drank gin and bitters because he did.

Fortunately, or unfortunately, Herman and Peggy loved making babies. By the time I met them at the very end of 1959, there were two of them, Sarah and Susan, with three more to follow. Herman loved being a father, loved the idea of being a patriarch, and, whatever else was going on in his life, he passionately loved his children. Given a choice between being a starving actor and providing for his family, he made the one that seemed obvious to him: he quit his professional theater career, though he dreamed of making a return to it for many years. Meanwhile, he had to earn a living and was supervising construction on the Kips Bay housing complex on the East Side of Manhattan and teaching English to immigrants somewhere in Brooklyn.

Peggy was from Gainesville, FL. She was a gifted poet and playwright and earned her living as the head copy editor for Condé Nast. But Peggy was most devoted to writing her plays and poems and occasional short stories, as she would be for the rest of her life. Even in her last days in a nursing home in Florida, stricken with multiple sclerosis (apparently triggered by the birth of her youngest child), bedridden, able to move only one finger, she would slowly peck away at her keyboard. It may be that Herman had decided that if anyone was going to be successful as an artist, it would more likely be Peggy, and he would do what he could to allow her the freedom to make that happen. I don't think he ever told me that, but it wouldn't be atypical of him. Nor do I think it would be atypical of Peggy to insist on it.

They lived in a brownstone in Brooklyn Heights, on State Street, and I was a frequent visitor. Herman and I would sit and talk for seemingly hours on end. Well, if you knew Herman, you know that it was mostly Herman who talked and I listened. He would tell me stories of his boyhood in Tampa, about being a Jew in Tampa, about his very strict father, about being taken to a whorehouse by that same father when he was a boy of sixteen to lose his virginity. Would that my father had done the same.

The first time Dad mentioned sex was when I was 20 years old. I met him for lunch in a Cantonese Chinese restaurant on the 2nd floor of a building on the corner of 59ᵗʰ Street and Lexington Avenue, near his office. It was a rainy day, with occasional claps of thunder. We sat at a table, my foot tapping impatiently underneath.

"Uh, um," my father said.

"That's all right, Dad. I know all about it." But, of course, I didn't know *all* about it, though I knew some of it, and I thought my father wouldn't be likely to tell me much more, not with that beginning.

Anyway, Herman would talk about the teachers he had had, about the plays he had directed in Gainesville, about his friends from Florida who were in New York or in Europe, about José, about his fellow members of the Circle in the Square, about Peggy's poetry and plays. In (small) return, I would talk about my parents, about my confusions, about what I had seen that afternoon at the Hotel Bossert. "Call up Barbara Eliot," the head of the Heights Players, he said, "and tell her you want to stage-manage a play."

So I did. Thus began one alternate life that would continue until I left New York again. The first play I stage-managed was Noel Coward's *Private Lives*. I also worked on a production of Samuel Beckett's *Waiting for Godot*. Did I stage manage Herman's production of Enid Bagnold's *The Chalk Garden,* or was that Amy? I've forgotten as I have the names of the other plays I worked on. If by day I was working or, later, going to school, at night I was often at rehearsals, and I loved it. I was no less interested in the process than during the rehearsal for *Epitaph for George Dillon* and decided that I, too, wanted to be a director. Having decided that, I also decided that I could now return to school (provided a school in New York would have me). Fortunately, NYU decided to take a chance.

That summer of 1960, I left my job at *Value Line* and returned to summer school at NYU, taking Italian History and Political Philosophy courses. Lo and behold, I did just fine on both, and I entered NYU as a full-time student in the fall.

If the University of Maryland had thousands of students, NYU seemed to have even more. If Maryland was largely a school that emptied out on the weekends while everyone went home, NYU was a school that emptied out daily and in which almost everyone I knew lived at home anyway, including me. If Maryland was a foreign and unfamiliar land, NYU was in Greenwich Village, just a few blocks from EI; I was on my home turf.

I took a normal course load and went to classes regularly for the first time in college. For the most part, I was getting by, mostly taking English and history classes along with math and French. My English class was in Irish literature, which I mostly loved, writing one paper on time and space in *Waiting for Godot* that I quite liked (I still do, though I haven't been able to find it). We were required to read *Ulysses*, which definitely was not fun. Admire it, yes; like it, no, except for some sections. We had a test on the book once, one of the kinds of tests I particularly abhor: 25 lines from the book and then wanting to know who said them and what was going on at the time. Let's say that I didn't do well on that one.

As 1960 turned into 1961, there was still a piper to be paid, one that had lain in wait for ten years. I registered for the spring semester, got my list of assigned textbooks, and went off to NYU's bookstore. The store was packed with students, as one would expect just before the beginning of a new semester. I picked up a couple of books for my English and history courses. I had another math or science course to take, and I slipped a math textbook inside my coat, paid for the books I was holding in my hands, and left the store. Outside, I was stopped. "What've you got inside your coat?" I was asked by a man, his hand on my shoulder. I took out the math book. "You know we'll have to report you to the school." I nodded.

My parents, needless to say, were shocked. I had no explanation for them other than I had done what I had done. I didn't tell them that I had been doing it for years; that in Maryland, I even had a coat in which I had made holes in my pockets wide enough to slip books into, something I did almost every week or two. My father offered to have his boss, Dr. Hexter, the Executive Director of Federation, write or talk to the university's president. I asked him not to. I didn't want anyone to do anything. Whatever would happen would happen, and I wanted to make no defense, wanted no one to plead for special consideration. I would pay whatever price NYU decided to exact.

Within a couple of weeks, I was told to report for a hearing before a committee of three professors, one of whom had been my professor in the Irish literature course I had just completed. It was embarrassing. I didn't mind three strangers passing judgment on me but having someone in the room that I knew was uncomfortable, perhaps more so because I had earned my discomfort. They wanted to know why I had stolen the book. I had no explanation, certainly none that was rational. Was it a question of money? Was I unable to afford the book? No, I had enough money in my pocket to pay for it. They mumbled and grumbled and told me a decision would be forthcoming. I was suspended for the semester.

I was relieved. I would have understood and accepted it (as if I'd had a choice) had the professors decided to turn the matter over to the police, but a suspension was undoubtedly preferable. Beyond that, I felt as though a great weight had been lifted off my shoulders. For some reason, being found out and punished meant I never had to steal again. I can't tell you why this is so, but there it is.

Thinking about the "why" in the above paragraph, I wonder if it isn't just too glib. A larger question: Do we, or at least most of us, as sentient beings, as immortal souls, if you will have an innate ethical sense, an innate sense of justice? Is it possible that there is such a thing as ethical behavior in the absence of a moral code, whether devised by religious groups or governmental or other institutional bodies or other groups? Increasingly over the years, I've come to think that there is. If it becomes obscured to some degree by the circumstances into which we're born and by the lives we have led (what we have done, what others have done to us, and what we have witnessed), that doesn't mean it isn't still there constantly looking over our shoulder, asking if we really want to do that, while we look at or shut our eyes to it. Looked at in that way, the relief I felt at being caught and punished would simply (or not simply) be the manifestation of that ethical sense insisting on itself and, therefore, an unburdening of a long-existing weight on me. That's worth thinking about, don't you think?

And so I entered a pause in one part of my education and, concurrently, now had time to take part in another part of it. Herman Shonbrun asked if I would stage-manage a production of his wife's play, *Makepeace's Blackouts*. Although unanticipated, over time the play came to have a powerful effect on my life, on ideas I have contemplated, and on goals to which I've aspired. To this day, it is never far from my thoughts.

> Twinkle, twinkle, little me,
> Up above the world so free.
> All the logic of the stars
> Cannot move my milky thighs
> To embrace the Major bear.
> Twinkle, twinkle, I don't care.
> But if I am nicely wooed
> And if I am in the mood,
> Little comet come and tickle,
> I am yours, so sweet and fickle.
> Twinkle, twinkle, little me,
> Up above the world so free.

Another little piece of verse, a bit of doggerel, a rewriting of a nursery rhyme — a rhyme that each character writes their own version of that I still remember as I do so many lines from Peggy's play.

In the spring of 1960, I turned a very young 20. At the time, of course, I thought I was plenty bright, no doubt intelligent enough to understand this play about three people from the South, Thomas Makepeace, his wife Mary "Peaches" Honeypiece, and their Black childhood friend, Joe Honeyman. Herman was undoubtedly smart and experienced in the theater. As Peggy's husband, he surely understood what she was up to, what she thought she was up to. Having lived with this play for almost sixty years, I'm no longer so sure. I don't think either of us understood much of that play. Maybe Peggy didn't either.

Herman's favorite metaphor for the play was a string of paper dolls cut out from the same piece of paper. They touched at hand, and hip and foot, but never at their hearts. A lovely metaphor. I have since come to think that he was wrong, as was I, one hundred percent wrong, 180 degrees wrong. The place they actually touch is each other's hearts. They have a death grip on each other's hearts, love each other passionately, and hate each other just as passionately;

they fight for each other and fight off each other, Honeypiece, in particular, both participant and instigator.

Herman used to think I had a crush on Peggy, but he was wrong about that too. I'm not sure I even liked her very much. But I loved Honeypiece just as I loved Lena, the angel in another of her plays, *Men and Angels.* Goddess-women, both. Though I loved them, I didn't understand either character. I didn't understand well enough that though they may have loved men, they were angry with them, too, perhaps, even, sometimes viewed them with contempt. And they were, maybe, angry at themselves as well for wanting and needing men. And their men, all men, were so fallible, easily manipulated, and so vain — far more so than women no matter how much Honeypiece loved hats — so blind.

Is that an inevitable consequence of being a goddess? Of being all women? Of being Woman? Is that the question, the question that Peggy was really asking? And if so, was she aware of asking it?

What man could not love Honeypiece? Even Joe Honeyman loved her, hoped that she might love him even though he knew that was impossible, that she would never be able to truly see him, that she and Makepeace were bound together. But, whatever their destiny, Honeyman was doomed to be the odd man out, the *other,* the invisible man, the Black man at the end of the line with the mocking minstrel man's laugh, even as he would refuse to go gently into the night.

> Look at them locked in each other's arms. Is it a beginning? For them yes. But not for Joe Honeyman. Joe Honeyman would scream if he could. Imagine that scream till it rings in your ears, in your mind, in the place you call heart – in the suburbs of heaven. It would be a relief to hear that scream...
>
> LOOK! LOOK AT ME! ...
>
> Hyah, hyah, hyah, hyah.
>
> (to the one-man band)
>
> Friend: a little traveling music if you please. It's late and we all have far to go.
>
> (one-man-band starts playing "Bye, Bye Blackbird" as Joe does a soft-shoe on his way off stage and the lights come down)

All these years later, we still have far to go. And those two phrases — "the place you call heart" and "the suburbs of heaven" — still reverberate within me. Rereading it, I'm still moved by the play. If it feels a bit dated now, the advent of Black Lives Matter reminds us how little has changed even while we think that so much has. Too many Black Americans are still shouting, still pleading, still demanding, "Look! Look at *me!*" and too many white Americans find nothing to see.

In a small example of how small the pond is that we all live in, consider the following: One of the producers was Julia Miles. Julia was either married then or would soon be married to Sam Cohn, who became the most powerful movie agent in New York for ICM, Hollywood's most powerful talent agency. He represented my *NewsHour* colleague and friend Roger Rosenblatt in later years when his play, *Ashley Montana Goes Ashore at the Caicos*, was produced at the Flea Theater in 2006. Julia was the founder of the Women's Project and, when I became aware of it, it was located within Wyn Handman's American Place Theater. Amy was part of the Women's Project's Director's Lab for a short time and later directed a play for Wyn at the APT. Wyn also produced one or two of Roger's one-man shows, and Roger and I did an essay about him and the APT when the theater (though not the producing company) shut down. Intersecting ripples in one small but big pond.

In the fall, as I returned to classes at NYU, my suspension lifted, we opened *Makepeace* at the Provincetown Playhouse in the Village. Unfortunately, regardless of the reviews, the play didn't catch on, and it closed after a couple of weeks.

Of all the lines in the play, there was one that I took very much to heart. It was a line of Tommy Makepeace's, the would-be writer, a writer who could neither confront the page, his wife, his old childhood friend, his life, nor himself, much less the world in which he lived. He says, after one magical moment before he destroys it, as much to himself as to anyone else, daring himself to confront everything ... anything,

Say something real, true, heartfelt.

For years, I remembered Honeypiece said that line, but I was wrong. It was Makepeace challenging, berating, and failing himself. Whatever Tommy Makepeace said, it was rarely what he meant because he refused to see, refused to look in the mirror, and, therefore, could never meet his challenge in either his art or life. In the end, Honeypiece is the only one who could always say, who could always see what was real, true, and heartfelt. It is Honeypiece who issues a final challenge to save their marriage.

Really look. Don't make up. Don't invent. Don't ... juggle words while looking in a mirror. *Only* look.

It's not that I identified with Makepeace, but I took that line into my own heart just as I took Honeypiece's challenge as my own. The two of them, conflated into one, became my own mantra, my own goal, my own desire, my dream, even when I knew that I betrayed it and was unworthy of it. If I could only do that, if I could "Really look," if I could only "Say something real, true, heartfelt," then I might be worthy of the world, of Honeypiece, of myself. I discovered that process —the mechanics of directing a play, editing a sports film, imagining an essay, or doing almost anything else — was, for me, everything and yet absolutely nothing without it leading to that end. I had discovered my end no matter what the process might be. I might forget it for a while, maybe even for years, but not for always; I might not know how I would go about doing it, but I would find a way or a way would find me.

So, on to classes, survey courses in British and American writers, classes in Melville and Hawthorne and Poe, in Hemingway, Faulkner, and Fitzgerald, in Restoration drama, classes in 20th century American history, Soviet foreign policy, and historiography. And French, too, always and forever.

I was writing poetry (I never said that I didn't have a considerable amount of cliché built into me, earth person that I am). Ideas, words, phrases, filled my head in a physics class for non-physicists. Lots of theory, little math; it was right up my alley. Interestingly, given that this course was in 1961, the professor's notion of physics mostly stopped at Newton, or, more accurately, the universe he described was Newtonian. The ideas of Einstein and relativity, of Niels Bohr and quantum mechanics, simply didn't exist in this class. So I would sit half-listening to the professor and writing lines of poetry. Never complete poems, but lines, ideas. Somehow the two, physics and poetry, went well together. I wrote one poem that semester, a short poem, that I liked very much. I still do. I called it "Christmas Eve," thinking very tangentially of a quintessential New York experience when I was in EI, going to the midnight mass at the Cathedral of St. John the Divine.

> Night's shadowed drippings
> caress the earth
> in eulogy of remembered mirth.
> Shattered red fingers
> of a flaming doom
> dip in defeat to the ashen moon
> and the decayed skull casts no glance.

There I was thinking of war, and hydrogen bombs, and churches, and candles lit for the dead and the dying — for the human race — and I was told by someone who read it many years later that it was about sex. Why not? Who am I to tell someone what should reverberate in their soul. I still liked it even if I'd never given a thought to sex when writing it. At least not that I was aware of.

And then there was this poem, the first line scribbled on a yellow pad in physics class while thinking of historiography and America's history in a different class.

> Sink low in the stirring wind
> The dying chorus of past renown. Changeless change:
> The Manifest Destiny of a Golden Age.
> Was it a reality to match a dream?
> Or a dream to match a reality that never was?
>
> Scattered wide through eternity:
> The dream,
> The reality,

(Neither itself,
Neither the other).

I gave them, along with some others, to the editor of the NYU literary magazine, who was in one of my classes. "Too personal," he said, dismissing them all. I blinked in amazement. I might have understood if he said that he didn't like them or couldn't understand them or that great standby for turning down work that you don't like but want to be polite about, "It's not for me." But "too personal?" I still don't know what that means. What is poetry, all fiction writing in fact, if not personal?

I sometimes wonder what would have happened if he had said, "Yes," I'll publish one in the magazine. Would that validation have meant something more than printing a few lines in a magazine? Would I have written more poetry? Taken my writing more seriously? Over a half-century later, I watched the Bradley Cooper/Lady Gaga version of *A Star is Born* and found myself thinking how consequential validation was, how important the nature of the validator was, how important the timing of the validation was. Those things coming together can be transformative. All that and the importance of staying true to yourself, of looking in the mirror.

I wrote one more poem that year, a longer one, and this time it was entirely personal. It was written long after the girl I was thinking of, my first real love, after we had broken up. It was never read by anyone until decades later. If "Christmas Eve" felt old to me, this one felt young, and I still don't know exactly what I think of it (although, admittedly, there's a lot in it that I like), and it doesn't matter. What matters is that it meant enough to me to keep it. It still does.

ADAM

"Into the valley of Death rode the six hundred!"
"What was *that* for?"
   "Nothing," he said,
Lowering his voice from its oratorical heights,
"but he shouldn't have done it that way."

"Why?"
and the wind sighed
an apple blossom perfume through the room.

She smiled; she knew. Yes.
Of course she knows,
he thought, she always knows,
while the moon climbed high,
its ghostly light
raining through a midnight sky.

Moon, Lune, June, croon,
foolish so young foolish boy becoming a man,
a moon for your thoughts.
No, no moon. Lune, singing an unsolved riddle. Moon,
poets and love and the reality of dead rocks.
What is your smile, woman-in-the-moon? You wink at me
a Mona Lisa paradox.
Moon of all mystery. Yes. A man-
made symbol for woman.
And when they whitewash that smile
with a man-in-the-moon
it will no longer be a mystery.
What will be our moon then?
No more June-moon, crooning Lune,
What will replace you as
the symbol of our ignorance? woman of a moon
who has let us deceive ourselves for so many
thousands of years.

Yes, I understand that smile.
You are sad,
for man makes his own destiny,
it is the path he has chosen,
you will not interfere,
you have your own way to go.
And while the drums roll and the trumpets blare

and the thousands of cheering feet go
marching off to victory,
you quietly cry of the defeat.

"He should have let them die in peace and dignity and
quiet instead of with horns trumpeting, degrading their
humanity, exalting their ignorance with bizarre and grotesque
fanfares."

Her fingers calmed his worried hair,
a faint smile of pleasure tingeing her cheeks.
He bent forward and kissed her, just barely
touching her lips in a grateful caress.

He laughed.
"Damned funny things to be talking about in a bed with
you. Here I am talking of death when I should be dreaming of
...
living love."

"But you are."

"Hmmm?"
and he reached over to the chair
near the bed and found some matches
(although not a cigarette)
in the pocket of his shirt
and held them in his hand.

Ah, boy almost a man,
don't indulge yourself with
now-meaningless questions,
thinking you've discovered something new
and wanting to give it to the world.
Beware of Greeks bearing gifts.
But she knows, she has always known
forever since Eve. Yes,

and the old men knew it too, sitting down
in the sterility of their lives to
write their *Genesis,* knew that it was
never Eve who sinned but rather Adam
(who wished he might live in the ignorance
of youth, the placidity of old age),
against Eve, against life, against Eden
and the springtime smell of apple blossoms.

And the old men
made their gift of
an Adam god
to an innocent and gullible world. Ohhh,
Man, *BEWARE OF GREEKS BEARING GIFTS!*
Listen to the song of the Lune,
Man, who was never in the moon,
what knows more of life, of death
then the womb, the woman's womb.

And the match in his hand flared brightly
and he looked at her, and he saw
(yes, moon of a woman, I see you now)
                                        Her,
her face haloed in love,
her wanting eyes so deep,
deep and her apple blossom body bursting
ripe with its gift and the warmth
and the perfume of her love,
her arms stretching towards him,
her hands now touching him,
and as the match burned out
(the boy become a man
says, "Eve, I shall not sin")
and as the room plunged into darkness,
the everlasting fire rose.

The girl never read the poem.

By Thanksgiving of 1961, I had made a decision about my future. No matter how many plays I saw or how many productions I took part in, I couldn't figure out how to actually make a living in the theater. I knew, obviously, that some directors were very successful, but most were not. There were too many who had to supplement their income in other ways, usually by teaching, among other things. If there was one thing that I wasn't going to do, it was to teach. I couldn't have cared less about academic theater (meaning teaching), and I had deliberately chosen not to major in theater.

Even more, there was the state of theater itself. Despite all the plays I had seen in my life and those I worked on, it felt like the theater was dying. The lure of Hollywood and the amounts of money that could be made seemed to be luring too many talented young writers, and I thought it would spell the end of serious theater. Other factors included the increasing cost of mounting plays on Broadway, the shifting demographics of both the city and the country, and the growing role of television in our daily lives. And that doesn't even begin to include the impact of the ascendancy of the singer/song-writer on American culture, the lure of budding poets and writers (not to mention musicians and composers) to the glamor and impact of pop music. Also, the day of New York as the intellectual center of America was ebbing. With few exceptions, Broadway was losing its hold on the intellectual imagination of serious people. Not that there wasn't good theater, but it was increasingly being shoved off to off-Broadway. The theater was quicksand. Moreover, as I said earlier, I had come to think that process was merely a tool, useful only to achieve an end. Like many others, I decided that there was another similar path to that end: Hollywood.

Thanksgiving dinner at my parents' house that year was, as usual, a family affair with 20 or more family members who gathered for the traditional turkey, including Mom's cousin, Ruth Zimmerman, and Bill, her husband. Bill was the vice president of Joe Levine's Embassy Pictures, the most important distributor of foreign films in America. Remember, this was the heyday of foreign art films, of Frederico Fellini, Michaelangelo Antonioni, Luis Bunel, Francois Truffaut, Karel Reicz, Tony Richardson, and others — so many extraordinary films and filmmakers — and Bill knew them all because Embassy was distributing most of their pictures. It was reportedly said of Bill that he was the only American Sophia Loren would talk to.

After dinner, I told Bill what I was thinking of doing and asked if he had any advice. He said that I should go to graduate school, preferably at USC, but UCLA would be all right also, and then, after a year and a half, he'd send me to work in Europe with whoever he thought was doing good work at the time. No, I didn't need to get a degree; what I needed was to learn the language of film. Needless to say, I was excited at the prospect. As for that little problem I had with foreign languages, I decided that could be worried about later.

I took the Graduate Record Exam and did well enough. My application to the USC Graduate School of Cinema, or whatever it was called, was provisionally accepted. They liked the GRE results, but my academic record was a mixed bag, although my grades in my major and minor from NYU were quite good. I was ready to go but I had one other stop to make, even if I have no idea why I thought I should.

One night during the Christmas break, I went to see Lee Hays. I always thought of Lee as being the glue that held the Weavers together, the one who brought Pete Seeger, Ronnie Gilbert, and Fred Hellerman into harmony with each other and kept them there. I'd known him for several years because he rented a room or apartment in Earl Robinson's house in Brooklyn Heights. He wasn't a friend; we just had a nodding acquaintance. He had moved out of Earl's house because Earl had left New York and returned to Seattle. Regardless, Lee was now living on Willow Street across the street from the old carriage house that Arthur Miller and his wife lived in while still together in his pre-Marilyn Monroe days.

Why did I go to see Lee? Did I initiate it? Did he? Does it matter? There I was, knocking on his door. We chatted; we had a beer. I picked up a guitar, and we sang songs from the Weavers repertoire, plus some others that we both knew. After a while, I put the guitar down, walked over to the piano, and played a few notes. There was a bit of a melody that I had created around the same time Avi had asked me to compose the music for a song he had written and was directing while he was at the University of Wisconsin. It was incomplete except for the central theme. And there was a bit from another part of ... well, whatever it was. I started playing, starting with one hand just picking out the notes, then adding the left hand, and then just playing and playing, the theme expanding, shifting, becoming something else and yet itself, lines and themes twisting together and separating, floating through the lamp-lit room. I was aware of nothing, could see nothing, feel nothing, sense nothing, except whatever was in my mind, in the place we call heart, finding its way through my fingers into the keys of the piano and engulfing me in its sound, the sound being everything, the sound being the world, the universe, being forever. A half-hour, forty minutes, and it was over. I stopped. I had no idea what had happened, though I knew that something profound had indeed happened. I was emotionally drained and yet enormously energized.

There was silence. Lee cleared his throat. "Well, now.... I didn't know you could do that."

"I didn't either. I never did that before."

And so we said, "Goodnight. Let's stay in touch."

Sure. I was about to get on a plane.

There is a follow-up to this story that might as well get told now. Many years later, after my first wife and I had separated for the final time in 1977, and after Lee died in 1981, my mother told me that in March or April following that Christmas meeting, Lee called my parents looking for me. My mother asked, why? Pete Seeger was leaving the Weavers, and Lee wondered if I would be interested in the possibility of making a final tour with them, no guarantees, but would I be interested? Mother said, no, she didn't think so. I was in California after having at long last decided what to do with my life, and she didn't think I'd want to leave school to do this.

Of course, by the time I heard about the phone call, it was way too late to do anything about it. The tour had long since happened, the Weavers had disbanded, and Lee was dead. Those I told about the phone call thought I should be angry at her, but I wasn't. I knew what she knew. I had made a career choice after a long and difficult struggle and, even if I was interested in Lee's inquiry, it would be a serious diversion. I understood why she was so concerned about me. I was concerned, too. But still. I would have liked to have the choice. I've often wondered what that choice would have been. Would "sanity" have ruled, and I would have chosen to stay in California? Would I have decided to roll the dice and returned to New York to make that final tour if they really wanted me? Today, I think I would have come back. But back then? I'll never know for sure.

In early January 1963, within days of my last class at NYU, I got on a Boeing 707 and left for Los Angeles. It was time to take another leap into America.

Chapter 7
IT NEVER RAINS IN SOUTHERN CALIFORNIA

1963 - 1964

It was pouring rain. Southern California, sunny LA, was not sunny this day.

Not having the foggiest idea of where the USC campus was, after landing at LAX, I took a jitney to the Hilton, then a new hotel, and practically the tallest building in downtown LA. I took a cab out to the campus and the housing office the following morning. I found an apartment listing that sounded promising and not too far from the campus. Another cab (how I found one that quickly, I'll never know, particularly in LA in the rain) took me to S. Burlington Avenue, three blocks east of Macarthur Park. Not so close, after all.

There was a white clapboard two-story house owned by two actors, Rod and Georgia (I don't remember their last name). They had a three-room apartment for rent on the 2nd floor, a large living room, a small kitchen of sorts, and a small bedroom, more or less (more less than more) furnished, and at a rent that I could barely manage to afford.

Once I moved into the apartment, I found that I loved the neighborhood. There were three movie theaters within easy walking distance. One showed re-releases of old movies, one showed relatively recent new films, and the third showed foreign films. What could be better for a film student? I went to the movies at least three times a week and sometimes more. There was a used bookstore and a new one as well. There were restaurants, worse on my side, the eastern side of Macarthur Park, better on the other side, reflecting their different neighborhoods. There was even a seedy strip club down near Olympic, a few blocks away, that I went to once or twice. There was a bus that would take me to school. Those at school who knew LA were generally aghast at the neighborhood I had chosen to live in. To them, it was the slums. To me, it was the closest thing I could find to being home.

The film school was in a separate building across the street from the main campus and bore no resemblance to the structure that houses today's film school. At the time, it was a small, square, one-story wooden building with an interior courtyard onto which all the classrooms and offices exited. There was a sound stage on one side of the building, and classrooms, a screening room, and offices filled the rest. There weren't many students, certainly not more than a hundred, if that. Being Southern California, with lots of sunshine, when we weren't in classes, people could always be found on the grass in the quad, as it was called. Very convivial. After so many years with thousands of students, I was back in an atmosphere more like EI. The physical separation from the main campus emphasized that for me more than the undergraduates taking film courses who still had classes on the main campus. I took courses in camera, editing, scriptwriting, production management, and a directing seminar. I enjoyed them all, particularly the directing seminar and editing class. I had no interest in operating a camera myself, but I wanted to know how they worked and the effects of various lenses and lighting. My scriptwriting left a lot to be desired, but I faithfully churned out the required pages. I probably liked editing most of all, and my later career reflects that. I got a job as a technician in the school's film lab, where I learned much about the physical properties of film that I would later find useful, at least until film virtually disappeared from the industry.

Sitting around the quad one day, I met Bruce Feldman, and we quickly became friends and remained friends off and on for many years. Born in South Bend, Indiana, Bruce was still an undergraduate. He had enlisted in the army and had then written speeches for John Brademas when he was running for Congress in Indiana with (failed) ambitions of becoming President of the United States, and later settled for becoming president of NYU. Bruce zipped around LA on his Vespa motor scooter, sometimes with me on the back. We spent many hours in his apartment close to the campus, talking long into the night. I discovered just how far my apartment was from USC when the buses stopped running at 11 pm. Since I didn't have a car, I walked home two or three miles more than once. Occasionally we went to bars or clubs together, visited the down-at-the-heels strip club in my neighborhood and the considerably more upscale Pink Pussycat in Hollywood.

Most days, we'd have lunch in a bar across the street from the campus. We were kicking around ideas for a short film that I thought I'd like to make during one of those lunches. I wanted to shoot at dawn in downtown LA. A girl in the middle of the street dances as she enters the city. She is happy, joyful, free, spinning, twirling, leaping down the street exultant at her freedom at the dawn of a new day. Gradually there is traffic. There are people. More and more. And she slowly disappears from view amidst the crowd on Broadway as it hurries along, focused only on the daily grind.

Bruce suggested I ask the head of the dance department for the names of dancers who might be interested. She said, "There's only one person here who's crazy enough to be willing to do this. Lynne Henderson." Somehow, a message was gotten to Lynne, and it was agreed that we were to meet at 2 pm in front of the Tommy Trojan statue on campus.

I'd never been on the main campus except when I registered and had no idea where to find the statue. Eventually, I found it. I was standing there when this very tall, quite striking girl, wearing a sweatshirt and tights with woolen leg warmers, came striding towards me. So this was Lynne. I fumbled around a bit, sort of explained what I was thinking about, but I'm sure it wasn't as much as I described above. In fact, I had no idea what I really wanted to do beyond the concept of a girl who is free but becomes trapped within the city's throngs. Was she interested? Maybe. How would she feel if I shot some footage just to see what it/she looked like? Why not. And so we did. I got a Bell & Howell camera from the school, and we shot a few minutes of film in a parking lot.

Lynne was certainly good-looking. Long dark hair in a ponytail, gray eyes, high cheekbones, an exotic, perhaps Indian-influenced face. She was tall, maybe 5' 11", and I think she weighed only 120 pounds with legs that seemed to go on forever. As thin as she was at what she called her dancing weight, she didn't feel or look fragile. She had the body of an athlete, real muscles and shoulders. Pretty stunning. She looked good on film, too.

Later on, she said that she didn't like me when we first met and who could blame her? I didn't know what to say to this extraordinary creature and so didn't say very much, which she took to mean that I was hostile for some mysterious reason. I wasn't; I was just intimidated. Lynne told me that she couldn't do anything with me right away because she was busy preparing for her Master's Degree thesis concert. It was just as well because I hardly knew what I wanted to do anyway. (We never did make the film, by the way.) Every night for the next couple of weeks, she'd be spending sewing costumes. Would I like to come over and we'd get to know each other while they were working? Yes.

And so, for the next two weeks, I'd go to Lynne's apartment in one of those motel-like apartment buildings on West Adams Boulevard where she and another girl were busy sewing. Her music composer was often there and other friends as well. Someone had a guitar, and I'd sing folk songs, and they would drink wine, and Lynne and I would talk.

Not only were we spending these long evenings together, but we were spending afternoons together when she wasn't rehearsing, usually at the bar with Bruce and other film students. Within a few days, we were being described as a couple, and jokes were being made about our getting married.

At the end of the two weeks, we decided to do just that.

An absurdly impulsive decision? Yes. Unwise? No doubt. Foolish? Of course. Did we actually get married? Yes. Did it last? No.

Thirteen years later, in April 1977, after years of mutually increasing dissatisfaction, of formal and informal separations, we separated for a final time. In our wake, we left two children who, somehow, managed to grow up into reasonably happy adults, simultaneously managing to love both their parents, despite how different they were from each other and how tumultuous we caused their lives to be.

Some of our differences were obvious. For starters, I was Jewish; she was not. I was very much an East Coast boy; she was very much a West Coast girl. No matter how different the worlds and cultures we grew up in, the differences seemed bridgeable, even irrelevant. After all, we were just two people who thought they loved each other. But over time, all those, as well as other differences, would prove insurmountable. Love conquers all, right? Well, no.

Lynne's mother and father were divorced. Her mother, Miriam Reynolds Henderson, was a schoolteacher; she played the flute and piano and taught music in an East LA elementary school. Her father, James Robinson Henderson, owned his own business, Las Vegas Building Materials, in Las Vegas, where she'd grown up. When she was seven, Lynne, her sister, and two brothers moved to San Gabriel with their mother after the divorce. After leaving Las Vegas, Lynne had gone to public school in San Gabriel and then to Mills College in the Bay Area, one of the top liberal arts schools for women in the country. While at Mills, she'd also been the "girl in the fishbowl" at Bimbo's 365. When her dad had a heart attack, she'd taken a year off and gone to Vegas to be with him and while there was the lead dancer at the Flamingo on the Strip. Now she was getting her Master's in dance from USC.

The day after our decision, we drove out to San Gabriel, a primarily middle-class town of modest homes to the east of LA but still in LA County, to tell Lynne's mother of our decision. I had met Miriam once before when Lynne had borrowed a tape recorder from her school, but we had never talked.

We were standing in the kitchen when I said, "Ummm, uhhhhh, we'd like to, uh, get married."

Miriam's eyebrows arched. "I'm sorry, I didn't get your last name."

I'm sure I laughed. That may have been the funniest line I'd ever heard, said so spontaneously that she couldn't have made it up beforehand, had it lying in wait, could she?

Miriam suggested that we wait until the summer rather than getting married at once (we were prepared to drive to Las Vegas the same day). We could move in with her (separate bedrooms, of course); we might get to know each other a bit better. Very logical.

Good idea, actually. And do we really want to go to Las Vegas to get married, which is, after all, the territory and home of JR (he was called Jim or JR by most everyone)? Hmmm. Maybe not such a good idea after all. But if we don't go there, who could marry us? After all, there is this difference between you, Michael being Jewish, and you, Lynne, being Christian? How about the Ethical Culture Society, the salvation of we Eastern secular Jewish intellectual inter-faith marrying types? Oh, yes, of course. Perhaps we should even consider meeting JR before the big event. And then there was the older brother. Shouldn't I meet him? Of course. And the younger brother, and the younger sister, shouldn't we tell them? Maybe before actually meeting JR, Lynne should tell him of our plans. That would be sure to garner an invitation, disinheritance, or both.

So, the phone call. Lynne was sitting in the dining room, tele-phone in hand. I stood in the kitchen watching through the swinging door. Miriam watched us both.

"Yes, Daddy, I'm going to get married. ... He's Jewish. ... Well, we thought we'd get married by the Ethical Culture Society."

Lynne was silent as a voice could be heard coming through the handset, even as far away as I was. Since I couldn't hear the voice before, the omens weren't good.

A few minutes later, after hanging up, face slightly flushed, Lynne said, "He was very upset about the Ethical Culture Society. He never heard of it. I tried to explain to him that it was legally registered as a Church in California, even Nevada and that it was a good way around the problem of you being Jewish and me not, and he said, 'But you're both Christian, aren't you!!!?'" And by the way, don't you think you should come to Las Vegas next weekend?

On to Las Vegas.

Jim and Jane Henderson lived in an English Tudor house on the 9th fairway of the Desert Inn golf course, and the story (not told by Jim) of how he got it may be apocryphal. Then again, maybe not.

Jim poured the concrete for the DI sewer system when it was first built. When payment for the job was too long in coming, he threatened to stop the toilets from flushing into the sewer system and was given the house instead. As I said, no doubt apocryphal, but who knows? We're talking about Las Vegas. Dreams in the desert.

Hallucinations, too. The land of Bugsy Siegel's imagination, murder, and burial.

Jim lived next door to Moe Dalitz, who bought the unfinished DI in 1950. For those who've forgotten their Americana, Dalitz was (before LV, of course) a gangster, a member of the Cleveland mob. He was a bootlegger, an owner of illegal gambling joints, an associate of Meyer Lansky's (as was Bugsy), an investor in Cuban casinos, and, reputedly, a frequent killer of enemies (as was Bugsy) before he moved to Las Vegas. Once there, among other things, he was a conduit for the Teamsters Central States Pension Fund money into Vegas casinos and other real estate ventures that got Jimmy Hoffa into so much trouble. And he was the main backer of Pat McCarran, the right-wing Republican Senator from Nevada. In 1976, long after he "cleaned" himself up, the Las Vegas American Cancer Research Center and Hospital named him its "Humanitarian of the Year," an honor he gracefully accepted still packing heat under his armpit. Even B'nai B'rith got into the act by awarding him the "Torch of Liberty Award" in 1982. He died in 1989. Reading his biography sounds like he could have been a model for the über Godfather, Michael Corleone. Then again, Las Vegas had so many candidates.

I've always liked to think that Dalitz's biography was proof enough that the story about how Jim came to own the house next door was apocryphal. If it really happened the way it was supposed to, Jim is lucky he didn't wind up in the sewer himself. On the other hand, maybe it really did happen that way. Maybe Moe and Company were so flabbergasted by Jim's threat that they gave in to him because they thought it was all so funny; that Jim really *didn't* know who or what they were. After all, Jim always insisted that the Mafia didn't exist in Las Vegas. The city in the desert was clean as the desert sand used to be. Sometimes we see only what we want to see, and maybe Jim really didn't want to know who his friends or neighbors were, or at least who they used to be. I can think of no other possible reason why he would urge Lynne to dance with the big goombahs with big bulges under their very expensive jackets.

The night we arrived in Vegas, while Jim was busy barbecuing steaks, Lynne and Jane were off talking about whatever step-mothers and step-daughters talk about while Jane got drunk and wound up going off to bed, which she often did. Jim and I were on the patio as night crept on and the last of the golfers went by in their electric carts. We got into an argument. No, it wasn't about Lynne, about marriage, about being Jewish or Christian (he was, at best, no more Christian than I was Jewish except on Easter Sunday when he'd go to church), about my career or lack thereof, or any of the other expected things. Instead, we argued about politics and public policy, an argument that lasted through the whole weekend. We argued about three things, as I recall: 1) Social Security was a fraud; 2) government regulation of business was evil (as in forcing users of the land like himself — he was in the ready-mixed concrete, rock, sand, and gravel business — to restore the land they destroyed; 3) Unions. You can figure out who was in favor of what for yourselves.

Lynne and I left on Sunday to return to San Gabriel, a wedding date having been set. Am I delusional? Did Jim, despite our obvious differences, actually find me acceptable? Was the fact that I was willing to argue with him, not back down in the face of the obvious motivation to do so, actually please him? Maybe. Jim was nothing if not an alpha male, a "self-made" man who thought of himself as a "man's man," and a misogynist with all that implies. If the weekend and our argument had been a test, I apparently had passed or, at least, hadn't failed.

There was, in fact, much to admire about Jim. According to Lynne, Jim was a half-breed (Blackfoot), which he always denied but which pleased her, a tall man, around 6'2", rangy build (he'd played tight end at the University of Pittsburgh, he said). After college, he'd made his way west to California and the Ojai Valley, where he worked for a building supply distributor. He met Miriam Henderson, a native of Ojai who came from a long line of schoolteachers (all of whom seemed to wind up divorced), and they married. Lynne and her older brother were actually born in Ojai.

After the Japanese attacked Pearl Harbor, the government, fearing the possibility of an invasion of California, set up support bases on the eastern side of the Rockies. Part of that effort was Nellis Air Force Base outside the practically non-existent town of Las Vegas, and Jim packed up his family and went off to pour the concrete for the landing strips. After the war, they stayed in Vegas, Jim going into business for himself by establishing the Las Vegas Building Materials Company and taking part in the rise of Las Vegas, becoming a relatively wealthy and influential man in the process. I was told he headed the successful "Right to Work" anti-union drive in Nevada and, I believe, was a onetime president of the American Mining Association and on the board of American Manufacturers Association. Jim would testify before some congressional committee in Washington most years I knew him. Miriam had left him in 1946 after she found out he'd been having an affair with his secretary, Jane, who he married soon after.

Years later, in the 1980s, I thought I understood much of Ronald Reagan's politics and, indeed, the thrust of western conservative Republican politics because of my exposure to Jim Henderson. Objections to taxation and unions, federal land ownership and regulation of land use, welfare and Social Security, and virtually any other social programs were a consistent theme. The one thing that made Jim (and even Reagan) not seem out and out evil was that on a personal level, they appeared generous, aside from their ability to be simply sociable and charming. If you knew Jim personally, you could ask him for anything, and you might get something, at least once. He believed in generosity on a one-to-one basis, not on a one-to-many basis. For Jim, at least, it seemed he thought that what happens to you, what you see for yourself, is what is real. Everything else is a lie. The man in front of you is real. He is the only thing that is real. To see beyond what is immediately in front of you, you must be willing to see things beyond your experience. But that is something else, people generally only being ready to see, to experience what they are willing to accept as being real. Just like Moe Dalitz (for Jim) and Reagan's famed welfare queen.

Decades after Reagan, though, we have witnessed other ways these attitudes can develop and be distorted. We in America, who long decried "crony capitalism" in third world countries, have been unwilling to acknowledge how far it has become ingrained in our own country in both political parties. One could certainly see it in the rise of George W. Bush and the Republican Party, especially after they took over Congress in 1994. God knows one could see it throughout the Trump administration. One can see it in the pervasive influence in both political parties of corporate America. What does a government "of the people, by the people, and for the people" actually mean when corporate money and billionaires seem to be so influential?

Not surprisingly, my parents weren't thrilled with the idea of my impending marriage. Aside from the haste of the marriage, they were disappointed that I had decided to marry a non-Jew. Mom flew out to California to meet Lynne and concluded she wasn't completely nuts. She and Miriam got along. I seemed resolute. Dad got a Dun & Bradstreet report on Jim and found him not wanting. Everybody was, if not exactly happy, at least accepting. Maybe resigned is a more accurate word. The wedding could go forward.

But who would marry us? And where now that a Las Vegas chapel was out of the question? Lynne had the answer: Dr. Headley, the chaplain at her *alma mater*, Mills College. He had done this sort of thing before and would be happy to do a non-denominational ceremony mostly of our devising, and so we cooked one up full of poetry and pretty sentiment. And where to actually have it? Lynne decided on a Methodist church in San Remo, a decidedly upscale area next door to San Gabriel. And where should the reception be? In a hotel ballroom in Pasadena, of course. So how many invitations should go out? Was it 100 or 200 of our nearest and dearest friends?

We had all of a sudden gone from a nice quiet wedding in a small non-denominational chapel with no guests to a WEDDING wedding with people who, for the most part, I neither knew nor cared about. It was no longer a wedding about Lynne and me (well, maybe a bit about Lynne) but one mostly about Jim Henderson. In fact, Lynne had really wanted a church wedding all along, something she never revealed until years later. (I wonder what I would have said if I had known it at the time.)

There was the usual wedding planning fuss, which I absented myself from as much as possible. Invitation designs to choose from, guests to invite, seating arrangements, wedding dresses to try on, wedding rings to buy, tuxedos to rent. My mother supplied an engagement ring, the diamond that had been my grandmother's, which Lynne lost a few years later — in the washing machine, I think. Bruce Feldman would be the best man, Lynne's sister the maid of honor, and a friend of Lynne's from Mills, the bridesmaid.

On August 8, 1964, the San Remo Methodist Church chapel was filled. The Henderson's were there in force, as was Miriam's family, the Reynolds. There were many business associates of Jim's from wherever they were from, almost all people I had never met before and would never meet again. Of course, Mom and Dad were there, along with my cousins, Henry Wortis and Emily Wortis Leider, along with their respective spouses, Sheli and Bill, but that's it as far as people I knew. Amy was in Europe that summer, in Zurich on that day, and couldn't get back. My mother told Emily how glad she was that Emily and Henry were there because she felt so lonely in the throng. She wasn't the only one.

Do I need to tell you that I was a nervous wreck? I wasn't sure I wanted to be doing this, but it was way too late to back out, and I wasn't sure I wanted to. Lynne looked lovely, as (almost) all brides do. Do you think she was nervous? A friend of hers sang some opera thing, and there was a children's chorus from Miriam's school. Where was that quickie Vegas chapel?

And so the service started.

Dr. Headley was drunk.

Instead of Khalil Gibran's poetry (whose did you expect in 1964?), Dr. Headley forgot what he agreed to do and shifted into the straight, unvarnished, unmodified, Episcopalian service. "In the name of the Father, the Son, and the Holy Ghost," once, twice. I could barely breathe. I was shaking. I imagined my mother trying not to show how shocked she must be. I clutched Lynne's hand, or she clutched mine. I could not imagine what I was doing there.

And then it was over, or at least the service was. There still, however, is the reception filled with strangers. A frilly red garter with a little pistol in a little holster had to be stripped off Lynne's leg and tossed to the throng. There was a bouquet to toss and cake to cut and shove into each other's mouths. What universe was I in?

The honeymoon itself was better, mostly spent with people I knew. We drove up the coast and stayed with Henry and Sheli in Palo Alto, where Henry was doing post-doc work at Stanford. I probably knew Sheli better at that time than Henry, even if I'd known him all my life. I think it was in 1960, when they were living in New York, that I got to know Sheli. Henry had gotten his Ph.D. and an MD to boot and was interning at Bellevue, along with Emily's husband, Bill. Sheli had grown up singing folk songs too, and we spent quite a few Saturday afternoons singing together. In fact, we were the entertainment at a big party for Grandpa's 70th birthday.

We went on to Lake Tahoe for a few days, where we met a dealer at the Cal-Neva Lodge who Lynne had known from her dancing days in Vegas. He was deep in debt to the casinos, which, apparently, is how the casinos managed to make sure their dealers didn't change their professions. Every night at about 4 am, he and other dealers would go to a casino and play and lose just like everybody else.

Then on to Fallon, Nevada. Fallon wasn't much of a town, but Lynne's bridesmaid lived there on a ranch with her rodeo cowboy husband, and we spent a couple of days riding horses and lazing about.

On a Sunday night, we left Fallon, driving through the relative cool of the August night, dropping straight down through the Nevada desert toward Las Vegas. All through the night, we were the only car on the road, driving Lynne's Ford Fairlane convertible with the top down, all black and silent around us except for the sound of the car. Gradually, starting around 4:30 or 5 am, as the dark sky began to lighten in the east, the first in a miles-long stream of headlights began to appear, rushing north towards all the military bases surrounding us hidden from view after a weekend's leave, mile after mile after mile of headlights.

In Vegas, there were a few nights of big shows on the strip and the usually more enjoyable acts in the lounges and days spent with Jim and Jane. Then we headed back to LA and a final two-week stay in Venice, where we rented a two-bedroom apartment on the beach with Bruce Feldman and his high school sweetheart and later wife. Then it was back to LA to an apartment a few blocks from the USC campus and the hot Santa Ana winds blowing in off the desert.

The honeymoon was over.

In the midst of all these goings-on, other things were going on, too. When Lynne and I were just beginning to know each other, I'd told her about *Makepeace's Blackouts,* and she suggested that I ask to direct it for the Theater Department that summer.

To my surprise, the department's head agreed to the idea after reading the play. One reason is that he wanted to increase the ties between the film school and the theater. I don't know the others. Could it be that he actually liked the play? He not only agreed to my directing it, but he agreed to my using professional actors rather than cast it from among the other students, and it would be performed both at the school and at the Idyllwild Arts Foundation. In exchange, I had to be willing to act in something myself, *Purgatory*, a one-act play by William Butler Yeats, basically a long monologue.

Much of June and July was taken up with rehearsals both of *Makepeace* and the Yeats play. I liked meeting the other people in the Theater Department. Josh White, who'd been a freshman at EI when I was a senior and who went on to be the quintessential designer of light shows for rock bands in the 70s (*The Joshua Light Show*), was there as was his girlfriend at the time, Swoozy Kurtz, among others. What I remember most about these kids (and most of them were younger than me, a real change for me) is that I generally liked them all much better than the film students.

I don't think I did a particularly good job directing the play. Having accepted Herman's view of it and its characters, I don't really see how I could have. I like to think I'd do a better job now that I have learned more about life, about love, about emotions, about people in general. It's only taken another half-century.

On the other hand, I'm not sure exactly how much I've learned about women. There is something about women that I don't quite understand, which probably makes me just another guy. More than once, it has occurred to me that if I am no longer under Herman's spell, I am still under Peggy's. Peggy never would have thought that men and women were the same. For her, there was an essential difference between them: Women could have babies. I think she would have said that it's too simple to say this is merely a matter of biology. For her, like all acts of creation, having babies is a mystery that cannot be understood solely by either reason or biology. She might have said that women have a direct pipeline to God. "Moon of all mysteries," Peggy called Honeypiece, or was that me in that long ago poem I wrote about another woman, a girl as much a figment of my imagination as a real person? Maybe both. I think Peggy might have understood the notion of God as a woman; it might have made far more sense to her than that old man with a beard. It is Woman who gives birth, endures the past, and creates the future. It is Woman who cares, who nurtures, who *mothers*. It is Woman who is hard-wired to her emotions. Oh, yes, men can be fine; they, too, can care, can be loving, they can play with their children and laugh and sing, they can strut and pose. They can even do the dishes. They are even necessary, in part anyway, to create a child. But they can never, ever be a mother.

I can't help but wonder what Peggy would make of today's attempt to de-genderize language and people, to de-genderize the person who grows a baby in her-their-its womb.

Non-specific gender designations aside, Lee, my ever pragmatic and altogether extraordinary wife, would say (in fact, has said) that I over-romanticize women; that women can be every bit as mean, spiteful, vicious, self-serving, vain, hateful and hate-filled, as men. More so, even. I am sure she is right. And yet ... Lee, too, is a mystery to me, and it is the mystery within her that I love as much as anything else.

This feels like a good place to end this chapter, don't you think? Sorry, I can't. Life isn't always so tidy.

Lynne and I returned from our honeymoon, as I said, to our apartment and the Santa Ana winds. It was so hot that first week in September that we spent much of it in the bathtub trying to cool off. Then married life began.

Lynne had finished her Masters and got a job at one of the Kaiser-Permanente hospitals. She was also still taking dance classes; dancers are *always* taking classes. I was going to classes, too. At night we'd go get ice cream sundaes — coffee ice cream with hot fudge — at the local diner on Hoover Street amid the used car lots or drive to the 24-hour supermarket on Adams Boulevard late at night. We'd listen to classical music because Lynne didn't care for most popular music and read. We'd watch a TV that one of Jim's business friends had given us. We saw her mother and sister. We visited the neighbors who lived in the little house behind ours. JB, Lynne's black, orange, and white calico cat, would come in and out of the bedroom window and leave dead birds or mice on the stoop of their house. Folk singer/songwriter Buffy Sainte-Marie, a house guest of our neighbors for several months, would sing her songs for me sometimes, and we sometimes sang together. I still remember her singing "Universal Soldier," "Co'dine," and "Until it's Time For You to Go" on our living room couch. I still remember their melodies and lyrics all these years later.

Bruce Feldman convinced the Pasadena Board of Education to film a school program to help kids with speech disabilities. We started shooting *In Terms of Speech* in October. Bruce was producing and directing. I was the production manager and editor. Other students in the film school filled out the rest of the crew positions. By early November, we were finished shooting, and I started cutting the film.

On the morning of November 22, 1963, I was in the editing room huddled over a Movieola (a machine used to edit motion picture film in those days) editing a sequence about a boy from Barstow who would only talk through the use of puppets. At about 11:30 am (PST), someone rushed in asking if I'd heard that JFK had been shot. I stopped, and we turned on a radio for a few minutes and then shut down my machine and went home. Like everyone else in America, I spent the following days glued to the TV in shock. I had voted for Kennedy, my first vote for President. I had watched every moment of the convention that nominated him on television, on NBC, with Chet Huntley and David Brinkley as the anchors. I had watched the Republican Convention as well. I had followed the campaign closely, read — devoured — Teddy White's *The Making of the President*. I knew, just as every single American knew, whether an Irish grandma with a lace antimacassar on her overstuffed armchair in Boston or a member of the John Birch Society in Orange County wearing his hatred like a medal, that something fundamental had shifted in America and that the future was a gaping black hole.

We finished the film, and the School Board accepted it. Bruce wanted to start a film production company with a couple of other students. However, he couldn't help being a micromanager. Regardless of whether I was doing something well or not, I hated being micromanaged. I hated to be managed at all, to feel the weight of someone trying to control me, and Bruce and I stopped talking for many years.

When the 1964 spring semester ended, my time in school came to an end as well. I had never been interested in getting a graduate degree. Nor had Bill Zimmerman (who had assured me of a jump start in my career) thought there was reason to get one. Unfortunately, not long after JFK's assassination, I learned that Bill had lung cancer. Six months later, he was dead. I was on my own.

I banged my head against the doors of Hollywood without success. The one job I found was working in the basement of a mail-order movie rental company splicing ripped and torn film so that it could still run through a 16 mm projector even if the film had become so chopped up over time that it was virtually incoherent.

As 1964 drew to a close, Lynne asked if I thought I could do better in New York. I didn't see how I could do worse, and we made plans to leave LA.

I was sorry to leave. When I came to LA, I felt free and unshackled in a way I never had before. I had left the deep depression of Maryland behind. I had left my parents behind. I had found the beginnings of building blocks around which my life could coalesce.

On the other hand, I was in a marriage that, at the time, I hadn't been exactly sure I should have entered into. At the same time, it never occurred to me that I should end it. I thought I loved Lynne, whether, in retrospect, I did or not. Moreover, both then and later, I took the idea of commitment seriously: For better or worse, richer or poorer, in sickness and in health, until death do us part. If our marriage didn't always seem better, it also didn't always seem worse either, certainly not then, at least to me.

As for Lynne, I didn't know what she was thinking about our marriage. Clearly, we were both unsure if we had done the right thing, at least in retrospect. Perhaps we just closed our eyes to what we knew was true and turned away. Instead, we packed up our belongings and left for New York.

Chapter 8
THE WINDING ROAD

◆

1965 — 1974

Every day is a winding road.
I get a little bit closer.
Every day is a faded sign.
I get a little bit closer to feeling fine.
—Sheryl Crow

It would be wonderful if our paths through life followed a steady, simple direction, one step in front of another leading in a straight line to what ... nirvana? But, unfortunately, that was not my path, not the way things happened. I had embarked on a bumpy road in both my personal and professional life and had no idea where it would end up — where I would end up. One step forward and then two steps back and sometimes more. One thing is sure: I was nowhere close to feeling fine.

Lynne and I left LA on a sunny January morning. We arrived in New York amid a cold, gray January winter a week later. I was home. Lynne was in a place she'd never been, and I don't simply mean New York. I mean winter as a daily grind, daily snow, daily dirty gray slush, constantly surrounded by massive buildings and endless concrete, throngs of people, screeching (and crowded) subways, a feeling of being under constant bombardment. Where was the sun? Where was the space? Where was the car with the top down and endless miles of open freeways? Of no less importance, she found herself in the center of a close-knit secular Jewish

123

family. The family, in general, was acutely aware of being Jewish despite a lack of religious belief. Many of its members (including my parents) were sure that a latent anti-Semite lay in wait within every Christian heart. I'm not sure that Lynne was ever completely at home in the city or with my family, no matter how hard she tried.

Enough of that. For the rest of this book, you will not hear much more about Lynne since its real focus is supposed to be about my work, and that journey was about to begin. Besides, if my personal life was going to be unstable over the next few years, so would my work life. If you think that the instability of each was mutually reinforcing, I'd say that they were both a reflection of me.

Now that Bill Zimmerman had died and I wasn't going to be sent off to Europe to work for whoever, I had to find a job. So I went to see Burt Hanft. Burt, you will recall, had been a vice-president at Screen Gems during the summer I worked for him. Now he was a vice-president at Paramount Television.

We had now known each other well for about six years. Bernice, Burt's wife, had worked for my mother at JFS during the war years while Burt was in the military. Around 1959, they rented the house next door to ours on Lake Copake. Just as our house was filled with people on weekends all summer (usually relatives), so was the Hanft's but not with relatives. Though there were few people from the entertainment industry, there were many interesting folks, mostly research scientists or administrators and advertising people. I liked them all. The weekends would be a free-flowing event with everybody moving back and forth between the houses. Burt, Bernice, and their friends were always willing to share their time with me, and I'd have long conversations with Bernice and would spend time with Burt after he came back from playing golf.

The time I spent with them both had been significant to me; I had needed adults to talk to who weren't my parents. So, when it came time to look for a job, I felt entirely comfortable talking to Burt about it. He sent me to see Les Winik, whose company, Winik Productions, was also in the Paramount Building on Broadway. The company was actually run by his two sons, who shot all the footage for their productions, and I was hired as their editor.

The Winiks made sports films. In those days before the existence of NFL Films, they shot the home games of the Jets and Giants, and I would cut highlight reels for teams and the various local TV stations. They also shot for the Mets, and I edited their annual highlight film and the "Meet the Mets" short that ran before their TV broadcasts for several years. In 1965 and '66, movie theaters still often ran one-reel short subjects (meaning they were about 10 minutes long) along with the feature, and Winik was contracted to provide six of them a year to Paramount. Those were the most fun to cut. If there was a disappointment, it was that I couldn't get credit for cutting them. Because Paramount was a union shop and because most theaters wouldn't show films unless there was a union seal on the film, the name of the negative cutter (who was a union member in a different company) was listed on the credits as the editor. When one of those films, *The Winning Strain*, a film about track and field athletes shot in super slow motion, was nominated for an Academy Award, it was the negative cutter who got the credit for editing it, and this was a picture that was all in the shooting and editing.

Despite the eyestrain and the headaches I'd get from constantly watching the flickering images on a Movieola, I was anxious to do something else with my time aside from sports. So, in the fall of 1966, I started working on a production of Arthur Miller's play about war profiteering, *All My Sons*, at Herman Shonbrun's suggestion, for a community theater in the Park Slope neighborhood in Brooklyn.

What I remember most about the actual directing of the play was devising different movement patterns for each of the three acts. I think the first act was done as a series of random-seeming interrupted movements along more or less straight lines. The second act was done in circular patterns as if the characters were constantly circling around each other. Finally, the third act mainly was long straight diagonals, generally, the strongest movements on a stage (or, indeed, a movie screen), as the characters attacked each other. I was having a pretty good time.

After we finished rehearsing around 11 pm in Park Slope, I'd go back to Brooklyn Heights and the Bossert Hotel, where we were mounting the play and helping with building and painting the sets and hanging the lights. I'd generally get home sometime between two and four in the morning and then try to get to the office by nine. I didn't often succeed. Needless to say, the Winik's weren't happy with my extracurricular activities or, at least, the effect it was having on my job performance. I was summoned into Les Winik's office in the middle of Christmas week and fired.

There is never a good time to be fired. Christmas is not worse than other times; they all suck. If I didn't sink to the depressive depths that I had in Maryland, I came close enough. I sent out resumes, had the occasional interview, went to movies on 42nd Street just to get out of the house. I was flailing without effect.

After being out of work for several months, with the urging of Lynne, I reluctantly decided that I had to be at least willing to do something completely different and started going to employment agencies looking for "management trainee" positions wherever I could find one. Then, finally, I had an appointment for an interview.

On a chilly spring day, I got out of the subway somewhere in Queens or the Bronx, wearing a suit and tie, on my way to my first interview in my attempt to find some kind of employment as far away from the entertainment industry as I could imagine. A *zipper* manufacturer of all things! Who would have guessed?

> **The street stretches out before me, stretches on forever. I don't really want to see where it ends. At the corner, I know there is a doorway, a doorway that I don't want to enter. The brick wall next to me is all cracked and dirty, its surface rough, hard, impenetrable, seemingly without windows as I look up at a patch of blue sky too far away to reach. I walk down the block swimming through quicksand, each step becoming slower and slower as I near the building's entrance. I stop. I can't move. I can't make my hand reach for the door.**

I knew then, as surely as I've ever known anything, that if I went through that door, that all would be lost. That *I* would be lost and not just for a day or for the life of that job, no matter if it lasted a day or a decade. I would be lost to myself forever. I had struggled. I had fought to gain some sort of foothold in my life. Those struggles hadn't been noticeably successful, but at least I had gained a foothold, a toehold, even if it was hanging by a fraying thread. I could not, I *must not* break that thread. My very life depended on it. I turned and walked away.

Finally, I got a job.

Ruth Zimmerman, the widow of Bill, worked for Titus Films on a freelance basis. While Bill was alive, she had become a director of the dubbing of movies into English from various foreign languages, and she continued doing it after his death. I would meet with her from time to time, and she arranged a meeting with Howard Lester, who did whatever editing was necessary for the films she worked on. Howard had a job available at one of his companies, Douglas-Lester Productions, and I went to work running their day-to-day operations. Little did I know that the people I met there would wind in and out of my life for the next thirty years and more.

Douglas-Lester was (to me) an odd company. It had only one client, National Educational Television, or NET. NET was the original national programming arm of public television, funded largely or entirely by the Ford Foundation. In the days before PBS came into existence, they were the source of just about all of the national programming, particularly public affairs programming, of the various educational or public TV stations around the country. In effect, NET was the network. Under their charter, NET wasn't allowed to hire below-the-line personnel — all the technical people who make a film, the cameramen, the editors, etc. To get around the problem, they had Howard officially supply all these people — union and non-union since NET didn't want to be hobbled by union contracts — and the facilities to edit the films and the equipment necessary for shooting and editing. Douglas-Lester had thirteen editing rooms in two locations (one was used by union personnel, and the other was for the non-union folks) that were all in use most of the time and would run a payroll of around eighty free-lancers a week.

Although I didn't know it, the people I met would become more important than the actual work, particularly the various production managers at NET. People like Mike Brooks, Hal Hutkoff, Don Sussman, and Bill Lynch would all play roles in my life in the years to come.

Take Bill Lynch, for example. Bill came to NET as the head production manager in 1968, a year after I'd gone to work for Douglas-Lester. I first met Bill when I worked for Winik because he worked for the DuArt film lab where Winik had its film processed. After arriving at NET, he decided he wanted to get out of the deal with Douglas-Lester. I don't know why. Maybe he didn't trust Howard, maybe with good reason. I know, for example, that when we billed NET, we'd add on a percentage to the bills we got from equipment suppliers, and NET knew all about it. On the other hand, I don't know if NET also knew that we'd get a kickback from the suppliers every quarter. Was that the reason? Neither Bill nor Howard ever said, at least not to me. At the beginning of 1969, NET moved its arrangement to a different company, Howard shut down Douglas-Lester Productions, and I was again out of a job. Bill and I, though, would meet again when, much to my surprise, he turned up as the vice president of MacNeil/Lehrer Productions when it was created in 1984.

Then there was Mike Brooks. He left NET and went to work for Reeves Sound Studios and encouraged them to hire me. I also replaced him for a brief time at TNT Productions, and after NET disappeared and merged with Channel 13 in New York, becoming WNET-TV, he let me know about an opening there in 1974. A few years after that, I got him a job as my replacement as the production supervisor on the *MacNeil/Lehrer Report* as I moved on to producing.

Don Sussman never left NET, became the head production manager of WNET after Bill Lynch left, and hired me in 1974.

Hal Hutkoff was another production manager at NET, and when I went to work for WNET, it was on a show he was working for while he was recovering from an illness.

None of this, I discovered, is unusual. No matter how large, all industries are, in reality, small. We meet people we once knew, worked with, worked for, knew through work, over and over again through time. Things keep folding back on themselves, the circumstances changing, but nothing, no one ever really disappearing. The same people, friends and enemies alike, run like threads through our lives, other ripples in the pond.

And just because I had a job or two or three doesn't mean that I had stopped wanting to write despite never writing another poem after *Adam.* Sometime during that depressingly lengthy period of unemployment, I wrote my first actual screenplay, an adaptation of William Styron's *Lie Down in Darkness.* I must have shown it to Howard Lester. Why else would he have asked if I would be willing to write a screenplay of Sylvia Plath's *The Bell Jar?* The only other writing that I know he saw of mine were some segments for *Kukla, Fran and Ollie* that I had written at his invitation on spec (i.e., without being paid). Howard had a long association with Fran and company in another part of his life. Although the sketches were quite charming (in my eyes), they were never used. Besides that, I'm not sure how writing amusing, even funny *Kukla, Fran and Ollie* sketches could translate into understanding Sylvia Plath's desperation, depression, and eventual suicide.

In still another part of his life, Howard was a sometime partner of Mike Todd, Jr., the son of Mike Todd and stepson of Elizabeth Taylor, who, Howard said, owned the movie rights to *The Bell Jar.* It could even be that this all happened after Douglas-Lester closed its doors. In any event, Howard wanted me to write the script on spec, and I said no, mostly because I didn't trust Howard and maybe, too, because it was such a daunting prospect, and I was afraid I couldn't do it justice. In other words, I chickened out.

I had read Styron's *Lie Down in Darkness* while at USC and was haunted by Peyton Loftis, the girl in the book. Peyton kills herself, and nothing in the book seems to explain why. Why did this beautiful, caring, torn girl find that death was preferable to life? What made it a better alternative? Can the emotional pain and confusion in one's life be so great that death is preferable? Not merely preferable in the imagination, but as a specific, intentional act? Was her love and anger at her parents so great that their only possible resolution was to turn them against herself? Was that resolution intended to turn her death into an accusation? That dissolving herself into nothingness would be a respite from the impossibility of separating herself from them? What problem was she solving? I thought by writing the screenplay, I might find out. Did I believe that I was facing similar challenges myself even if I didn't think of myself as suicidal? Maybe. I don't know. But I was haunted by her, and it is not likely that it was entirely coincidental.

The adaptation came out pretty well, and I sent it to Styron. He said he liked it and sent it on to a producer friend or acquaintance who wasn't interested. There was no interest in it from everyone I sent it to in Hollywood either. The general opinion was that it was too depressing, whatever its virtues (or flaws). I remember a lunch at the Sportsman's Lodge in Studio City. Now, the studio exec said, if I could only *do* something about that end…. No, there was nothing I could do; there was no happy ending possible. Peyton had to die; her father had to be destroyed by his guilt. The best I could do was hope that her mother could come to understand the role that she had played in Peyton's life and death, too late to do Peyton any good.

I didn't seriously disagree with Hollywood's assessment of the script. I thought I had been very clever about it, weaving the past, present, and future in and out of their lives. It wasn't only the Loftis family's personal past I was weaving, but our collective past of post-World War II America: JFK, Johnson, King, Nixon and Vietnam and Watergate, our recent collective history of political assassinations, civil rights, and anti-war demonstrations, the violence of the Black Panthers and the Weather Underground. I may not have been publicly engaged in these tumultuous events, but I was hardly unaware of them. And so, one way or another, through newspaper headlines and TV news bulletins, radio broadcasts as backgrounds, as Peyton Loftis's family was disintegrating, so was America. I thought it would be a powerful and moving film for people to see. On the other hand, I didn't know that I actually would go to see it. Seeing it, I thought, would be like taking bitter medicine. In later years I resisted seeing *Schindler's List* for similar reasons. Eventually, though, I swallowed the pill and went to see it with the expected results.

Many years later, someone else bought the rights to the book, and I sent him my script. He wasn't interested in it. Whatever his plans, they came to nothing. But looking back at my screenplay today, I think I would do it a bit differently but not much, change the language somewhat, shorten it up some. It still wouldn't get produced.

Interestingly enough, when Styron's *Sophie's Choice* was published, Stingo, the narrator of the story, tells of a girl in his hometown who committed suicide and says that however much he tried, he couldn't understand the act. In my reading of that, I understood that she became Peyton in *Lie Down in Darkness* and that Styron had no more inkling of why Peyton killed herself than I did. And that Styron wrote the book, at least in part, to try to understand the suicide of one of his classmates in his real life, not to mention, given his history of depression, his own suicidal thoughts. No matter Peyton's father's alcoholism, her mother's puritanical, self-proclaimed martyrdom, and her assignment of blame for any and everything to others, it still was not enough of an explanation. Perhaps it is that the acts of others can never fully explain the decision to end one's life. There must be an act of comparable magnitude. How bad does one's life have to get to decide to end it? How desperate, how despairing must one be? How angry or disappointed in oneself? In others? After all, suicide is not always, maybe never is, an entirely private act. I didn't know then; I don't know now. And Styron never knew either. As for Peyton, she took her knowledge with her to the grave.

There wasn't a very long gap between my leaving Douglas-Lester and joining Reeves Sound Studios, no more than a month or two. Mike Brooks, who had been at NET, was now at Reeves and encouraged them to hire me in the post-production scheduling department in the fall of 1969. Reeves was the largest independent video post-production company in New York and, perhaps, the country. The place worked pretty much around the clock. During the day, it was busy editing programs for the networks and NET along with commercials and film transfers to videotape. At night another crew made hundreds of dubs, mostly of commercials, to be shipped out the next day to ad agencies or stations around the country. It was a busy, high-pressured atmosphere. It was fun. I met all sorts of interesting people, and I got along well with the engineers. And I was learning the ins and outs of a whole new industry, the video industry, which was quickly displacing film. The various technicians — the editors and supervisors in particular — were helpful. From their viewpoint, the more I knew about their jobs, the better I could do my job, which, in turn, would help them do their jobs better.

I'm not sure the equipment used by Reeves in those days still exists except in museums. Color videotape was a recent innovation, and Reeves had been an early adopter of the technology, which partly explains their eminence in the industry. As different as videotape was from film, the process was similar, even if not identical. In our editing rooms, there were three machines, each about five feet high and four across. On these were mounted two-inch tape reels. One machine would hold the edited master, all the sequences and effects in a program. Mounted on the other two machines would be videotapes with all the visual elements that had been gathered. The editing process basically required copying material from one machine to the other. To create an effect like a dissolve from one shot to another, the third machine would hold the final sequence, and the other two machines would play through a switcher, which would, in effect, make the gradual transition. That's not much different from the Movieolas that I worked on when I edited sports films for Winik. Despite intrinsic differences between film and tape, the same basic editing techniques and principles were used. In fact, that's still true today when almost everything is done digitally through computers, those hardware behemoths able to be replaced by a single notebook.

NET was one of Reeves' most important clients, and they became one of my responsibilities because of my earlier relationships. Reeves' general attitude was that NET was a necessary form of income but nowhere near as important as their commercial clients. It became my task to shift their attention from the editors that Reeves thought of as their stars to others.

Reeves had recently bought three sound stages on West 67th Street, now owned by ABC. One of my favorite public affairs programs, David Susskind's live show, *Open End*, initially aired from those studios every Sunday night. Debuting in 1958, I watched it every chance I got. The show was as unadorned as possible. Susskind would sit in a blacked-out studio with one to eight guests arrayed like a horseshoe on either side of him. The show would go on for at least two hours. In those days, TV stations usually went off the air late in the evening, usually around midnight. If Susskind's show was going well and was still interesting to him and his guests were willing, he was free to continue it as long as he liked. Eventually, as broadcasters moved to program 24 hours a day, the show was limited to a two-hour slot. There was no set format to the show, no subject was off-limits (that I know of), and there were no regular guests. As far as I know, there had been nothing like it before and nothing like it since. The show lasted until 1986, a few months before Susskind died in 1987. If I were running a cable TV news network, that's a show I'd want on the air.

After Reeves bought the studios, one of the control rooms was turned over to NET, which had begun transmitting as an actual broadcast network to the various educational television stations around the country. After a year or so, PBS was formed and took over the network broadcasts from NET. Either NET or Reeves wanted to shift the network transmission from the studio building to the control room in the main building on East 44th Street where I worked. I, in fact, argued against the change, saying that it meant that our commercial clients wouldn't be able to use the control room and would move their business to our competitors. The NET network operation was moved with or without good reason, and the predictable happened. The large commercial production houses and advertising agencies began to move their work to our competitors, including ancillary services like the very profitable dubbing business. When PBS was formed, they moved the broadcast operation to Washington. It was one signal that the end for Reeves was coming.

During that first summer of 1969, the Children's Television Workshop chose the 67th Street studios to shoot the pilot episodes of a new program, *Sesame Street*. My relationship with the show was purely tangential, but watching the feeds of completed segments sure was fun. Kermit was my guy. Then, in August, the union representing the technicians went out on strike. Since I was part of management and, therefore, not in the union, I was stationed at the studios every evening, and I got to know the various stagehands and cameramen on the picket line whom I'd never met. I'd let them in the building to use the bathroom or drink water to the displeasure of management. By the time the strike was over, I had a beard, and *Sesame Street* had moved to a competitor. Although Reeves hung on for a while longer ... tick-tock, tick-tock.

There were occasional ancillary benefits from working at Reeves. One night Simon and Garfunkel came in to transfer their *Bridge Over Troubled Water* television special to tape. I still remember the title song's sequence, the film shot in black and white, the song being sung over Bobby Kennedy's funeral train. It reminded me of Earl Robinson's cantata, *The Lonesome Train*, about the train carrying Lincoln's body.

> **A lonesome train,**
> **On a lonesome track.**
> **Seven coaches painted black.**
> **A slow train, a quiet train**
> **Carrying Lincoln home again.**

I was moved by my memory of the cantata, Simon & Garfunkel's song, and the video itself. With them came a surprise, Peggy Lewis. Peggy had been our receptionist for a while at Douglas-Lester, the ex-wife of Simon's manager and another connection of Howard's hidden (to me) life. She was now Paul Simon's wife, a girl with a gray streak in her hair who had become, I always assumed without other evidence, the silver-haired girl of "Bridge Over Troubled Water." While Paul and Art supervised in the control room, Peggy and I went off and chatted. Following that night, I never saw any of them again.

After Reeves sold the soundstages in about 1970, they tried to get into the helical scan tape business by buying the Actron company, which developed into the VHS tape business. A small stage on Fifth Avenue came along with the purchase, and they put me in charge of it and a couple of video technicians. It had some work, though not enough to sustain its cost. We shot commercials in the studio and did some small remotes, but not enough. In 1971, the theater director Alan Schneider came to shoot Samuel Beckett's one-man play, *Krapp's Last Tape*, with the great Beckett Irish actor, Jack MacGowran. Since MacGowran died in 1973, it was one of his last performances. Although intended to be televised, it has never aired. A DVD of the production can be bought through www.phfilms.com.

The other thing that I did that year was direct a five-minute in-house promotional video for the Sears Roebuck Women's Store. It was the first time I'd directed a video. Sears was happy with it, and so was I.

Meantime, my time at Reeves was coming to an end. Actron, the VHS tape subsidiary of Reeves, was failing, as was Reeves itself, and I was out of a job once again. Within months, Reeves itself was gone, a victim of bad business decisions, the strike, and a considerable investment in a new computerized digital editing system that never worked.

The twists and turns of my life were difficult to navigate both professionally and personally. Lynne and I, though still married, were going through multiple official and unofficial separations. In between those episodes, Brandon and Michelle, our two children, were born. And there was another job or two or three.

The most personally rewarding one was as a director for Visual Information Systems. I was hired because of a woman who had worked for Howard Lester and was now working at VIS. The company's primary business was making medical films for physicians' continuing education. Most of these were shot at locations in New York or around the country. I shot films in New York, Atlanta, Miami, and LA on diverse subjects: childbirth, angiograms, drug addiction, and emergency medicine. I was editing a film on traditional Tibetan medicine when the Watergate Hearings began, and I'm sure I paid more attention to watching the hearings on PBS than the film. I paid no attention to the hosts, Robert MacNeil and Jim Lehrer, much less the producer, Linda Winslow. And I certainly had no idea that all three would play a role in my future.

As for the film on angiograms, I certainly remember it all these years later. The procedure was pretty new at the time, and it was fascinating watching the dye as it was pumped into the heart. When it came time for my own angiography in 1999, I could still hear Dr. Watson of New York's Memorial Sloan Kettering Cancer Center in 1973 calling out, "Hot flash coming!" as the dye was pumped into an old woman's arteries. But by the time of my angiography, hot flashes were a thing of the past.

There were some live-action, multiple camera shows that I directed as well. I made a discovery: Live-action multiple camera shoots, scripted or unscripted, were not my forte. They required a kind of hand/eye coordination, a kind of multi-tasking that I was not good at. I would get interested in what someone was saying and forget that I had to change shots. It was a valuable lesson for the future.

Towards the end of the year, I was asked if I'd like the opportunity to shoot some commercials. I should have said no. I was supposed to shoot twenty-four fashion commercials in a day, thirty-second spots with two or three models. There was no script. On the shoot, I had no idea what I was doing. I froze, and the producer took the shoot over. It was no surprise that I was fired a couple of months later.

Another job lasted for just a few months that I got, again, through Mike Brooks. This was at TNT, a company that supplied large-screen video projectors to movie theaters for big fights in the days before satellites and cable TV. It was a logistical nightmare of a job with projectors stashed all over the country and trucks that had to get them and move them to theaters and technicians who had to check and repair them. I did one Ali championship fight, and then the owner and I agreed that this wasn't a job for me.

In the summer of 1974, out of work again, separated from my wife again, and once again feeling desperate and depressed, I called my former boss at Reeves. She was now working for EUE/Screen Gems, the same Screen Gems, much changed and reduced, that Burt Hanft had once worked for, as had I in a summer job while still in school. I practically begged her for a job, any job, for whatever she could pay. She hired me to schedule post-production facilities again and paid me what she could, which wasn't much. It didn't matter. I was enormously grateful to her then and now. I stayed from the summer and into the fall.

And then things started to change. At last.

Part Two

THE MAGICAL MYSTERY TOUR

Chapter 9

THE MAGICAL
MYSTERY TOUR

◆

1974 — 1981

Maybe while I was stumbling around in the dark, the road with all its twists and turns was leading me to where I was going, even if I couldn't see it. Well, yes, of course. Wherever you end up is where you were going, even if you never intended it or expected it. Or maybe your experience in this life is different. Maybe you got to where you consciously intended to go all along. Lucky you (maybe).

On Monday, November 25th, 1974, the day following the Thanksgiving holiday, I started work at WNET-TV, Channel 13, the PBS affiliate in New York. Once again, Mike Brooks told me about the job. It's not as though we were personal friends; we never saw each other socially outside of work. I can't remember having more than one or two lunches with him in all the years I knew him. Yet he had been directly responsible for my working at Reeves and then at TNT. Now, again, he intervened in my life. He was back with public television as the head production manager for public affairs shows at WNET. I had stayed in touch with him off and on while I was out of work, and in mid-November, he told me that there was a temporary job opening at the station if I wanted it.

Don Sussman was now the head production manager for all WNET's programming. He offered me a three-month contract as a production manager reporting to Hal Hutkoff, who I knew from my days at Douglas-Lester and Reeves. Fifty years later, Don told me that I was hired because of his and the rest of NET's experiences with me in those earlier companies. He neither asked for nor received an

139

official resume from me. So other than their day-to-day contact with me, no one at WNET had the foggiest idea of my background.

Aren't perceptions a curious thing? Whereas I thought I had been failing or, maybe, flailing, at least some other people had the impression that I was succeeding. Regardless, Hal had gotten hepatitis and didn't have the energy to handle all the location shooting that *Assignment America*, a 1/2 hour series, required.

The executive producer of the series was Al Perlmutter, who I also knew from my days at Douglas-Lester when he was the executive producer of NET Journal, one of TV's legendary documentary series. When I was at Douglas-Lester, he owned a small sound stage in Chelsea. When the Rolling Stones wanted to shoot a music video for "2000 Light Years from Home" from the *Their Satanic Majesties Request* album, they asked Howard to find a studio to film in and to supply the equipment and personnel. I oversaw the shooting for our part of the responsibilities. The director was the still photographer who created the album cover for *Sgt. Pepper's Lonely Hearts Club Band*. The video, as I remember, was simple: a girl is shot jumping on a trampoline in very slow motion in black limbo, and images of her from different angles were layered over each other as she floats through empty space. Another video dating from 1967 can be found on YouTube, but it isn't the one shot in the Chelsea studio. No matter. It's still one of my favorite Stones songs, and there aren't too many of those. And no, I never met the Stones; they weren't there. As close as I got to that was when I knew Mick Jagger's sister-in-law in later years, and that wasn't anywhere near close.

There were four hosts for *Assignment America*: Maya Angelou, Studs Terkle, Doris Kearns, and Harvey Cox. In addition, George Will did a couple of shows while I was working on the series. One of the producers, Howard Weinberg, went on to work for *The Robert MacNeil Report* and, later, CBS's *Sixty Minutes* and *Sunday Morning*. Al Perlmutter left soon after I arrived to become Vice President of Documentaries for NBC News. His replacement was Carey Winfrey, who came to the show from *The New York Times*.

Within a few days of starting at *Assignment America*, I was off on my first shoot in Woods Hole, MA, to interview Albert Szent-Gyorgyi, the brilliant, witty, 1937 Nobel Prize-winning biochemist.

Howard Weinberg, the crew, and I checked into the motel the night before. The receptionist was a pretty South African girl with short black hair and violet eyes. Howard furiously flirted, and she was amused. After Howard went to his room, I talked to her for a few minutes and asked when she got off work. She told me, and I said to her offhandedly, "Why don't you knock on my door when you get off?" She laughed. Imagine my surprise when at 10 o'clock, accompanied by her startling intense eyes, she actually did knock on the door. We had a lovely night and, early the following morning, took a long walk on the beach, and disappeared from each other's lives.

We shot the interview with Szent-Gyorgyi in his lab. He was witty and brilliant. It went without a hitch. Who cared? Maybe life as a single guy needn't be a tragedy. I'd just had the best time I'd had in what seemed like forever. Was it possible that my personal life needn't depend on my marriage to Lynne?

I was already well acquainted with James Baldwin's work when I went to LA with Maya Angelou to interview him. I had read and admired *Giovanni's Room* when Bill Levy had given it to me while we were roommates at Maryland, and I had read *Notes of a Native Son* and *Go Tell It on the Mountain* and was looking forward to meeting him. Unfortunately, this shoot was not as rewarding as the last one. Maya was a prima donna, a diva, something I didn't (and still don't) find very endearing in anybody when working with them. However, that in itself wasn't the real problem. We arrived at Jimmy's house at about 10 in the morning. He didn't like to get up too early, probably because he was hungover. Jimmy started to drink, and Maya matched him, water glass for water glass (no shots for these two). By the time we were ready to shoot a couple of hours later, both of them were drunk. No, not high, drunk, staggering drunk. I urged Maya to cancel the shoot, but she refused and insisted that she was okay. The result was predictable: An incoherent babble. Yes, we managed to piece together something that seemed sort of comprehensible in the editing room with great effort. Then again, if one actually read the show's transcript, maybe it wasn't comprehensible after all. I was asked a couple of times if I'd be interested in doing something with Maya while working at the *NewsHour*. I always said no, and, happily, was never asked to justify my unwillingness.

Aside from my Woods Hole romp, the most engaging shoot for me was in Las Vegas. This documentary would be one of the first to be shot entirely on videotape for broadcast television. Portable professional video cameras were a very different beast than they are today. The PCP-90 was very much a beast, weighing something like 50 or 60 lbs. and maybe more. That's a lot to carry on your back for a whole day.

There was a new producer for this one, Steve Glauber. I had known Steve when he was a lawyer for the old NET while I was at Douglas-Lester and then for WNET when I was at Reeves. My recollection is that this was the first time he'd been a producer, and he later went on to produce for *Sixty Minutes*. We also hired a director for this one, Duke Struck, perhaps because Steve was so new at this. Duke was at least 6'2", if not more, and weighed well over 300 lbs. The rumor was that he'd been a lineman at Wisconsin. I believed it. He could be a pretty intimidating figure. I think this was Carey Winfrey's first segment after he'd replaced Al Perlmutter, and we had a new correspondent, George Will.

Steve had gotten permission to shoot the gambling tables at Benny Binion's Diamond Horseshoe. Binion, who wouldn't be interviewed, was one of those Vegas characters whose past my still father-in-law refused to acknowledge. He had a long history of criminality in Texas as a thief, running a numbers racket, and murderer, among other things. Whatever the pretensions of the Nevada Gaming Commission, many criminals, past or present, found a place in Vegas. Regardless, we could shoot in the casino as long as we promised not to show the faces of gamblers. After all, you never know who was with who they weren't supposed to be with or was doing something they didn't want anyone else, particularly their husbands or wives, to know. Steve had also lined up other interesting people to shoot. There was a cocktail waitress who, when asked if she ever "dated" any of her customers, batted her eyelashes and said, "Sometimes." There was a madam from an out-of-town legal brothel who we shot on the grounds of the Convention Center. Hank Greenspan, the editor of the Las Vegas Sun, talked with us on the tee of a golf course, and Steve Wynn spoke to us in his office at The Golden Nugget.

If you think George Will looks young now, imagine him 40 plus years ago. Then, he had a baby's face with his wire-rimmed spectacles. He was prim-looking, almost prissy. Aaron Freeman, a Chicago-based sometime comedian who wrote essays for me in the mid-'80s, once did a piece about all the young men around Reagan and Gorbachev. They all seemed to have baby faces and glasses. He called them Young Fogies. George was the spitting image of a Young Fogy. Even today, there is something fogyish about him. Duke decided to tease George about what Duke presumed to be his prudishness. We were shooting in the Diamond Horseshoe, and George was sitting at the bar, a glass of seltzer in front of him, when, by pre-arrangement with Duke, a cocktail waitress whispered in George's ear. George turned beet red, and I don't think he responded to her. Duke and I, at least, laughed. I don't think George was amused by Duke's prank, but he never mentioned it, at least not while I was around.

Other things were not so funny. At least at the time, Steve was not the most articulate of men. As a producer (at least if you have a director), you must be able to communicate how you visualize the final piece: what you expect to see, how you imagine the various elements will go together even if you're not exactly sure how it will really play out in the end. The director (if you have one since, in news and documentaries, the producer often performs both functions) has to have some idea of what he's doing and why he's doing it. The problem was that Steve didn't really know or, if he knew, couldn't or wouldn't tell Duke in a way that Duke could understand. It also could be that Duke was simply unwilling to listen. The situation kept getting worse with Duke threatening to quit, and I couldn't get the two of them to talk to each other.

Finally, I called Carey in New York and asked him to get on the next plane because we were headed towards a disaster. Carey arrived at around midnight, and at two in the morning, the four of us sat down at an empty blackjack table in the Union Hotel casino with Steve on one side of him and Duke on the other. Carey said, "Steve would you tell Duke what this story is?" And Steve, haltingly, started to tell the story, Duke listened, and after a half-hour, the problem was resolved.

Duke and I went to Nashville to edit the show at Opryland Productions. We had a great time watching *Deep Throat* during some technical downtime and watching Linda Ronstadt from the wings of the Opryland theater while the stagehands told us all the rumors about the sexual exploits of various performers.

And the show? George wrote a beautiful script — "Dreams in the Desert," he called it — and the show was a terrific success.

Aside from the Las Vegas show, all the shows were edited at WNET, and I sat in on all the edits for the months I was on *Assignment America* and not traveling. The station was bustling in those days, and the editing rooms were working 24 hours a day. Our editing schedule worked in three-week blocks, each taking a different shift. I'd work from 10 am to 6 pm for three weeks, then 6 pm to 2 am for the next three, 2 am to 10 am for the final three weeks, and then the cycle would start again. I was at the edits because I knew something about editing on videotape and film and because the producers mostly came from film backgrounds. The station's union contract with the Director's Guild also required that assistant directors be at the edits, so I got to know them.

Whatever the ups and downs of my past jobs, I had obviously learned something from them all. The film editing at Winik, the directing and remotes at VIS, management of resources at Reeves, the trucking at both Reeves and TNT, etc., had left me with a relatively wide range of experience and competencies. Not only that, but I was able to work with lots of people, including the technicians — the editors, cameramen, and all the others. We might not have been friends, but we all seemed to like one another and, more important, respect each other.

More important than all of this, though, was my feeling that I was finally involved in doing something that mattered. Of course, in itself, doing a good job wasn't important, aside from the necessity of earning a living. But it was doing the job in the service of an end that I thought mattered, which made the work meaningful and more than just a job. It wasn't, after all, entirely an accident that I found myself at WNET, the flagship station of public television. It's not that there weren't other major stations, but WNET was the biggest and most important of them all.

I was a byproduct, remember, of EI. I had read voraciously from the time I stole my first Zane Gray novel when I was 11 — highbrow, low brow, it didn't matter. I read everything from Thomas Mann to Mickey Spillane, not to mention all the books on science and American, German, and Russian history that I had plowed through. I had been interested enough in America and its history to have enough credits to have had an official double major at NYU. I had watched every minute of every presidential nominating convention since they started broadcasting them. My parents had been vitally involved in the social problems of my hometown and often discussed them at the dinner table. I was the grandson of Grandpa as we pushed pins into the map of the war in Europe and stood in the Lincoln and Jefferson Memorials. I had sat in Grandma's lap while Bach wove his many strands, and I had heard Joe Honeyman scream, "Look at me!"

I had been watching America with sadness, cynicism, apprehension, wonder, and sometimes anger ever since the assassination of JFK. The whole litany of Civil Rights, the Black Panthers, the Free Speech Movement, the Mobilization Against the War, the Weathermen, the SDS, the assassinations of Martin Luther King and Bobby Kennedy, the deaths of civil rights workers — black and white — Chicago's Days of Rage, riots at Columbia and Harvard, murder at Kent State, the Weather Underground, My Lai, Watergate. The list is/was seemingly endless. So how could I not care what was happening in and to my country?

And then there was this: One night, sitting with my parents, during my first extended period of unemployment, my father asked, "Why couldn't you have picked a profession that we could have helped you out in, like medicine or accounting or social work or law?"

I said, "It's all your fault."

My mother straightened in her chair, an orange-ish upholstered armchair, the same chair in which she would sit some eighteen years later and announce that time had come for her to die. I remember her back stiffening, her neck stretching as her chin rose and drew back combatively. I could practically see the hairs standing at the back of her neck. And then the official office voice, the feared voice of my childhood, "What do you mean?"

"It's just that I learned everything that you taught me to value, everything that you thought was really important. Art, the act of creation, the past. All the people you admired, the writers, the poets, the painters, the sculptors, the directors. Grandma, Eliakum, Shomer, Sheila, and all the others, including both of you." So many of us, all descendants of the Zunser/Shomer clan, had all become infected with the virus.

She relaxed back into her chair and nodded. She understood.

Through the years of wandering on my twisted path, I had concluded that if I couldn't make movies in Hollywood, then maybe public television was the place where I could best put to use all of those events on my journey: standing with Grandpa in the Lincoln Monument, the endless dinner table conversations — even fights — with my father, the arguments with Harold Kirshner, the loss of my friendship with Joe Louis, the love of W.B. Yeats and T.S. Eliot, all the books and poems I had read, and what I had learned from Mary "Peaches" Honeypiece.

At the end of my three-month contract, Don Sussman asked me to stay on, not permanently but week to week. From April until July, the work was hectic. New York was in the midst of its dire fiscal crisis, the one that produced the famous "New York Drop Dead" headline in the Daily News. I was the production manager for several special hearings in New York and Albany and the remotes for the Nursing Home Hearings (a problem that never seems to go away). In addition, there were soccer games in New York and Boston, the shooting and repackaging of The *Fifty-First State* for summer reruns, and a film series called *The First Rebellion* produced by Dan Chaykin. In later life, as I discovered in an internet search, Dan turned out to be the producer of the HBO series, *Pornucopia: Going Down in the Valley*, the arc of American rebellion from the American Revolution to the Sexual Revolution.

Towards the end of June 1975, Jerry Toobin, the Director of Public Affairs Programming for WNET, handed me a preliminary budget done months ago for a proposed show with a former NBC correspondent, Robert MacNeil, who was now living and working in London for the BBC.

A brief time out.

Robert MacNeil has never been called "Robert," at least so far as I know. He's always been known as "Robin," at least informally. There have been occasions when guests would call him "Bob," perhaps thinking that was his informal nickname. That would always give us a chuckle because it was a sure indication that the two had never met. So, Robert is Robin forevermore. And *never* Bob.

Back to the story:

"Here," Jerry Toobin said, in his gruff fashion, "Fix it."

"What's wrong with it?" I asked, quite reasonably, I thought.

"Just fix it. Go on, get out of here."

That was Jerry. One might think he was a madman. He'd yell, though rarely, if ever, at me. He'd rant and rave, and most of the time, he didn't mean a word of it, of the ranting and raving, though he did mean what he meant to be saying. No matter how much he yelled at his small staff, they were fervently loyal to him. He was a man whose bark was far worse than his bite, although he certainly knew how to bite. Jerry had become a supporter of mine, without my really knowing why. Maybe it was because there had been all these shows that I had worked on that had gone exceptionally well (well, let's not mention the Maya Angelou incident since I never said a word to him about it, and I don't know if he ever heard of it). His support certainly wasn't because I worked for him, at least not directly. At 13 (as WNET is usually called), the production managers all reported to the Director of Finance. That was primarily because of the financial debacle that had resulted from *The Adams Chronicles*, an elaborate historical series in the tradition of the BBC's *Masterpiece Theater*. However successful the series was to audiences, the station never recovered from the financial aftershocks, at least not as long as I was there, and was never the same production company.

I went off and studied the budget as it was laid out. I had never done anything like this and was quite aware of the consequences of any significant mistakes. There is no counting the number of errors that can be made in budgeting for 260 shows. I tried to imagine the show, what it might look like, how it might function on a day to day basis, how many people it would take, what materials and equipment they would need, what was required for the studio, for the sets, what editing facilities would be required, how many playback machines during the show would be necessary, how the control room should be staffed, and on and on. On the other hand, there would be predictable fixed costs such as salaries and time in the studio. As it turned out, I didn't make massive changes in the budget. After all, the station's production managers were competent at the very least, and several had experience with strip shows (i.e., shows airing five nights a week). But I did make some changes.

For one thing, the show was conceived of as having a Washington, DC component three days a week, with a part-time anchor/correspondent in Washington, Jim Lehrer. I didn't know any more about Jim than I did about Robin, although I knew he had been Robin's Watergate partner because I had watched the hearings on PBS while in the editing room cutting the show on Tibetan Medicine while at VIS. So the first thing I decided was that once Washington was in the show, it would likely never leave, and I budgeted it for five days a week. Next, I realized that there had to be a way to get information and scripts back and forth between the two cities; telephones and typewriters wouldn't do. I could just imagine people having to dictate information to each other. Fax machines were pretty new in those pre-computer days, and I budgeted for a high-speed stand-alone fax machine for each city tied together by a dedicated full-time phone line. I also budgeted for a telephone tie-line between Robin and Jim so they could talk to each other by simply picking up the handset, subscriptions for daily newspapers from all around the country, and the Associated Press wire service. I submitted the budget and continued with other tasks until August 4th, when Robin was due to arrive from London.

As scheduled, Robin arrived in early August. Since we had never met, never had a conversation, I had no idea how he imagined the show. So within the next couple of days, we sat down to see what he wanted to actually do with the money we were being given out of WNET's discretionary funds. We repaired to Nirvana, an Indian restaurant that used to be in the penthouse of a building on Central Park South with fabulous views of the park and city stretching to the north beneath us. Later on, the city shut down the restaurant, which had a penchant for keeping its illegal immigrant help virtually enslaved.

When I met Robin for the first time, I had no idea who he was as a human being, much less who this person was that I was detailed (at least as I saw it) to both protect and enable. To enable, meaning to make sure he had what he thought he needed to do his job while at the same time keeping the budget under control. To protect, meaning to help keep him from making mistakes regarding his handling of personnel and, even more, to make sure all the technical aspects of the show performed in the way they were supposed to.

Robin was 44 when he arrived at WNET. Sandy-haired, about 5' 11", and Canadian (he didn't become an American citizen until 1997, two years after he retired). He had an easy smile, a twinkle in his eye, and a somewhat formal, reserved manner. I never knew if he was naturally shy, or simply reticent or hesitant in social situations. Yet he had a wonderful sense of humor. One of his favorite pastimes was writing ribald limericks, which surprised me when I first learned of it. I never thought we were ever friends, but we were colleagues, and I think we came to trust and rely on each other. After the show's debut, we rarely shared a meal together unless traveling together, which didn't happen all that often. I don't recall either of us ever talking about our personal lives together, certainly not in any significant way. Nor, by the way, had Robin or anyone else who ever worked for the show ever seen my resume. Nonetheless, from the very beginning, for the purposes of the show, we were allies. As I said about my early life, sometimes having an ally is more important than having a friend.

Robin was always the show's steady center, the calm in the middle of the storm. He hardly ever raised his voice, although you never misunderstood when he was annoyed by something or disappointed in you. Outward displays of passion were not in his wheelhouse. Instead, he was always thoughtful and rational, always willing to listen and seriously consider anything you had to tell him. The door to his office was always open; any staff member was welcome to come in and talk. That so few did or did so reluctantly had more to do with his reserved manner. Or, maybe, everyone respected him and his quiet but determined leadership so much that they didn't want to intrude.

From the first moment I met him, he was willing to trust me, to assume that I knew what I was doing even if I didn't, and was willing — wanted even — for me to succeed because if I succeeded, then he could succeed. If I was going to fail him, I would have to do it on my own. I like to think that I never did, at least not in any critical way.

Does that mean that I thought he was infallible? No. None of us is infallible. And I didn't always agree with the choices that were made. Whatever criticisms I had of the show (and I will not hide them from you), they were never of Robin, the person. Nor were they necessarily correct. They are simply how I saw things from my vantage point, a place that evolved over time, and I'm not talking about my title in the show. If you were a viewer of the show, I'm sure you will make your own evaluation of anything I may say.

So, onward.

It turned out that Robin, despite his background as a correspondent and weekend anchor at NBC and as a BBC producer/correspondent, had decidedly non-TV-oriented ideas of how he wanted to staff his show. Rather than the usual cast of producers, associate producers, production assistants, and the like, Robin wanted to base the show around reporters, people whose primary skills were journalistic and who may never have been involved in television. Indeed, it often seemed that any television experience a reporter might have was a negative in his eyes. There would be two producers who would function more like print editors than anything else since there were no plans to shoot news or documentary footage. Whatever actual videotape responsibilities there were could be left in the hands of production assistants. Conceptually, things remained remarkably similar, at least until Jim Lehrer's retirement. When we left Nirvana, my napkin was full of scribbled notes about changes I'd have to make in the budget.

There were some noticeable changes as the show evolved into the *NewsHour*. After the *NewsHour* began, the biggest was that some actual TV producers were added because of the various videotaped elements introduced like documentaries and essays. But most of the ½ hour show's producers were without significant TV production experience when they were first hired. Although Robin and Jim frequently and publicly expressed their gratitude to the show's reporters over the years, it wasn't until the show's 30th anniversary that I ever heard either of them publicly thank the producers for their contributions. Their general lack of acknowledgment of the producers was surprising, grating, galling, and disappointing, at least to me. Even more, one might conclude that their disdain for television was a significant contributor to some of the show's long-term problems.

Regardless, Robin agreed to hire Ray Weiss as the executive producer at Jerry Toobin's request, as long as it was understood that he, Robin, would run the show. He didn't want any interference by Ray, especially when it came to editorial matters. Ray's responsibilities were to be pretty much limited to the day-to-day operational management of the show, a sort of office manager with a bigger title. Unfortunately, the most effective thing Ray seemed able to do was to reduce our production secretary to tears.

We wanted one director to work on all the shows in NY, and there were several candidates. As it happened, both Robin and Jim had worked with Duke Struck, who I had worked with on *Assignment America*. I encouraged them to pick Duke. I thought Duke had several skills that would be very useful. For one thing, he was well-seasoned in dealing with live, multi-camera shows in high-pressure situations. As a director of NFL football games on weekends for CBS, there wasn't likely to be anything we would do that was too challenging for him or any crisis that would leave him altogether at a loss. Not only that, but he was so big both in size and personality that no one could intimidate him, and there wasn't anybody who he wouldn't try to impose his will on if he thought it necessary. Then, too, there was the fact of two locations. Duke couldn't direct both places simultaneously, but he had to be able to control what the remote city was doing. Finally, the most important quality was that Robin and Jim trusted him. Ultimately, the director's most important job is to protect the anchor, just as it is with everyone else working on a live show. You never want to cause the anchor to look foolish, ill-informed, or have his facts wrong. There are plenty of opportunities for an anchor to do that all by himself. I don't know if I was simply concurring in a decision that Robin and Jim had already made or if my recommendation made any difference. Still, I liked being consulted on the decision-making.

I wanted a permanent assistant director for the control room and asked that Judi Elterman be assigned. I had worked with her many times in the editing room during *Assignment America* and the other live shows I did before the *Robert MacNeil Report*, as it was initially called. Because of the shows we worked on together and the meals we had shared at 2 or 3 am during or after late-night edits, I had complete trust in her ability and dependability, and Duke accepted my recommendation.

Bob Wightman designed most of the studio sets that 13 used, and neither Robin nor I knew anybody that we preferred. After some preliminary sketches, Robin came up with his notion of Lois Nevelson-like sculpted walls. But Robin's main concern was the anchor desk. He didn't want people to be sitting in a circle like most TV talk shows or in chairs opposite one another. The slot desk, rather like the copy desk at a newspaper, was his solution. It would allow him to be equidistant from all his guests, it would give him and them a place to put papers or water or whatever they might need, and it allowed them to sit quite close to each other without it looking like their legs were getting all tangled up. It was a clever solution to a real problem, and it became a mainstay of the show. However, it did have one drawback: it occasionally forced us into an awkward shooting situation, namely, something called a jump cut, where someone seems to be looking in one direction and then in the next shot seems to be looking in another. Nevertheless, Robin felt that the other advantages outweighed the one disadvantage. He was right about this as he was about most things.

The other big design decision had to do with handling Jim's presence on the show. Robin wanted it to appear that Jim was his co-equal whenever he was on the show. The idea was to place a monitor on the set so that, ideally, Jim would almost appear to be sitting at the same table. Of course, it never really looked that way, and we later moved to a larger screen, but the intent was clear. Even more than that was the fact that we would not trumpet the presence of someone in another city. We would say that Jim and his guests were in Washington once, but we wouldn't make a fuss about it. This was unusual in an era when every technical innovation would be loudly and frequently trumpeted on TV shows. Even more, interconnects between different cities during a live news show were extremely rare, if they happened at all. The most famous of them, NBC's *Huntley-Brinkley Report,* wasn't really an interconnected show at all. The NY and DC segments were taped separately, with the Washington portion fed to NY and edited into the final show.

Although the only cities we were interconnecting at the beginning were New York and Washington, that would change by the end of the year. Even then, though we announced where we were connecting, we wanted to make it feel like everyone was sitting at the same table.

Bernie Hoffer wrote the music theme for the show. I don't remember how we got to him, whether through Robin, the head of the 13 Music Department, or some other person. The original music Hoffer wrote, rearranged several times through the years, is still the show's mainstay.

There were two producers at first. Linda Winslow moved to New York from Washington, where she worked for WETA. She had been Robin and Jim's producer for the Watergate Hearings, which they hosted. In 1978, she returned to WETA as Vice President of News and Public Affairs and then returned to New York in 1982 as deputy executive producer to aid in the transition to the *NewsHour*. Linda, obviously, had considerable experience in live television. Eventually, in 2006, she became the *NewsHour's* executive producer and remained so until she retired in 2014.

Howard Weinberg, the same Howard Weinberg with whom I had worked on *Assignment America,* became the other producer. Robin decided to leave Howard's salary negotiation to me. I told Howard that we were prepared to offer him the same salary he'd made for *Assignment America,* which did not make him happy. We discussed it back and forth, and I insisted that what we were offering already exceeded what our budget called for. As I typically did in similar situations, I also said that he was always free to appeal his case to Robin. In fact, that was why I was negotiating this and some other salaries. It was always valuable to have someone with greater authority make a final judgment. So, Howard went to Robin, and Robin increased the offer by $5.00 a week. Howard wasn't too pleased with the final figure, but he accepted it, having been at least somewhat successful. I thought the result was perfect. Robin had shown that he could be flexible, yet the end result was that we essentially held the line.

Howard's experience and interests were primarily in documentary production. Although Robin and I never discussed it, I thought his hiring partly satisfied Jerry Toobin's interests by having a WNET veteran on board and, perhaps too, he was keeping an eye on the show's future direction. But Howard was frustrated by the general lack of documentary production, and it was probably one reason he left before the transition to the *NewsHour*. Indeed, after leaving, he went on to produce documentaries at *Sixty Minutes* and CBS's *Sunday Morning*.

The first reporter we hired was Shirley Wershba. Shirley had a long career and had been at CBS News for many years. She was married to Joe Wershba, a producer for *Sixty Minutes*. If you saw George Clooney's film about Edward R. Murrow and Joe McCarthy, *Good Night and Good Luck*, you may remember Joe and Shirley's secret romance as part of the story. Robin wanted to have at least one highly experienced reporter on the staff since most of them were going to be young and, for the most part, relatively inexperienced. So he tracked her down in Spain, and we added her to the staff. By the end of August, Robin and Jim had hired the remaining reporters in New York and Washington, and the rest of the staff — the production assistants, production secretaries — all the people vital to getting a show on the air, were on board.

At the end of August, Robin and I headed off to London for a couple of weeks. Before he arrived in NY, one thing pre-planned was his participation in *Goodbye, America,* a drama co-produced by the BBC and WNET. I presume Jerry Toobin suggested that I go with Robin and represent WNET's interests. Or maybe it was Robin's suggestion, and I didn't know it. Regardless, off we went to London on my first trip out of the country other than that uncomfortable trip to Montreal with ZBT.

Goodbye, America was a reenactment of the last session of the English Parliament before the thirteen colonies in America issued *The Declaration of Independence*. It was to be done as a *faux* news program. In modern dress, Robin and his British counterpart acted as the anchors overseeing the parliamentary session, with the other actors in 18ᵗʰ-century costumes. There were scenes of the parliamentary debate about what to do about the obstreperous colonials, interviews by the anchors of various participants, and filmed reports of other goings-on, like the reaction in France to the British conflict with their colonies. I'm not sure how good the program actually was, but it went off without major problems that I knew about.

On October 20ᵗʰ, 1974, after a couple of weeks of rehearsal, *The Robert MacNeil Report* went on the air. I won't say that it was always trouble-free because no show ever is. But, with some exceptions, it was a relatively trouble-free broadcast and remained so as long as it was based in NY. After the show moved to Washington, I'm less sure about that consistency because I was less involved in the live broadcast and rarely in the control room. All that means is that the actual machinery of the show, the cameras, lights, etc., worked well most of the time. The problems most often had to do with people, as is usually the case.

Duke, our director, loved problems. If there wasn't a real problem, he would manufacture one as often as not. Usually, these had to do with the interconnection to Washington. Indeed, the video quality from Washington was always a bit soft, the picture looking a bit out of focus. Whether that was because of inadequate quality control at WETA or a loss of quality as the signal hopped from microwave tower to microwave tower between the two cities was never entirely clear to me or anyone else.

Even after satellite transmissions became the norm for PBS, the connection between the two cities was via microwave links. When a signal is transmitted to a satellite, there's a time delay of about 3/4 of a second because of the distance it has to travel. The delay can be even longer if the signal has to bounce from satellite to satellite before arriving at its destination. Those delays became common throughout live television during the pandemic in 2020, and I guess everyone became somewhat used to them. But there is virtually no delay when the transmission is via microwave or landlines because the distances are much shorter even if they seem long, so that manner of connection between the two anchor cities was maintained.

Beyond that, I always thought there were two reasons that Duke liked a sense of crisis. One was that he felt that he needed to keep everyone on the crews in both New York and Washington on their toes; it's easy for crews to become blasé in a show that, for them, repeats itself day after day. The other was to keep himself from being bored; he needed a way to get his own adrenaline flowing. Somehow, whatever crisis Duke manufactured would be resolved with about thirty seconds until air.

For me, it was an exciting time as it would be for the next three years. In the show's first year, I was in the office from about 9 in the morning until nine or ten every night. Perhaps, after all, I was my father's son. There were always numbers to crunch after the evening's broadcast. There were bill payments to authorize, expenses to approve, personnel schedules and problems to sort out. Most important was calculating how much money we had left to spend in the month, mostly meaning what we could afford to do with the money set aside for discretionary spending. The truth was, outside the running of the editorial end of the show, Duke and I were pretty much running everything else, at least until Ray Weiss was replaced as the executive producer in 1977. Increasingly, every morning it would seem as though there were people outside my office door. They all wanted some problem solved that usually had to do with hurt feelings or thrashing out some policy that was sort of ill-formed and needed either tinkering with or inventing. There wasn't any official written "policy" for the show regarding personnel matters in the early days, so I made it up as we went along. Eventually, Ray's successor had a policy manual drawn up that made things much clearer to everyone.

In December 1974, Robin asked if we could try something new. Because we were a local show airing only in New York, we had a reporter, Dan Werner, whose beat was New York City. He wanted to get Manfred Ohrenstein, the Majority Leader in the New York State Senate, on the show from Albany. Could we do it? After talking it over with Wayne Grenier, our Engineer-In-Charge, or EIC, we figured out a way. And thus was the official birth of "the interconnect" to other cities as an integral part of the show. Once we knew we could do it, it was hard not to want it regularly.

Although, as I said, we were a local show, we primarily covered national issues. Not surprisingly, Robin wanted to expand our reach. When I started making up a budget for the following year, interconnections lay at the heart of the increase in our budgetary request. As a justification for the rise, I wrote something like, "Not all wisdom resides in New York and Washington." True enough. On the other hand, over time, I found out that one can find someone anywhere in America who will mirror what someone in Washington or New York thinks they should be thinking.

For us, this mirroring effect occasionally manifested itself in decisions made in the daily planning meeting on how to cover a story. Knowing what the story was supposed to be, the reporter would look for guests around the country who mirrored the viewpoints being looked for by the producer and/or Robin and Jim. If a reporter found that the story was somewhat different than the senior staff understood it to be, it could be difficult to impossible to change their minds. And if a potential guest expressed viewpoints that weren't being looked for, then that person wouldn't get on the show. This isn't a problem that was unique to our show. You will hear similar stories from newspaper and television reporters all over the country who get told what should be reported even if they find that the reality on the ground is different.

Sometimes a guest would say something completely unexpected, occasionally with unhappy results. On one famous show, Sen. Pat Moynihan and his Republican counterpart were to be on the show for the whole ½ hour debating some aspect of foreign policy. The two had widely divergent views in their pre-interviews with our reporter and their public statements. Moynihan's response to the first question went something like, "Well, we don't really disagree at all." Robin was left wondering where his whole plan for the show went. If it threw him, it only did so for a moment, and he continued on as though nothing had happened.

On another occasion, Jody Powell, Jimmy Carter's press secretary, was being interviewed by Jim about a report on the Burt Lance banking scandal. Powell asked Jim if he'd actually read the whole report, pointing out differences between what the Executive Summary said and what was really in the body of the report. It completely flustered Jim because he hadn't read the report at all other than the summary and whatever he'd been told about it by the reporter. Jim never allowed himself to be caught in that position again.

I can't resist one more famous story. On the Friday morning after the 1976 Republican Convention in Kansas City, we taped a show to air that night after we left. The subject was the looming crisis of the depleted Ogallala Aquifer that supplied water to much of the agricultural mid-West. Quite naturally, Robin asked the guest how soon it would be before the crisis was upon us. "In about fifty years," the guest replied. In the control room, at least some of us practically fell on the floor laughing. I'm pretty sure neither the producer nor reporter of the segment found it so amusing, much less Robin. On the thirtieth anniversary of the *Robert MacNeil Report*, I asked Robin if he thought the Ogallala was about to run out of water anytime soon. He laughed a lot harder than he had in 1976.

There were experiments we tried that we never tried again. For example, we once devoted the whole show to a debate about the virtues of Pringles, which had just been introduced, versus regular potato chips. Aside from guests, Robin became an advocate of one and Jim of the other. I think they tossed a coin to decide who would advocate what. That was the last time we did that. I also remember a show about the weather. We had Professor Irwin Corey begin the show with a weather report. For those of you who never experienced Corey, he was a comedian dressed as a homeless clown and spoke absolute gibberish that somehow contained bits of wisdom. We never did that again either.

It seemed we were much more adventurous in the first few years of the show than later on. Maybe it was simply that we were discovering what the show could be. As time went on, Robin and Jim had a better sense of what they thought worked and what didn't. The more successful we were, the less they wanted to tamper with the formula. Don't fix what isn't broken. But, on the other hand, it sometimes felt like we were too willing to be cautious, no matter what was said to the staff.

Robin or Jim would come back from vacation feeling energized and wanted to energize the staff. So one or the other would say, "Let's do things differently, let's find some different people, different ways of covering stories." Whatever they said, over time, and with their encouragement, things would slip back to the way they had been. A reporter might suggest a new guest, and one of them might say, "Gosh, wasn't so and so really good on this issue. We know what he's like. Let's get him."

In the ½ hour show, the general rule, almost without exception, was one topic per night. This usually meant that more than two guests would appear. It may seem obvious, but policy issues are complex affairs with many aspects to be considered. Three or four guests with differing viewpoints would be more likely to get at the nuances of policy debates than two guests. More and more guests, particularly the politicians, would obviously have had media training as time went on. They learned to have prepared talking points and tried not to deviate from them. The cleverer of them knew how to sidestep any question they didn't like and return to their talking points. Just watch any White House Press Secretary, and you'll see what I mean. The result, over time, is that interviews became less interesting as answers became more predictable. For me, as the format evolved into the *NewsHour,* the discussions had less potential for the unexpected or, for that matter, interest.

Really good White House press briefers are masterful spinners. They can take a set of facts and make them seem to be saying something other than what anybody else might make of them. Nicole Wallace (now an analyst and moderator on MSNBC) was masterful when she did briefings for Bush 43. She was so good at it that I couldn't bear to listen to her. So was Ari Fleischer. At the other end of the scale were Trump's briefers, who simply lied when or if they bothered to talk to the press.

Before we ever went on the air, Robin (and Jim) established the basic principles of the kind of journalism that the show would follow for as long as both were involved. The most basic ones were pretty simple to explain: Every issue had at least two sides. If possible, in any policy discussion, both sides should be represented. There were some exceptions. Certain people, like the president or vice president and cabinet secretaries, or senior members of the White House like the chief of staff or the national security advisor, might get solo interviews. On rare occasions when at least two people couldn't be found to discuss an issue, a journalist might be used to explain both sides. But they always wanted the highest ranking people available as guests. In the case of congressional representatives, this meant the committee chairman and ranking member from the other party. In other words, they wanted guests who had the responsibility for and power to make decisions.

If the show had wanted an accurate slogan, it might well have been "Fair and Balanced." I guess no one thought of it until Fox News came into being twenty years later in 1996 and used it as their slogan. What Fox meant and what Robin might have meant were totally different. At least in its nighttime schedule, Fox imagined that its network would have a specific political bias different from the supposed liberal perspective of every other news organization in the country, print or TV. In other words, Fox News was deliberately conceived of as a conservative propaganda machine. There has never been anything "fair and balanced" about Fox News.

On the other hand, our show actually had a bit of a slogan embedded in the show's concept. Since it aired after the network evening news shows, the idea was that people should watch the evening news and then watch us to better understand the day's leading issue. In fact, the daily topic of the show was usually the lead item of the network shows. That's not because we were copying them. Instead, it was because it's generally pretty obvious what the day's main story is, at least if you read the AP wire copy as it's constantly being fed, 24 hours a day, to every major newsroom in the country.

Robin had his own slogans that he repeated in interviews about the show. One was, "We dare to be boring." This was during the hyperinflation in the late '70s, and we talked about monetary and fiscal policy a lot, which could often be sleep-inducing. Nevertheless, Robin thought these issues were vital, and we covered them as thoroughly as possible, no matter how many people we put to sleep.

I seem to remember that he had a sign posted on his primary camera for a time. "KISS," an acronym for "Keep it simple, stupid," meaning, for him, keep things as direct and straightforward as possible, don't get sidetracked and caught up in the weeds. The phrase originated in the Navy, and Robin's family background was naval. In fact, at the time, I think his brother was a NATO naval commander based in Norfolk, VA.

There is a problem with live shows: their very unpredictability can make you want to limit the risk or possibility of the unexpected. Experiences like the Moynihan episode could make you uneasy. In the first couple of years of the ½ hour show, one of our volunteers kept suggesting extraordinary and often unlikely combinations of people for guests. She'd think of each show as if she were planning a dinner party and was inviting people who might bounce off each other in unexpected ways. Robin loved the suggestions, was delighted (I think) by the possibilities, and hardly (I think) ever took them seriously. Too bad. As time went on, live conversations and interviews were virtually pre-scripted, designed to bring out the information and viewpoints that had been revealed in pre-interviews, and rarely leading to a sense (to me) of spontaneity or the unexpected. Over time, my own experience led me to conclude that one could rarely expect the unexpected for the first twenty minutes of an interview. After all the stock answers were handed out, after all the answers that a guest had prepared had been said (usually with the help of their PR advisers), only then might something real, genuine, and surprising happen. Increasingly, those were the moments I looked for. Increasingly, particularly as the show moved into its hour-long version, those moments became both less frequent and less possible, not to mention less desirable. Ironically, as the show's length stretched to an hour, program segments and interviews became shorter and even more predictable.

Sometimes it felt as if the adherence to the show's basic format was as much a fundraising device as a devotion to journalistic principle. That is to say that our attempt at evenhandedness meant that a potential funder couldn't complain that we tried to lean in one direction or another. Not that we weren't accused of that, but that was always by people who wanted us to lean their way.

I don't know many fundraising stories because it wasn't something I was involved in, and Robin rarely talked about raising money, although he was often responsible for underwriting decisions. But, if nothing else, he was willing to meet with potential funders. The rumor was that the decision of Exxon's initial underwriting of the ½ hour show when it went national resulted from a chance meeting of the president of Exxon and Robin at a cocktail party, after which

Robin sent him a short letter saying, in effect, "Why don't you fund us?" And Exxon did, underwriting the show for several years.

Jim thought it improper to meet with potential funders no matter how much it was urged upon him to do so, particularly during the years when the *NewsHour* was financially pressed after Robin's retirement. I personally know of one instance when Jim's willingness to meet with a potential donor was likely to result in a substantial check. But he was always concerned about the appearance of propriety and conflicts of interest, and those concerns were always present when it came to raising money. So no check.

On the other hand, in Terence Smith's book, *Four Wars, Five Presidents: A Reporter's Journey from Jerusalem to Saigon to the White House*, he recounts a meeting between Jim, him, and the Pew Charitable Trust asking for funding of Terry's position as the show's media correspondent. So there were obviously exceptions to Jim's unwillingness to meet with funders. It might have to do with his perception of the difference between charitable organizations like Pew and business corporations, but I don't know.

As an example of the kinds of pressure that funders can bring, here's a story that I think is mostly accurate. When it came to providing gavel-to-gavel coverage of the 1980(?) political conventions, we had to look for underwriting since there was no money for covering this kind of event so extensively. Herb Schmerz, Mobil's vice president for communications, offered to underwrite the coverage. Herb had practically invented the corporate newspaper op-ed. Once a week, in the lower right-hand corner of the *NY Times* op-ed page, you could find Herb's columns, which looked almost like every other column on the page. Regardless, he said he didn't want any control over who was invited to be on the show. However, he did want to determine who would get to speak first. Robin said, "No," to both the request and the funding.

Naturally, there was more to the funding story. The rumor was that Bill Moyers offered to help raise the money for the convention coverage provided he shared the program with Robin and Jim. They turned him down as well. There was considerable competition between them. Bill, supposedly, was annoyed that WNET had underwritten Robin initially with discretionary money that might otherwise have gone to him. Instead, he was forced to raise money for his show from outside sources, something he apparently managed to do for a long time. So far as I know, that competition never filtered down to the staff. My office for a time was next door to Charlie Rose when he was Bill's executive producer, and we'd sometimes chat in his office or when we ran into each other in the elevator. The same was true of Joan Konner, Charlie's successor. Later on, after Joan became Dean of the Columbia University Journalism School and Robin had announced his retirement, she asked if I would like to join the faculty. I declined because I wasn't interested in teaching. Joan, by the way, was the long-time girlfriend and eventual wife of Al Perlmutter.

Small world. Small pond. Ripples forever running into each other.

I've never gotten over the adrenaline rush of walking into an empty control room, something I liked to do, particularly in the earliest days of the show. It was always a moment of possibility, of an entire world about to come to life. It was also potentially perilous because the clock was the clock, and time was a tyrant, and disaster was always a real possibility.

The control room was dimly lit before and during a show. When I walked in, an engineer would be in the video pit, turning on the cameras and making sure all was working. Gradually others would drift in. Usually three or four cameramen, the sound mixer and audio assistant, the Chyron and teleprompter operators, tape operators, make-up artists, all the technical people it takes to get a show on the air. Red Chumbly, the technical director (TD) for almost every show while it was in New York, would stroll in and start testing out the controls on the mixing board and talking to his crew. The audio guys would check out the soundboard and the various microphones. Judi Elterman would come in, preparing for Duke. Various show staff members would rush in with guest lists, videotapes, and scripts. And then came the executive producer, the news desk editor, the producer, and the reporter of that night's show. Duke would come in about a half-hour before showtime, his ever-present leather bag over his shoulder, and would look at the script, make his plan and start running through instructions to Judi, the TD, and cameramen and sound engineers. Then he would talk to the director and cameramen in Washington if they were in the show that evening. Robin would come in at about fifteen minutes before air, chat for a moment with the guests, and pre-record the opening. And then, as the clock approached 6 o'clock, Judi …

"10, 9, 8, 7, 6, 5, 4, 3 …"

"Roll tape," from Duke. And then, to Red, "Take tape," and we were on the air.

I would immediately look at the monitor displaying the actual show as it was being aired, first on WNET and later on PBS, and breathe a sigh of relief. We were on the air, and, with rare exceptions, the show was in the hands of everyone else. My job as the production supervisor, the person responsible for all these people coming together in NY, DC, or anywhere else in the country, was done unless there was some kind of emergency. Even after I no longer had that responsibility, whenever I walked into a control room, I would automatically check to see if everyone was where they should be, if everything was happening as it should, and try to feel the emotional temperature of the room. As I said, it was always an exciting moment for me, a moment pregnant with possibility, no matter how many years I worked on the show.

In January 1975, Jim was no longer an officially part-time participant. As part of a campaign to have stations in the PBS network air and help underwrite us, the show's title was changed to *The MacNeil/Lehrer Report,* and we fed it to the entire PBS network free of charge. The campaign to transform the program into a national show aired to the whole country succeeded.

The other significant change that winter was that Robin and Jim increasingly wanted guests from locations other than NY and DC on the show. I tried to accommodate them within the limits of a budget that had never anticipated such things. In today's world, when we seem to think nothing of connecting people in different cities or from their homes using Zoom or similar technologies, not to mention foreign countries, at a time when we broadcast live reports from battlefields, it may be hard to remember that there was a time when this was rare.

Whenever there was one of these interconnects, Wayne Grenier (the EIC or Engineer in Charge) and I would fly to the location and oversee the production of the insert. It always involved getting AT&T to either install a video landline or microwave link to a switching center or, at the very least, to turn on a pre-existing link. Then there was the installation of additional phones to serve as a backup audio system in case we lost both picture and audio through some technical problem, as well as separate phone lines between the show's director and the local director, and a phone line between the studio in New York or Washington and me. None of this could usually be done overnight, much less the last minute, but we would try, and there were only a few times when I'd have to tell Robin that we couldn't do what he wanted, at least as long as we had the money because these things weren't cheap. Gradually, as stations became more and more familiar with what we needed, as technology improved and satellite uplinks became more common in both PBS and commercial stations, it became increasingly unnecessary for Wayne first, and then for me, to take these trips. Commercial TV stations sometimes became a more viable option after *Nightline*'s debut following the Iranian hostage crisis because they, too, were interconnecting to stations all over the country and world.

At the end of March 1976, Robin and Jim decided to cover that summer's national political conventions. Duke Struck, Wayne Grenier, and I flew to Kansas City, the location of the Republican Convention, to work out a way to originate the show from the local public TV station. KCPT was a small station, nowhere near the size of WETA or WNET, and we were talking about moving most of our staff there for more than a week, leaving only a few people back in Washington and New York to prepare for the following week's shows. Producers, reporters, production secretaries, production assistants, graphic artists, a couple of anchormen, an executive producer, a director, an assistant director, and me. The station manager was accommodating, and we figured out where to stuff all the bodies, what to do with the studio, and how to meet all the show's technical requirements. I also made arrangements with the Republican National Committee for hotel rooms, credentials, and convention floor passes.

The Democratic Convention that year was going to be in Madison Square Garden, so it presented less of a challenge. However, arrangements for credentials, floor passes, and a few hotel rooms for the Washington staff still had to be made.

By mid-May, all of our convention arrangements were complete. But the rest of my traveling was beginning to pick up. I was at an OPEC meeting in London for a week at the end of the month (working with the *Wall Street Journal*'s Middle East reporter) and LA a couple of times.

In June, Robin announced that they had decided not to cover the political conventions after all. He said that just because everyone else was going to do it was no reason that we had to. We could deal with whatever news came out of the conventions through our usual show. There was no need to make the enormous effort and expense to take the entire show to Kansas City. I asked him if he was sure that he wanted me to cancel all the arrangements with the RNC and DNC. Absolutely, he said, their decision was irrevocable.

I should have known better.

The Republican Convention was going to open on August 16th. On July 29th, Robin said that he and Jim had reconsidered their decision; they didn't see how the now national and newly renamed show, *The MacNeil/Lehrer Report*, could avoid covering the conventions. I about fell over. Did Robin realize we had canceled all our arrangements with the RNC, the DNC, and KCPT? Yes. He was sorry to have caused the problem. Did Robin see the steam coming out of my ears? There was no indication that he did, and I was doing my best not to show it. Robin and Jim both seemed to have this unshakable faith that a way could be found to do something if they wanted it. I'd like to say that their faith went unrewarded every once in a while, but those occasions were rare. I said that I would do what I could to reinstate everything.

KCPT was the easy part. They'd be happy to oblige. AT&T complained a quite bit more than usual about reinstalling the telephone and long line video transmission lines after we had canceled them since they were now in the middle of the massive installation at the KC Convention Center. But they got the work done in time. The RNC said they were sorry, but they had given our floor passes to others, and there were none left; there was nothing they could (or would) do about it. As for hotels, they had given our rooms away, too, and very nice rooms they had been, they made sure I knew. However reluctantly, they agreed to find rooms for the staff, though they wouldn't vouch for their quality, and they'd find something better for Robin and Jim. I never saw the hotel that the staff stayed in, but I gathered it lived up (or down) to the RNC's promise. As for myself, I was so annoyed that I didn't want to be anywhere around anybody and stayed in a motel with, I think, the Oklahoma delegation, about forty miles west of Kansas City. As for the lack of passes, I got Hal Hutkoff, my friend from *Assignment America*, who was working on another show shooting at the conventions, *USA: People and Politics*, to share his floor passes with us.

No sooner had we arrived in KC than Ray Weiss proceeded to act in his most effective manner, reducing our production secretary to tears and leaving me to try to repair the damage and talk her into staying instead of getting on the next plane to New York. That was topped by Shirley Wershba, our ace ex-CBS reporter, who decided to berate me for supplying both an inadequate number of floor passes and useable for limited periods of time. I told her to take her complaints to Robin. She and I may have become good friends later on, but I didn't talk to her for the rest of the week. As for the shows, they went off without a hitch as far as I was concerned. There were no real technical problems that I remember. The cameras worked, the switcher worked, we hit the air on time. There were two lovely times for me each day. One was driving to my motel to the west in the gathering twilight on the rolling plains; the other was the drive into the sunrise on my way to the studio each morning. Once at the studio, I did my job and stayed out of everybody's way except when I couldn't avoid dealing with them. The same was true for the Democratic Convention in New York.

Of course, I couldn't stay mad forever, and I didn't. Besides, things were to become more complicated, and being mad wouldn't help. On September 13th, I was in Austin, Texas for a show, when Ray Weiss told me that we would provide live coverage of the presidential debates that would start just ten days later in Philadelphia. Did he know what the shows would consist of? No, not really, but they would originate in each of the cities of the debate. Linda Winslow would be the producer; she didn't know what would be in the shows either.

Presidential debates are big deals, as we all know by now. In 1976, they were a bigger deal because they hadn't become the staple of a presidential campaign they have today. In fact, there hadn't been one in 16 years, not since the famous Nixon-Kennedy debate that many thought had decided the election. Their significance has not abated as time has gone on. In the past forty years, every presidential debate has been pivotal, sometimes decisive, in each election campaign.

I called Jim Karyan, a long-time fixture in the public television universe. He was now the station manager of WHYY, the public TV station in Philadelphia. Could we use their studios to broadcast the show? Yes, he'd do whatever he could to help us out. KQED was also willing to accommodate us in San Francisco. I remember least about the third show in Williamsburg, Virginia. So I presume that I got a lot of help from WETA on it, including, probably, them arranging for the remote facilities. However, I have a suspicion that I may have called upon Opryland Productions, where Duke and I had edited during *Assignment America*, to supply the remote truck and gear.

I called Linda. Did she know what the shows would consist of? No, but they were working on it. So I asked her to meet me in Philadelphia on Friday, the 17th, along with her reporters. I also made arrangements for the studio production supervisor at WNET and Bob Wightman, the set designer, to meet us. Duke and Wayne agreed to come down, as did Chubby, a trucker I had used many times at Reeves and was sure I could depend on. And then I flew to Ann Arbor to do another show, arriving back in Philadelphia on the afternoon of the 16th.

Early the next afternoon, six days before we had to be on the air, we gathered in an empty studio in WHYY. By now, Linda knew what elements would be in the show. There would be an anchor position with guests; there would be a panel of twelve local citizens with various viewpoints to discuss their reactions to the debate in response to questions from one of the anchors. The Roper organization would conduct an instant national poll following the debate, and there had to be a place for the phone banks and Roper himself. All that meant that we needed three separate set areas, along with new sets that had to be designed, built, and painted, along with all the cameras, phones, etc., to go with them. In addition, there would be the pool feed from the debate site (yes, I made arrangements for that, too, somewhere along the line) that had to come into the control room, as well as video loops to feed the network. And hotels. And everything had to be trucked down to Philadelphia and then out to San Francisco, and, following a week's break for the vice presidential debate, we all had to reconvene in Williamsburg for the final debate.

Did everybody understand what had to be done? Yes. Could they do it? They all said they could, and they did. I don't know how they did it, but they did, and, at our scheduled airtime, the network switched to us, and there we were on the air, originating from WHYY's three separate studios simultaneously with three different sets. I was never so glad to have Duke as the director. For him, if this wasn't exactly child's play, it wasn't any more complex a task than the network football games he did every Sunday during the football season, and probably less so.

Those of you who watched that first debate might remember that the audio dropped out in its midst. In the control room, miles from where the debate was occurring, we had no idea what was happening. Had we lost the audio feed? I yelled for someone to get one of the other networks up on a monitor so I could see what was on their air. Meanwhile, I was on the tie line to the pool coordinator, which I think was ABC, trying to find out if it was just us that was down or the entire pool. The last thing I wanted was for us to be the only ones without audio. No, the coordinator finally said, the audio feed had been lost for everybody. I breathed a sigh of relief; we weren't going to be the only ones to be embarrassed. Finally, after 27 agonizing minutes, the debate's audio link was repaired, and it resumed without further interruption. Somehow, aside from that technical problem, the rest of the show went off without any major hitch.

After the debate, Chubby made his way to San Francisco with the set, and I flew to Miami, with Duke and Robin to follow. We were to shoot an interview with President Ford on Monday, September 27th, by the pool at the Fontainebleau Hotel. We'd then feed it from the local affiliate to WNET, where it would be integrated into the live show as it was being aired to the network. The shoot went fine, though it ended, shall we say, a bit late. Duke and I got into a car, with Duke driving, and we tore up the freeway to WPBT, our local affiliate, without being stopped by the police. Upon arrival, I leaped out of the car and ran into the station where they were waiting for me. The tape was loaded onto the playback machine while I was on the phone to the control room in New York, making sure they had something to air in case we didn't make it in time. Ten seconds before air, I told them we were ready. "Three, two, one, roll tape." I left for San Francisco the next day to set up for the next debate.

And so it continued. San Francisco went off fine, except for the night the assistant director called me at 2 am to tell me she had just awakened from a nightmare. I must say that stumped me. Why exactly was she calling me? What was I supposed to do? So we talked for a few minutes, said good night, and went back to sleep.

From San Francisco, I went to Houston for the vice presidential debate, the first-ever televised debate between vice-presidential candidates. We weren't providing live coverage of the debate, though Hal Hutkoff's show was. We nonetheless were interconnecting to the station there for the regular show. From Houston, I went to Williamsburg to plan for the final presidential debate and then on to La Grange, Texas to survey the courthouse for a show we were preparing for after the debates, then to Austin for another show, and then back to New York for one night, and finally down to Washington and Williamsburg for the final debate on October 22nd.

My calendar from that year is a bit barren in spots, more barren than was actually the case, not because I wasn't doing things but because I never got it all down on paper. I think it was the week after the debate that I returned to La Grange for a post-debate reaction show along with Jim, Duke, a producer, and a reporter.

La Grange had been the home of the Chicken Ranch, an illegal whorehouse that operated with the protection of the local sheriff and much of the town from 1905 until publicity by a Houston TV station forced its closing in 1973 despite the sheriff trying to present the governor with a petition with 3,000 signatures to keep it open. And it was the subject of the Broadway musical, *The Best Little Whorehouse in Texas*.

Washington's political staff had arranged for us to shoot in the courthouse, a beautiful old limestone building built in 1891. The sheriff, a leathery old man, looking every inch like he had stepped out of the Old West himself, was happy to help us out, but he made sure to tell me he wouldn't talk about the Chicken Ranch, on or off the record, much less the role he might have played in helping it to stay open for as long as it did.

I no longer remember what disasters struck this show. I know we got it done somehow, but Duke and I were furious at the producer. This was neither Linda nor Howard, but someone else added in the new fiscal year, which, with its enhanced budget, enabled us to add more staff. In those days, it seemed that the last thing anybody needed on their resume, particularly if they served in an editorial capacity on the show, was prior experience in television. So the fact that a producer was called a producer didn't mean that they could produce a thing, at least not in TV terms. As I said, I don't remember what this producer had done to so botch things up, but Duke and I were mad enough that we flew to Washington and asked Jim to fire her. Jim, shall we say, did not take kindly to this request. How dare we judge one of his people! It was the first and last time I was ever directly lambasted by Jim. It wasn't fun.

Finally, I arrived home on election eve for only the second night since the middle of September. Lynne and I were back together by now. I woke up in the middle of the night, the room pitch black. I felt a body next to me. Oops. Who's this? I turned on a light on the nightstand and saw it was Lynne. Oh. I turned off the light and turned over. We were hurtling to the end of the marriage.

The next day, Election Day, November 2nd, I got back on a plane and flew to Chicago for an election night show and then back to New York.

On Friday night, November 5th, I went to Tarrytown, New York, and the Tarrytown Conference Center. Amidst the frenzy of the past couple of months, I arranged for Robin, Jim, their assistants, Ray Weiss, the producers, Duke, and me, to spend a weekend talking about the show, what we'd done in the past year, and what we wanted to do in the future. Jim brought along Kate, his wife.

Friday night was uneventful since we all arrived pretty late. On Saturday, we spent most of the day in meetings. All proceeded convivially enough that night at dinner, with lots of eating and drinking. Too much drinking, as it turned out. After dinner, we all gathered in a lounge and started chatting. For some reason, Kate Lehrer decided to tell the producers based in New York that she didn't like how Jim was being treated, particularly by Howard Weinberg. Jim was being ignored, she said, and he was hurt by it. He was every bit as important as Robin to the show and deserved to be treated with the same respect and consideration that Robin was. Howard, unwisely but understandably, thought it necessary to defend himself and did. That upset Jim, who believed that Howard was attacking Kate, and if there was anything he wouldn't stand for, it was someone, anyone, attacking his wife. Duke was sitting there doing what Duke always had a great deal of enjoyment doing: egging everybody on, helping to make things worse. I think the rest of us, including Robin, just sat there aghast at what was going on. Finally, it petered out, and everyone went their separate ways, with considerable ill-feeling hovering in the air. Discussions continued the next day without much enjoyment, and we all got out of there as fast as possible. Robin swore he'd never do anything like that again, and he never did. Even later on, when we did have once-a-year meetings, they took place in the office during the day and ended before dinner. And no spouses. Eventually, those gatherings also came to an end.

It was regrettable because Robin's inclinations as a boss or manager were quite collegial. For as long as Robin led the show, there was a staff meeting every morning at which everyone in both New York and Washington (and Denver, too, when it was added) was free to attend. It was required for producers and correspondents to be there for sure, but anyone else, even the interns and production secretaries, could be there as well. Anyone was free to ask anything they wanted, could make any suggestion they wanted, make whatever comments they chose. There also was a once-a-week planning meeting when we'd discuss what was anticipated for the next couple of weeks. In the first couple of years of the show, I loved going to the meetings because we talked about all sorts of things as we were discovering what the show really was going to be and what it should be.

Aside from discussing that night's show and upcoming ones, Robin used the time to, in effect, conduct a class in journalism, the kind of journalism he was interested in. There were frequent discussions of journalism ethics and the idea of fairness when applied to guests. He was not interested in generating heat but rather in calm and rational discussion. When asked if we were too polite to guests, allowing them to avoid and even, sometimes, lie, he always said we had a well-informed audience. They were intelligent and knowledgeable enough to know when guests were dishonest; he didn't need to point it out.

I've always thought that was too generous to our guests and audience. Yes, it was true that our audience skewed to older and college-educated people, people who were interested in the news and policy. Teachers were a significant part of our audience, as were corporate CEOs (or, at least, someone in their public affairs offices), government workers, and politicians (or their press folks) were all sure to watch the show, just as were my parents (naturally) and their friends. But I'm also sure that we overestimated how aware our viewers were of everything going on in the world. After all, we had a relatively large audience, something like two or three million people a night, something like 10 million different people a month. Not all of them were news junkies.

As for Jim, during the first two or three years of the show, he would tape it at home and watch it after he left the studio. In the meetings the following morning, he would often start anything he said with a critique of his performance the previous night. In truth, there were sometimes things worth criticizing or at least that were noticeable. For example, he had difficulty asking questions directly in the early days. He'd hem and haw a bit, circle around the question, his eyes would turn this way and that; in fact, sometimes his eyes would actually close as he looked at the guest and finally asked the question. It was a flaw that he worked hard to correct and, after a time, he did so. I never knew if his self-criticisms were based on his own estimation of his self-worth, a desire to point out his own flaws before anyone else had a chance to, or simply a determination to be better. Or, perhaps, before criticizing the performance of others on our staff, it was only fair that they should know that he wasn't perfect. Maybe it was all of the above.

One more thing was made clear in these meetings. This was Robin's show, first and foremost. There was nothing he could say that Jim would really disagree with, certainly no policy decision. Any disagreement would be taken care of in private during their many phone conversations during the day. Similarly, after Robin retired, the show was completely Jim's. Robin once told me that he never called Jim to talk about the show and never would. When he was done with it, he was done.

After a time, the morning meetings seemed mostly rote exercises, but I would faithfully go if I was in New York and not busy on other things. However, after Robin retired and Jim took over the meetings, that broad collegiality disappeared. Jim seemed only interested in having the fewest people necessary to planning that night's show at the meetings.

After the Tarrytown disaster, my schedule continued at the same hectic pace: Chicago, Washington, Montreal, Salt Lake City, New York, back to Montreal, back to New York, and then to Austin before the month's end.

In December, Lynne's stepmother fell gravely ill, her alcoholism finally destroying her, and Lynne flew out to Vegas with the kids to be with her father. I flew out for her funeral on January 5th, 1977, and flew on to LA later in the day. Lynne decided to stay in Vegas for another week or two and then came home.

I met her at the airport, and we started driving home. Lynne asked if I remembered that before we had moved from California, I had promised that someday we would return. I remembered, but I don't know whether I told Lynne that I remembered. She said that she was going to return to California, with me if I was willing to go, without me if I was not. After thinking about it overnight, I told her that I wouldn't be going with her. It was time to put an end to the marriage. I don't think we discussed it at all. We both knew why we were ending it. We had worn each other out. Whatever feelings we had for each other were long since evaporated, at least on my part, and there was no point in recriminations or in a lengthy discussion trying to rationalize, justify or explain the decision.

We called the kids into the bedroom to tell them. Michelle, now eight, was devastated. Brandon, now ten, said, "It's about time the two of you made up your minds."

We remained in the same apartment for another few months, sleeping in separate rooms while Lynne made arrangements to leave NY. Besides, I was rarely in NY anyway, maybe one or two nights a week at most. We were leading virtually separate lives and had been for quite a while, and though there wasn't any great animosity between us, there wasn't any particular affection either. I'm not sure we even liked each other by that point. In mid-February, I flew to Sarasota, FL, to tell my parents what was happening to my marriage. They weren't in favor of the breakup. More accurately, their concern was about Brandon and Michelle, that they'd be damaged by the split. I understood the possibility of that, the likelihood, in fact, but I didn't see how the marriage could continue.

I have often thought about marriage and relationships over the past decades and wondered what makes a successful relationship, forgetting about love. A psychiatrist once told me that any two sane people could manage to live together. That seems obvious, though the word "sane" is the tricky word, don't you think? How many totally sane and rational couples do you know? If you think you know a lot, I'll bet you don't know them as well as you think you do. And I'm sure you noticed the word "love" didn't enter into the formulation.

When my mother died in 1993, I wrote a eulogy in which I tried to understand what I had learned from her about love and marriage. Like many children, certainly when I was younger, I couldn't understand how my parents had stayed married for so long. Yet their marriage was, I thought in retrospect, enormously successful. I knew about the "compromises" my mother had made, what she had given Dad. I thought I knew, too, what she had gotten in turn from Dad. Dad was too sick by then to ask him what he thought of it all, but it was always obvious that he adored her.

Remembering everything about marriage and relationships I had heard over the years, I recalled the idea of the perfect Marxist state: "From each according to his ability, to each according to his need." I doubt if I had any real sense of what I needed when I asked Lynne to marry me in 1964, much less what it was that I had to give her that she needed. If I had a better sense of those things thirteen years later, it was way too late for us. It was never that I hated Lynne or, even, disliked her. On the contrary, forgetting about love, I think it's fair to say that we always liked each other, a few occasions notwithstanding. But liking is not enough. Love is never enough. Those things are only a beginning.

A week after leaving my parents and a stop in Miami to do a show with Larry Flynt, the publisher of *Hustler*, I briefly returned to New York before going on to Washington. On the morning of Tuesday, February 22nd, I was with a crew from WETA, pulling into a parking spot at the Executive Office Building to set up for an interview with Vice President Mondale. Robin and Jim would both be there to do the interview, which had been arranged to start after lunch. This was a big deal for us. The only president we'd interviewed was Jerry Ford at the pool at the Fontainebleau in Miami the previous year, and I think we interviewed Nelson Rockefeller in the WETA studio when he was vice president. Interviewing those folks was always a big event, and I wanted to be there in plenty of time to make sure everything was ready.

I knew the WETA crew well by this time, having spent a lot of time in Washington since the show had started. Once they had the cameras set up and cables run down to the control room in the truck, I put on the headphones so I could listen to whatever was going on between the cameramen and the video operator while they tweaked the cameras. Then, suddenly, one of them said, "Why did they give us this damned sticky lens."

My ears pricked up immediately. "Hey Huey, what do you mean about a sticky lens?"

"Aw, we've got this zoom lens, and it sticks all the time."

"You mean when you use it to zoom in and out?"

"Yeah."

"Whose camera is it on?"

"Mondale's."

Whoops. What to do? I called WETA and asked if they had another lens that was working. No. I then called the Director of Engineering in New York and asked if they had one they could put on a plane that could get to Washington in time to make the switch before we were supposed to shoot. They could. Then I told Huey to put the sticky lens on Robin and Jim's camera so that Mondale's camera would be okay even if the replacement lens didn't make it time. As it turned out, WNET's lens arrived in time, the switch was made, and the show got done without further problem. But that was not the end of the story.

I was fuming. I thought that WETA's engineering department had acted carelessly and recklessly. At the very least, they should have let me know that there was a problem beforehand. If I hadn't overheard Huey talking over the intercom, we would have done the show, and the first time we zoomed in on Mondale, it would have been a bumpy ride. So I wrote a memo stating what had happened and sent it to Gerry Slater, the Director of Public Affairs Programming of WETA. At the same time, I called Jerry Toobin, Slater's counterpart in New York, to tell him what had happened and to be ready for a storm.

The storm broke. Gerry Slater called me into his office. Why had I sent him a memo about this, he asked, holding his head in his hands? Couldn't I have just told him about it? Now, since it was on paper, he had to do something official about it. He had sent a copy to Gene Swansea (I'm not sure about the spelling of Gene's name), WETA's engineering head, who was livid since it reflected directly on him and his department. Gerry wanted me to meet him and Gene for breakfast the following morning to calm the situation. I thought a moment and said, "Sure. Can I bring someone with me?" Gerry shrugged, he may have even sighed, and off I went.

Later that night, I told Duke about the meeting and asked him to come with me. He, of course, knew all about the situation since he had come down from New York to direct the show, and I had told him what had happened. So Duke said he'd pick me up in the morning, and we'd go to the restaurant together.

The following morning, we walked into the restaurant, and there were Gerry and Gene, along with Kathy Test, the head production manager of the station, and Rosemary Murphy, who oversaw the production requirements for the show in Washington. I was amused that Gerry felt the need to ensure that WETA outnumbered the foreign intruders from up north. I don't recall Kathy or Rosemary saying a word during the meeting.

Gerry asked me to explain what had happened and why I had sent the memo, which I did. Then Gerry talked about how we really were all one big family, and we had to learn how to get along with each other. Duke got this big smile on his face, reached into his breast pocket, pulled out a piece of paper, unfolded it, and handed it to Gerry. "Gerry, have you seen this yet?"

It was a memo from Gene to the Washington technicians forbidding them to talk to anyone from New York without getting his specific permission first.

Gene's face turned red and then furiously white, while Gerry threw up his hands. The meeting was over. Later that morning, he told me that I had to get his permission before showing up in Washington again. I called Jerry Toobin, told him what had happened, and said I hoped he'd be able to fix things with Gerry Slater because I had no intention of asking Gerry's permission to come to Washington to do my job, and I never did.

That was the end of the story. It wasn't too long before Gene left WETA and went to PBS, where if I ever talked to anyone from their engineering staff and asked if Gene was behaving himself, they would simply roll their eyes.

And, by the way, I don't think I ever told Robin or Jim what had happened and have no idea if they ever knew. In fact, I didn't really work for them, at least not officially; I worked for WNET. Initially, my official boss was Jerry Toobin, not Robin. In either 1975 or '76, the production managers were transferred to the Chief Financial Officer of the station because of the financial debacle of *The Adams Chronicles*. Nonetheless, it was Jerry Toobin I would tell about this kind of problem because it affected the relationship between the stations and had nothing to do with money.

Finally, Lynne, Brandon, and Michelle left NY at the beginning of April, moving to Las Vegas to stay with her father for a few months before moving on to LA. There was nothing left of the marriage, not even tears.

On Friday, April 15th, I flew to New Orleans for a survey on Saturday. There was a program we were planning on doing from there, and, for some reason, it was advisable to see WYES's facilities to make sure they could handle what we were hoping to do. I was supposed to meet the station's Director of Programming, Bill Hess, the following day to inspect the studio. I called him when I got in.

He asked if I'd ever been to New Orleans.

No, I hadn't.

Well, he said, we're not going to have a meeting tomorrow. We're going to Jazz Fest instead, and we'll meet about the studio on Sunday, and do you want a date tomorrow night, and are you doing anything tonight?

No plans for tonight, and yes, I'd like a date tomorrow night.

I'll pick you up at nine, he said

And thus began another first day of the rest of my life. Or, to put it another way: the winding road hadn't stopped winding. If my professional life seemed more stable and fulfilling than it had ever been, then the life of what Peggy Shonbrun called "the place we call heart" was still twisting and turning.

One of Bill's passions was New Orleans Jazz. For most Americans at the time, New Orleans Jazz meant trumpeters Al Hirt and Pete Fountain, who played Dixieland for the most part. For Bill, though, jazz in New Orleans was something else. It was that funky mélange of rhythms and expression that came from the city's unique cultural and racial mixture: Cajun, Caribbean, Afro-Cuban, Afro-American, and Native American, all mixed in with blues and rock and roll. No band exemplified that tradition more than the Neville Brothers. Although they were relatively newly formed and largely unknown outside of New Orleans, they were enormously popular with younger people far away from the tourists on Bourbon Street.

That Friday night, Bill took me to Tipitina's, a club on the outskirts of the Lower Garden District. It was a new club, having opened on January 14th, 1977, to honor the legendary (at least in New Orleans and among musicians) Professor Longhair and give him a place to play during the last years of his life. The club's name came from one of his most famous songs, "Tipitina."

> **Tipitina tra la la la**
> **Whoa la la la-ah tra la la**
> **Tipitina, oola malla walla dalla [little mama wants a dollar]**
> **Tra ma tra la la**

There's a lyric for you.

Four months after the club opened, the place was packed when we arrived. If there were usually tables in the club, they had all been moved out. There was barely room to stand. A small stage was bathed in red, orange, and amber light, the smell of beer pungent in the air. Bill grabbed a couple of beers from the bar. Before long, the lights on the stage went out, and there began to be clapping and cheering. Then, the lights came up, and there were the Neville Brothers. Art, Charles, Aaron, and Cyril. Maybe there were one or two others who I don't remember. But the next two hours were among the most exciting, musically, that I had ever enjoyed. It was non-stop pulsating rhythm, syncopated in all those off beats that Professor Longhair had passed on to every musician who ever heard him play.

Bill was not done introducing me to New Orleans, the New Orleans that he loved. The following afternoon we went to the Jazz Festival and more music, music of every sort from zydeco to blues, to gospel, to, well, if it existed it was probably there. And then there was the food: andouille gumbo, crawfish bisque, po'boys, a whole new world of tastes and sensations with the sun beating down and the sweat pouring out. All I could think was that New Orleans is unlike any other city in America.

That evening, I arrived at the entrance of a modest-looking house (at least on the outside) on the corner of Annunciation and Leontine Streets in the Lower Garden District, just a few blocks from Tipitina's, to meet my very first blind date.

I've always kind of liked blind dates. Most people can be relatively interesting for a couple of hours over dinner. Of course, sometimes it's a complete bust, but I can only think of one blind date that I've ever had that was a total disaster. To be fair, the girl was probably bored silly too, but that experience was an exception. Showing up at Susan Willard's door, I had no idea what to expect.

We left for dinner at a small, un-touristy restaurant in the French Quarter, where we rarely went on subsequent occasions. Susan had returned to Louisianna not all that long ago. She was recently widowed. Her husband had been either an intern or a resident at a hospital in Boston, and she had been pregnant when, one evening while sitting in an armchair, he had a brain aneurysm and died instantly. She had her son, who I think was now about three, and had returned to New Orleans to rebuild her life. She had two sisters who lived in the city with their families.

We talked at dinner, laughed, and found that there were things we both liked, things that we had in common, things that we admired and respected in each other, values that we seemed to share. We had a wonderful time and dated for the next several months. I frequently returned to New Orleans on weekends since I was constantly traveling, and it didn't really matter if I was in New York. Eventually, the relationship ran its course, and, much to my regret, it ended.

I tried to answer this question:

What is love?

Joe Honeyman said in *Makepeace's Blackouts*, "Love, is love, is love."

> Love (luv) *n.* 1. An intense affectionate concern for another person. 2. An intense sexual desire for another person. 3. A beloved person. Often used as a term of endearment. 4. A strong fondness or enthusiasm for something....
>
> —*The American Heritage Dictionary*

Does that help?

Little Tommy Makepeace, his mother having died in childbirth, asked Joe Honeyman's mother, Aunt Hannah, "What is love?" She said of the dictionary's definition of love,

> Ain't none of them say what love really is. Love is ... a twist in the heart. Something sweet sudden come to mind is love. Hand feels good touching somebody, that is love. Take everything bad and mean in the world – and everything left, that is love.

It's so easy to fall in love, even if it's only for a minute. I'm not talking about how to sustain love, but just that moment when you know you're in love. It lies at the center of most of our hopes, of our dreams, of our lives. And yet, after all the scientists, psychologists, writers, and poets have had their say, we still don't really quite know what it is. Perhaps that's because whatever it is, it's different for every person, time and circumstance; the contours of our love of a particular person are shaped by the object of our affection and desire and by that specific moment in time.

Whatever else it is, it is always different, and it is always young. Being in love at sixteen is neither more nor less than being in love at thirty or sixty. Hormones don't get any older; synapses firing wildly in the brain don't know about age. The need and desire for love never disappears, not entirely, always lurking in the background, waiting to spring to life. The collapse of my marriage did not spell the end of love.

Adam, my so young Adam of long ago, who was dizzy with the springtime smell of apple blossoms, was still there on an April night in New Orleans in 1977. He has never gone away.

And, by the way, I've never stopped asking that question: What is love?

Much later, in February 2006, I returned to New Orleans again, for the first time in many years, to do an essay about the first Mardi Gras celebration after Katrina. As we landed, the airport was empty. Taxiing, I saw two cargo planes, and that's all. All the passenger airplane gates were open. Lumbering down the runway, ours was the only passenger plane in the entire airport. I dreaded what I knew awaited me: the devastated lower Ninth Ward, shuttered, shattered buildings and businesses, empty streets, and those who were left or who had managed to return struggling against the dark, the title of my essayist, Chris Rose's book, *One Dead in the Attic*. Yet, I couldn't help but remember the excitement and joy with which I had always arrived at the airport, knowing that Susan was waiting for me at the gate twenty-nine years before. Driving into the city, I remembered it all. My eyes burned with tears, the loss of what had been a magical time as fresh in my mind as the empty airport and the expectation of what I was about to witness.

We are often fond of saying that we'd like to live our lives again knowing what we now know. I've never wanted to do that. I've always said that I never wanted to be a child again because I was too sad, too lonely, too frustrated, too often. I wouldn't want to repeat any of that without a guarantee that it would be different, that the path through life wouldn't be so painful, so twisted. Well, nobody is handing out promises that I know of. It's more than that, though. To live my life again, knowing what I know now, would mean losing the life I've led and not just the bad parts. It would mean losing the good parts, the joy I've had as well. And if I managed to avoid the mistakes I've made the next time around, there are plenty of others to make. So no, I'll take what I've had — all of it — and what I will have.

Life continued on as it always does. If anything, though, these next few years would be even more event-filled as my engagement with the world both widened and deepened. Like most people, I lived several different lives simultaneously, and only sometimes did they intersect. There was my life at *MacNeil/Lehrer*, which was shifting as time went on. I had not lost my interest in creating programs or movies for public television or Hollywood. There was the life of a single man at loose in the world. Though I didn't see my children all that often, I was still a father, an ex-husband, a brother, and a son.

Much of my life at *MacNeil/Lehrer* continued at a relatively frenetic pace through the next four years before it started to slow down, and much of it was rather uninteresting, at least in terms of the work. By the end of 1978, I don't think any engineer was traveling with me except in unusual circumstances, such as my trips out of the country.

Sometime during 1977, my title at *MacNeil/Lehrer* changed. I was no longer the production supervisor with my responsibilities covering both NY and DC operations but was now called a field producer, the meaning of which was fluid. Sometimes it just meant that I arranged for and supervised the interconnects in the field as I had been. At other times it meant something more. And I was no longer officially reporting to WNET. Instead, I now reported to the show's executive producer and Robin.

Also, by this time, the original executive producer, Ray Weiss, had been replaced by Al Vecchione, a veteran production manager. The change was no surprise. In late August 1976, Robin, Linda, Duke, and I had sat around a table on the patio of a hotel in Pasadena following a show at the Jet Propulsion Lab after the first landing on Mars. Our discussion was mainly about Ray and the necessity of making a change. If I remember correctly, Robin and Linda talked about the virtues of Al. (Not so coincidentally, since I had booked it, the hotel was the same one where Lynne and I had our wedding reception.)

Having met Robin at NBC, Al went on to the Public Broadcasting Laboratory and then to WETA as the Vice President for Public Affairs. When we met in Pasadena, he was a media adviser to the Democratic National Committee during the Carter presidential campaign. He joined *MacNeil/Lehrer* in 1977, sometime after Carter's inauguration. I felt that our show, the day-to-day running of the show, was now in competent hands, and I was free — insofar as Robin and Jim (and Al) would let me — to pursue other objectives within the show. If you think that sounds like I felt a propriety interest in the show, you'd be right. Whether Robin or Jim was aware of that feeling or what, if anything, they thought, much less cared about it, I couldn't tell you.

Chapter 10

FOREIGN AFFAIRS

◆

1977 — 1985

During the first week of December 1977, I flew to South Africa to oversee an interconnect with Prime Minister John Voerster. The Friday night I left New York, December 2nd, a South African magistrate found that Stephen Biko, an anti-apartheid Black leader, had died from brain injuries suffered in prison but nevertheless exonerated the police of any criminal responsibility. Today, as then, everyone who wasn't wearing the rosiest of glasses knew that to be untrue. The American State Department's spokesman said, "Mr. Biko's death clearly resulted from a system which permits gross mistreatment and violation of the most basic human rights." The Prime Minister's response in the interview was, "Well, all I can say is, in that case, then the State Department knows more about my country than I ever heard of." The rest of the half-hour proceeded in much the same vein, with Voerster ducking and weaving and obfuscating. I, for one, had to wonder whether Voerster actually believed any of the things he was saying. Do bigots know themselves to be bigots?

I wish I could remember who first told me that only those who wonder if they might be bigots themselves are those who are least likely to be bigots. And, of course, the corollary: the more people insist on their lack of any trace of bigotry, the more likely they are to be infected by the disease. I wondered about it most when watching American politicians through all these years, particularly Republican politicians from Southern states, who capitalized on the alienation that the Democrats created in white voters by putting an end to legal

185

segregation. Did Jesse Helms and Strom Thurmond truly become color blind as they asserted? That Thurmond fathered a bi-racial child did nothing to answer the question since white fear of miscegenation only emphasized the illicit commonplace that it was, at least when it came to relationships between white men and Black women. It sort of reminded me of my fraternity brothers at Maryland and magical hymens. Just as, at the time, I wondered what Trent Lott (the one-time Republican Senate Majority Leader) honestly thought of James Meredith and the desegregation of Ole Miss during the time he was a cheerleader there.

My impression back then (undocumented by any sort of evidence) was that I most often heard the phrase that we live in a "color-blind society" coming out of the mouths of Southern or border state Republicans than anyone else.

By now, none of us should be under the delusion that we live in a color-blind society. Did you think the explosion of the Tea Party and its hatred of President Obama had nothing to do with color? And only the insistently oblivious could believe that Donald Trump's political campaigns weren't transparently racist. One of the most distressing aspects of contemporary life and religion is the extent to which so many Southern Baptist preachers, in particular, have returned to their racist southern roots when they would proclaim that God was a segregationist. And then there are the identity politics propagated by both Republicans and Democrats. It often seems that it matters more what race you label yourself or what country your family came from than if you're an American. The virtuous dream of America as a melting pot during my childhood seems to have become an anathema to everyone other than political centrists, and I'm not entirely sure of them.

Has it never occurred to you that the sin, transgression, and crime that someone rails about loudest may very well be the sin he is guilty of?

In my experience, Republican politicians are especially adept at this kind of messaging. They've also been flagrantly guilty — and usually more so — of the things they rail at Democrats about. It's not that Democrats are sinless. But they rarely seem to have as effective a messaging operation as Republicans.

The morning after the Voerster interview, it took about 30 seconds for the head of WNET's engineering department (who had accompanied me) and me to decide to visit the Kruger National Park for three days. The alternative was to be a "good" journalist and visit Soweto. I thought that I could see poor people living in terrible and degraded conditions on any day, anywhere in the world, even if it might not be exactly the same as in Soweto. But the possibility of seeing lions and tigers and, well, oh my ... who knew when I'd get that opportunity again? Oh, you mean there are no tigers in Africa? I stand corrected. But there definitely were lions and elephants and elands and giraffes and ... As I said, it took 30 seconds to decide. Maybe less.

In April of 1978, I flew to Panama to produce another interconnect. This time the trip was occasioned by the attempt to ratify the Panama Canal Treaty by the US Senate. When I arrived in Panama City, I was hooked up by arrangement with George Nathanson. He was a freelance reporter who lived in Mexico City and had spent much time in Panama. He supposedly knew all the players in Panama and could help line up guests.

The city was filled with narrow and dusty streets. Or maybe it just seemed that way because we were trying to avoid the raucous street demonstrations while at the same time trying to find Panamanian politicians who never seemed to be anywhere they usually could be found, or alternatively attempt to reach them by telephone. Maybe they didn't want to be found. All this while simultaneously trying to stay in touch with Al Vecchione so that we knew what was going on in Washington, and he knew whatever we knew about guest possibilities. The closer it got to air time, the less likely it seemed that there would actually be a vote in the US Senate before the broadcast. It equally became clear that no Panamanian would talk on the record before the treaty was actually voted on. So while George was on one phone frantically trying to find someone — anyone — for us to talk to, I was on another with Al as we approached a final cutoff. Finally, I told Al we weren't going to make it, and we should pull the plug on the satellite, canceling the interconnect. It was one of my rare failures in all my time at *M/L*. However, all was not entirely lost. That night, as George drove me around the Canal Zone, he pointed out all the whorehouses that existed to primarily serve American military personnel, which ones were for enlisted men and which were for officers, and would I like to go to one? Apparently, as a journalist, I could go to either. I turned down the offer.

In mid-September, I returned to Central America due to a full-blown revolution in Nicaragua. General Samoza, another dictator long propped up by the United States, was clearly on the defensive in this uprising by the Sandinistas. What most impressed me about this trip was the terrible poverty. On our drive from the airport, hovels made from cardboard cartons lined the highway and on the road from the Intercontinental Hotel to the Presidential Palace. Buildings were pockmarked by the bullets smashing against them. The faces of the general's personal security force all appeared to be in their forties — apparently, the young weren't to be trusted near the president. Shooting from rifles or machine guns could be heard on the presidential palace grounds in the distance, the bullets occasionally whistling overhead or nearby. And then there was the presidential bunker. It really *was* a bunker built into the side of a hill from which Samoza was trying to run his government. We did the interview, and I returned home thinking that if you were a dictator and your subjects across the entire economic spectrum were in full-scale revolt against you, and you had to live your life in a bunker, then you should be looking for a safe exit.

Perhaps I should note that on these trips I always felt somewhat protected by my press status since I was always in these countries at the invitation or acquiescence of the government. But press credentials are no protection against bullets and random violence, as we should all know by now, and a certain degree of fear is always present when you cover events with the potential for violence. That's true when covering domestic or foreign events like the revolution in Nicaragua. And that was not my last encounter with the potential for violence in foreign lands.

By the end of November 1978, the long-simmering Iranian Revolution was underway, and the Shah's American-supported (and sponsored) dictatorship was slowly being throttled. On December 2nd, Robin, producer Jo Franklin, reporter Rob Hershman, and I flew to Paris to interview Ayatollah Khomeini, the leader of the opposition to the Shah, who was in exile, living in a small complex of houses in Ponchartrain on the outskirts of Paris along with his closest advisers.

Our primary contact with Khomeini was through Ebrahim Yazdi, who was in charge of the Ayatollah's communications with the outside world. After the revolution, he would become the Deputy Prime Minister and then the new government's first Foreign Minister. As I recall, we had gotten to Yazdi through his son-in-law, a student at Princeton who had been on our show one or more times. It was either Rob or Jo who connected initially with the nephew. It served us in good stead. Yazdi was to be the interpreter during Robin's interview.

The other contact we made in Ponchartrain was with Sadegh Ghotbzadeh, who was in charge of Khomeini's personal security. After the revolution's success, Ghotbzadeh would become head of Iran's telecommunications ministry. Still later, he was arrested for plotting to overthrow the Ayatollah and executed. I understood that he and Yazdi were rivals for power and favor in Khomeini's eyes. The fact that Yazdi was our "rabbi" in the court of the Ayatollah may have had repercussions for us a year later, but that is a separate story (I find it ironic to use that very New York phrase, "rabbi," when discussing the vehemently anti-Semitic Iranian Shiites).

If memory serves me right, Khomeini and his followers were living in a gated compound of several small houses. The interview took place in a dusty room with no decorations other than flower-patterned wallpaper and several area rugs. Robin and the Ayatollah sat shoeless and cross-legged on the floor. Robin (I think) was dressed in a tweed sportscoat — the ever polite interviewer — while Khomeini sat wrapped in his black robe and turban, and glowered, not a hint of levity before, during, or after the shoot.

The day following our interview was to be the beginning of the end of the Shah, the period when Khomeini urged Iranians to use "any possible means to overthrow the regime of the Shah." Khomeini told Robin that his followers would use whatever means they had at their disposal, from demonstrations to strikes and, if necessary, violence, to achieve their ends. No compromise was possible. As for America, the Ayatollah said, "They have committed the biggest crime by imposing on our people the Pahlavi dynasty. Through this support, they have plundered our natural resources, and instead, in return, they have given us things that do not help our people in any way." If that sounds similar to some of the accusations later made by Osama bin Laden, well, such complaints were hardly unique to those two.

A month later, the Shah was gone, and the Ayatollah was in Tehran.

I cannot help but point out some of the differences between the revolution in Iran and America's second war in Iraq. When we interviewed the Ayatollah, the revolution was supported by a broad cross-section of the Iranian population. All the various political factions inside and outside Iran that were opposed to the Shah had coalesced under the Ayatollah's leadership, including several that were by no means radical Muslims. He was supported by religious Shiites and many secularists in the middle-class, poor people, students, and even Jews. Although the army was among those most highly favored by the Shah and his American supporters, it, too, eventually turned against him by refusing to shoot demonstrators.

In Iraq, all attempts to produce similar results had failed. It is not simply that Hussein was ruthless in stamping out opposition within his country, just as the Shah did. In all their years of exile, the various political and religious groups who opposed Saddam could never agree about anything other than their desire to be rid of the dictator. No matter how much pressure had been put on them by Bush 41, Bill Clinton, or Bush 43, they could not agree on anything. Various Americans, most famously Don Rumsfeld, Dick Cheney, and George Tenet, had their own preferences of who should lead the country after the invasion, most notably Ahmad Chalabi, whose lies were utilized by the US to help justify the war. But the exiled Iraqis couldn't agree on a candidate among themselves before or after the invasion. As for the Iraqi people, they didn't seem to be much more prepared for compromise.

Of course, regime changes by revolution and invasion are not the same thing, are they? And if many (and perhaps most) Iranians did not get the kind of government that they hoped for, they at least got rid of a government that many, if not most, had hated. It's hard to know precisely what the general population in Iraq has gained after the invasion. One thing is sure: whatever it is, it isn't anything they chose; it's something we chose for them. No matter how often the Bush 43 administration said that the future of Iraq was in Iraqi hands, the fact is that it isn't or wasn't until we decided to decide for the Iraqi people what was in their best interests. It is hard for me to know if the Iraqi people think they are better off today than before Hussein's ouster.

May I tell you what I enjoyed most about that trip to Paris? No, it wasn't sitting in on a conversation with one of the most significant figures in post-colonial Middle East politics and violence. But, lest you think something magical had happened to my linguistic abilities after I had left NYU some fourteen years earlier, it hadn't, and I had hired a friend of an old friend and NYU classmate as a translator. The night before the interview, she took me to a small restaurant, the name of which I never knew. I remember rough whitewashed walls and bare timbers, a roaring fireplace to warm the late fall air, candles on the checkered tablecloths. But most of all, I remember the first time I ever had *foie gras*, pan-seared rare duck breast, and earthenware jugs of just made *Beaujolais Nouveaux*. Now that was heavenly, a heaven that was infinitely preferable to the very dark and scowling visage of Ayatollah Khomeini.

Sometimes the various strands of one's life converge in a tight bunch, each one different while at the same time touching one another, sometimes in unexpected ways. For example, on Tuesday, February 13th, 1979, I was in the waiting room at Beth Israel Hospital while my father underwent surgery for an aneurysm, the first of two such operations and the beginning of his fifteen-year-long physical disintegration.

The next day, I flew to San Francisco for an interconnect. That night I had dinner with Kathy Test, who had been present at the post-Mondale interview breakfast with Gerry Slater and Gene Swansea and who I had helped get a job at KQED, the San Francisco public TV station. Kathy was working for Zev Putterman, who, I discovered at a wedding I attended many years later in Hillsdale, NY, had been the bride's father.

The following day, Thursday, I had a call from the show saying they were trying to arrange something from Tehran, and we did the San Francisco interconnect. I flew to Tampa the day after that to visit Brandon and Michelle, now living in Florida with Lynne.

On Saturday, in addition to talking to various people at *M/L*, I spoke to Allison Miner, Professor Longhair's manager in New Orleans, about arranging a meeting with Longhair, and then continued to New York and Paris before going to Tehran.

And when in Paris, I met an old friend of Herman Shonbrun's in the kitchen of the Scottish embassy making haggis with his wife.

See what I mean?

By Sunday, February 18th, 1979, the Iranian revolution had succeeded, and there was now an interim government in place headed by so-called moderates with the Ayatollah scowling over the whole mess. I'm never sure I understand what is meant by "moderate." If I describe an extremist as, say, to the right of Attila the Hun, then does that make Attila a moderate? If Donald Trump is a conservative, what was Richard Nixon? Or Ronald Reagan, for that matter? Our political shorthand vocabulary is sorely lacking, or at best, has meaning only in relation to a specific time and place. But I guess that's something else. More to the point is that I wrote something about the trip shortly after I returned from Iran. Though never completed, it is a pretty accurate account of the first part of the trip and how I saw it at the time

WELCOME TO TEHRAN

She asked why I would even consider going, much less be willing to go, not to mention actually wanting to go.

I wasn't even sure I understood the question. Perhaps it was just politeness, a way of expressing care or concern. How could anyone not want to go – to see – to experience? So I said that. I talked about wanting to see, to taste, to smell. I talked about death, about life, and the roiling turbulence that had to be there. I wanted to come into contact with the elemental.

She said that was insane.

Perhaps so.

It was, I thought, just a matter of time until we went. The call I had gotten on Thursday in San Francisco felt real. You get to learn the difference after a while. The tone isn't quite the same, and you know that the trip has become a fixed part of the universe on some level. Fine, I said. Just let me know when and, by the way, does my insurance cover me for war zones and getting shot, etc.? And now, here I was in Florida visiting, by chance, my kids for the first time in seven months and my separated wife whom I hadn't seen in a year, and talking of life and death, *my* life and death, and waiting for word to go to Iran.

Sunday morning, the plane for New York was late coming up to Tampa from Sarasota. Fog. So, as usual, when I am forced to idleness, I get on the phone. Rob Hershman, our foreign affairs reporter in Washington: There is no word. It doesn't look like we can get in unless there was a charter going in from Amman, and we weren't willing to spring for the money by ourselves. If there was a change, he'd call me later in New York. Alan Ziring, the production controller (the man who now kept the show's financial records) in New York: Yes, the insurance covered me. Wayne Grennier, the show's chief engineer in New Jersey: He wouldn't go unless he flew first class; if he's going someplace where he might get killed, they can damned well send him in comfort. I sympathize and tell him it looks like nothing today. Be prepared tomorrow. The plane comes, and I go home.

Sunday night in New York is cold as it has been for weeks, and once again, I wonder what I'm doing living in this city. At six, I'm about to eat dinner when the call comes. I'm booked on the 10 pm flight to Paris. Can I make it? Of course. Will I call Al Vecchione, the executive producer? Sure. First, I call Wayne. He's already gotten the word. Al has words of confidence in me; he thinks it should be safe – the worst seems to be over, do the best you can, stay in touch. Right. I call Air France. Upgrade the seats to first-class and make hotel reservations at Hotel George V (I'm no different from Wayne, it turns out).

Wayne is already at the Air France counter when I get there. He says they've got our reservations already upgraded to first class. I shrug. I have managed to find a good rationalization for the change. Naturally, Wayne's considerations don't enter into it. We're going to be going non-stop for the next forty-eight hours if everything works out. Sounds good. But that feeling of being even the slightest bit pampered makes us feel good. It's too bad we're the ones who had to think of it. But it really does make sense, doesn't it? Wayne is apprehensive about getting shot.

Meanwhile, where is Rob? Coming up from Washington. Due in at 8:40. It's after 9. We ask the girl if she can check. The flight's been canceled; it was a continuation from Atlanta, and Atlanta's been closed down by snow. It's snowing in Washington. He's been re-booked on a National flight, which might have gotten out; the airport in Washington is now closed. Rob arrives ten minutes before flight time.

The champagne's not bad. The ice-cold vodka is really terrific with the Beluga. So there really were good reasons for doing it this way. Maybe we'll get an hour or two of sleep before landing in Paris Monday morning.

The Air France counter at Charles de Gaulle tells us that the airport in Tehran is still closed. Maybe that night's 1 am flight will leave, but no one knows at this point. Two girls behind the counter disagree: One thinks maybe, one is sure not. Can we be booked on it anyway? Waitlisted. It'll have to do. How about the 8:30 flight the following day out of Zurich? No word. Pan Am out of Frankfort? Still only running charters for the State Department. We've already tried that route, and so far, nothing; they won't let us on. But there's supposed to be a meeting that morning in Washington. We'll find out later.

Off to the hotel. It may be high priced, but it's only a couple of minutes by taxi from the Iranian Embassy. Good excuse, that.

You can tell it's the Iranian embassy from a block away. No, it's not the architecture. It's the police bus in front of it. Inside, they don't look like diplomats; they probably aren't. A big conference table is deep in ledgers. I think they're records of Iranians who are in or who have passed through Paris. They're trying to figure out who they are. Who they should let back in and who they shouldn't. Who is a revolutionary and who is a Savak agent. I go to get a passport photo with an expatriate jazz musician who we've picked up to interpret for us. We get visas, thanks to Rob's contacts in Washington who have supplied him with a visa and us with a letter filled with indecipherable writing and official-looking stamps. I wonder what it says.

Wayne and Rob go back to the hotel. I find the Iranian bank that has supposedly opened up for the first time that day in several weeks. There are people in the bank who obviously know what they're doing. They've been in banks before. But who are those semi-scruffy looking types intently watching everything, and why do I think that they are not quite sure what they're looking at or why they're looking for it. By the way – at the embassy and at the bank – no chadors. My first surprise.

Back at the hotel to call CBS's Paris Bureau. We've heard of a pooled network charter operating out of Amman. Yes, there is one, and here's the number of the CBS man in Jordan. No, arrangements for flying in and out are made in Amman and not in Paris. Now I know that even if we can't get in through regularly scheduled airlines, and if the Pan Am charters won't take us in, we can at least get in through Jordan. Just a matter of money. And by the way, with all the talk that I remember in the papers about the difficulty of getting clearances for the evacuation flights, how come the network charter gets in and out without apparent problem?

By now, it's 3:30 and time for a nap. We have a rendezvous at 5:30 in Rob's room. First, a couple of State Dept. types, friends of Rob's, will meet us for dinner. Next, a call to Air France. It looks like the 1 am flight is really going to go out. We forgot to ask what time we should get there and call back. This time we're told the flight isn't going out. But someone just told us that the fight was planning to leave. Well, no Iranians are being allowed on the flight. An Air France decision? No, the Iranian Government. Be there early. The ticket counter opens at 10 pm.

A call to the States. The meeting with Pan Am and/or the State Department. Washington is snowed under with its worst storm in fifty years. It looks like we're going to get in on the first commercial flight into Tehran since the airport was closed by the Bakhtiar government. [Shapour Bakhtiar was the Shah's last prime minister and, having fled the country, was assassinated in Paris in 1991.] Mike Brooks, the production supervisor, has hotel rooms and flights scheduled for me all week in Philadelphia, Salt Lake City, and Dallas. Cancel them all. We won't call again from Paris unless we don't get out.

Down to dinner with someone from AID, the Agency for International Development, who has been scheduled to go into Chad (civil war now in progress) and so has been redirected into Senegal, and the U.S. embassy doesn't want him there, and we talk about it, about what he does, and it sounds impressive, and I can't remember a word he says. I'm in half a fog, and if it doesn't have anything to do with what I'm there to do, I don't want to know about it, and I won't remember it.

8:30. Time to go. We check out, asking them to hold our rooms until morning in case we have to come back.

De Gaulle-Roissy is practically deserted. The counter isn't open yet. A group of people, presumably Iranians, are also waiting. Although it's late, we get them to let us into the first-class lounge and sit down to wait it out. The counters open at about 10, and we check-in, wait in the lounge until 11 and go to the duty-free shops searching for diversion and a short wave radio. It's the only way to keep in touch with the rest of the world and, sometimes, with what's happening where you are. Another long wait. A few fellow travelers straggle in. Journalists or at least related (e.g., an AP photographer) and a couple of French business types. Are they trying to take advantage of France's having given sanctuary to Khomeini? Probably. By 2 am, we are on board. Although the plane had been fully booked there are only 29 people with us. The rest were probably Iranians. It's a five-and-a-half-hour flight, a two-and-a-half-hour time difference. We land at about 10 am local time, Tuesday morning.

Rolling down the runway, looking at the mountains (they seem to fold differently than I'm used to seeing), looking for signs of violence, fighting, the Air Force. The Air Force is there. Rows of fighters. Troop transports or cargo planes. Helicopters. A fighter, its afterburners flaming, streaks off. We roll to a stop. We are told there will be a slight delay before disembarking. Welcome to Tehran.

The door is opened, and men with rifles come in. They come down the aisle, these self, or otherwise appointed guardians of the revolution. Our passports are checked. What are they looking for? Iranians? Visas? Troublemakers of some never defined sort? Whatever it is, it isn't us, and we are allowed to leave the plane.

As we descend into the crisp morning air, hazy as it usually is – with mist or smog or desert dust, I cannot tell – a Pan Am 747 thunders to a landing – an evacuation flight. The irregular Islamic Guards (as they have been named by themselves or by some mysterious Committee) always near us and always the guns – the rifles, the AK 47's, full magazines, held loosely, held carelessly, pointed every which way except deliberately away from us. Into the bus and we are taken to the terminal building.

These are not the regular customs officials. They look through their books, their lists of names. How long have they been drawing them up? Deciding who is desirable and who is undesirable. He studies my visa for a long time. What is he trying to decide? What has the Paris consular official written in a (to me) indecipherable hand beneath my visa stamp? It is, perhaps, my most anxious moment. Knowing that something has been written that I cannot read. Knowing that it is telling this person something. He stamps my passport, and I pass through. A few days later, I ask our interpreter to translate it. It's just someone's name and their title. Oh.

We collect our baggage and move into the central part of the terminal. It is packed. Crowded. Americans awaiting their evacuation flight. Tired eyes. An air of tension, not from high expectation, I think, but anxiety. Women and children and animals in cages. The flotsam and jetsam of American policy. We don't talk to them. We have other business to take care of.

If we didn't know we were in the Middle East, it soon becomes clear enough. The regular price into town is 600 rials, the taxi driver tells us (anywhere from 68 to 90 on the dollar depending on where you have bought them – mine, from the Paris bank, were 68). Because there are three of us, he couldn't possibly take us for less than 1,000. Who are we to argue? When I don't tip him later, he glowers.

The drive into town. There is a large amount of construction that has been going on. All over Tehran, there are unfinished high rises, which I assume are apartment buildings. They are to become as familiar as the fixed construction cranes that stand like so many metalized flamingos standing guard over the lifelessness. We have heard how the people of Iran have returned to work. Not here. The construction sites have been closed for weeks, if not months, with no sign of reopening. We are to hear hints of that about other things. The major industries – factories and the like – have not been reopened. Except for oil. The oil workers are returning to the fields.

The Shiite monument, a more graceful Arc de Triomphe, stands in the middle of a large traffic circle, which itself stands in a vast space, empty except for the sentinel cranes and the naked shells of the unfinished buildings. There were millions of people crowded into that space not so long ago. I remember the pictures on TV. There is no way the TV screen can do justice to that. The FCC won't let you broadcast sound that loud. Minimally, it should be in 70mm Panavision directed by David Lean. No, bring back Cinerama. Better yet, IMAX. Maybe that would have given it the proper size. Not really. The decibel level would blow out the Quadraphonic speakers. My mind tries to fill it in. The ghosts of that so recent hugeness still seem to reverberate and crowd in, and I smell the sweat of the four million and feel the immense weight of that crush and the overwhelming, "Allah Akbar, Allah Akbar, Allah Akbar." God is great … No wonder the Shah fled. No wonder the Army disintegrated. I have begun to understand. I think of Chairman Mao, who said that "power grows from the barrel of a gun." Really? Ask the Shah.

The Intercontinental Hotel, home of the Western press. The last time I was in an Intercontinental Hotel, it was in Managua, Nicaragua. Another revolution. They are not so different. There are armed guards. In Nicaragua, they were Samoza's National Guard – long-termers in uniform, no two rifles or machine pistols the same. In Tehran, they were members of the Islamic Guard – no uniforms at all, but the rifles are all the same.

Xerox copies of Newsweek's cover of Khomeini are on each of the hotel's glass doors. A hand-lettered banner in Persian hangs over the entrance between two poles stuck in potted bushes. It says that the hotel staff supports the revolution and the Ayatollah or Imam Khomeini (as he is now frequently called). Not too long ago – the previous week? – the hotel was attacked by some group or other, and the ground-floor Persian restaurant was bombed out. The telex room hasn't been functioning in weeks. Everything else, though, is functioning pretty normally. The newspaper stand sells the two local English language newspapers, the Persian papers, two weeks to month-old magazines, paperback books in English and French. A Persian rug store opens at 4 pm daily. There are also antique or curio shops. They are expensive and don't look like they do a particularly brisk business. There is also a travel agency. I think it was closed when we arrived, although it had reopened by the end of the week. Two restaurants on the top floor are open. One, Polynesian, is only serving a buffet for breakfast, lunch, and dinner. But it is open 24 hours a day and serves the room service menu (hamburgers and chiliburgers, of all things) the rest of the time. After a couple of meals there, it all tastes the same. Pretty much the same can be said for the French-*ish* restaurant that serves a lot of frozen food. On the other hand, the things they do serve are vaguely Caesar salads and caviar. That, I eat. Downstairs in the lobby, coffee and tea are available, and it is the principal place for exchanging gossip, which is constant. Liquor is still being served. It's a bit like five-star hotels in South Africa where Blacks could stay before the end of apartheid and the only places in the country where Blacks and whites could eat at the same table. In Tehran, you can drink at the Intercontinental. So far.

My room overlooks the mountains to the north of the city. They are snow-covered just above what looks like the end of the city. Off to the northeast is a large red and white transmission tower. N.I.R.T. National Iranian Radio and Television? Also, the tower of the Tehran Hilton where the American evacuees have been holed up.

Wayne's room overlooks the South. No mountains but lots of cranes. He also has a tin of rotting caviar in his refrigerator. The fridge is also missing its complement of Cokes, 7 Up, beer, gin, and scotch. It takes two days and an Assistant Manager to get it filled up.

There is a reason why journalists stay in the same hotel. We are no different. As soon as we have unpacked, we're off trying to find if anyone we know is there. We decide to try the networks first. They all have suites and, since ABC is on the highest floor, we go there first and will work our way down. That was not an editorial comment. I could have said that we started at the bottom with CBS and worked our way up, but that wouldn't have been true either factually or symbolically. As it happens, Wayne knows the ABC producer, Paul Cleveland. They once worked on a project together in New York. We chat and tell him why we're there. We're trying to secure Prime Minister Barzagan and Deputy Prime Minister for Revolutionary Affairs Yazdi [the same Dr. Yazdi whom we met in Paris with Khomeini and who later became Foreign Minister] for a satellite hookup to the States. He is doubtful. They've been trying to get Barzagan for three weeks, as has everyone else, and he hasn't budged, at least not for TV, although he is now willing to do at least some print interviews. We've read the one he gave jointly to the Times and Newsweek. They, together with CBS and NBC, feed the States at 8:30 every night. Phone calls are tough to make. Long delays. They've been unsuccessful in getting a four-wire co-ord line installed. For the uninitiated, a four-wire circuit is essentially two audio lines – transmit and receive – which are of much higher quality than telephones and highly useful for coordination and other purposes, particularly in countries with unreliable telephone service.

We also meet the translator they have hired. Does she know anyone who might be free to give us a hand while we're here? She'll find someone. It's lunchtime. Paul wishes us luck and obviously thinks we'll need it.

We have not come to Tehran empty-handed. On the contrary, Rob has established strong contacts within the revolutionary government. We are in Tehran because Shahriar Rouhani, the new government's main man in Washington, has told us that Yazdi, the aforementioned Deputy Prime Minister, has guaranteed the two interviews. Rouhani, it so happens, is also Dr. Yazdi's son-in-law. But there is a problem – how do we get in touch with Dr. Yazdi?

That's as far as my narrative went. However, I remember much of the trip, at least in its bare bones.

ABC's translator found someone to help us, a young Jewish woman who had been a student at the University. She had been a supporter of the revolution. However, now that it was successful, she was beginning to feel uncomfortable with the growing ascendancy of the radical clergy and its anti-Semitism. In fact, some months after we left, I made inquiries about her wellbeing and was told that she and her family had fled the country.

Since Rob couldn't reach Yazdi by telephone, we decided to simply take ourselves to his office and wait until he appeared. Though I don't think we saw him, we were told that both he and Barzagan were, in fact, committed to the interview, and we just needed to tell them where and when it would be. So Wayne and I went to Sadegh Ghotbzadeh's office at N.I.R.T. We exchanged pleasantries about seeing each other once again and found out that he already knew about the interviews. He was willing to make his own facilities and personnel available to feed the tape back to New York. Also, for the interview itself, we needed to make sure that we could get two telephone calls to New York, one so that Robin and Jim could ask questions and the other for Wayne and me.

We were stopped by the Revolutionary Guard on the way back from Ghotbzadeh's office or returning from the one dinner we ate outside the hotel. People with guns were all over Tehran, and cars were often stopped. Often these were very young people, and they very seriously waved guns in front of your face. I've had guns pointed at or near my vicinity several times in my life by professional soldiers. But, frankly, a professional pointing a rifle at you is very different than having a sixteen-year-old or younger pointing the same gun at you. Children with guns make me particularly nervous. And so it was in this case, as a car filled with young males pulled us over to the side, stuck their guns in the windows, and demanded to see our identification. The incident passed without further problems, but it certainly didn't make me feel like walking around the city, something that Rob, in fact, did.

One thing I've always found true of journalists actually covering a story (as opposed to those sitting back in their offices) is that they are almost always willing to help out their colleagues if they can. Unlike their superiors up the chain of command who have other priorities, journalists covering a story, foreign or domestic, recognize that at that moment, they have more in common with their fellow journalists on the ground than they do with their bosses. So there is always a willingness to exchange information and actively help one another as long as they are not being asked to share an exclusive or scoop with a direct competitor. Thus, you will have a newspaper reporter covering a story with a magazine or TV reporter, etc. So it was in Tehran.

We hadn't brought our own camera crew to Iran, hoping that we would find one of the many freelancers or networks willing to help us. Since we had already established a relationship with ABC, Wayne and I went back to Paul Cleveland. Would he and ABC be willing to help us? What did we need? A camera and sound crew and someone familiar with the videotape and satellite transmission facilities. We didn't want to be totally reliant on N.I.R.T. getting it right. Paul would help, he said, provided we could help him with something. He brought Jack Smith, ABC's correspondent on the ground, into the meeting. Jack, who, like everyone else, had been trying to get an interview with the prime minister, wanted to come with us so that he could at least make a direct pitch to Barzagan.

I said that if Jack stayed in the background until our interview was over, I'd introduce him to Barzagan before the crew packed up. He agreed, and the deal was set. At the appointed time, we all went to the prime minister's office, set up, established the audio links to Robin, Jim, Duke, and Al, and shot the interviews, after which we took the tape to N.I.R.T. and fed it to the satellite. Robin and Jim had been recorded separately in NY, and our feed was edited into their video and aired. Done. As promised, I introduced Jack to Barzagan before we left. I have no idea what resulted from their meeting.

We finally left on Tuesday, February 27th, and I did so happily. It had been an interesting, if a bit nerve-wracking experience and one that I hoped I didn't have to repeat.

No such luck.

Nine months later, on November 4th, 1979, the American Embassy was stormed and its personnel taken hostage. After Khomeini supported the hostage-takers, Prime Minister Barzagan resigned, followed by other government members.

Ten days later, on November 14th, I was on my way back to Tehran. I'm still not sure how this was arranged. In fact, I don't think I knew about the trip until the morning we left. On Friday, the 9th, I had lunch with Burt Hanft. He had left Paramount and now was the managing partner of a law firm that protected the major motion picture distributors against illegal skimming by theater owners and piracy. Dinner was with another friend, Joan Golub. On Saturday, I went to see a dance recital given by a friend's dance company, and on Sunday, I flew to Las Vegas, returning on Tuesday night. This doesn't sound like a schedule of someone who knows he's about to go to a city in the midst of ... revolutionary excess, does it?

I vaguely recall arriving at the office at around 10 am on Wednesday morning. Robin called me into his office and said we had arranged something big: We had been guaranteed the first and exclusive interview with the Ayatollah since the hostages had been taken. Could we pull it off? Maybe. When would it be, I wanted to know? How soon could we get there? Robin wanted to know. He was clearly expecting a miracle, and I said I would try to make it happen. At the regular morning staff meeting, which started at about 10:20, Robin announced the plan and asked everyone to keep it quiet. In the meantime, I headed for the phone.

Since Robin and I would be going to Tehran by ourselves, it only made sense to talk to ABC about helping us out. Dealing with the same people I had dealt with in February would undoubtedly make it easier. I told them what we had — an exclusive with Khomeini — and what we needed — a two-camera crew and transportation to and from the holy city of Qum, where we were told Khomeini would meet us. ABC agreed, provided they could have something meaningful in return. I promised them five minutes of our interview to be used on their nightly network newscast, even if that was before we aired ours, as long as they gave proper onscreen credit to *M/L*. The deal was made. I went back to tell Robin that we had a way to do the show and that we were booked on a redeye to London that night and another redeye to Tehran the following day.

How did WNET's photography department find out about the trip? Did Robin tell the general manager of WNET about it? The station's head of programming? Maybe Cheryl Gruver, in charge of our relations with other PBS stations, told her boyfriend, a WNET staff photographer she later married, about the trip. Whoever told someone about it, word got to the photography department, and they asked if I would take pictures of Robin and the Ayatollah together. I had a camera but was only a very occasional photographer and didn't really want to be distracted by the obligation to take pictures. Reluctantly, I agreed. They offered me one of their cameras but said I'd prefer to bring my own, but I would take their film. They poured a dozen rolls into a lead-lined bag for me. Robin and I headed off to the airport.

I don't remember a thing about the flights to London or Tehran the next day. However, I remember landing in Iran at dawn. Arriving in Tehran previously, the airport had been packed with people trying to get out of the country. Now it was virtually empty. Robin had a bottle of liquor in his bag. The Revolutionary Guard poured it into an oil barrel.

The rest of Thursday and Friday is pretty much a fog. A cab took us through a silent city to the Intercontinental Hotel. I think I got hold of Paul Cleveland (presuming that he was still in Iran), the ABC producer, and told him we'd let him know what was going on when we knew. But what was going on was nothing. The arrangements for the interview had been made through the foreign ministry, where Rob Hershman had strong contacts. But some of the government had simply disappeared. Foreign Minister Yazdi, whom we had interviewed in February when he was the deputy prime minister and who had translated for us when we interviewed Khomeini in Paris, had resigned. The ministry was now silent. Robin wasn't getting anywhere with them (I'm not even sure he could get through to them), and Rob wasn't getting anywhere in Washington. Once in a while, I'd talk to ABC and say I still didn't know what was going on. We were soon to find out.

Robin and I were sitting in the hotel lobby wondering what, if anything, we could do that we hadn't done. While sitting staring dumbly at each other, there was a stir at the entrance and in swept *Sixty Minute*'s Mike Wallace all trench-coated, his producer trailing behind. Greetings all around. What was he doing there? He was there to interview Khomeini. Oh. Wallace was shortly followed into the hotel by Peter Jennings, then ABC's top foreign correspondent, and then, I think, by Tom Brokaw.

So much for our exclusive. So much, maybe, for ABC's technical help. Robin decided that there wasn't much point in staying. The difficulties of doing the interview, one that was no longer an exclusive and, even more, was likely to be much the same for each of the interviewers, seemed pointless since the networks would have it on the air at least a day before we were able to get it on. So we decided to withdraw gracefully, if not with good humor, from the field.

The following morning we took ourselves to the airport, wanting to get the first plane that we could find out of Tehran as long as it went somewhere towards the West and away from the Middle East. I think we got to the airport around 8 am. I'm a bit hazy about the following sequence of events. Did we have to go through security before being allowed into the waiting area to buy our tickets? Yes. People with guns all around. It's more like kids, the Revolutionary Guard, with guns. They want to check my bag as we pass passport control and customs. Inside, of course, is the lead-lined pouch filled with unexposed film. They spill the rolls onto the table. "What's that?" I am asked, by somebody above the age of 18, pointing accusingly at the film.

Some would claim that I am among the calmest of men, even-tempered, well-controlled in times of crisis. While everyone around me is having hysterics and panicking, I am keeping everything under control, making rational decisions, finding solutions to problems, creating order out of chaos.

"None of your business."

Kalashnikovs snap to the ready. Robin has a horrified wide-eyed look on his face. As various officials or non-official officials start to crowd around me, Robin at least has regained his calm. He snaps his briefcase open and pulls out a picture of him with Khomeini from when we were in France and explains that we have been in Tehran at the invitation of their government and the Imam, who knew us well. And he has a Canadian passport, which doesn't hurt.

Meanwhile, I actually answer the original question. "There isn't anything on the film." And, no, they are welcome to it – as if they needed my permission to do anything they chose with it.

It will not surprise you to learn that they pulled the film out of the canisters and threw it in the garbage. You might be surprised that I didn't wind up in jail. It certainly surprised me, and both Robin and I expressed sighs of relief as they let us through customs into the waiting room.

I've come to think of this episode as a Frank Fenza moment, thinking back to my sudden and possibly irrational (unthinkingly virtuous) impulse to defend the honor of Ruth Nagashima in the fourth grade. To this day, I have no better explanation for it. Why I decided to insist on a First Amendment right in a place that wouldn't have known what freedom of the press meant other than as something to be shot down — literally — as quickly as possible, I don't know. But it really was the First Amendment that I was thinking of at that moment. Honest. I really believe that I have a right to freedom of speech, of thought, of assembly, of religion, of the attempt to gather information and make it known to anyone who wants to see, hear, or read it. I had learned many lessons when Grandpa took me to Washington all those years ago. When the customs agent (or whoever he was) asked me, "What's that?" he wasn't asking just anyone, an everyman who assumes he has no rights except those granted by whoever is holding the gun at the moment. I know that's the way we're supposed to behave, and most of the time, I was willing to go along. But not that time. I was not a featureless, stateless, rights-less man. I was an American and a human being who assumes that he *does* have rights, *inalienable* rights, and insists on exercising them, even, on occasion, when it makes no sense. It's good to remind yourself who you really are every once in a while. There's a Waylon Jennings song that I'm reminded of, "I may be crazy, but it's kept me from going insane."

All that said, it wasn't with any great self-satisfaction that I entered the waiting area. Rather, it was more like trembling with the shock of my foolishness and the relief of it having no consequences. The first plane we could get on was an Air Italia flight to Rome that night with connections to New York late the following morning. During the long wait, we both bought kilo tins of caviar. I bought two, which made for a couple of delicious feasts with family and friends over the coming weeks.

Meantime we took off at around 8 pm and ordered drinks as soon as the stewardess could serve them, meaning once we exited Iranian air space. We landed late in the evening in Rome and took a cab to our hotel, the Hassler, on the top of the Spanish Steps, a favorite of Robin's from his foreign correspondent days. Whatever its state today, it was old, elegant, and beautiful in 1979, a perfect antidote to Tehran's dirt and dust, anxiety and fear. We sat down to a bit of a meal with a bottle of Barolo, the first time I'd ever had it.

At seven the next morning, Sunday, Robin and I met in front of the hotel at the top of the steps, the city spread out before us, and we set off on a walk around the barely awake city while the sun gradually rose, spilling soft golden light through the ancient streets. I don't think I've ever enjoyed a walk so much. Partly, it was just having left a place where it didn't feel safe to so much as take a step out of the hotel. Part of it was the sheer beauty of the morning. Part of it was Robin, who had been in the city many times, happily pointing out this and that, himself relieved to have escaped from Iran unscathed. Part of it was the sidewalk café where the proprietor swept the sidewalk in front and served us freshly brewed coffee and just-baked rolls. Part of it was strolling through Vatican City, empty and silent but for the fluttering birds and the armed Swiss Guards.

And then we were on a plane back to New York, and it really was over.

Over the years, I've often wondered how word got out to all three networks what we were up to. ABC obviously knew about it, but it was in their interest, I thought, to keep it to themselves. Of course, many *M/L* staffers knew about it, and word had certainly gotten around WNET quickly enough. The first person through the Intercontinental Hotel's door was Mike Wallace, so my suspicions fell on two specific people. One was reporter Shirley Wershba whose husband, Joe, was a producer for Wallace's show, *60 Minutes*. The other was our studio director, Duke Struck, who did NFL football games on Sundays for CBS. However, the truth is that far too many people had known about it if we were serious about keeping it a secret. One other possibility intrigued me. If our "rabbi" had been Yazdi and the foreign ministry, it was long rumored that CBS's "rabbi" was Ghotbzadeh. If so, he possibly let CBS's producer in Tehran know about the interview in a bit of gamesmanship with the rival foreign ministry. Aside from curiosity, it no longer matters if it ever really did.

None of our work on the Iranian Revolution would have been so successful without Rob Hershman, one of the best and brightest reporters to have ever worked for *MacNeil/Lehrer*. After he left us, he went on to produce documentaries for CBS. Tragically, he died in 1995. He was only 41.

On Saturday, March 15th, 1980, I flew again to Johannesburg, but it was only to change planes on my way to Salisbury, Rhodesia before it was renamed Zimbabwe. I was accompanied by Pat Ellis, one of our foreign affairs reporters, who had arranged for an interview with Robert Mugabe.

Rhodesia by then was in the midst of the transition from the pariah white government of Ian Smith to the revolutionary Black government of Robert Mugabe. Mugabe and most of the leadership of his political party, ZANU (PF), were living in the capital, Salisbury. A month later, on April 18th, 1980, the country would change its name to the Republic of Zimbabwe, and Mugabe would be installed as president of the new government. In the meantime, Mugabe's lieutenants were all jockeying for power and position among themselves and their rivals, particularly Joshua Nkomo and his party, ZAPU.

Although we had been told the interview was guaranteed by Mugabe's representatives in Washington, the truth on the ground in Rhodesia was not so certain. Perhaps it was the general nature of third-world countries where very little seemed to happen when or how it was supposed to. Or maybe it was the inexperience of the various people involved, or perhaps it was the fluidity of the status of different Mugabe representatives, each of whom insisted that he spoke for Mugabe. The truth was that no one spoke for Mugabe when it came to what he really would do or when he would do it except for Mugabe. As a result, we spent much of the following week going to meetings with various Mugabe representatives or running around Salisbury trying to find them. We visited ZANU's headquarters and ZAPU's, met with Nkomo, and, finally, met with Mugabe and his wife. Only after we met with Mugabe were we sure that the interview would actually happen.

At night, most of the top Black politicians and/or revolutionaries would be found at some point at our hotel, which was filled with various people from the UN, trade missions from all over the world, not to mention diplomatic representatives. They were all trying to get a sense of what was actually going to happen in Zimbabwe and who was going to make it happen, who would be in control of what. Gradually things sorted themselves out for us. The time and date and various technical arrangements for the interview were sorted out. The interview would be in Mugabe's house with an audio link to New York. After that, I'd take the videotape to the country's television facilities and feed it to New York through South Africa, where it would be edited into the show. All of that went off fine.

Pat and I didn't spend all our time together during that week. While she was off doing her reporter thing, I was off doing my own thing, i.e., roaming the city and its art galleries. I had gotten a minor bug for African art, particularly masks when I had been in South Africa. I'm not a serious collector, but I've bought a few masks from various parts of Africa over the years. I didn't find any that I wanted, but I did come across an art gallery (Gallery Delta? which may not still exist). There I found the work of the extraordinary sculptor, Nicholas Mukomberanwa, who died in 2002. The work of Zimbabwe's Shona sculptors has become increasingly popular over the years, but that of Mukomberanwa is without peer, at least in my entirely amateur opinion. Even today, over 50 years after my first afternoon spent with his work, I find myself still moved by it whenever I see it. It's not his technical expertise that I so much admire, though he has plenty of that. For me, though, his work is imbued with an enormously powerful spirit. I don't know how he does it or how any great artist does it, for that matter.

I visited the gallery several times over the next few days and eventually bought a piece called "Sleeping Woman," a traditional Shona theme, and carried all 50 or so lbs. of it back home with me on the plane. Mukomberanwa's sculptures can be found in museums all over the world and online.

Following the taping on March 24th, there were another few days that we had to spend in Rhodesia before we could leave. So rather than stay in Salisbury, Pat and I flew to Victoria Falls, where we spent the next few days in enforced idleness. Unfortunately, there really wasn't very much else that we could do. There were still plenty of marauding bands wandering the countryside, and it was unsafe to go anywhere without an armed escort. So we lounged by the pool and watched the mist rising from the great falls. Sometimes the life of a journalist on assignment is truly difficult.

There was one excruciating aspect to Victoria Falls. A radio station played through one of the channels on the TV in my room (there weren't any television programs on that I recall). Twenty-four hours a day, it played one song over and over again. I can never think of Rhodesia or Zimbabwe without Neil Diamond's "Forever in Blue Jeans" running endlessly through my head. It can take days to get rid of it.

Finally, on Saturday, March 29th, we flew back to Johannesburg and then to Geneva, where we had lunch with friends of Pat's while waiting to change planes, and then on to New York.

I made one more foreign trip during the half-hour show's

existence. On May 6th, 1981, after several years of increasing tension between the United States and Libya over Libya's expanded territorial claims regarding offshore boundaries, their support of Mideast terrorist organizations, and their assassination of opponents of the Qaddafi regime in foreign countries, President Reagan ordered the Libyan embassy in Washington closed and expelled some or all of their twenty-seven diplomats for supporting terrorism. Six days later, I left for Tripoli for an interview with Qaddafi.

This time, I was traveling with an engineer, Ed Goldberg. Ed was a nervous sort of fellow, and being Jewish, he was particularly anxious about going to a Muslim country with a decidedly anti-Semitic record. I kept telling him that since we were going at the invitation of the Libyan government, he had nothing to be afraid of. That is, as long as he wasn't tempted to buy liquor from our driver on the way to the hotel, who assured us there was an ample supply in the trunk of the taxi. And as long as he didn't try to exchange money anywhere but the hotel. And don't take documents or anything else from any Libyan we happened to meet. And, given the current state of relations between the US and Libya, it probably wouldn't be too smart to wander the streets without an escort. I'm not sure that my assurances calmed Ed down at all.

Be that as it may, when we got to the hotel, we turned our passports over to the front desk and watched as they were put into a drawer with lots of others. There was nothing unusual about this, but it certainly meant that we couldn't leave the country without official documentation. We also told them when and on what flight we were booked to leave the country. Ed was biting his lips, his fingernails, anything within reach.

The following day, we made our way to Libya's telecommunications headquarters. Or, at least, I think that's what it was, though it could have been the foreign ministry. Everybody was pleasant and polite and, by the way, there is no guarantee that the interview will happen. Why not? Col. Qaddafi would like to know what he is going to be asked. I'm sorry, I say, but that is against the show's policy. We never tell guests what we are going to ask them.

We are all very polite and equally insistent. I finally say that I'd like to call the States and discuss the problem with my boss. It apparently isn't so easy to place a call out of the country in Libya without official permission. They agree after some more back and forth and make sure that I have a direct line to New York and access to a telex machine. Al Vecchione, to no surprise, is confident that neither Robin nor Jim will agree to give Qaddafi a list of questions in advance. Once again, I discuss our position with Qaddafi's representatives. Suppose, I say, that we were willing to tell them the general subject areas we might want to talk to the Colonel about. Would they be satisfied with that? They leave the room and, after an hour or two, they return and say my proposal might work.

Once again, I get through to New York, and Al says he will take my proposal to Robin and Jim. An hour or two later, the telex starts chattering, and there appears a list of nine subject areas ranging from terrorism to oil sales to assassinations to territorial claims, the whole panoply of contentious issues that had contributed to the escalating tensions between our two countries. In other words, we want the latitude to ask him about anything except where he sleeps each night. Again, much muttering and a retreat by the Libyans to discuss the telex privately and with whomever they consulted. Finally, they come back. The telex is accepted as the basis of the interview, and it will go forward. I'm not sure I know what was gained since there wasn't anything that we were being asked not to talk about. Maybe they just wanted to see if we were going to be truthful from the outset and not going to say we were going to ask about one thing while planning on ambushing him with something he wasn't prepared for. If that was the case, the telex reassured them since it said that we would ask about everything.

Early the next afternoon, Thursday, Ed and I make our way to Qaddafi's official office, where we meet up with the Libyan technical crew that will help us. We help set up the audio lines in the office and place the camera where we want it. We put a TV monitor next to the camera because the Libyans have insisted that Qaddafi see a return feed of the program. Since I will not be allowed in Qaddafi's presence, I ask the cameraman to urge Qaddafi to look at the camera when talking or, instead of that, towards the monitor. He agrees. Finally, everything having been arranged, we go to the remote truck to wait.

Because of the time zone difference between the U.S. and Libya, we have a considerable wait since the Libyans have insisted that this be done live so there can be no editing after the fact. The Libyan crew invites us to eat dinner with them, and we sit down for the meal. I can't tell you what we ate because I have no idea. We sit on cushions in front of a large, low table, close to the floor, when enormous platters of food are brought in. Everyone reaches in with their hands and dips into the meal. When in Rome ...

Finally, it's time to do the interview, and the satellites come up as planned, the audio connections are made, Qaddafi appears when he is supposed to, and he and Robin chat for a few moments before the show hits the air. I'm on a push-to-talk handset connected simultaneously with Duke Struck and Al. Qaddafi isn't looking at the camera, and he isn't looking at the monitor either. Instead, he's showing us his left profile in what seems like a deliberate choice on his part. Duke fulminates as only he can. "Where the hell's that idiot looking?" Duke expostulates. "Anywhere he wants," I say calmly. Duke laughs uproariously, and the interview goes on without incident.

The next day is Friday, and our plane isn't due to leave until early Saturday morning. Since we don't have our passports, Ed and I go to the front desk to make sure they are easily accessible. There is a problem. The hotel no longer has them; they've been sent to the foreign ministry. Can they be brought back to the hotel? Oh, no. It's Friday, the Muslim day of prayer, and the ministry is closed. If nobody is at the ministry, how can we be sure that the passports will be back at the hotel early enough in the morning in time for us to leave for the airport to get a 7 am plane? A shrug. Ed is visibly sweating by now. He is sure that we are never going to leave. He has visions of two Jews rotting away in some dark and filthy prison cell, and that's just the most optimistic version of his imagination. After insisting that the hotel try to contact the ministry and give the manager all our contact numbers, we sit and wait, not knowing if we will leave. Finally, at about three in the afternoon, the manager appears all smiles, shows us our passports, and assures us we will get them in the morning. So sorry about the confusion. Ed is dying for a drink, but the best we can manage is a Pepsi (no Coke in Libya, among other things). The next day we leave for London and then back to New York on Sunday.

No, I didn't wear a trench coat on any of these trips. I probably had one somewhere at the back of a closet. I was not a foreign correspondent. I was not one of those intrepid and incredibly brave (or foolish) producers or cameramen who dive into perilous situations and stick with them month after month. I have great admiration for those who are courageous, dedicated, and foolish enough to bring us the news of the wars and revolutions of our times.

At the most, I was able to, allowed to, asked to dip my toe into the enormous turmoil in the world beyond America's shores, and I'm grateful for having had the opportunity. Revolutions in Iran, Rhodesia, and Nicaragua, upheaval in Panama, South Africa inching its way towards transformation, a dictator in Libya with territorial ambitions, I had seen something of them all: The Middle East, sub-Saharan Africa, Northern Africa. Only Asia and the Indian subcontinent were missing.

And what did I learn? Where do I begin? Maybe three things most of all.

1)Western Europe, in particular, had made a terrible botch of its colonial adventures, most notably in the Middle East and Africa. Perhaps it's too much to expect that any of the great imperial powers of Europe (and America, too) would have had the foresight to imagine that their empires would come to an end. How those empires were created and administered usually meant that unmanageable and ungovernable entities were left behind at their demise. These states, whose boundaries had been drawn by Europeans, were no more nations than European countries themselves had been a thousand years before. When Europeans left Africa and the Middle East, they left geographical entities divided by never resolved tribal, religious, and ethnic differences. They often left a barely educated population and had rarely established institutions that could help the transition to self-rule, much less pluralistic democracies. The result was continual distrust and war between various groups within those countries. It was almost inevitable that these countries would come to be ruled by dictatorships that looked to benefit mainly themselves and their families and tribes, along with massive corruption, and would deny the idea that one should govern for the benefit of all people of the nation. And it left people with an understandable mistrust of their former colonial masters and allies in the West.

There is a corollary to this of which America has also long been guilty. There is the assumption that military strength, economic power, and religious conviction mean cultural and spiritual superiority. It also, of course, implies the assumption of cultural and spiritual inferiority of all others. From the beginning of America's colonization in the 1600s, we've seen the effects and fallacies of these assumptions. But, unfortunately, they aren't limited to the distant past. In contemporary times, these errors have been evident in every war we've fought, beginning with the Vietnam war. The costs in lives, dollars, and influence have been incalculable. That cultural arrogance has been a constant presence in America through the centuries.

2)The past never settles anything with finality. Wars rarely end anything. Treaties do not finish things. History continues, and the problems that existed before such things continue to evolve and need to be worked out. In particular, the extent to which foreign policy decisions made by America in the post-World War II era were guided, almost entirely, by Cold War considerations, along with the long-term problems caused by corporate adventurism, particularly in Latin America and the Middle East. America propped up dictators and tyrants and tolerated all the murder and brutality that their support required, and tried to influence the course of elections throughout Europe to prevent Communists from coming to power. Finally, America had few qualms about overthrowing democratically elected governments if it thought they might look too favorably on the Soviet Union or might be under their control. The necessity — if indeed it was necessary, something that might be seriously questioned — of such extreme *realpolitik* helped create a sense of American hypocrisy and sometimes enmity towards the USA in Third World countries that persists to this day. And always, suspicion of American motives. William Faulkner wrote, "the past is not really dead. In fact, it's not even past."

3)That America lives too far from the rest of the world, no matter the ease and speed of modern-day communications and globalization. Our physical separation from most of the world and our great military and economic power keeps us from personally witnessing the direct impact of our policies. The people of other countries (generally with much smaller populations), even more than their governments, feel the direct effects of those policies. We do not feel them, except minimally and only over time. We often don't even notice them unless there is an exceptional event like the supply chain disruptions during the Covid pandemic. We do not like to live in the past (except occasionally, and then it's usually an imagined past rather than a real one) and cannot imagine that people in other parts of the world remember a history that we've forgotten. So we like to tell ourselves and others that it's time to move forward. It's a convenient way to deny responsibility for what has been done to others in our name, a way to proclaim America's innocence, always America's innocence. Where did that insistence on our innocence come from? It is, perhaps, the greatest American lie, a lie that helps make it impossible to deal forthrightly with real problems by its very insistence.

But beyond anything, there are billions of people throughout the world, most just trying to survive as best they can. Too often, they live under intolerable conditions, suffering from the heavy hand or indifference of leaders, governments, and institutions that are more interested in their own power, self-perpetuation, and self-aggrandizement than the people in whose name they exist. I didn't have to go to Soweto to know how miserable the lives of far too many Black South Africans were. I didn't need to see the cardboard box houses of the poor in Managua, Nicaragua, to know in what intolerable conditions they lived. The degradation in which so many people live is beyond belief, their willingness to tolerate it even more so. The true tragedy, though, is how often they've been betrayed. Even when they revolt, in Cuba, in Nicaragua, in Haiti, in Iran, in Zimbabwe, in Egypt, in Syria, most people never get what they bargained for, what they fought for, what they hoped for, what they died for, much less what they were promised.

As for America, the land of the free, the home of the brave, neither do we.

I made one final foreign trip for *MacNeil/Lehrer* in 1985 for the *NewsHour*. Roger Rosenblatt, the only essayist we ever had under contract, spent a month traveling all over the Soviet Union preparing a cover story for *Time* magazine. Simultaneously, a book was being published, *A Day in the Life of the Soviet Union.* The book (which had nothing to do with Roger) contained the images of 100 still photographers who had shot daily life all over the country. So we thought it would be a good idea to combine Roger's observations with video we would shoot in Moscow along with photographs from the book. We met up in Moscow on September 25th, shot five essays with a Russian crew over the next week, and then returned home. On the plane on our way back home, I jotted down some impressions of our trip.

RUSSIAN MEMORIES
Five Days in September

LEAVING HOME

My passport is pristine. Newly renewed. Never been used. Its clean, unstamped pages waiting to be filled with reminders of places, adventures. Memories.

My jet floats towards Moscow, its nose pointed up throughout its flight, as though it's going as slowly as it can. As if to say, "Don't shoot. It's only us. We come in peace."

Because it is a long flight, I have brought a long, easy book to read — "Red Storm Rising," a story of a war between the USA and the USSR. Taxiing to the gate in Moscow, I decide to leave it on the plane, the last 100 pages unread.

The idea of Moscow coaxes fear. Caution.

PASSPORT CONTROL (COMING)

The uniformed agent in the glass booth takes my passport and its separate visa. He examines me, and he looks at them, then returns them.

As soon as I am through the control point and safe, I think, I am stopped by another officer who examines my passport and visa again. No problem.

I look at my passport. It is unmarked.

CUSTOMS (COMING)

A Syrian is in front of me on the line. He has many bags. The customs agent looks inside one. All new clothes in their cellophane wrappers. The agent empties every bag. Much discussion with other agents. Officers. They finally let him through.

I am let through without so much as a glance at my belongings. What, actually, does my visa say?

GOING TO TOWN

A man approaches. "Taxi?"

"Sovincenter Hotel?"

He nods, takes my bag, and hurries out the door. I scurry along behind him. "How much?" He continues on. "Wait a minute. How much?"

"$100," he flings casually over his shoulder.

"$100?"

"$100 only."

"Too much." I lunge for my bag. "Too much." We each briefly tug on the bag. He gives it up, looking hurt.

Just like New York.

When I do get a car, the cost is $16. Not quite like New York.

On the way to the city, we pass one high-rise housing complex after another. Reminders of Lefrak City going to seed. Everything I see is falling apart or being built.

SOVINCENTER HOTEL

Looks and feels like a ten-year-old cross between a Hyatt and a Holiday Inn, slightly down at the heels. It, too, is going to seed. Things obviously made in the Soviet Union—shower curtains, etc.—are shoddy. There are towels and toilet paper and tiny bars of soap that hardly diminish with use.

Armand Hammer built the hotel. In the lobby/atrium, there are trees set in green circles. The trees are plastic; the grass, carpet.

There is also a cuckoo clock. The clock is 50 feet tall, and it looks to be made of the same "wood" as the trees. On the hour, there is a trumpet fanfare. The mechanical rooster atop the clock flaps its wings and cock-a-doodle-doos. Twice. Doors around the clock open, mechanical figures turn, and paddle-boats move and do other things I can't quite figure out.

Hammer is reputed to be a man of acumen, intelligence, and taste, reportedly with many millions spent in the collection of art and Arabian horses. He is supposed to have spent $1,000,000 for the clock and an undisclosed amount for the trees.

A Russian girl tries to enter the hotel. The KGB (?) agent at the door inspects her papers. With exceptions, the Russians are not permitted contact with foreigners in their hotels. She is allowed to enter.

Radio Moscow is the English language entertainment in my room. It gives me an interesting perspective on the news of the day: There is no evidence that the Iran Ajr was laying mines. A transport plane carrying 15 civilians was shot down by American Stinger missiles in Afghanistan. 150 civilians traveling in transports have been shot down by American Stingers and British Blowpipes. American arms are interfering with the policy of National Reconciliation. Country-Western music has its roots in one of the Soviet Republics.

ON SIGHTSEEING

I have arranged for a car and an English-speaking driver to show me the city to get my bearings and have some idea of what can be shot when I finally get to read Roger Rosenblatt's essays.

The driver talks a great deal, gesturing emphatically to make sure I understand. He obviously knows a lot about his city. The trip lasts three hours, and I've seen the outside of every major building in Moscow except Lubyanka.

Unfortunately, the driver speaks no English.

MEETING ROGER

I get back to the hotel. Roger has arrived. He has spent the past month traveling 8,000 miles from Leningrad to

Samarkand. He has seen the future, and it doesn't work. Roger's mood matches his experience.

Why does everyone in this hotel look like they have just committed a crime or are about to commit one?

Roger receives the kind of phone call for which the Sovincenter is so famous. It is the middle of the night when the phone rings.

"Hello? My name is Maria. You would like massage or sex? I can be there in ten minutes."

SEEING MOSCOW

We shoot hundreds of people on the street.

One smiled at us.

One made faces at the camera.

One asked if we would take her picture.

Two smiled at each other.

Of the others, many cast suspicious (?) furtive (?) sideways glances. Many carefully (?) intentionally (?) ignored us.

The most colorful (literally) sights in Moscow: The flower-strewn graves in the cemeteries.

The place where feeling and emotion are the most visible in Moscow: The cemeteries and the church in the graveyard.

The most moving and tragic thing about Moscow: The cemeteries.

I look for Lara everywhere. She is nowhere to be found.

ON LEAVING

Moscow—love it or leave it.

I'm leaving in the morning.

On each hotel floor, there is a woman whose prime function is to give you a piece of paper. To leave the floor with your luggage, you must have this piece of paper. The desk clerk must stamp this paper. The KGB (?) agent at the door demands that you give the paper to him before you leave.

CUSTOMS (GOING)

A woman in the line next to ours has every single item in her baggage individually x-rayed. I pass through once more with no baggage inspection.

PASSPORT CONTROL (GOING)

I give the man my passport and visa. He stamps many things. My visa is kept; my passport is returned.

COMING HOME

We are landing at JFK, and I have filled out my customs declaration. I take out my passport and open it. There are no stamps. No marks. It is as bare, as virgin, as unused as the day I got it.

Is Moscow an experience only to be shared by them and me? A secret between us? Something to be hidden?

Is Moscow only a memory?

As I reread these words after so many years, it seems that not so much has changed. There was a brief moment when the Soviet Union disappeared and was replaced by the democratically oriented Russian Federation. Still, as the KGB and its henchmen have gradually reestablished government control, it is clear that not so much has changed after all. Gone is the pretense of "Communism," leaving in its place what seems to be a kind of state fascism in which power and money are the only values of importance, in which the state controls all major industries and sources of information. Perhaps the best way to see it is as a criminal enterprise, something like Las Vegas, which was created by various bootleggers and murderers who had legitimacy bestowed upon them by their success in corrupting everything around them. For us, though, Russia is a country that has inherited its fundamental foreign policy objectives as they have been passed down from the Tsars to the Soviets to the Putinists — expansion and/or control of the territories that surround Russia and perhaps beyond, warm-water ports, access to and control of the Black Sea. In this iteration, though, the Russian actually have one product they possess that the West may not be able to do without: oil and gas. It affects the balance of power in significant ways. Russians felt free to invade Georgia, at least in part to forestall the building of an oil and/or gas pipeline that would bypass Russia. America was reluctant to embrace the Nord 2 pipeline. Belarus threatened to cut off fuel supplies to Europe until Russia told them to back off; there was the expropriation of the Crimean Peninsula and then, seven years later, the indirect armed invasion of eastern Ukraine. And, of course, there was the threat of an even wider war if NATO did not bend to Russia's will regarding security support or guarantees to all the countries on Russia's periphery. These were all long-time Tsarist/Soviet/Russian goals, even predating 1854's Crimean War. And not long after I wrote these lines, Russia did, indeed, invade Ukraine. As Faulkner said (once again), "The past isn't dead; it isn't even past."

Chapter 11
DOMESTIC AFFAIRS

1977 — 1981

Of course, my domestic traveling continued at a hectic pace, though it started winding down in the early '80s. But from the very beginning, my long-term interests were not in the technical nuts and bolts of getting programs on the air but in creating program content. So, in 1977, within the *MacNeil/Lehrer Report* and apart from it, I began to try to do just that.

In October 1977, I was asked to go to Miami with a reporter to cover the Ronnie Zamora trial. Zamora was a fifteen-year-old boy accused of murdering an elderly neighbor. His lawyer, Ellis Rubin, decided on an insanity defense claiming that Zamora had been temporarily insane because of "television intoxication." In other words, Zamora intentionally murdered someone because he had watched so many TV murders. The trial was televised, a rarity back then, and the day the guilty verdict was announced, I cut together a half-hour summary of the trial, and we aired it.

Rubin's argument may not have been the first instance of the idea that everybody is a victim and no one is responsible for anything. Still, it will do as an early example of the lengths some people were willing to go to intellectually justify the idea. For example, a year later, San Francisco Supervisor Harvey Milk and Mayor George Moscone were murdered by Dan White. In his 1979 trial, he argued that he was not responsible for his actions because of his "diminished capacity," his life's history, and the ingestion of too much junk food and sugar. This became known as the Twinkies defense, even if that was a mischaracterization of the argument.

It will come as no surprise that I met many of the general managers and program managers throughout the PBS system through my continual traveling around the country. In fact, I considered that to be part of my job. No PBS station was forced to air *M/L*. When PBS underwrites all or part of a show, the money usually doesn't come from PBS itself but from the stations that air it. Since *M/L* was partially funded by PBS, if a station wanted to air the show, it had to pay for it (I don't know anything about the current funding of the *PBS NewsHour*, but I assume it's similar). The amount an individual station paid was decided by the relative size of the market the station served. Thus, New York City, for example, would pay much more for a show than, say, Wichita. Aside from the editorial desirability of interconnecting with other stations, my visits played at least a minor role in creating a personal relationship between the show and the stations' executives. Aside from making many friends, those efforts paid off more directly.

Six months after the Zamora trial, at the end of March or beginning of April 1978, I went to Robin. I asked if he'd be interested in *M/L* doing a series of specials in conjunction with other PBS stations leading up to the '78 elections. He wasn't interested, thinking we could cover them adequately on the show. When asked if I could propose such a series to Jerry Toobin, WNET's director of public affairs programming, he didn't object. Jerry liked the idea but said he didn't see how WNET could find the money. I asked if he minded if I talked to Lee Clark (now Lee Cullum), the Vice President for Program Development at KERA, the Dallas PBS affiliate, who I knew from earlier trips to Dallas. He didn't.

Not coincidentally, I was scheduled to travel to Dallas on April 11th, and before I left, I called Lee and asked if she and I could have lunch. I had a program proposal I wanted to discuss with her. So on the 12th, we had lunch at a Mexican restaurant. I suggested a series of several shows about the upcoming 1978 elections, using them to look at what was happening politically around the country and looking forward to the 1980 presidential election. The programs would be co-produced by a group of stations from different regions of the country. The stations would be able to provide particular insights to elections in their own areas, but, equally important when thinking of programs for PBS, the fundraising by a group of stations acting cooperatively might be a powerful inducement.

Lee was enthusiastic and volunteered to take the lead in the venture as I had hoped. The day after I returned to New York (and just before I left for Panama), I sent a memo to her, Jerry Toobin, and Linda Winslow (now head of public affairs programming at WETA), with a copy to Robin, outlining the idea in broad strokes. And so, *Election '78*, as it came to become known, began to move forward.

While Lee undertook to raise the money (it eventually was funded by CPB, the Corporation for Public Broadcasting), we started filling out the show's staff and deciding on its structure and our partner stations within the PBS system.

Lee thought the executive producer should be someone who had a national reputation. Despite my role in the show as its generating spirit, I really couldn't disagree. She suggested Chick Cherkazian, who, at the time, was at the Smithsonian. I had known Chick from my days at Douglas-Lester when he was one of *Your Dollars' Worth*'s producers and had liked and trusted him. So I agreed. Chick couldn't have acted more graciously. He said he shouldn't be the executive producer, and I should; he'd be happy to work as a consultant. However, Lee's reasons for wanting him were understandable, particularly when it came to finding underwriting. Besides, if I were to be the executive producer, it would mean taking a leave from *M/L* for about ten weeks or so, and I understood that Robin might object; it would take me away from the show for too long. So, with Lee's agreement, Chick and I worked out our mutual roles. He would take primary responsibility for the live segments of the shows and their composition. I would handle the documentary pieces that the stations would produce. But I would also have primary responsibility for our relationship with the stations, the producers, correspondents, and studio managers that were essential to the show since we would originate the programs from each of their studios. My title would be coordinating producer, and I think I got credit for creating the series (though I don't remember the screen credits).

We asked five stations to participate: KERA-Dallas, WNET-New York, SCETV (the South Carolina Educational Television Network) in Charleston, WTTW-Chicago, and WGBH-Boston. At the urging of Larry Grossman, then the head of PBS (before moving to the presidency of NBC), we wanted Washington's WETA to also be part of the group. However, Linda Winslow said she didn't have the personnel or facilities available.

Zev Putterman (at KQED) objected to calling the series a co-production. Because it would be centrally controlled from Dallas and New York, he argued that it really wasn't one since the participation of station management (meaning him and his equivalents at the other stations) would be practically nonexistent. Although he had no objection to using his on-air talent and was supportive of our efforts, he wanted to distance himself from the project slightly by not calling it a co-production. I understood his position, as did Lee and Jerry Toobin.

For our on-air talent, we asked Marilyn Berger to be the host. Marilyn was a well-established journalist. She had been the White House Correspondent for NBC and was working for the Council on Foreign Relations. We also chose two commentators, one a liberal and one a conservative. Our conservative was Kevin Phillips, best known as the author of *The Emerging Republican Majority*. This book laid out the strategy that Nixon followed to capture the South and turn it into the base of the Republican Party that it still is today. Ken Bode, the then political editor of *The New Republic*, was our liberal.

This was an unusual production model for PBS stations, and I'm not sure how often it had been used before. But, as far as we were concerned, it worked very well. The producers, correspondents, and stations did their job, and we did ours. Initially, Lee suggested that we air the series on five consecutive Monday nights with a sixth show on election eve and another following the election. Unfortunately, although I have many pieces of paper from the series still in my files, I have no record of whether there was the sixth show, and I am sure there wasn't a seventh.

On the other hand, I was in Dallas the week following the election, so maybe there was a follow-up show. Regardless, I successfully urged Lee to reconsider her plans for five weekly regional shows and, instead, to air them on the five consecutive weekday nights before the election. I wanted whatever information and polling we presented to be as accurate and up to date as possible, and the picture can change quite dramatically in the space of five weeks. Besides, I thought stripping the show would make for a more comprehensive and cohesive look at the election for viewers and make it easier to promote. Each show, although similar, would be different because there were different races, different issues, and different trends to follow. We had pollsters on some of the shows and other experts in the local elections and, in the case of Chicago, an audience for John Calloway, WTTW's chief correspondent, to interact with. It was all to be moderated by Marilyn while Kevin and Ken would analyze and discuss the implications for the presidential contest that was just two years away.

Although both Kevin and Ken had their ideological bent, they were both willing to be non-ideological and reasonably honest in their approach to their analysis. They were more interested in exchanging viewpoints and discussing them than keeping score. In fact, they understood that this was the point. This is not, by the way, to claim that we invented this form. After all, I'm pretty sure I got the idea from what we were doing on *M/L* in its half-hour version. This approach became institutionalized on the *NewsHour* after it began in 1983 with the weekly analysis by David Gergen and Mark Shields, a decision that I'm sure had nothing to do with what we did on *Election '78*. In fact, I don't know if Robin or Jim even saw the shows since they never said a word about them. As for Al Vecchione, he argued that I shouldn't be paid separately by KERA for my work on the series because I was being paid by *M/L*. It was an argument that he won.

CPB agreed to underwrite the shows by the summer, and we went ahead. While Chick was making plans with Marilyn in New York and his staff in Washington, I met with producers and correspondents in the originating cities. Lee oversaw the production in Dallas. And so it went. The shows aired, and they were credible. I don't know that they were brilliant, but they were solid and serious. They dealt with the most interesting races and issues — sunbelt vs. snowbelt in the south, the fight to break the power of Democrats in Texas, and the possible effects of Proposition 13 in California. And the overarching question, what the election meant to the future of potential presidential hopefuls like Jerry Brown, Ronald Regan, Jack Kemp, etc.

And what did all this mean? Not a thing. Almost a year later, the hostages were taken in Iran and upended the political landscape and all the presidential calculations everyone had been busily making.

Many of the people I met traveling around the country were women, some of whom I dated casually, and some became friends even if we never dated. One of the latter was Kathleen Kinderman, a producer I met when I visited the Denver PBS affiliate, KRMA. Whenever I was in Denver, we had dinner and, since her father, Arthur Schlesinger, Jr., lived in New York, I tried to see her whenever she came to the city. We remained friends until she left Denver and moved to Boston in, I think, the early 80's, after which we gradually lost touch with each other. Every once in a while, I would think about finding her again but never did. It was only when I read her father's obituary in 2007 that I learned that she had died in 2004.

In late 1978, Kathy told me about Ruth Earnshaw Lo, a woman with whom she was writing a book. Ruth was an American who had lived in China since the mid-1930s. She'd only been allowed to leave China after the death of Chairman Mao in 1976. As a student at the University of Chicago, she met a Chinese graduate student, Lo Ch'uan-fang. They married in 1935 and in 1937 settled permanently in China, becoming English teachers in a university. They supported the Chinese Revolution following the war but gradually became disenchanted. By the time they wanted to leave China, it was too late. During the Cultural Revolution, which began in 1966, Dr. Lo was "put up on the wall" and regularly denounced as a "rightist" and a supporter of bourgeois ideology. Although they were allowed to stay in Shanghai, their living quarters were repeatedly ransacked. Dr. Lo was often reviled in public and subject to many interrogations. Their children were exiled to the countryside. Although both wanted to leave China, they could not do so before Dr. Lo died of a heart attack in 1969. Despite his death and being an American citizen, she was not allowed to return to America.

Ruth sounded like a fascinating woman, and I asked Kathy to meet her. In early December 1978, we drove to Boulder, where Ruth lived in a small apartment. She indeed was a lively and engaging conversationalist, and over tea and cookies, she told a fascinating and horrifying story of life during the Cultural Revolution. Of course, we've learned much more about the Cultural Revolution in the years since, and there have been many extraordinary firsthand accounts. Still, Ruth's is one of the very few eyewitness accounts by a native-born American and is unique in its perspective. Unfortunately, her book, *In the Eye of the Typhoon*, written with Kathy, is no longer in print, although you can still find it on Amazon.

Ruth's story was so unique that I thought it would be of interest to the *M/L* audience, and I asked Ruth and Kathy if I could try to interest Robin and Jim in interviewing Ruth. They were enthusiastic, and so were Robin and Jim. A month later, Jim flew to Denver, and on January 5th, 1979, we taped the ½ hour show with Ruth, which aired on January 9th.

In the final couple of minutes of the show, Jim asked her what America looked like after a forty-year absence.

> Beautiful! (*Laughs.*) I had no idea that it was going to be such a moving experience. But when I saw those mountains back of Boulder, it was really ... it really made me cry. ... The people here are so beautiful -- these tall young people with their long hair, even their beards, I find really astonishingly beautiful. The way they walk and their friendly atmosphere. The first few days I was here, I went out for a short walk. I met absolutely strange young people on the road and, "Hi, Ma, how are you? Beautiful day, isn't it?" Well, it was such a change from the atmosphere of being very careful: "Do I know this person? Dare I speak to that person?" It was just like a new world, and I loved every bit of it. (*Laughing.*)

Jim was tearing up as the show ended. He continued on to the annual PBS meeting that weekend, and I was told he talked about the show during his speech on Saturday night. For several years it was the highest-rated show we ever aired.

I made two other attempts to interest Robin in someone I found worth spending a half-hour with. The first was with a young, disabled playwright who Amy told me about because she was directing the premiere of one of his plays in Chicago. The second was with an old, rediscovered musician.

RON WHYTE
A proposal

Ron Whyte is a playwright who lives in New York. He is, I would guess, in his forties. He is also a double amputee, has a deformed left hand, is legally blind, and is slowly losing his hearing. He is, without question, one of the forty or fifty million people that this country calls "disabled" or "handicapped."

He is a produced playwright. In New York, it has been off or off-off Broadway. Out of town, it has been in such places as the Arena Theater in Washington and St. Martin's Theater in Chicago. A young writer developing and honing his craft in what is becoming the new way – through America's regional theaters. His plays have included *Welcome to Andromeda, Disabilities,* and to be opened next week, *Funeral for a One Man Band.*

After a couple of postponements (side trips to Iran, e.g.), I met with him on Friday, March 2, in his home.

Ron lives on West 99th Street between West End Avenue and Riverside Drive. It is not one of New York's better blocks. But, as he said to me when I left that evening, "You'd better walk up the left side of the street. Too many vacant buildings on the other side." His apartment, which is five or six rooms, is overflowing. Floor to ceiling books. Records. Tapes of plays (his own and others). It is a perfect reflection of himself and his interests. He is interested in everything. But the books are almost a metaphor for him as he talks. The words pour out of him when he talks. Ideas, observations, and most continuously, his point of view – what he sees in the world about him.

I should mention, before I forget, that despite the lack of two legs he walks. He has two artificial legs, and he uses them, usually with one crutch. He says people think about you differently if you have only one crutch. When you have two, people think there is really something wrong with you. With one crutch, you are obviously on the mend from a skiing accident or something.

My grandfather used to say in his declining years, as he was putting on this or that brace, "I used to get up in the morning. Now I assemble myself." Ron Whyte does the same thing, although it is more than a matter of putting on braces. It is, in fact, the conscious construction of an attitude toward the world, toward life and living, as well as the daily putting on of a pair of legs. "When I grew up," he says, "I had two choices. I could be either Helen Keller, or I could be Captain Hook. I decided to be Captain Hook." This basic stance of aggressiveness and assertiveness characterizes his relationship with the world. It is not, it should be understood, a particularly hostile stance. On the contrary, it is one that insists on not being taken for a cripple – someone who needs to be taken care of, someone to feel sorry for, to feel guilty about, to be ashamed of, to hide away in the closet.

This daily construction, for example, starts with his clothes. He wears denim and leather and chains and, sometimes, dark glasses. He can be, I daresay, a rather menacing figure. Yet, despite the neighborhood in which he lives, even though if you pushed him, he would simply fall over, he has never been mugged. He seems to be saying that people will take you for what you tell them you are. If by his dress he is telling the local toughs and junkies that he is a hell of a tough dude and to not be messed with, they seem to have gotten the message.

He wears a sweatband around each wrist. Those have a purpose, too – they define the separation between arm and hand – not something too important for most of us. But as he shows me, pointing to his right arm, his normal arm, first, "You see, arm ... hand." And then, taking off his sweatbands, he points to his right arm again, and no, there is no problem in discerning the arm and the hand. But then he holds up his left arm – shortened and the hand that has, I think, only two fingers – a thumb and one finger – neither of which even look normal – and says, "But what is this. You can't really tell what it is. But if you put the bands back on," which he does, "all of a sudden it makes sense. You see? Arm ... hand." He's right.

He notes about clothes, "It's a $35 solution to a $1500 design problem." Doctors suggest wearing baggy pants that can easily be taken off, but he doesn't. He just leaves them on his legs and takes the legs off instead. Of course, if he liked the way baggy pants looked, he might change his mind. But he doesn't, and besides, he figures it takes him about 20 minutes to put on or take off a pair of pants, so why do it when you don't have to? He also notes that denim wears well, and most other fabrics don't, so there's a money consideration as well. If he were to wear different kinds of clothes, they would have to be specially designed and sewn, and he sure can't afford that. He does have one suit that he had designed for him. Cost? $1500.

He further notes about his clothes that they are really the closest thing to showing on the outside what is inside: Leather and straps. He seems to be saying, don't hide anything. Be what you are and be it forcefully.

Ron is, informally, a product of mainstreaming. Growing up in Montana, the disabled were either put away in institutions or went to school like everyone else. He went to school.

In his younger years, aside from kids in the Shrine hospitals, where he spent a good deal of time for arthritis and other problems that finally claimed his legs, he went to the regular school where there were no other disabled children. His parents, his father in particular, continuously thrust him forward. If he were home on a Saturday night in his teens, his father might berate him for not having a date. Between that parental attitude and his decision to be Captain Hook, he has obviously survived. He notes, by the way, about hooks: If you're going to have one, why have it blunt: Have it sharp.

Be able to use it for whatever you can. Maximize it, don't min-imize it. It is a characteristic viewpoint.

Just a couple of other notes on things we talked about. He points to Homer, Beethoven, O'Neil, Steinmetz, Cole Porter – all disabled or handicapped and asks where would we be without our disabled artists? Without the *Eroica*, without the light bulb, without the *Iliad*? With forty to fifty million dis-abled people in this country, we need them even more. Not merely for what they can tell us about themselves and about life and living, but for role modeling purposes. He would point, for example, to the women's liberation movement and say that the handicapped are involved in and need the same kind of thing. After women, he says, the handicapped are America's largest minority. He also talks about the credibility of artists. He mentions Kopit and *Wings*, for example, or *Elephant Man*, and likens them to white playwrights writing about blacks and their lack of credibility or, rather, credentials.

I would be remiss if I didn't mention at least a couple of other stories. There is, for example, how Ron got to be 6'1" when he actually started out at about 5'8". He kept trying on different sizes of legs until he found a height that he liked. His shoe size is his doctor's, and, as he says, it's a good thing that his doctor had big feet. There is also a story about trying to give his foot (the real, original one) to a sculptor friend in San Francisco, much to the horror of the hospital (his friend never got it). There is also a hilarious story about a taxi that stopped with its tire on his foot and him trying to get the cab to move.

He has a great fund of these stories with a real point but range from amusing to hilarious rather than somber and serious. It is a characteristic of him and his plays. He says he is an entertainer, and his plays are meant to entertain. It is true, but it is also disingenuous. But it is also one reason why an interview with him would be unusual.

The rest of the proposal contained elements that I thought should be in the program and are irrelevant here. What matters, ulti-mately, is that we didn't make the program. What matters more is that *Funeral March* opened in Chicago to glowing reviews. What matters (to me, at least) is that Amy won Chicago's equivalent to that year's Tony Award, one of her finest moments in the theater.

Ron Whyte died in September 1989. He was 47.

On Sunday, March 11ᵗʰ, 1979, nine days after meeting Ron Whyte, a month after returning from Tehran and the Iranian Revolution, I spent an afternoon with Professor Longhair and his young manager in New Orleans. On my return, I sent a report of my meeting to Robin.

PROFESSOR LONGHAIR
a legend no one ever heard

He's been described by others as "a living legend" and as the "Bach of rock and roll." His name is Henry Roeland Byrd – Professor Longhair – and hardly anyone outside New Orleans and the music business has ever heard of him.

We've become used to thinking of music and the music industry in the terms which it has wanted us to view it. Platinum and gold. Months spent in the recording studio. Multimillion-dollar recording contracts. Huge promotional campaigns. SRO in Madison Square Garden and arenas around the country. The Bee Gees and Fleetwood Mac, not to mention the Beetles of not-so-yesteryear, are examples of the most visible and highly promoted part of the music business. However, we don't often hear of the others who live on the fringes of success – those who are, despite their frustration and lack of monetary success, true creative artists by any definition of the word.

Professor Longhair belongs to the legion of artist – black or otherwise – who have struggled to make a living at their chosen art. What makes 'Fess's experience so touching and frustrating is that his was and is an authentic and unique musical voice which has affected the aesthetic experience of this country by his influence on popular music in the early fifties in particular. His reward for giving us what was best in him has been poverty, fifteen years of virtual seclusion, drunkenness, and being taken advantage of by the business professionals of the music industry. It has also been rediscovery by a small group of people determined to have 'Fess given his due.

Of course, you have to hear his music to hear 'Fess. Otherwise, nothing else matters. He plays me a few bars of a B_b shuffle, a relatively standard blues-type progression. And then he plays it the way he might choose to play it. It is not the same, and the differences matter. First of all, they are noticeable to anyone. Second, and most importantly, there is a joyousness in 'Fess's style, which is simultaneously free and tightly controlled, and there is an almost impossible to control the desire to tap your toes, to move, to feel the beat, the rhythm, the pulse.

Why, then, has it been so difficult for 'Fess to make a living from his music over the years? He talks about New Orleans. He says that one of the problems in his hometown is, in effect, an overabundance of good music. People don't really expect to have to pay to hear music. They can go down to the French Quarter, stand outside the door, and listen to it for nothing. They can stand on the streets and listen to the street musicians.

And how about outside New Orleans, where most New Orleans musicians playing New Orleans music have never really been able to break through? Allison Kaslow, his manager, says that for some reason, people outside of New Orleans can't seem to "get down" with the music. It is almost too free and pulsating with life for people in the north.

'Fess plays another example. It is a complex piece where two separate things are going on between the left hand and the right hand. Some critics have said that it is difficult for sidemen to play with him. Andy Kaslow, Allison's husband and a member of 'Fess's band, says it is because of the contrapuntal nature of much of his music. His music is filled with its own particular quirks and gimmicks. The polyrhythmic structure of his work. I mention Dave Brubeck, remembering his playing with varying rhythms in *Take Five*. 'Fess doesn't remember Brubeck at all.

The hardest thing about it for 'Fess is that because his music is challenging to play, it is difficult to have sidemen stay with him when he isn't getting much money to pay them. He'd rather have a drummer who really didn't know how to play so that he could train him his way. One of the fundamental problems, he says, with the recently released *Live on the Queen Mary* album is that the drummer, aside from being only 18, had never played with him before. It sounds like it. Any drummer leaving 'Fess and going to another band would find that he would have to completely change his style.

That, of course, is one of the ways that 'Fess has managed to be such an influence. There were all those people who played with him who he insisted play his way. He tried then and now to create music that other musicians would want to play because it was interesting for them, and the audience so obviously enjoyed it. He tells a story of how in the '40s, he was asked to sit in with a band that wasn't drawing on Bourbon Street. The people walking by would stop and listen, and gradually the place began to fill up. He might have just been sitting in, but he was playing his music.

Of course, to keep a band with you, you have to be able to pay them. Not just for performing, but for rehearsing, too. It's the only way for them to learn your material, and it's the only way to allow it to develop and mature. He has a band now, but they only play 26 songs because he doesn't make enough to have the rehearsal time to teach them the dozens of other songs he has written over the years.

II.

He's 60 years old now. His face is lined and grizzled by age and hard times. His eyes sometimes have a slightly devilish twinkle, and his impish grin is dominated by the single gold tooth which stands out in obvious contrast with the empty spaces surrounding it.

Esquire music critic Albert Goldman wrote of 'Fess, "What did he get for giving Elvis his *Blue Suede Shoes* voice? Little Richard, his boogie frenzy? Fats Domino, his rumba left hand?

Dr. John his catchy, quirky, off-the-wall licks? Why the usual poverty humiliation and indifference that our great country has traditionally bestowed on its black musical geniuses."

Except for his first few months, 'Fess has lived in New Orleans for all of his 60 years. His mother, a musician herself, taught him what he knew of music. She taught him to play the guitar, bass, drums, piano, Jew's harp, and harmonica. When he was around 10, they would play together whenever she was home. In his early teens, he either left home or traveled with his mother in various minstrel and sideshows, mostly doing stunts of one sort or another.

His first attempts at earning money playing music were of a pretty amateurish sort when he was 18 or 19 years old. "A dollar was a dollar in them days. It was the depression. I got slapped around pretty good, and I decided I wanted to study something that I could do myself, and I decided that I could become a musician if I had something to become a musician with. I didn't have any money to buy any instrument, and I got to thinking; about it. Build me something. At that time, guys was comin' up with tubs with one string and makin' a bass out of it. If he could make a bass out of a tub, I could make a drum out of a box. I got me a soapbox and some tin cans. Broken bean cans. Sardine cans. And I went down by the Lafayette Theater, and I got these big reels that the films come in that they show in the movies, so I made a cymbal out of one and a snare drum out of the other, and I fixed me a box drum so with the tub and the drum we used to go up and down Wortham and _____ Street playin', you know, in the street, and guys dancin', pick up a few bucks and we divide it up. And one guy got smart and wanted to stash some money, and we get into a fight and break up the whole band." His first foray into music as a street musician ended in failure and frustration.

He went into the Civilian Conservation Corps working at every job there was -- hard physical labor. But at night, there was often a piano around, and he would play. And if there wasn't a piano, someone would find one and bring it over in a truck so that he could play. It was his real apprenticeship.

It was when he began to find out that not only did he enjoy playing, but that others enjoyed his playing – that he might actually have something to give.

After he came out of the CCC, he formed his first professional band and received a piece of advice, which obviously influenced him a great deal. It wasn't enough just to play. He had to take a song – a piece of music – and find a way to make it uniquely his own. 'Fess's thoughts about music – about playing, about sidemen, about audiences, about other musicians, about other's compositions – all revolve around this single driving obsession. 'Fess talks about working all the time. He dreams. And his dreams are about songs, about playing and singing. How to do it so that it will entertain an audience. He rehearses it in his sleep. It is a never-ending process, and the songs and the music constantly evolving.

As with all improvisers, Andy Kaslow notes, music constantly evolves. Listen to a Jelly Roll Morton number, for example, recorded in 1920 and then in 1939. His manager says that his songs even change from month to month. 'Fess wishes the one album from 1949 (on Atlantic) would disappear. He doesn't like the way it sounds anymore. It is no longer his. He won't even play a song for me the way he did in '49 and the way he does now so that I can hear the difference.

But all this striving for perfection, for change, for having his own voice, did not help him make money. On the contrary, it may even have hurt. Someone once wrote that most of the hard-luck stories coming out of New Orleans seemed to involve Professor Longhair.

If there is something which 'Fess has on his mind almost as much as his music, it is money. It's pretty hard to pay the rent and feed and clothe yourself, much less a family, on $9 a night, which is what he would make in the early days. That's assuming you worked every night, which you didn't. That is, assuming you were paid every night, which you weren't. "Sorry," the club owner might say, "I just don't have it tonight." And you would play anyway because that's all you really wanted to do. And the pressure would start to build, and maybe you would start to drink. And drugs were always around. And you would start hiding from people because there you were, Professor Longhair, famous musician, and people would want to know you and they would ask you for money or a cigarette even. There was no way to tell them that you probably had even less money, were even poorer than they were. And maybe you would write a song that someone liked, and you would sell it and the copyright for a few bucks so that you could eat for a little while, and when the song became a hit, you got nothing. If you were ever able to collect on all those royalties to which you sold the rights, you would probably be a rich man by now. And maybe the pressure of it all – the poverty, the drinking, the drugs, being the Professor Longhair, the humiliation – would finally get to be too much. You would gradually just disappear from sight, and for all anyone might know, you had probably died, and they just hadn't heard about when it happened.

Professor Longhair sank out of the music scene almost entirely for fifteen years. By the end of that time, no one knew that he was still alive, and he had become a legend, "one of the Fathers of Rock and Roll." He was rediscovered by accident in 1971 by Quint Davis, one of the producers of the New Orleans Jazz and Heritage Festival. Davis had purchased some records which this aging black man was carrying out to the car for him. The old man was addressed by other store employees as "Professor" and "Longhair." The legendary Professor Longhair was reborn.

I have a few final thoughts about 'Fess. We (and perhaps I mean "I" as much as anything) often talk about integrity, whether journalistic or artistic. It is never very far from our thoughts, even if we don't actively think about it. And we are very middle-class and educated, and we rarely have that integrity seriously tested. Yet, gradually, after talking with 'Fess, I realized that somehow that was precisely what we had been talking about. Here was this aging man, uneducated, not very knowledgeable about what goes on in his business, perhaps a real innocent in so many ways, who had never been able to compromise. He always played his music. And if he couldn't play his music his way, then he just wouldn't play. And if that meant that he would drink to forget and to sweep out stores to earn a dollar, then that is what he would do.

That is, I think, what he did.

We didn't do the program, and a year later, Professor Longhair was dead.

Why did Robin turn down these proposals? Perhaps because neither was tied to any current public policy issue. The battle over the *Americans with Disabilities Act* was far off in the future. Ruth Lo, at least, had been a witness to one of the most tumultuous events in recent history, so her story had a public affairs interest. But Professor Longhair, no matter how influential, was just another poor black musician who had been cheated and bamboozled by better educated, more savvy businessmen. It was an old story in the music business that still happens today despite all we know about it, not only Black musicians. Think, for example, of Taylor Swift, among so many others. Maybe it was because few people had ever heard of 'Fess, even if they were pop music fans. And perhaps it was because Robin didn't seem to like rock and roll or much that smacked of popular culture. He didn't appear to know much about it and didn't want to. Or maybe it was something else.

To me, though, 'Fess's story was tragic and heroic. It was tragic because he cared so passionately about what he could create and was too often denied. It was tragic because the society he lived in wanted to ensure that he wouldn't be too successful and that he should always know his place was at the bottom of the barrel. And it was tragic because what happened to him had to happen because of who he was. It was heroic because he never compromised his integrity and would almost inevitably fall. There may have been better ways to live his life, but he lived it as best he could. But at the end of his life, it was also a hopeful story because he found two people in Allison Miner and her husband, Andy Kaslow, who believed in him, in what he had given them, and could still give to others. They wanted to help him do just that and not simply make money off his greater talent.

And Ron Whyte's story was no less tragic and heroic, doomed by his body, tied to the mast of his sinking ship, and refusing to go gently into the night, he died as he lived, "raging at the dying of the light."

To me, Ron and Fess's stories were no less important than anything else *M/L* did that year. I understood why Robin and Jim might have felt that these stories didn't really belong in the *MacNeil/Lehrer Report,* but I also knew why I thought they did. It wasn't that 'Fess's music was so remarkable or that he was poor or Black. Instead, I cared that he struggled and persevered, that he cared enormously about this one thing, and that finally, before he died, his gift was recognized.

These were things that I felt were as important as "news and public affairs" for a show such as ours to do, not all the time, but sometimes. Of course, people need to know what is happening in government and politics and understand their stake in those areas. But they also need to know how to live in the world. How to survive. How to have courage. How to love. How to die. They need to know how to lead a life of personal integrity and fulfillment and that such a life is possible even for them. If these things had a particular resonance with me because of all my past struggles and current personal concerns and explorations of my own life, then my gravitation towards them was natural and understandable. But my self-interest doesn't and shouldn't diminish the importance of the point.

On the other hand, to Robin and Jim's credit, when the hour-long show began, I was allowed to see my concerns and interests reflected even though we never ever discussed them in those terms in all the years between 1984 and 2009. Did they ever know or even think about what I was trying to do? I have no idea, but I don't think so.

In the meantime, my life outside of work went on. Herman Shonbrun was still very much a part of my life. By now, he and Peggy were divorced after many complications. She had developed MS and moved back to FL. He was a recovering alcoholic and had had a major heart attack. Now Herman had a new wife along with a new, sober life. All this is to say that one December night just before New Year's Day, 1979, a week before the Ruth Lo show, Herman asked if I would like to join them at a dinner party at a friend's apartment. Among the guests was Joan Golub. Joan was working for the William Morris Agency. I soon took advantage of our meeting and asked her to introduce me to the agency, an important relationship over the next few years, even if fruitless. In the longer term, Joan and I became good friends. Her connection to William Morris became particularly important after the incident at Three Mile Island on March 28th, 1979, just three months after we met.

I sometimes think that all TV news shows are mostly "full of sound and fury signifying nothing." They are placeholders, if you will, a time reserved to hold viewers' attention until something significant happens, and then we all know where to turn to find what we need to know. At those times, TV news becomes a vitally important window through which we get to observe, contemplate, and sort of experience the external world we really live in, a world of life and death, and events that directly impact our lives in very significant and immediate ways. Journalists live for those events. Like soldiers and athletes, journalists thrive on adrenaline. When something really big happens, and the adrenaline rushes in, they are ready to charge off and do whatever is necessary to get the story to their audience. The bigger the story, the bigger the rush. Just look at what happened to the cable news networks, the NY Times, and Washington Post during the Trump years when sales and ratings soared only to subside after Joe Biden's election.

On the other hand, television's addiction to the "big" story and noisy controversy can be manipulated. Donald Trump is the prime example of a politician's ability to gain coverage and popularity. By continually making outrageous speeches during the campaign for the 2016 election, CNN became convinced to air entire campaign events for weeks on end. I don't think that had ever happened before. As president, Trump made sure that he was the lead story on almost every news broadcast day after day. He achieved this by always making a statement personally and being totally outrageous. I don't think it mattered to him if something was true or false as long as it got him coverage. And it didn't matter if the coverage was positive or negative as long as it was there. In fact, I think he preferred negative coverage. It gave him one more enemy to fight.

In the process, Trump gained a fiercely loyal following. He may not have had quite enough votes in battleground states to win reelection in 2020, but it laid the groundwork for either a future victory in 2024 or a mechanism to overthrow the government. At the time I'm writing this (in early 2022), I'm not sure the American experiment in democracy will escape intact.

But back to *MacNeil/Lehrer*.

The partial meltdown at the Three Mile Island nuclear plant in 1979 was a brief and very scary moment in our relatively recent, purely domestic history. It was one of those stories that gets the adrenaline flowing. And the more we found out about it after the initial headlines and aftermath, the scarier it got. Two weeks after the incident, transcripts of the Nuclear Regulatory Commission's secret meetings were published in the *NY Times*. They were stunning. They were so unusual that I thought they should be dramatized and I began a two-year effort to do just that.

Although I don't have the final memo that I wrote for Hollywood about TMI, I do have bits and pieces of drafts from which I have cobbled together the following pages, which were written on July 9th, 1979, six months after the incident. They are the clearest recollection I have of what happened at TMI (as seen through my eyes only), how *M/L* reacted to it, and my ideas about its dramatic possibilities. I am sure there is some hyperbole, particularly about my role in this tale. Nevertheless, I include the whole thing, somewhat edited, because it is probably as good a nuts and bolts description as I know of how *The MacNeil/Lehrer Report* reacted to one truly important news story. Besides, I still think it was an important story all these years later.

The incident at Three Mile Island began in the early morning hours of Wednesday, March 28th, 1979. Regardless of what the final determination is of the cause of the incident – mechanical failure, design mistake, human error, or some unforeseen or unforeseeable act of God – the basic element is simple: A valve was stuck, or an instrument gave an incorrect reading, or somebody misinterpreted data, or someone turned something the wrong way, and the core of the reactor was uncovered and was proceeding to heat up uncontrollably thus threatening a meltdown and the actualization of a China

Syndrome, and threatening to spew massive amounts of radiation into the atmosphere.

It is vital that what happened, what actually caused the accident, or the series of accidents doesn't matter in a dramatic sense because so much was unknown. But what people thought, guessed, or hoped was happening was everything. So the story we are going to tell is one of the perceptions. How did the NRC perceive what was happening? How did the White House view it? And what did Pennsylvania's governor think? What did you and I think was happening? How did the people of Harrisburg, Hershey, and Middletown perceive what was happening? And how did everyone react?

For me, TMI really began in the middle of the afternoon of Wednesday, the 28th. I had seen the wire bulletins, and there had been some discussion about the advisability of doing a program on Thursday, the next night. Finally, we decided to originate a program out of Hershey on Thursday. Early indications were that it would be easy. Three guests: someone from the state, someone from Metropolitan Edison (MetEd), which was the operating power company, and somebody from the anti-nuclear groups. The government and MetEd indicated their willingness to cooperate. We didn't bother calling the "moaners" because they tend to be eagerly available most of the time. I arranged for studio facilities at the local PBS affiliate in Hershey as we prepared to leave that night. I would pick up a clean pair of socks and underwear locally sometime the next day. I should have known better.

As I was preparing to leave for TMI that night, I listened to the CBS Evening News. Walter Cronkite called it the worst nuclear accident in the history of nuclear power, and I thought that this really was one hell of a story – even bigger than I had thought – and what kind of mess were we getting into? Later, MetEd blamed the press for exaggerating the danger. Indeed, they later made a promo film that said there never really was anything to worry about. It was a blatant lie. In later testimony, Richard Thornburgh, the Republican governor, said that through the first three days, press reports were more reliable in what they were printing than the information he was receiving from official sources, meaning MetEd in particular and possibly the NRC as well.

Thursday morning proved bright and fair. It was early spring, and the weather for the past few days had been chilly enough for me to be wearing my sheepskin coat, but the morning was warm enough for me to leave it in my room. While MacNeil and the show producer went to a press conference held at the Hershey Inn by MetEd, I went off to the TV station to coordinate our efforts and start putting up sets, lighting, graphics, etc.

Later, MacNeil told me that the press conference was like being in "amateurville." The officials of MetEd had never faced a crowd of ravenous reporters covering a major national breaking story and didn't know how to handle it or themselves. It was, he said, a bloodbath.

While he went to shoot an opening for that night's show in the shadows of TMI, I sent someone else to cover the anti-nuke rally in Harrisburg in which Professor Sternglass made his recommendation that pregnant women be evacuated. It was, needless to say, pooh-poohed by everyone in authority who could be gotten say anything.

Meanwhile, a reporter was starting to line up specific guests. MetEd agreed to appear on the show, then equivocated, and finally backed out, although they never specifically said they wouldn't appear. Finally, a representative from the Atomic Industrial Forum (AIF, the prime industry-wide organization) agreed to appear in MetEd's place if they didn't show up. He later backed out too on instructions, he said, from the organization's headquarters in Washington. We wanted an anti-nuke but not a "crazy." It seemed as though it was mostly the crazies on the scene.

Senators Hart and Heinz, in the meantime, arrived by helicopter to be briefed by Gov. Thornburgh. MacNeil came back to write his opening copy (what was understood about the cause of the accident so far) and another producer went off to see Heinz and Hart come out of their meeting with the governor. When they emerged, they said they weren't happy with the information, and there was too much that no one knew. Heinz agreed to appear if we would take him in Washington. I thought he wanted to get out of Hershey as fast as he could. We agreed, and I ordered the DC studio fired up. Lieutenant Governor Scranton of PA said he'd appear. There was a representative of the NRC rumored to be somewhere on the scene. I tried to track him down and failed. The Washington office of the NRC wasn't helpful. Was it possible that the NRC really didn't have a rep somewhere in the vicinity or on the site?

Henry Kendell, a founder of the Union of Concerned Scientists, and definitely not crazy, agreed to appear from Boston if we could arrange it. We could, and WGBH's facilities were arranged for, video and audio lines were ordered, and a three-city hookup was in place. However, we still lacked an industry spokesman and finally convinced the AIF in Washington to send us someone. In the meantime, the TV station's VP had been in and out all day feeding me contacts and information, as were their local news producers and reporters.

We went on the air and had as good a handle on the situation as anybody did that day. We congratulated ourselves for being on top of the story, to have hit it at its peak, to have once again provided something far more solid than the commercial networks had. We had a drink with our Washington staff, which had come up to help. Then, MacNeil and I drove off to meet our charter flight and flew home, watching the containment shell and stacks bathed in floodlights almost beneath us as we drifted towards New York. The pilot assured us we were upwind of any possible radiation emissions. For us, TMI was over.

Right?

Wrong.

In fact, TMI had barely begun.

In New York, Friday, March 30th dawned bright and fair. But, at TMI, the weather was not so good. A low-pressure system had moved in. The skies were probably gray or at least somewhat overcast and hazy. There was the possibility of rain. The winds were light, maybe 5 miles per hour.

In the early post-dawn hours, something unexpected happened. For some inexplicable reason, a puff of vapor, maybe steam, was automatically ejected from the TMI plant. It wasn't supposed to happen — it just did. And that puff was loaded with radiation. 1200 millirems worth. It rose high above the stacks and then drifted like a plume to the northeast in the light breeze.

Somehow, word got to the NRC. At 9:15, an NRC staffer called the Pennsylvania State Police and suggested that an evacuation for an area five miles downwind of the plume might be in order. The State Police could do nothing of the sort without the governor's direct order. Somehow, word of the uncontrolled release and the NRC staffer's recommendation got to the governor's office. Someone in that office apparently called the NRC (presumably the Bethesda Incident Center) and asked for the Commission's official advice. Should the governor order an evacuation?

Was that staffer right? If right and nothing was done about it (someone in the governor's office notes later that morning), the governor is going to "have a problem."

This fundamental question lies at the heart of the NRC transcripts and at the heart of this drama.

You will recall what I said at the beginning – that what physically happened to the reactor and how it happened doesn't matter for the purposes of this show. This program deals in perceptions, the perception of apparent reality while the event was occurring. Decisions, after all, are based on what one thinks is happening, or on what one hopes is happening, or on what one pretends isn't happening. This program will be based on the real world and how things happen. It will not use hindsight to justify actions or non-actions. Instead, it will use what was known and let us see the decisions as they were being made. In so doing, we will be making those decisions for ourselves as well.

A week or two after the incident, NRC staffer Dr. Roger Mattson (I think), who had made an impassioned plea for evacuation on March 30th, was asked in testimony before a congressional committee if evacuation had proved to be necessary. He said no. He was not asked if, given the same data available on that day, and without knowing the future, he would have come to a different conclusion. I presume he would probably still have recommended evacuation.

To return to our story.

Who was it that first picked up what was happening inside TMI? I don't know. At around 9:30, urgent bells ringing, lights flashing, the AP wire started chattering the first bulletins in a day that would build in tension until it partially broke 13 hours later.

When did they hear about it in Harrisburg? Probably around the same time. It is not too difficult to imagine what was happening. Most people were already at work. The kids were busy in the first school period of the day. The dairy cows were probably back out in the meadows after being milked. Farmers were plowing their acreage, getting ready for the spring planting. A mom might be doing the breakfast dishes or making the beds. It was a typical day in this semi-rural area, except for one thing. Everybody was listening to the radio or had the TV on.

For two days, they had been living under a shadow, and it was a particularly menacing sort of shadow. Some people lived virtually beneath the three stacks of the containment structure of TMI. Those stacks dominated the landscape of an area of Pennsylvania that is essentially flat and rolling. And something was going on inside them. It was something that you couldn't see and you couldn't touch, but it was there nonetheless. And it wasn't entirely under control, no matter what MetEd had to say. Some people who were afraid of it have already picked up and left to visit a relative somewhere else. But most people had stayed. After all, nuclear power was really safe. Everything that could go wrong with a reactor was known and planned for. There were backup systems on top of backup systems. Every possibility had been checked out by computers. So there was nothing really to worry about, right?

Right?

And then the latest word came over the radio. There was this uncontrolled thing, this puff, this cloud, this thing that you couldn't see or touch or smell, and it had escaped, and now what was to be done? How dangerous was it? Where is it? I just can't pick up and leave, I mean, I've got fifty cows over there in the pasture, and you just can't leave them ... Florida would be lovely. Still, I sure can't afford to go stay in a hotel for God knows how long ... It was thoughtful of my son to call when he heard the news, but I don't know what to tell him, and I wonder if maybe I just should go and spend some time with him and his family since we haven't seen each in the past few months.

At 9:57 (?), a call comes in from an anonymous staffer at the Bethesda Incident Center telling headquarters to gather the Commissioners, tell "Congressional to get on the stick," and start "banging this up to the White House Situation Room." This is serious stuff. Things just don't get "banged" up to the White House unless they are damned serious.

Do they?

And so the NRC gathered in official session behind closed doors to consider what should be done. They gathered in Washington in the Commission's headquarters on H Street, the top staff people in Bethesda. The Governor of Pennsylvania gathered with his advisers in the State House in Harrisburg.

What should be done?

What should be done about this plume of radiation streaming out from TMI? Should the NRC officially recommend evacuation? That's the first question. What are the radiation levels? What's the weather, the wind? How many people are involved? What's the situation inside TMI? Can this happen again?

So it begins, the continuous closed-door sessions of the NRC dealing with the worst nuclear energy crisis yet experienced in the United States, one that, if they don't get under control, will affect the lives of thousands and potentially millions of people. It is the NRC, successor to the Atomic Energy

Commission, upon whose shoulders these momentous decisions rest.

Who are the leading players in this part of our drama? First and foremost, there is Joe Hendrie, Chairman of the NRC. He is a man in his late fifties or early sixties. Tall, I would guess, and rather spare. A decisive face. A leader. A scientist-politician. A technocrat. Physicist. Formerly with Brookhaven. Longtime supporter and advocate of nuclear power.

Second, there is Harold Denton. A man in his forties, probably. Unlike the commissioners, he is a professional staff person. It is he who will ride off like the cavalry to TMI to bring order out of chaos. Not only does he know his profession, but he is skilled at handling people and the press, as he demonstrates that night.

Third, there is Roger Mattson. Another physicist and staff member and clearly in his thirties, bearded, and by far the most passionate person we hear from. He has no hesitation in saying what is on his mind. If Denton is the ideal person to be dealing with the public, then Mattson is the right guy to be hammering at MetEd, B&W, and anybody else who he thinks is either trying to con him or just not willing to look at the truth.

Victor Galinsky was initially the Acting Chairman since Hendrie was away the day the incident began, although he returned by the time of the closed-door meetings.

Others, including Joe Fouchard (probably a press or PR liaison), are present. But of the major players, there are a couple of things to note. First, staff people may be free to make recommendations, but they don't make policy decisions. It's the commissioners who must make those decisions, who must weigh, through whatever means they choose, the various risks and cost/benefit ratios, etc., of any decision. How big a chance should they take? On my behalf? On yours? Second, there is an apparent generational difference between the commissioners and their staff. This is not merely reflected in age but also in points of view. It is no accident, I think, that the staff is in favor of evacuation while the commissioners are opposed. For example, early the following week, when the commissioners discuss Governor Jerry Brown's request to have Rancho Seco closed down, they reject it. A week or two later, it is Mattson who, on behalf of the staff, recommends that Rancho Seco, as well as all the other B&W plants, be temporarily shut down. This time he prevails. To these younger scientists, the situation at TMI is much far more complicated and dangerous than the commissioners, particularly Joe Hendrie, ever seem to think it is. Are the commissioners out of touch with reality, or is the staff?

Yet, a decision must be made by the NRC commissioners. What information do we have? Not much. Where can it be gotten from? TMI. So what's the problem? They won't call us back with the data. Meanwhile, Joe Fouchard keeps saying they've got to call the governor. But they don't. They need more information. But they can't get the information. Well, what's the weather like there? Winds of about 5 mph. Hmmm. That means that it's traveled about this far downwind. Spread out pretty wide. And they start talking about something else. How likely is the event to reoccur? Denton says very likely. They should evacuate a part of the population. Hmmm. They talk about something else. Anything else other than should we, the commissioners, recommend evacuation or not.

That morning, Friday, March 30th, I arrived at the office at about 10 am happily attired in clean clothes. As I was the first one in that day of the crew that had gone to TMI, I was handed an AP bulletin that spoke of an uncontrolled release of high dosage radioactivity into the atmosphere. I could not help but remember the large geodetic survey map of the TMI area adorning the wall of the room in Hershey, out of which I had worked the previous day. More than once, I had stopped to look at it – looking at where we were in relation to TMI and where the airport was and thinking that in taking off, we would have to pass close to the stacks and also knowing where everyone was at all times so that in case we had to get out fast it could be accomplished with a minimum of fuss. That bulletin scared me more than anything had to that point. Every piece of news that had come out since word of the accident first appeared seemed to get worse and worse. No matter how hard MetEd had been trying to downplay the event, the facts always seemed to imply hidden dangers. The more MetEd tried to minimize things, the more worried I got.

With the NRC keeping a quiet and low profile, with the White House standing mute, how could we not do another story? Maybe we have been wrong all along about some things. Perhaps we should have one of the "crazies" on. They seemed to be righter than anyone else was so far. And where were the Feds? Where was President Carter, who actually knew something about nuclear power?

Al Vecchione, the Executive Producer, came in, and I took him the copy. He had just seen *The China Syndrome* the previous week and had visions of meltdowns dancing in his head. He went into a fit and talked for fifteen minutes before running out of gas. We had to do something!

MacNeil came in, ever the voice of reason and calm in the storm. There really isn't anything to be alarmed about yet. Radiation dosages thus far released have been relatively small. Even the announced release of the cloud didn't amount to too much when you figured on the spread. We have never done two shows in succession on the same subject. We were on top of it, and we had done a first-rate show last night, better probably than the networks had done. We were about to have our weekly planning meeting and could discuss it briefly then.

As the meeting was gathering in New York and Washington, I went off to phone up the TV station in Hershey. What was happening? They didn't really know more than the AP bulletin but had people on the move to find out. Could they supply us news crews if needed? Could they provide a studio? Would they continue to keep me informed? Yes, to everything, and could they now go and continue their emergency planning for moving the studio and on-air operations should an evacuation be ordered?

Our planning meeting was in progress. MacNeil didn't want to do anything unless events further deteriorated. If we did decide to do a show, what would it be? Two things are decided – we want a Commissioner from the NRC, and we want to talk about the dangers of low-level radiation. And what about the weather? I told them. Low pressure, not much wind. Good, he said. I think we all felt the same. A call from Hershey. The Governor would make a statement at 12:30. They would feed it to us.

At 12:30, the Governor announces the evacuation of pregnant women and children. People should stay inside. He has talked to the White House, and they are sending up a special representative, later revealed to be Harold Denton of the NRC; information, he says, has been difficult to get.

There is no question about it now; we will do a story and gear up. Hershey agrees to send a crew out to an evacuation center. If it is good, we will take up to a five-minute story, a minimum of two. They will keep their studio on standby. And how, I wonder, does the engineer with the pregnant wife who lives on the banks of the river in sight of TMI feel now? Hershey doesn't know. They haven't seen him yet today. And yes, of course, they will re-feed the press conference because there had been a video problem in the original transmission. They'll also feed an impromptu press conference held earlier by MetEd. Feed schedules of various local network video lines are rearranged with a combination of negotiation, arm twisting, pleading, begging, and, I hope at the time, without lying. I move to the studio control room to better maintain the liaison with Hershey and various editorial, production, and technical strands as they are being woven together. It is now 2 pm. I will spend the next nine hours in the control room, trying to hold everything together.

Our reporters in Washington are doing everything they can to get someone from the NRC to appear. We go to the NRC and get turned down. We try going through the White House. That, finally, works. We will get Commissioner Gilinsky, who will stop at the White House before coming to the studio. The radiation experts are reluctant to come on, but we are confident that we will find the right pair.

The feeds come in roughly on schedule and are being edited as they come in. I think we've thought of almost everything to keep up with the news. A new wrinkle – there will be another press conference by the Governor at 8:30 pm, and PBS wants us to anchor a network feed. A truck from Pittsburgh is setting up for it now.

Meanwhile, the telephone lines to the Harrisburg/Hershey area are tied up. I try every trick I know. Although the phone company cooperates, there is a problem – the operators in Harrisburg won't pick up the phone. They're either too busy, or too few have shown up for work (I bet on the latter). We finally figured out a way of connecting the Engineering PL (Private Line) of the Eastern Educational Network with the PL of the Pennsylvania TV Network, where they intersect in Philadelphia. Will someone in the Harrisburg Network Master Control get somebody to the Pittsburgh truck and have them call me? I get Hershey on the same line and thank them for their help and drop the studio.

The truck calls. We negotiate the format – their talent and our talent. Have I heard that Jody Powell (President Carter's Press Secretary) is about to make a statement in Washington? They hold on, and I get Washington to run it down. It proves untrue. We agree to leave the line open until we're done for the night – whenever that is.

6:30 pm. Half an hour to air. It may be that Gilinsky won't show up. He's been delayed at the White House. So we make plans: We will do the show without him at 7, if necessary. If he shows up a little late, we'll just shove him in. If he shows up really late, we'll hold him and redo the show live at 7:30 for the normal refeed. We notify the network of our plans and settle arrangements with them about that night's special.

8:00 pm. We're ready to go with the special at 8:30. If it gets delayed, we'll hang on. It gets delayed.

By 8:30, the rumors have started in Harrisburg. A general evacuation order is being prepared. Why else the long delay? They are obviously writing up the final order, maybe clearing things through the White House.

Meanwhile, the Governor's press secretary will hold up the Governor's appearance for us if he's ready to go by about 5 minutes before the hour so we don't have to break into a program unnecessarily.

10 pm. At about 30 minutes after the hour, the state officials start to file in for the press conference. We're on the air. It's not an evacuation, and we breathe a sigh of relief. A spare engineer volunteers to go to the bar across the street from the studio and get the executive producer and me a couple of martinis. The problems of the past few days seem to be contained. The evacuation order for pregnant women is still in effect. Harold Denton, the nuke (and NRC) version of the cavalry, has ridden to the rescue, and he sounds believable. A pro is finally on the scene. He sounds like he knows what he is talking about, which is more than any of us have heard for the past three days. He is calm and deliberate. The immediate danger is over. There is a hydrogen bubble that is a source of some concern. They are sure they can lick the problem. The Governor's Press Secretary has been trying to end the conference for ten minutes. He finally does, and it doesn't occur to me for a couple of weeks to wonder why. MacNeil and the local talent in Harrisburg wrap it up. We're off the air.

PBS asks us to do a special over the weekend. We say no unless there are more significant developments. We've already done more than anybody else, and we don't have anything more to add at this point.

Monday, there is a rumor that if the hydrogen bubble doesn't respond to attempts to dissipate it, they will order a general evacuation. We send a reporter to Hershey: Find a family or two to follow in the case of an evacuation. We get a crew on alert.

Tuesday. No evacuation. We do another show on TMI. We give the reporter another day or two in the field before recalling him. The crisis is over.

Once again, we congratulate ourselves; we've done a pretty terrific job on this story. It is really only MacNeil, I think, who catches on that maybe the hydrogen bubble is as serious a problem, if not more so, as what has gone on until now.

It was not until two weeks later that the transcripts of the closed meetings of the NRC began to be published. I missed the original break on NBC Thursday night but saw the New York Times story on Friday night. It was a bombshell for me. No matter how bad we, or rather I, thought the whole thing felt, the transcripts confirmed that it was at least as bad if not worse.

It even began dramatically with that call to NRC head-quarters about gathering the Commissioners and start "banging this up to the White House Situation Room."

Mr. Gossick

Bill, we have got a deteriorating situation up there with regard to some releases. The Governor is asking us to confirm what he is getting from the plant, which says that they had an uncontrolled release of stuff, which may result in something like up to 1200 millirems per hour. Anyway, I have called John Ahearne, I tried to call the Chairman, and he is en route somewhere. Would you get it to Gilinsky and Bradford? We have just started banging this up to the White House Situation Room and everybody else, okay?

NRC transcripts tell us, particularly about Friday, March 30th, that the NRC still did not (maybe) have a representative on the scene two days into the incident. It becomes clear, I think, that neither MetEd nor Babcock and Wilcox (who built the plant) were anxious to have them there. They seemed to be trying to con everybody, including the NRC. They couldn't even get reliable, accurate information. They couldn't get anything, accurate or not.

That is where my notes about the events at TMI end.

Within minutes after reading the NRC's transcripts, I walked into Robin's office. I said that I thought they were extraordinarily dramatic and that something could be done very quickly to put a reenactment of the meetings on the air. Would he be interested? He would and gave me permission to see what I could put together.

Bruce Feldman, my old friend from USC and the best man at my first wedding, was still living in California. He had won an Emmy for his docudrama, *The Defection of Simas Kudirka*, and was willing to adapt the transcripts. Jerry Toobin, Director of Public Affairs Programming at WNET, was interested and ready to support the idea if PBS got behind it and if the money came from somewhere other than WNET. Barry Chase, the Director of Current Affairs Programming at PBS, was prepared to clear time on the network for the show but said that they had no money for the venture. I talked to someone, I don't remember who, at the National Science Foundation and asked for the money. They were very interested, *really* interested, they said, in the possibility and would get back to me right away. A couple of hours later, they came back with their official answer: They had finalized their grants for the year, and no more money remained in the till. Was that really true? Did they really have no money, or had they decided they didn't want to contribute to the foul odor that had suddenly permeated nuclear power?. It's not something I think I even considered, but as I discovered many years later, those suspicions were validated.

Even if it was too late to do the kind of dramatization I had initially envisioned, it gradually occurred to me that there nevertheless was the potential for a dramatic and serious TV movie. I thought, again, it was something that could be turned around fairly quickly. So I called Joan Golub at the William Morris Agency, and she sent me to Steve Weiss, a young agent at the agency. After we met on May 14th, he, too, liked the idea and approached Roger Gimbel, the US head of EMI (the largest producer of Movies of the Week for TV, or MOWs), about the project. Roger was interested, and a meeting was arranged for 9 am on a Saturday morning at his home in Bel Air.

It was a typical morning in the western part of LA, cool and sunny. His house's long, curving driveway was green with trees and shrubs and fenced in pastures where horses grazed. I pulled up to the kitchen door and knocked. No answer. Knocking again, I wondered if Roger had forgotten about the meeting. A third knock. In the dim interior, a woman appeared through the entrance in the far wall of the kitchen. She was blond, wearing a worn blue terrycloth robe, and looked like she was rubbing the sleep out of her eyes. As she neared the door, I gradually recognized her, and she, me. She opened the door. "Jennifer?" I exclaimed as she exclaimed, "Michael?" Of all people to see in the middle of Bel-Air! There I was in sunny LA, talking to Jennifer Warren, a girl who I hadn't seen in 22 years, not since I was 17 and she was 16, a girl I'd had a crush on when I was in the 9th grade at EI, and she had been in the 7th.

Jennifer and I sort of caught up with each other, perhaps neither of us quite knowing how to react to each other in this situation. At least I know I didn't. Were we both feeling terribly awkward, or was it only me? And then Roger came out, and Jennifer left. I think. Or maybe she sat there silently while I explained what I was interested in doing to Roger. He was still interested, and the process would continue. I promised to write something of my thoughts about TMI and the NRC for him and Marion Rees, his Director of Development, after which we could begin to fashion a drama (the memo you've just read).

As enthusiastic as Roger was, there were immediate objections, not from the development people at EMI but, instead, their lawyers. Their reaction was swift and discouraging. On July 12th, Marion Rees (whose enthusiasm for this project never died until the final nail was driven into its coffin) sent a memo to Roger. A copy was sent to Steve Weiss at William Morris, and Steve sent a copy to me.

> In follow-up to yesterday's development meeting specifically with respect to the legal position on proceeding on the 1500 page transcripts, which Mike Saltz has brought to our attention, Gunther Schiff's immediate response was an emphatic "no." His reasons can be amplified separately, but basically that the "privilege" in a congressional hearing is one thing that would certainly not apply to us.
>
> Secondly, there are people who designed THREE MILE ISLAND, including Westinghouse, who can and would sue. Additionally, the people of THREE MILE ISLAND have not waived their right of privacy.
>
> His recommendation is that a better show with less problems would be to fictionalize a THREE MILE ISLAND

story dramatically telling what happens to a community when such a warning is alerted. We should take this under immediate consideration before progressing any further in developing this project.

I'm not a lawyer, and I don't even play one on TV, and now, as then, I thought the objections of Schiff were nonsense, particularly the first paragraph. My guess is that any First Amendment lawyer would tell you that the published transcripts were in the public domain and could be used in any way we saw fit. Consider the *Pentagon Papers*.

The second paragraph, the fear of lawsuits by the corporate interests involved, was where I thought the actual problem lay and, in the long term, would probably prove to be the death of this project. But I wasn't willing to give up on it. So, after talking to Marion and mulling it over, on July 17th, I sent her back another memo detailing the basis of a *roman a clef*. I think it's called being a realist, basing it on Governor Thornburgh's decisions.

This notion apparently didn't appeal to Roger. I can't say that I blame him. I thought it was workable as a story but nowhere near as exciting as a factual docudrama. It was clear from Roger's letter to me at the end of August that he thought the potential legal problems weren't worth fighting. "I'm sorry too – but there just wasn't any way to do the Three Mile Island project without getting us all in a big jam."

I think that it was sometime late that summer that Marion and most of her staff left EMI to start their own production company, NWR Productions. In late September, she was in New York, and we had lunch together. She had not lost interest in TMI and was interested in pursuing the fictionalized version. The attempt to get something done, to get a development deal done with one of the networks, dragged on for a couple of years. A letter to Steve Weiss about the project, written in the summer of 1981, indicates it dragged on at least that long.

The bottom line was this: NBC was very interested in the project even if they recognized some of the potential problems and was interested in making a deal to develop the story. In fact, the project was presented to the Board of Directors of NBC for their approval, and they turned it down. Steve Weiss told me how and why it was rejected.

All TV movies, particularly docudramas, must undergo a rigorous fact-checking process to ensure that allegations can be backed up by credible sources, just as is true of journalism. I remember Bruce Feldman telling me that when he wrote *Kudirka,* he had to validate every line in the script before it was given the green light. This effort protects the network from liability suits.

My understanding from Steve Weiss was that the liability insurance at the time for NBC and, I think the other networks, was underwritten by the Fireman's Fund insurance company, which had a representative on the board of NBC. The Fireman's Fund was also the underwriter of the liability insurance for Babcock & Wilcox, the builders of the steam generation boilers at Three Mile Island.

That's all that Steve said, all he needed to say. The implication was clear: The Fireman's Fund was telling the board that their other client, B&W, would sue if this picture was made. Was it worth fighting the suit to make the picture? Was it *that* important to the network? I know the answer to the question as well as you do. And, in essence, it was the same problem that EMI had been warned about by their lawyers.

Was I disappointed by the decision? Yes. There is no use in pretending that the broadcast TV networks are something other than entertainment providers, a device to attract viewers' eyeballs so that advertisers can reach them. They want to do good work, or as they like to say, "important" work, but that isn't what the networks are really about. Most ... well, maybe not most ... many producers and writers also want to do "important" work in television, and most find out just how much they have to compromise themselves to do it, within short order. For the most, they will shrug and say it's the business. Fight the fights you have a chance to win and forget about the rest. Live to fight another day.

Money, too, is the grease that eases the skid towards compromise. That, along with celebrity or rubbing elbows with celebrities. Success in Hollywood can bring lots of money with it and, of course, fame to the outside world, power in the inside world, and a different kind of celebrity — the kind that brushing up against the real thing leaves you with pixie dust sprinkled on you and lots of gossip to tell. On the other hand, lack of success often breeds hunger and yearning like an addiction. Hollywood can be a terrible disease.

Today's media world is not the same as when I tried to get TMI and other programs produced. The explosion in streaming services like Netflix and Amazon Prime that aren't dependent on advertising means that a considerable amount of original material can be created without regard to the likes or dislikes of individual advertisers. As a result, a project such as TMI might have had much less resistance, at least conceptually. Of course, it could still fail to gain support, but the reasons would be different.

Before I leave Three Mile Island altogether, I'd note the following. In 2021 I had a brief telephone conversation with Victor Gilinsky, a former member of the NRC, who said some things of particular interest about TMI and those closed-door meetings.

1) In their public statements, the NRC wanted to protect the reputation of nuclear power and that, inevitably, colored what they said. In other words, they tried to present a more optimistic picture of the situation than it perhaps warranted.

2) The NRC didn't know the actual condition of the plant until five years after the incident. What they learned was worse than anything that had appeared in any report or congressional testimony. Initially, they didn't know how hot the core was other than that the thermometers were maxed out. Since the highest temperature they could record was 600°, they had no idea how hot the core actually was at the time but merely guessed it was above 1000°. The actual temperature was probably several thousand degrees above that and more dangerous because of that.

3) The original designs for the containment building called for a 10-foot thick concrete base. However, years after the incident, they found that the base had actually been 20 feet thick and that the core had melted through the original 10-foot thick bottom. So, in other words, if I understood Gilinsky correctly, it was only because of this change in the construction, whether intentional or accidental, that we didn't have a China Syndrome or something as calamitous as Chernobyl. That's pretty chilling.

I brought project after project to William Morris and various producing companies like Lorimar, ITC, HBO, PBS, and Columbia. Some — most — were TV projects, some were features. But, almost all had some factual basis.

For example, the Monday before TMI broke, I was having breakfast with someone at PBS about a docudrama that Bruce Feldman wanted to write about the killings at Kent State in 1970. But there were lots of others.

One of my favorites was a TV series to be called *The Pirates*. The idea was based on a story I'd read in the *New York Times* in 1982 that had to do with the interception of boats smuggling drugs outside the territorial waters of the United States.

Since my first visit during the 1976 presidential campaign for our interview with President Ford, I had been to Florida many times. It was clear that the state was changing radically, no longer the Sunshine State, the place where oranges grew, where tourists lay about the beaches, and where everybody who lived there was over 65 and had emigrated from the snowy north. By 1982 six out of the ten American cities with the highest crime rate were in Florida stretched, as I recall, like beads on a string along I 95, the interstate highway connecting the state to the rest of the nation. Drug smuggling was estimated to be the largest industry in the state. Public officials at all levels of government were being investigated and indicted for their involvement in illegal activities. Despite an extensive Federal anti-drug effort, drug trafficking seemed largely unchecked. South Florida was an armed camp with dissident groups from practically every Latin American country, revolutionaries, counter-revolutionaries, criminals, and even law-abiding citizens. In the war against crime, the criminals were winning.

Against this background, I set a television series about a group of private citizens who had been granted a secret "letter of marque" to hunt for drug smugglers beyond the twelve-mile limit. And since what they were doing wasn't exactly secret, they, in turn, were being pursued on land by their foes.

I thought it was a good idea for a series, as did the folks in Hollywood with whom I was working. We kept at it for a year or so before CBS decided that they didn't really want to do it, explaining that no one (supposedly meaning in the viewing audience) would be interested in a series set in Miami.

A year later, in 1984, *Miami Vice* had its premiere. So much for CBS's acumen in judging the American viewing public, at least in this case.

I don't think *The Pirates* was as good an idea, much less a better idea than *Miami Vice*. *Miami Vice* was a brilliant show conceptually and in its execution, notably how it used popular music and its visual and fashion style, a style that ranged from the colors of buildings to the colors of Sonny Crocket's t-shirts. If Sonny wasn't entirely original, he was unique enough, and Don Johnson was terrific. It is interesting, though, that both ideas were mining similar territory. Michael Mann and I had both seen the same Florida and recognized its potential for television. Now, if I had only thought of Phil Collins ...

> **I can feel it coming in the air tonight, (Oh lord)**
> **And I've been waiting for this moment,**
> **for all my life, (Oh lord)**
> **Can you feel it coming in the air tonight,**
> **oh lord, (Oh lord)**
> **—Phil Collins**

Of course, a thousand other producers may have had the same general idea, and it was Mann's that got developed first. Who knows? It's even possible that CBS had been pitched and passed on *Miami Vice* before they had seen *The Pirates*. It wouldn't be the first time someone passed on a project simply because they had read something similar to it before. Networks are wary about potential accusations of plagiarism, as are writers and producers.

Another project was *Lavender Mountain*, an hour-long dramatic series set in a boarding school in the mountains near Rome, Georgia, that still exists. The original Berry School was founded in 1902. Though initially for white boys only, today, it is co-educational, multi-racial, and includes a college. The series was set during the Depression. It wasn't, like most boarding schools, for rich kids. Instead, it was a school for people who were poor either because of pre-existing conditions or as a result of the ever-grinding Depression. In particular, it was for the poor of the Lookout Mountains, one of the poorest areas of America. Almost everyone there was on a scholarship of some sort. But the school was conceived of as self-supporting. Everyone, youngest kids to oldest, worked on the school's farm raising produce that they'd eat and sell, and animals, too, for meat, for milk, for wool, and for sale. Martha Berry, the school's founder and guiding light, believed in the redemptive power of work.

"Too soft" was how one network put it about this show intended for the 8 pm time period, so-called "family time." And what was *Little House on the Prairie,* I wondered?

No matter. There was more where that came from.

For example, *The Murder Trial of Charles Head,* another docudrama, this time about the murder trial in Mississippi of a black Vietnam Marine veteran, a survivor of nine months of the long-range reconnaissance patrols deep into Viet Cong territory as a nineteen-year-old, who killed his first man just before his 20th birthday. A woman and an old man were among his six other known victims. His military career came to an end after his patrol was ambushed. He was the point man and the first hit, twice in the gut.

> Defendant, a resident of Houston, Texas, traveled to Shreveport in search of his wife and three children who had left the family home in Houston [4 days before]. After unsuccessfully deriving his wife's location from his wife's mother, defendant called the Shreveport home of his wife's sister. The sister's denial of knowledge of his wife's whereabouts arose his suspicion and defendant drove to her home though it was nearing midnight. No answers were made to his repeated knocks on the doors and windows. Defendant then kicked in a door leading from the carport, entered and found his sister-in-law's husband at the end of the bedroom hall, armed with a pistol.
>
> Though the evidence is not clear as to the precise moment when the shooting began, both the victim's wife and defendant's wife testified that defendant began firing his pistol shortly after breaking into the house. The sister-in-law's husband informed

the defendant that he, too, was armed and did not want to
be forced to shoot him. Defendant continued firing his pistol
down the bedroom hallway until he had emptied the pistol of
bullets. Defendant then ran to his car, retrieved a rifle from the
trunk, and returned, firing several blasts, one of which struck
the sister-in-law's husband in the eye, killing him.
—Louisiana Supreme Court, 385 So.2d at 231

Charles was found guilty of first-degree murder. However, the
conviction was reversed on appeal when the defense was allowed
to introduce additional evidence relating to post-traumatic stress
syndrome.

There was another docudrama about a rebellion by milk farmers
in Iowa during the Depression who were so desperate to raise milk
prices that they poured thousands of gallons out on the ground
rather than sell it at a loss.

There was the beginning of something about the Weathermen.

There was an attempt to convince Marion Rees to buy the rights
to Jane Kramer's *The Last Cowboy*. I still like the idea.

There was *Blow It Away*, a movie I was trying to develop with
Joan Golub about the use of drugs, particularly cocaine, among the
rich and fashionable of New York's Upper East Side, something she
knew a lot about.

There was even a sitcom called *Manhattan Plaza* about a group
of 20-somethings – actors, dancers, singers, directors – who lived in
the existing Manhattan apartment building of the same name. The
actual building houses hundreds of mostly young people in the performing arts who are struggling to create careers and lives for themselves. My proposal was long before *Friends* was ever a thought in
someone's mind (but who knows how long David Crane and Marta
Kaufman had been pitching *their* idea).

Finally, there was the story of Butch Bordoli. Another friend,
who'd been born in Nevada and had firsthand knowledge about the
effects of the above-ground nuclear bomb tests in the 1950s, told me
about it.

Butch was just 7½ years old when he died on October 24th, 1956,
at a hospital in Reno, Nevada. Officially, the cause of his death was

leukemia, a diagnosis that had only been made earlier that month. His illness first appeared in 1953 following the Upshot-Knothole series of above-ground tests of atomic bombs while he and his parents lived on their ranch near Ely, Nevada, a small town about 250 miles east of Fallon, NV, where Lynne and I had spent part of our honeymoon. Almost immediately after the tests, he started getting sick. At first, there were terrible legs cramps. Then a constant fever and stomach cramps. Nose bleeding. A diagnosis of appendicitis and a pill. Another of a virus. A pill for his bleeding nose. A doctor suggested arch supports for his shoes. Butch could only drink milk by then, and his fever was over 101°. And then he was dead.

Few doctors in Nevada knew anything about radiation disease, much less had been told that they might expect to see cases of radiation poisoning in their practice. Neither the Truman nor the Eisenhower administrations wanted to warn anyone that they would be affected by the above-ground tests. So when they said that there would be little effect, no one noticed that they didn't say that there would be no effect, and no one thought to ask, "Could that be me?" And in fact, it is not a certainty that Butch died because of exposure to radioactive fallout. But, on the other hand, no one ever had another plausible alternative. The federal government steadfastly refused to admit that it was possible. To recognize the possibility might mean there might be some liability, some responsibility for having caused his death. It wasn't because they had intentionally killed Butch, but because his anonymous death served a larger, greater, more important purpose than his life, present or future. Butch's life may have been precious, but when it came down to it, not all that precious to anyone except those who loved him.

In the 1950s, both Democratic and Republican presidents decided that the deaths of some American civilians were a necessary cost of the Cold War. They just didn't want to say that to any American, much less the most likely sacrificial lambs. It was only in the mid-'80s, after the courts and then Congress decided and/ or admitted that there really was culpability, that some grudging admission of liability and accountability was offered.

There was nothing new about this behavior, this unwillingness to level with the American people. We've seen it repeatedly by presidents of both parties. This is particularly true when it comes to things like war. We were lied to by both Lyndon Johnson and Richard Nixon about Vietnam and George Bush 43 about Iraq and Afghanistan. Even Barak Obama doesn't escape unscathed. As for Donald Trump, the real difficulty was always trying to figure out what he didn't lie about. We are poorly served by *so* many of our national leaders regardless of party. By letting them get away with it over and over again, we are also to blame. Their lies have cost us dearly. Thousands of lives lost, trillions of dollars wasted. Perhaps you'd prefer a softer word. Why is it easier to lie than to tell the truth? Do we prefer to be lied to? It can be much easier to accept the lie rather than deal with the inevitable complexity of the truth.

By the way, the Butch Bordoli film never got made. I don't know why. Some "important" people in Hollywood were very interested over several years. There were meetings and discussions, telephone calls, and other things that happen in the preliminary stages of a Hollywood project. But, still, it never quite got over some invisible threshold.

At lunch one day many years later, I asked Joan why none of these projects made any real headway. She said she didn't know. She always thought they were good projects, all of them. Maybe it was timing, or because my agent didn't have enough clout despite or because he was the son of Nat Weiss, the head of William Morris's movie department. Could it be that I wasn't a good enough writer? Or because I lived in New York? My personal favorite: An absence of four-leaf clovers.

So much for my Hollywood career.

Uh, maybe someone will decide this book would make a great movie.

(*Laughter off stage*)

Joking aside, what should I do about Ann Marie Venne?

She was a girl I never met, never knew. Her life never meant much except, perhaps, to a few whose lives she directly touched. But to the broader world, neither her life nor her death caused more than a temporary ripple, if that.

Ann killed herself the night of December 21st, 1979. She hanged herself by a bedsheet that she had tied to the duct of a ventilator in the ceiling of her cell in the Albany County jail five days before she was due to be released. She was sixteen years old.

On January 14th, 1980, a Monday morning, I was sitting in my office at *MacNeil/Lehrer* reading the *Times*. I had just returned from a week of traveling around the country. A headline caught my attention **"Suicide of Girl, 16, in Albany Jail: Troubled Life, Troubling Death."** The first lines of the story by Clyde Haberman intrigued me enough to read the whole thing. "By anyone's yardstick, Ann Venne had done a lot of living for a 16-year-old. Not much of it was good."

I would have left the story there, just another sad story like so many that one finds in newspapers, except for this: It was something that the girl wrote, Haberman said, while she was in the George Jr. Republic, a non-profit residential therapeutic shelter in Freeville, New York where she had been sent in June 1978 by the courts.

I AM
I am: a prisoner of love
I am: a prisoner of life
I am: a prisoner of the world
I am: a prisoner of sacrifice
I am: a prisoner of

Another girl, another suicide, another mystery. What was it about Peyton Loftis, about Ann Marie Venne, that I found so magnetic? Was Ann simply an overly melodramatic, overly hormone-inflamed teenager? Or did she actually see something that was all too real in herself and the world around her? Did she kill herself to escape her prison, the trap that was her life? Did she kill herself as a final thumb in the eye of everyone around her?

You will at least understand that I found the story powerfully attractive by the fact that I took a day off from work and spent a weekend trying to find out more than was in the NYT article and, possibly, something that I could turn into a … well, I wasn't sure what. And so on March 7th, a week before my trip to Rhodesia for *M/L*, I flew to Plattsburgh, NY, the closest airport to the town of Lyon Mountain where Ann had lived. I don't know that there would have been much of an airport in the city if it hadn't been for the large Air Force base located there. After all, the town had fewer than 20,000 inhabitants, and it certainly was not the center of an area of significant economic activity. But it is on the northwestern shore of Lake Champlain, where I had once gone on a multi-day canoeing trip when I went to a camp in New Hampshire while a kid. And it was a northern gateway to Adirondack Park and just 50 miles from Lake Saranac, where I had spent a summer with my parents, so there was at least an element of a tie to the story that stretched back into my childhood. And Albany, where she killed herself, was a mere 40 miles from my parents' home in Lake Copake.

I met Theresa Venne, Ann's mother, in a conference room at her lawyer's office. She was a practical nurse and worked in a nursing home (if I remember correctly). My impression was of a psychologically frail and exhausted woman who, perhaps, drank too much too often. She told me her version of Ann Marie's life, and we discussed more mundane things like rights and options: so much for a book, this for a TV film, that for a movie, etc. I left with a carton filled with copies of the papers Ann had left behind, primarily letters to her and letters that she had written but never mailed, random pieces of paper, and an orange notebook.

Ann was born on June 13th, 1963, and grew up in Lyon Mountain, officially a hamlet within the larger town of Dannemora in Adirondack Park. As of 2020, the population was 423, less even than ten years earlier. She was the sixth of Albert and Theresa's children and was a happy child by everybody's account, loving nothing more than her horse like many other young girls. However, things changed with the onset of puberty, and Ann grew wilder, more volatile, and increasingly difficult to control either by others or herself. It became too much of a burden for Theresa and Albert, who I think was out of work. Finally, in 1977, Ann, now 14, OD'd. Theresa, in desperation, asked the courts to declare Ann a PINS, a "person in need of supervision," and have the state take over the responsibility for her care. There followed a series of placements: six foster homes, two stays in the St. Lawrence Psychiatric Hospital in Ogdensburg, two suicide attempts, residences in the George Jr. Republic, and a shelter for adolescent runaways. There were lots of drugs and sex with several people. There was the possibility of a pregnancy and a miscarriage (it's not clear if the pregnancy was actual and, if so, how it was terminated). There were rumors (never confirmed) that Ann had occasionally earned money by prostituting herself in Albany. And there was a boyfriend, Steve Lawrence, whom she met in 1977 while still at home.

Ann had been with Steve in a car he was driving and in which they were living. The auto had different license plates on the front and back. Did Steve think no one would notice the difference? Well, the police did notice, stopped the car, and asked Steve to get out. Ann, who did not have a driver's license, slid into the driver's seat and sped off. The police gave chase and, catching up to her, arrested her. Who knows why she did such a thing. Maybe there were drugs in the car she wanted to get rid of. Maybe ... who knows? She can't tell us anymore.

Ann pleaded guilty on November 23rd, 1979, and the judge set her fine at $170. She had no money. Steve couldn't or wouldn't put up the money, nor would her friends. Her mother said that she hoped the stay in jail would teach Ann a lesson, a lesson that she hadn't managed to learn since becoming an adolescent, since, perhaps, writing to her mother, "I hate you, you bitch." But, unfortunately, the social service agencies supposedly responsible for her weren't willing to help, presuming anyone had informed them of Ann's plight. The same was true of the foster families she had stayed with.

So, Ann was sentenced to 55 days in jail, originally in Clinton County, where she was arrested, and Lyon Mountain was located. Because the jail was overcrowded, she was sent to the Albany County jail to serve the rest of her sentence. While there, she had no visitors, made no telephone calls, and cried a lot. She was a well-behaved prisoner. As a reward for "good behavior," she was scheduled to be released early, on December 26th, the day after Christmas. And on the night of the 21st, she killed herself.

Among her belongings was an undated note, perhaps written while she was in George Jr. or maybe the year before when she was in Ogdensburg.

To Whom It May Concern

Steve was the one who helped me first. I was on heavy drugs and always alone with my horse and all I wanted from the outside world was booze and drugs. Then I met Steve and he changed my life by wanting to be with people. But then people started using me and I ended up getting hurt. Steve never hurt me and never would so then Steve was added to the list of crutches. 1. Drugs. 2. Beer, alcohol. 3. Steve. Then heavy drugs weren't my crutch anymore. And then gradually it was just me and Steve. But when they sent me away I became dependent on people and when I did they used me again. Then I just didn't want to live because I was just too weak to handle this world. So then I went back to drugs and I loved hurting people and instead of hurting people I was hurting myself. These are things that flash in my mind and they are jumping off bridge, cutting my wrist, taking pills (OD), trying to hang myself, my grandmother in her coffin, the blood pouring out, when I stabbed Tony, my arm bleeding, the car accident. Seeing Cindy. There's more, getting a bit hysterical.

[Written later but on the same page, the handwriting looks different]

Steve please help me. I need you.

Steve couldn't help her any more than he could help himself. We had a long telephone conversation after my trip to Plattsburgh. He was filled with self-justification and self-pity, full of complaints about how everything was someone else's fault. He was out of work as he had been for most of his semi-adult years and wasn't interested in finding a job. He *did* have muscular dystrophy, and his legs were withering away. He mostly lived on disability payments, beer and pot, and the sympathy of others. I disliked him intensely, though that might have been because I so wanted someone to have been able to help Ann.

A letter from Steve to Ann is undated, though I think it was written in Ogdensburg, where she was sent not very long after they met. This also follows a (short?) period when he was sitting in a jail cell on

December 14th, 1977 (I don't know the offense). The court order establishing Ann's PINS state, by the way, was dated December 5th.

> I don't know who is telling you stories. I haven't looked at a girl since you've been gone. What the hell are you trying to do to me. I never tried to get anything from you except a little love in return for my love for you.
>
> The reason I haven't been writing is my conditional discharge wasn't over and Judy de Long [*Steve's probation officer*] sent me a letter that said I was breaking it because of you, but that's over.
>
> I tried to help you a lot you can't say I didn't. Now I will soon need your help. My legs are going slow but sure.
>
> Please write me back or I'll end up like you want me to end up. Dead. And just because of what we did in Millerton, believe me I wanted that because I love you, not because it feels good or not to take advantage of you.
>
> If I never see you again, you won't like it too much if I do go out and find you.

As I said, it's not easy to see his virtues.

The letters from her girlfriends are filled with the real and/or imagined melodrama of their teenage years.

YW (Ann's best friend), October 1978.

> Do you really think you are pregnant? Is Steve the father? What did you stab that guy for? Not going with Paul anymore. Do you want me to ask Steve? I hate him. Don't marry him (nobody will go to the wedding).
>
> Excerpts from a November 16th, 1978 letter from YW.
>
> I Hate Lori & Paula, as does Paul. She's a slut. Going to Boston and get shot. Paul going to Hawaii.
>
> Where are you?
>
> Doing badly in English (42), biology (65), social studies (70), math (83), typing (80). Failed English last year and social studies and math. Pot and Beer. Shot a partridge.
>
> Paul's mother gets mad when I don't go to school.

Tell me if you're pregnant. Thought I was last month. Paula thinks she is (no period for 3 months). Could be John's or Rick's. Ralph had ounce of pot.

Remember when I pierced your ears?

DS to Ann. September 30th, 1978.

How'd you get back in that hole [*St. Lawrence Psychiatric Center in Ogdensburg?*]. I'm glad to hear [*Steve*] proposed.

I've been here almost 9 months [*St. Ann Institute in Albany, "a private, not-for-profit organization dedicated to serving the critical behavioral and mental health needs of children and families."*] and it's pretty rough. My time is up in July.

Let's get to the lighter side of things like Sex and Drugs and Rock and Roll. As for sex – I only get that when I go home for visits. Drugs – not very frequent here – but whenever I can – Rock and Roll is always around so one out of three ain't bad.

I tried to find YW before returning to New York. I drove west from Plattsburgh, passing beneath the forbidding stone walls of the Clinton Correctional Facility, built in 1845, or Dannemora as it is commonly called, a maximum-security prison, and the dirt road that passed in front of the trailer in which YW and her parents lived. No one was home and I left a note for her. She wrote back to me saying that she wouldn't talk to me and asked, "why won't everyone leave Ann alone?" I thought it was at least as likely that she didn't want to be asked about the actual lives she and her friends were leading, their lives of "sex and drugs and rock and roll."

Driving past Dannemora, the poverty so evident along the dirt roads, the desperation (quiet or not) of Ann, her parents, and her friends, I got a far different picture of rural America than I was used to seeing or thinking about. This was the same countryside, the same Adirondack Park, that looks so beautiful and bucolic, that was the summer home to the wealthy like Dr. Hexter (my father's boss), that was the summer playground for tourists like my family. Who thought of these other lives, the lives of so many people who actually *lived* there?

Perhaps one could understand why "upstate" New York has such a dislike for the huge city at the southern tip of the state. And why Democrats, for whom poverty inevitably means Blacks and Latinos and not the impoverished whites of the northern part of the state, had such a hard time electing governors at least until the 2006 elections. Suppose one wondered why Hillary Clinton did so well in New York's senatorial elections and among working-class whites in the 2008 Democratic primaries. In that case, one need only understand that she campaigned in places like Plattsburgh and Lyon Mountain almost exclusively, leaving New York City to its overwhelming Democratic majority. Perhaps she learned while in Arkansas that post-60s identity politics excluded the plight of low-income whites and were a significant explanation for the "Reagan Revolution" and the success of the "Contract with America" and, eventually, Donald Trump. Today, upstate NY is predominantly Trump land. And maybe by the time she ran for president, she and some of her advisors forgot those lessons.

Rural America was clearly not all it was cracked up to be. All was not family farms and cows and corn and loving homes where all the virtue of America resides. Today, it's pretty clear to most of us that the underbelly of rural America can be as ugly and desperate as the underbelly of America's large cities. The difference is that we romanticize the rural while over-dramatizing the ugliness of the urban, not to mention the racial overtones in the comparison. If, at the time, I had any illusions about the "country," they were put to a final rest when I read Norman Mailer's *The Executioner's Song*, his tale of America's heartland. My admittedly jaundiced view could be fully on display when listening to America's politicians and others, like writers, who extol the virtues of the heartland having decided to leave it. My impression is that almost every heartland politician who lives in Washington for a significant amount of time never returns to Kansas when he retires. Like Bob Dole, who lived in the Watergate and became a lobbyist before he died, never moving back to Kansas. As for every writer living in New York or Chicago or LA who writes nostalgically of their rural childhood lives, I would simply remind them that they left for a reason and they're free to return whenever they want. But they don't.

As for Ann, the question that I started with at the start of my trip remained. What to do about Ann Marie Venne? What to do with this story of failure, of tragedy? It was a tragedy because the end was inevitable, at least in hindsight. It was hard to comprehend the totality of the failure, the failure of every single institution that we have constructed in America to prevent the end of Ann's life. It was a failure of the family, the social service agencies, the psychiatric profession, mental hospitals, therapeutic communities, the foster family system, and the judicial system. And if Steve truly loved Ann, it was a failure of the curative and transformative power of love. Finally, and ultimately, it was Ann's personal failure too. For every step she took forward, she took two back. And finally, there were no more steps to take.

It occurred to me then, as it does now, that the self-styled "prisoner of love" really was a prisoner. And it seemed to me then that her frustration, rage, pain, and loneliness were directed both outward and inward. No matter how much she hated her life, she hated herself for being unable to break out of it, break out of herself. She really felt trapped in her prison. Is it possible that suicide was the only rational solution to a life that neither she nor anyone else could help her with? What a terrible, awful thought.

I thought a book was the only way to do justice to her. So for three months, I poured over the letters, over my notes, made lists of people to talk to, places to visit. I tried to imagine being Ann on that last night, the night she hung herself. But the deeper I got into the story, into Ann, the more depressing it got. It was like a dark cloud descending all around me, and I felt it beginning to suffocate me. I began to wonder what the virtue of this book would be, so unrelenting was its gloominess, its pessimism, its lack of any glimmer of hope.

Finally, I said, "Enough," and I decided to put it aside, to put what was left of Ann, her notes and letters and scraps of paper, in a plastic bag that I still have. And yet, here I am decades later, still thinking about Ann, still writing about her.

Thinking about Ann and my earlier obsession with Peyton Loftis, I cannot help but recall Roger Rosenblatt's essay for the *New-sHour* about Robert McFarlane some years later. McFarlane had served a stint as Reagan's National Security Adviser and was deeply involved in the Iran-Contra scandal. In 1987 after his retirement, he tried to kill himself and failed. In writing about McFarlane, Roger said something that I've never forgotten. People, he said, "try to kill themselves for their own reasons, not ours."

An undated note from Ann:

> **My life is nothing. I keep screaming for help but no one hears me. I'm a prisoner of the family court. I tried for two years but I give up. This is the best peace and freedom I know.**
> **With all my hate and love, Ann, the prisoner of life.**

So, I have my answer to YW's question. Why won't I leave Ann alone?

Because she won't leave me alone.

Chapter 12
A FAIRY TALE

◆

1981 — 1983

I met Lee Garro in the spring of 1981.

It was not a notable event. At least, it didn't seem so at the time. One evening, we met through friends, and I spent a half-hour talking to her and her husband. Actually, I spoke to her husband, who was quite garrulous and sociable, while she sat, mostly silent. Alicia, their daughter, was almost three and asleep in another room. But I did notice Lee. A sort of ping that sort of said, I see you. So we chatted about this and that, and I left. Over the next couple of years, I'd sometimes run into her since I had friends in the neighborhood and the building in which she lived. We'd talk on the street for a few minutes, me thinking not much of it other than I liked her, and she was undoubtedly attractive with ping still pinging. On the other hand, I might have been single and dating, but she was neither. If there was one thing I never asked about, it was the state of her marriage, and she never volunteered a word about it.

Also, that spring, I read Milan Kundera's great novel, *The Book of Laughter and Forgetting*. I was flying to Washington, and I had picked up the book from the airport bookstore. I still remember the impact I felt when reading one particular sentence of Kundera's.

The struggle of man against power is the struggle of memory against forgetting.

It is a line that I have never forgotten. Over the years, it has come to mind repeatedly as we have witnessed history slide by us. I have watched and noted how politicians, in particular, try and too often succeed in convincing us to ignore the past or, even more, forget that it ever existed. We don't even need the airbrushing of a historical photograph by the Communists that was the stunningly graphic metaphor at the beginning of Kundera's novel. It is something we Americans do to ourselves without the benefit of Photoshop, being all too willing to cherry-pick our past so that only the good things remain. Sometimes, we knowingly lie about it.

We try to whitewash our history of slavery. We wax nostalgic about the 1950s, refusing to acknowledge that the evil of segregation and Jim Crow laws existed only because we allowed them to and because some of us wanted them. The same was true of the blacklist, refusing to recognize that we were all culpable. We talked about the innocence of the American Heartland after the bombing in Oklahoma City, forgetting the terrible violence that has often run through the Midwest's past, a river of blood as mighty as the Mississippi. We abhor the number of mass shootings, murders by guns, deaths by police action, and we find ourselves incapable of doing much of anything about it, paralyzed by slogans and our politics. We are angry about attempts of other countries to interfere in our elections when we have often interfered in theirs or are affronted at the thought of friends and enemies spying on us, although we assume the right to spy on them. We may not (or may have) tortured people during the Cold War. I don't know if we tortured people during Vietnam, but we certainly allowed or asked others to do it for us. Did that make us less culpable? During the wars in Afghanistan and Iraq and other places we have not learned about, we willingly admitted that we tortured people but made up a more benign name for it, "enhanced interrogation." We sometimes allow fear to take us to places we wouldn't usually go. There were no consequences for anyone who had command responsibility for these actions, except maybe damaging their reputations, presuming that we remembered who they were. We say we believe in the rule of law, and yet there are countless instances in which the law is simply ignored, or we refuse to prosecute and, even, investigate. We deplore the biases and prejudices of others while we embrace our own, refusing to recognize them for what they are.

I don't know that we Americans do this anymore than other people. The Russians seem to have a unique ability to accept the airbrushing of history. One wonders how many Chinese allow themselves to even remember the Cultural Revolution. How long will it take the people of Hong Kong to forget that there once was such a thing as democracy? The Japanese have an eraser regarding the Rape of Nanking, not to mention Pearl Harbor. And the French and other self-righteous Europeans? Let us not go there. We are *all* earth people, aren't we? Each of us is capable of doing all the things others of our species are capable of doing for good or evil, as we demonstrate over and over again. But that line of Kundera's is something we ought never to forget. *"The struggle of man against power is the struggle of memory against forgetting."* We ignore it at our peril.

Meanwhile, life went on. You already know about most of the important stuff, things that went on in the show, and the projects I was promoting in Hollywood. And, of course, I was living the life of a single male at loose in the world.

As 1982 wound to a close, two things happened that I haven't mentioned. One was that the days of *The MacNeil/Lehrer Report*, the half-hour show, were drawing to a close. The following year, the fall of 1983, would see the show's expansion to an hour. Robin and Jim and their PBS station partners in New York and Washington had worked hard to accomplish this. Each of the network evening news shows had wanted to do it but had been unable to convince either their networks or, probably, more importantly, their local affiliates to surrender the time. With the expansion would come greater opportunities, presumably, for those already on staff as the show changed and new people were added.

But to get back to Lee: Of course, I didn't really know her at all. We had met that one time in her apartment and ping though there was, there had been only occasional casual contact between us since. But whenever I saw her, there was just *something* about her. She never told me that her marriage was on the rocks, and she was dissolving it. Even more, she didn't tell me until much later that she had not been oblivious of me either. But she didn't want there to be any confusion between me, her, and the state of her marriage. So it would be better not to have anything to do with me (or any other male for that matter), at least for the time being.

In December 1982, I ran across her once again. She told me that she and her husband were getting a divorce. Actually, I was happy to hear it, but I'm sure I said something inane like, "Oh, I'm sorry to hear that." That is what one is supposed to say in situations like that, isn't it? I really had no idea what to think of it other than it seemed to be a fact. Lee didn't leave any room to think the decision had any wiggle room and she didn't seem upset by it. So, ping still pinging, I'm sure that I came up with another positively brilliant line like, "Why don't we have dinner sometime?" Lee said she'd like that but couldn't until her separation agreement was finalized. I thought that was a bit unusual in my experience, but I liked her for it. Besides, I wasn't in any hurry. Things would happen whenever they would happen if anything happened at all, and that's how we left things.

On a weekday night towards the end of the next month, January 1983, Lee was there again. Her separation was finalized, and we could now go out. And so, on February 5th, 1983, we had dinner together. I said goodnight to her in the lobby of her building in front of the elevator. She did not want to take the chance of her now four-year-old daughter, Alicia, being awake.

Did we make another date before I left, or did I say I would call her? Whichever it was, I at once stopped dating other girls. I called her again and again and again, and we saw each other over and over again. Finally, one Saturday morning in April, I said I'd like us to live together. She agreed.

Lee was born into an Italian-American, nominally Catholic family in the Astoria section of Queens, the land of Archie Bunker. Hers was a working-class family whose children all aspired to higher things. It was as different from both mine and Lynne's as it could be. Her father had a milk delivery route and a fish store at other times. He also liked to play the ponies. But, like most gamblers, he often lost. He died after a stroke before I came on the scene. Rosie, his wife, was a seamstress who had had to work to pay off his gambling debts despite her age. Lee had two brothers, one of whom had a PhD. in biochemistry and held various research and academic positions, finally becoming the provost at U Mass, Dartmouth. Her other brother was a drug addict and bank robber. The first time I met him was when he was in a halfway house in Brooklyn. A sister, younger by 18 years, was still in high school when we first met. She had been adopted as a 9-month-old baby by Rosie.

When I appeared in her life, Lee's family enthusiastically and unquestioningly welcomed me into their midst.

As for Lee, she was entirely self-made, much as my parents had been. She had wanted to be a lawyer, but her father didn't think girls needed any education beyond high school and insisted that the limit of her ambition should be to marry an Italian boy from the neighborhood. So she left home when she was 18, moved to Manhattan, and was entirely self-supporting from then on. Finding that earning a living and going to night school were incompatible for her, she dedicated her life to achieving her ambitions through her work. Over the years, she became one of the most respected buyers in the close-out retail business.

Lee was as interested as I was in living in and being aware of the real world. She, too, read the *Times* every day and sometimes the *Wall Street Journal* and one of the tabloids in addition. Her interest in politics and social policy was similar to mine, which was a pleasant discovery, though our views weren't identical. She loved to read books, go to movies, theater, and music concerts. She loved good food. She liked to entertain if I was there to help; I liked it too, though increasingly, our jobs didn't leave much room for it. She even laughed at my jokes.

It didn't take long to discover Lee was (and still is) the most honest, ethical, fair, and reliable person I know. She is the most "in the present" person I know and the most forthright. Her daughter's interests were paramount and would always precede her own as a mother. She could be absolutely fierce in defense of those interests. Her goal, she always said, was to make sure that Alicia could stand on her own two feet so as not to feel dependent on anyone, romantic partners included, for her survival. To me, Lee seemed the sanest and most rational person I knew, certainly more so than me. What a relief.

In other words, I admired and respected Lee enormously, not because she was the same as me but because she was so different.

That admiration and respect have never gone away, never wavered, not even for an instant.

As important as these things were, Lee was not overly impressed by what I did for a living, unlike more than a few of the girls I dated. In fact, I don't think Lee ever cared what I did other than that she wanted *me* to care. If that meant *M/L*, then that's where she thought I should be. I think she would have been satisfied if I had ever said that what I really wanted to do was drive a cab. She didn't care how much money I made as long as I contributed my share of our mutual obligations, and she always made sure that those were well within the scope of our incomes. She made one thing crystal clear: She didn't want to be a backseat driver to my career; she didn't want to be the woman behind the man (and, yes, some women thought that's what they should be). Thank God (or someone, or something).

And so, as the weeks went by, I came to love Lee. Feelings just grew as naturally as a flower being watered by rain. It was a love that developed within the reality of our mutual lives and our lives as individuals. Maybe, too, it was because Lee was always so much *there* without the threat or possibility, either real or imagined, of disappearing. I could look into the future and couldn't see an end to the story of Lee and Michael. We were simply there together.

When I moved into her apartment, there were pre-conditions. I had to agree that if we didn't survive as a couple, she would keep the apartment; it was rent-stabilized, and she had a child. I wouldn't insist that she go with me to any work-related functions. And I had to understand that she didn't do shirts.

I had to promise one more thing: I would never desert Alicia.

And what did she want out of this relationship? "I want a playmate." We've been playing together for many years.

In return, she gave me complete and total freedom, support, loyalty, and love. They would be there as long as they were returned in kind.

I wish I could say that I have never disappointed her, but that wouldn't be true, that there have never been bumps in the winding road, that ripples in the pond were never disturbed. But whatever turbulence there has been, it's been dealt with. We're still here, still together thirty-nine years later.

And so, in April 1983, we started to live together along with Kaneel, our German Shorthaired Pointer, who came along that summer and remained with us for the rest of her life. In some ways, there was much that was familiar to me. After all, I once lived with my own small children. I understood the necessity of waking at 6 in the morning rather than 9, getting Alicia off to school, and the ritual importance of family dinners. I knew about staying home on weekend evenings to be with Alicia. I knew what walking a dog required. And I knew what living within a budget meant even if I hadn't been living that way in recent years.

On the other hand, Lee had been living with a very tight budget for years; her husband had not been, shall we say, a significant contributor to the family's income. It took quite a while before she felt she could stop divvying up the cash from her paycheck each week into separate envelopes, so much for rent, for utilities, for groceries, for fun. Now, when we walked down the street, she would happily say, "Do you know how much we actually make between us?" It was something like $57,000, hardly a king's ransom in those days of hyperinflation. Fortunately, we managed to improve the amount over the years.

My parents, though, had yet to meet Lee. They were already in Copake for the summer when Lee and I had decided to be together. So we arranged to go to Copake for Memorial Day weekend.

Meanwhile, the *MacNeil/Lehrer Report* was hurrying on its way to becoming the *MacNeil/Lehrer NewsHour*. In the spring, I had lunch with Les Crystal, who was coming on as the new executive producer. He had a long history in the TV news business. He had been with NBC News during its most successful era, having been the Executive Producer of the Huntley-Brinkley Report. I had long been an NBC News fan. It had always been Chet Huntley and David Brinkley, who I watched during political conventions and on election nights when I was younger; they were the source of my primary education in national politics. And he had been the president of NBC News.

Perhaps I should pause here for a moment because the advent of the *NewsHour* was the harbinger of enormous changes that were about to overtake the TV news business during the next several years. The 1980s were far more transformative than any of us recognized at the time.

First, Les Crystal's departure from NBC was apparently a public signal that the attempt by ABC, CBS, and NBC to expand their nightly news broadcasts to an hour had failed. The networks' affiliated local stations simply weren't willing to surrender the additional time slots and their revenue to the networks. The expansion of *The MacNeil/Lehrer Report* to an hour meant that Robin, Jim, and their supporters in Public Television had achieved something at which the networks had failed.

Then, in 1987, Laurence Tisch took over CBS from William Paley. His interest was in increasing profits. One place he looked to improve profitability was CBS News, once the apple of Paley's eye regardless of profitability, the one-time home of legendary correspondents like Edward R. Murrow. One way to do that was to reduce costs. That meant cutting staff, including long-time correspondents and entire news bureaus, domestically and overseas. It meant that people with deep knowledge of their subjects were jettisoned and replaced by people with far less understanding. The ability to cover stories in-depth was reduced, and programming reflected the change. The other networks followed Tisch's lead. Hour-long investigative documentaries, once a staple of the networks, declined. Reporting from hot spots worldwide and domestically was too frequently done by younger reporters who weren't deeply versed in the background of the issues or by stringers (meaning freelance reporters). News bureaus came to be based far away from the geographic areas they covered or no longer specialized in anything. There were so many hot spots and crises that TV networks found it virtually impossible to cover them all.

Also, in 1987, Ronald Regan's Federal Communications Commission (the FCC) abandoned the Fairness Doctrine. This policy required that broadcasters present to viewers and listeners information about controversial issues. And it required that they present differing and opposing viewpoints. As a result, radio stations virtually abandoned their news broadcasts since they were apparently no longer needed to maintain their licenses. Other consequences would soon follow.

In 1988, Rush Limbaugh burst onto the scene on the radio. His kind of program, about as politically one-sided as you can get, became enormously popular and helped fuel the following years' increasingly polarized politics and culture wars. The program could not have existed under the Fairness Doctrine. Not that he couldn't have had a program, but it would have had to be different. And Fox News on cable TV —deliberately unfair and unbalanced — could not have existed as Rupert Murdoch and Roger Ailes created without the absence of the Doctrine. So, too, for MSNBC as it evolved, particularly after the election of Trump.

TV news was forever altered on June 1, 1980, by the debut of CNN and its introduction of the 24 hours a day news cycle, with its endless repetition of the same stories hour after hour, and the search for any story to be blown up into something worthy of a headline. It became as omnipresent as the AP wire service in every newsroom around the country.

Simultaneously, the 1980s saw another development that had enormous consequences for the news business in general and, more generally, America and the world. And that was the introduction of the PC by IBM in 1981 and the introduction of the internet in 1983. Over time, the digital revolution has come to affect every area of life that it has touched, including the news business. TV news and newspapers were forever altered by the proliferation of content through cable and then, more directly, by the internet. The internet was used to create new sources of information, news, and propaganda, as well as entertainment. Advertising flocked to the new mediums, depriving printed newspapers of crucial revenue, which, in turn, meant closing newspapers all over the country. And the explosion of social media sites could be — and still is — exploited for nefarious purposes.

The early evangelists of the virtuous potential of the digital age have tragically learned that all virtue can be corrupted, that where you find saints, you will also find sinners, where you find the honest and ethical, you will also find criminals and snake-oil salesmen. Everywhere you find earth people.

Before Facebook went public, investors asked how this social media platform could earn profits if it was free to users. We found out.

When Google proudly touted its motto, "DON'T DO EVIL," no one asked them to define what they meant by "evil" and what was excluded. The motto was dropped in 2018.

Frankly, it's hard for me to see where all this is going for the news business and all the rest of us. If you thought Facebook and Google were eager and willing to exploit every thought you've ever had, every piece of data in your life, why would you trust their move into virtual reality? Where did George Orwell go?

I'm not optimistic about the future of the news business and the continued invasion of our lives by the digital revolution. And that doesn't even begin to address the escalating social, political, and economic byproducts of global warming. Am I too pessimistic? Could be. I'll keep my fingers crossed, knock on wood, and look for four-leaf clovers.

But all that was in the future as Les and I had lunch, chatting about what I had done at *M/L*. He gave no inkling of what he was thinking.

On the Friday afternoon before 1983's Memorial Day weekend, the job assignments for the new show were announced. I was to be an associate producer.

I was devastated. I thought I deserved a producer's job given the extraordinary efforts I had made during much of the show's life. It was four o'clock. Lee was waiting for me to drive to Copake to meet my parents in her car.

"What's the matter?" Lee asked as soon as I got in the car. I told her. "Well," she said, her words floating across the space between us light as a feather, "you'll just have to show them what you can do. Have fun. Knock their socks off." A leaf floating on an early summer breeze, alighting on the surface of the pond ever so gently, barely creating a stir, only the slightest wave rippling across the water. She turned the key in the ignition, and off we went. "How do we get there," she said.

Do you believe in fairy tales? I have always wanted them to be true. I wanted the beautiful princess to kiss the toad who would be transformed into the handsome prince hiding below the ugly surface. I have always somehow hoped for, believed in the transformative power of love. It only occurred to me many years later that that moment, that leaf alighting on the surface of the pond, was my fairy tale moment.

No sooner had we arrived at the house on Lake Copake when my mother asked what job I would have with the new show. My father was there too, of course. Much hand wringing. Much worrying. My mother began doing her thing: her back straightening, her chin coming up, marshaling her views, her arguments, her directions as to what course of action I should take in the light of this news.

Lee took my hand. "Come on, Michael, let's take a walk." And so she extricated me, and we walked along the road that ran along the lake's shore in the gathering twilight. And that was the end of that, with the rest of the weekend continuing normally, without much, if any, talk of Friday's events.

What was normal dinner table conversation for my family that weekend was completely abnormal for Lee. If my parents talked about politics and books and various cultural events, Lee's family would talk about the more familiar, the actual content of their lives, what they did during the day, and what they thought and felt with their mother Rosie never passing judgment. On the rare occasion that Lee told Rosie something about her life that upset her mother, Lee would simply say, "Don't ask if you don't really want to know." Would that have been true of my family! On the other hand, I might still have maintained my inclination to silence, particularly in the face of my mother's implacable will. Still, I like to imagine things would have been different.

On Monday, I went to work with only one real question on my mind: Was Robin telling me that I had no future with *M/L*. I don't know what I would have done in the past, but I walked (nervously) into his office that day.

"Uh...I have a... uh... question about my job. Are you trying to send me a message?"

"No."

"Okay. Then I'll stay."

And I did.

Chapter 13
LOOKING FOR AMERICA

◆

1983 — 1995

"Kathy," I said as we boarded a Greyhound in Pittsburgh
"Michigan seems like a dream to me now."
It took me four days to hitchhike from Saginaw
I've gone to look for America
—Paul Simon

Whatever my title in the new hour-long show, my new role was hardly well defined. All I knew was that I was supposed to report to a newly hired producer. Whether or not it was what anybody else had in mind (since I was never told), in her mind, part of my role was to teach her the ethos, the culture of *M/L*. So not only was it not a role I wanted, but I resented it. Beyond that, I'm not sure she knew what she wanted to do with me, perhaps because she wasn't sure what she wanted to do with herself or what was really expected of her, what her actual role was.

But I know that I carved out a role independent of her; it was not entirely accidental. And intentionally or not, knowingly or not, Robin, Jim, and Les both facilitated and encouraged it.

In the ½ hour show, initially as the production supervisor, I was responsible for the daily and long-term logistical and technical oper-ations, along with the fiscal solvency of the entire show, including its NY and DC components. So, I was somewhat separated from most of the staff since I had to make certain personnel decisions or recommendations, oversee expense reports, etc. Those things create a natural distance. On the other hand, my office was on the same floor as the rest of the NY staff, except for the Graphics Department, and I interacted with most of the staff daily, both in the morning meetings and the general performance of my job, not to mention being in the studio most nights. My office was a couple of doors away from Robin's.

In Washington, WETA's offices were on L'Enfant Plaza, where PBS was based during the years of the *MacNeil/Lehrer Report*. Jim and his staff's offices were also there, and I would visit at least a couple of times a month just to keep an eye on things. I would always stop in to see Jim and see if there was anything that I could do for him. I'd also stop by to see Gerry Slater, WETA's Director of Public Affairs, the parallel job to Jerry Toobin's in NY.

Once I started traveling for the interconnects, I was mainly on my own. Obviously, I worked with all the other producers and reporters and generally liked them. But because most of my work took me increasingly away from the office and Robin and Jim, I was inside and outside the show simultaneously, an outside observer and an inside participant.

When it came to the early days of the *NewsHour*, I was just as separated. Aside from that distance, I don't think either Robin or Jim, neither of whom knew me particularly well, had any idea what they should do with me, what I could and couldn't do that would benefit the show. Neither of them (or anyone else who worked for the show, including Ray Weiss, Al Vecchione, and Les Crystal) had ever formally interviewed me, much less seen my resume. Besides my history on the show, my past was a mystery; I was a blank slate. It could be that was one reason I found myself in the predicament I was in. In effect, they left it up to this new producer to define my role. Or I would have to define it myself by my actions if nothing else. At least in retrospect, that's exactly what I did, even if I did it without conscious forethought, even if it happened in ways that I didn't expect.

In their initial conception of the *NewsHour*, Robin and Jim wanted to have scenic bumpers between segments of the show, a bumper being some sort of visual and audio transition between show segments. There was nothing unusual about that; they still exist in the *PBS NewsHour*. And in commercial TV news broadcasts, they're called commercial breaks. For the *NewsHour*, there would be three of them in each show. The idea was to have a visual image of some sort that would last 25 seconds. We were to think of them as postcards from various parts of the country.

Les told me that it was my job to create these bumpers in late June or early July. So, no sooner had I been assigned to this new producer, I was separated from her and assigned this other task that had nothing to do with what anyone else on the show was doing. I was reassigned to report to a different producer who had been with the show for a while. This, too, proved untenable since this other producer was all too involved in creating her role in the new show and had reporters to supervise who were also new to the show. The show was busy inventing itself. Within a couple of months, the only person that made sense for me to report to was Les, the executive producer, and that's the way things remained until I retired.

But was anyone able to tell me what they really had in mind with these bumpers? No, but they would know it when they saw it. And so began that process, which is not entirely rational but hardly unusual, of finding out what was wanted by finding out what was not.

I took a cameraman down to Greenwich Village to shoot in Washington Square Park to try out some ideas. I remember the one shot of the long row of chess players sitting on the concrete benches hunched over the boards, their hands reaching out to move the pieces and then quickly slapping the timers. The shot was terrific. It was so terrific that the 1993 movie, *In Search of Bobby Fischer* used something similar. Les and Robin loved it. Unfortunately, it was *not* what was wanted. It turned out that people wouldn't do. Whatever shots we used had to be neutrally juxtaposed against any story. If people were included in the picture, the juxtaposition might be construed as an editorial comment on what came before or after. At least that was clear. No people.

And then nothing. I barely did anything in July. I couldn't imagine how to go about doing something in the absence of some idea about what to do. But there was one idea that hung out there. Postcards. We wanted to have postcards from America. So I set out to discover America, to look for America, a different America than I had been seeing during my travels from city to city through the years of the ½ hour show. It would not be a land of social problems, political strife, urban decay, of experts in this or that. Instead, it would be an America of landscapes, of the shapes of hills, of trees, and streams meandering through "pastures of plenty" (in the words of my favorite Woody Guthrie song). It would be an America of the visual, of the sights one could see if only one had time to look, if one only stopped to look. The land of America the Beautiful. A land of postcards.

August approached. The September 5th debut of the *NewsHour* was practically upon us, The necessity for three postcards in every show, 15 new postcards a week, 780 a year. It loomed as a daunting undertaking, particularly for something that felt so nebulous in concept. So I plotted a trip.

Why did I choose to go to South Dakota first? I don't remember. Maybe because Mount Rushmore was the most American postcard I could think of. Or because it was far away. Those names! The Badlands. The Black Hills. Maybe it was those names more than anything else. Besides, they were places I'd never been. Regardless, that's where we went, shooting those faces on the mountain, the herds of buffalo, the scrub-covered hills, a rusted plow abandoned in a straw-colored empty field.

From the Badlands, we worked our way east, stopping in Kansas City in the heart of America. I picked Kansas City to follow the path of the Missouri River, shooting the lush pastures and herds of cattle so different from the sere landscape of the Badlands and then to jump east to the steep hills and valleys of West Virginia's coal-mining region.

The real reason I wanted to go to Kansas was not because of the rural landscape. I had been there, remember, during the 1976 Republican Convention. I wanted to go back to the stockyards, which were practically next door to the Kemper Arena where the convention was held. I remembered how drawn I was to the old structure sitting across from the Golden Ox Restaurant, which no longer exists. The restaurant claimed to be "where the steak was born," and I took our staff there for dinner when everyone arrived for the convention. The dying mammoth barn of a building stood looming in the twilight, the paint long gone from its sides if, indeed, it had ever been painted, its wooden siding eaten away by time and neglect, a building haunted by, inhabited by time.

The afternoon of Monday, August 8th, 1983, a day of bright sunlight and high heat, the crew and I drove down to the stockyards and got permission to shoot inside the structure. The air was filled with dust dancing in the shafts of light, the air redolent with the sweet smell of hay and straw, the sounds of squealing pigs echoing through the otherwise empty, dying building.

While the crew went off to shoot the building, I talked to Charles Edmunds. He told me about the stockyards, which were established in 1871. Since its founding, millions upon millions of head of cattle had moved through its pens. Over 2,000,000 heads a year were fed there at its height before heading off to the slaughterhouses in Kansas City and beyond. Now there might be one or two hundred on a good day. The stockyards once covered 600 acres, including the area on which the Kemper Arena now stood; it was now down to 55. There was a time when Kansas City was the frontier, the Wild West, and later the gateway to the new Wild West; now, it was flyover country, no one's destination. For 25 years, most of his adult life, Charles worked there.

With his sunburned arms, stocky build, and short sandy hair, Charles wore a red baseball cap with "The Living Well" insignia that I took to be a religious reference. "But whosoever drinketh of the water that I shall give him shall never thirst, but the water that I shall give him shall be in him a well of water springing up into everlasting life."

And a leaf drifted down upon the water, and I remembered what Lee said. "Well, you'll just have to show them what you can do."

So Charles and I continued talking, the crew returned, and I said to Bill MacMillan, the cameraman, "Can we do a bit of an interview?" Bill, of course, agreed, as did Charles. So we talked, maybe fifteen or twenty minutes, no more, about the stockyards, about the recession and the hard times devastating the industrial rust belt and the agricultural Heartland, about his life, about his job, about time.

...the whole thing is going so fast. We're in such a fast cycle. Seems like that people are going to have to – something's going to have to slow down. Something's going to have to give. People can't exist. How they going to keep going? The economy is – they talk about the economy is bad. I don't see where it's any different now than it was back when I was growing up. We're making more money now than we ever made. We're paying more money for everything else because everything else is higher, but everything's going along with the times. I mean, when I made $36 a week, now I make $200 a week, so I can't see no difference in it. I'm staying up – trying to stay up with the times as it goes. But the stockyards is – I don't know. It's something else. I wouldn't trade – I would rather work here than any place on earth. You're outside. You're with the animals. And I mean it's enjoyable. It's – I don't know, you get just a thing of being closer, I guess, to something old. I mean, you're like being a part of something that's antique. Maybe I'm antique. I don't know. But I like being close, you know. The point is that this is an old place, and it's like you're part of it. You've been here 25 years. It's like you're a piece of it.

The Kansas City Stockyards closed for good in 1991.

When I got back to New York, I found that we had discovered a formula for the postcards, one that would be duplicated hundreds of times until the show was revamped the following fiscal year. So the postcards disappeared, though happily not before I got to spend weeks wandering through the deserts and mountains of America. I meandered through Bryce Canyon, Zion, and Yosemite National Parks, boated on Lake Powell with its otherworldly red rock canyons and the blue water, motored through Death Valley, spent a fall week in New York's Adirondack Mountains, shooting as we went along.

What the show decided it liked was a simple 25-second zoom. The camera would focus on a close-up of something in the distance — a tree, a hill, a structure of some sort, most often an old barn (a new one wouldn't do) — and widen out from that to see the entire landscape as it stretched out before us and, of course, a postmark with the shot's location, just like a postcard.

I sometimes wondered why that kind of shot found such acceptance. Why was an obviously old barn preferable to a new one? Perhaps it was similar to Charles Edmunds and what he said about being an antique within the context of that old barn of a building. The forever-lasting land and the antique become one with the other. A new barn would be an imposition on the landscape. One is natural; the other, artificial.

Maybe, too, it provided, for the viewer, something similar to the walk that Lee took me on. To see something in detail and then move further and further away is to see that everything has a context. Everything fits into some larger world, that the world has space and distance and time, that everything isn't just *now*, and *here*, and you don't have to have your nose shoved up against it. We all need space and distance from time to time. And maybe, just maybe, we all need beauty and balance in our lives.

After returning from that first trip, I took a few days in the editing room to cut my interview with Charles Edmunds. My questions were not heard, his voice the only voice in the piece. Overlaying the interview were the images of the stockyards, sunlight streaking through the weathered cracks in the siding revealing the sawdust swirling in the air, the sounds of the few, far-off animals echoing through the silence and the dying. I asked Les to look at it. It aired on the third night of the *NewsHour*'s first week, and nothing was ever the same.

Looking back at my calendar for that year, it is astonishing how quickly everything at the *NewsHour* changed for me. At first, at the end of May, I was an associate producer, unsure if he had a place in the show. Then, after a couple of barren months, I was producing feature after feature and was promoted to a producer and then a senior producer within a couple of years.

Seemingly every new thing Jim and Robin wanted to try was thrown my way, from weekly book reviews to weekly political cartoons during the 1984 presidential campaign. A reporter was assigned to work with me, and then a production assistant was added. At the end of October, there was an all-day meeting of the senior staff from the New York, Washington, and Denver offices and Robin and Jim. Les played the Stockyards piece for everyone. *That*, he said, was what a feature should be, compelling visuals and a compelling story that had something to say.

I was browsing in a magazine store near Columbus Circle on a gray and drizzly day in September. The cover of *America West* magazine caught my eye. A black and white photo of a cowboy on his horse.

He sat motionless, still as a stone on his frozen horse, each feature of his face, each line in the timbered barn behind him crystalline in the silence.

There was a quiet to the image, a stillness, a feeling of antiquity. I wondered if this was a photo out of the past, out of the last decades of the 19ᵗʰ century when the West was the *West*. So I called the magazine's editor. No, the photo was the work of a contemporary photographer, Jay Dusard, and, yes, I could have his phone number.

On Sunday, November 21, 1983, I met Jay in Prescott, Arizona. The next day, it was unexpectedly snowing, and we went off to get me some waterproof boots. We met my crew (the same one that had been with me in South Dakota and Kansas City and with whom I would do many more pieces over the next few years) and drove 100 miles or so to a line camp in a remote section of the vast Yavapai Ranch in Arizona's Juniper Mountains.

Jay had learned "to cowboy" — how to ride, rope calves and brand them, and how to round up cattle — when he was in the Army and stationed in Fort Hood, Texas. He bought a horse and saddle, and whenever he could, he'd go off to the Fort Hood Reservation and talk somebody into letting him ride along and, at least for a little while, fantasize about living the life of a cowboy. Though he now made his living as a well-known landscape photographer and teacher, there was nothing he loved as much as being on a horse with nothing but steers for company.

He got the idea of trying to marry his fantasy life with his profession and started photographing cowboys all over the west, from the northern high plains states down to the Mexican border.

> When I photograph these cowboys and go around to these
> ranches, my custom is to – I take my saddle along, I take all my
> cowboying gear as well as my photographic equipment, and
> I've found the best way to get to know these people is to try
> and help them with their ranch work. And I'm sure that there's
> that selfish part of me that is going around and having this
> wonderful adventure of cowboying all over the West. I'm not
> qualified to do it under professional conditions, but the fact
> that I'm photographing kind of gives me a wonderful excuse
> to get in there and get into the game. ... I've had the chance to
> try and pay 'em back a little bit with what that I can do for the
> outfit, and it's a lot of fun.

Jay said that there were only about 200 "real" cowboys left near
as he could figure, primarily single men, itinerant laborers, really.
Though they had pickup trucks, they did their work on horseback,
drifting north and south with the seasons, leading lives of ... well,
if you've ever listened to Willie Nelson singing, "My Heroes Have
Always Been Cowboys," with its men who are "sadly, in search of,
and one step in back of, themselves and their slow-moving dreams"
you'd know what Jay was saying.

We drove on a barely-there dirt track for mile after mile, the only
vehicles to be seen, the newly fallen snow a light groundcover. Then,
in the distance eventually, a small, weathered wood cabin, a thin
plume of smoke rising in the quiet. There we met Joe Hall, a tall,
lanky cowboy who had agreed to let Jay photograph him and us to
tag along with them the next day while they rounded up strays. He
cooked us up some dinner on the wood-burning stove (not much
to it, as I recall), and we sat and talked awhile by the light of a
kerosene lamp as the dark night gathered around us and the temperature outside plummeted. But, of course, it wasn't any too warm
in the outhouse either. The camera batteries went into the bottom of
our sleeping bags so they wouldn't drain their power (no electricity
to recharge them) as the fire died and the cold seeped into the cabin
while we went to sleep.

In the morning, Joe broke the ice on the top of a bucket of
water and made "cowboy" coffee and steak and eggs. Since he was

married, he brought the eggs for us following an occasional stay at his wife's house (she never stayed with him in the line cabin). And then he and Jay saddled up, and off they went to round up the strays with us trailing behind, shooting all the while.

Jay unpacked his big, wooden 8 x 10 camera that used sheet film and mounted it on a heavy tripod when they were done.

> **I began to photograph the cowboys with the 8 x 10 camera because it was the camera I was most familiar with, and I'd seen that most of the photographs of cowboys were being done with a hand camera – 35 millimeter, very portable, very easy to use, and I thought, well, 100 years ago they were photographed with cameras on tripods. That was all that was available then. ... Somewhere between the romantic connection with the past and the fact that I know the big camera better than the little camera, I just started it that way.**

That's why Jay's cowboy portraits in his book, *The North American Cowboy: A Portrait*, look the way they do: Absolutely still. Frozen in time and space. They are expressionless because you have to be entirely still for the few seconds it takes for the sheet of film to be exposed, unlike today's smaller, faster cameras that can freeze the quickest motion. So, no, "Say Cheese" in these photos. In Jay's photographs, the cowboys look no different than if they had been taken a hundred years before.

I interviewed Jay for a few minutes, and then we packed our gear, waved our thanks and goodbyes to Joe, and were gone.

> **If it was possible for me to just pick and choose my dream situation in life, what I would really prefer to be doing right now, I can tell you this. I'd sure like to be doing quite a bit of cowboying. I'm not professional cowboy caliber, but I would sure like to be able to spend more time at it than I am right now.**

The last time I talked to Jay, nothing had changed. He still loved being a photographer. And he still loved cowboying.

Jay's photographs of cowboys, the images' stillness, the method of photographing, the similarity to pictures taken a century before were, in a way, a portrait of the mythology of the West in the American imagination. These, however, weren't mythological creatures; they were real people in the present, in the now, clinging to a past that was fast disappearing and, in fact, no longer really existed, if it ever really did.

In 1985 Richard Avedon published his book, *In the American West*. His photographs of ordinary people in western America, manual laborers, and, at best, scruffy people who led, at best, scruffy lives were the complete opposite of Jay's cowboys. Photographed against blank white backgrounds, they were, in effect, stripped naked, stripped of the context in which they were usually seen and, perhaps, never really seen as anything other than an unnoticed part of the background. If Jay's photographs were of people clinging to the past, Avendon's were of people very much living in the present. Avedon's would all have been at home in Norman Mailer's *The Executioner's Song."*

Some didn't like Avedon's book and the exhibition on which it was based, the photographs enormously enlarged, their starkness assaulting you, insisting that they be seen, these previously mostly invisible people. Maybe it was my imagination, but people in the east loved the photographs; but some western folks were less enthusiastic, much preferring the mythologized West.

Westerners, at least those in Texas, love their mythology. Just think about the Alamo. There is no Texas tale more mythologized than the Alamo's heroes dying valiantly in the battle against the horde of Mexicans for the sake of Texas and "liberty." Yet the reality of those "heroes" was that they were a bunch of quite unsavory characters, and the liberty they sought was the right to own slaves, a practice that Mexicans were trying to banish.

In 1988 I remembered reading Larry McMurtry's *Anything for Billy*. McMurtry was as fine a writer about the West of our imagination as we've ever had. In the book, Billy, the Billy as in Billy the Kid, is demolished as a myth by McMurtry and revealed to be a pretty despicable person. However, by the end of the book, McMurtry has managed to recreate a mythological Billy the Kid, seemingly despite his best efforts not to do so. Perhaps McMurtry was saying that the mythology of our West is too powerful to be erased by mere facts, by reality.

The co-author of Avedon's book was Laura Wilson, a Dallas photographer well known to Jim, AC Greene, and Cheryl Gruver, who was in charge of PBS station relations for the *NewsHour*. I think Laura was working for or with a PR firm at the time, and I think we had been introduced by AC, but I might be wrong about that. In any event, she arranged for me to shoot Avedon while he was photographing one of his portraits in Texas. Unfortunately, we never had a chance to interview Avedon directly because the project was abandoned when I was asked to devote myself to the essays on a full-time basis.

As an aside, in later years, *Hutterites of Montana*, Laura Wilson's book of text and photographs about this religious sect, became the basis of an essay by Richard Rodriguez wrote for the *NewsHour*.

Les, Robin, and Jim seemed to like these features almost as much as I did, and there were many more of them in the next year or so. In fact, they liked them so much that we created a series for them. We called it, for want of a better name, "The Road Series." I'd pick a stretch of road, and Nancy Nichols, the reporter assigned to me, and I would look for people whose story I wanted to hear, whose story I wanted them to tell me, whose story I wanted to retell to the rest of America.

In Charles Edmunds and, in particular, Jay Dusard, I had found what I was looking for: A theme that I cared deeply about and a form through which to express it: People who loved what they were doing or who would find a way to do what they loved. All of them did it well. Some were able to make a living at it, some not but did it anyway, at least some of the time, just because they loved it so much. Some were famous, most not. But in all cases, fame and money were not the reason they did whatever it was they did. They *had* to do it.

These were values that meant a great deal to me. They were, in fact, why I did what I was doing. God knows I wasn't in television, and certainly, public television, to get rich. The things that I tried to create for Hollywood were not proposed to make me rich, though I'd have had no objection if that had been a byproduct. I had something(s) in me that wanted to get out, that I wanted to say, express, and communicate to the world, and this was a way to do it, even if I wasn't always sure in advance what those things were. Thinking back to my days of greatest struggle, no, making zippers wouldn't do it for me. It wasn't that I had an agenda, that I had a list of particular things that I knew I wanted to say or communicate. It was more that I felt that there was a sensibility that I had, a sense of values, of things right and wrong, of greater and lesser importance, of the beauty and tragedy of humanness, of … I don't know. I would know them when I saw them.

I knew something else as well: That every time I made something, every time I put something on the air, it was not something that was apart from me, something that was distinct from me. It *was* me. It was what I had seen, what I had felt, what I had experienced, what I had learned from my lifetime of living. That was true even if I never appeared on camera or anyone ever knew my name. But I knew that what they saw was me, for better or worse. Sitting in an editing room, it was neither the first nor the last time that I would think of that plea in *Makepeace's Blackouts* by Tommy Makepeace, the ne'er do well-failed artist, failed man,

Say something real, true, heartfelt.

For the first time in my life, I began to feel that I was coming closer to doing that. Sheryl Crow sang, "Every day is a winding road. I get a little bit closer to feeling fine."

And so on I went. To be sure, I was asked to produce things that were of no particular interest to me, but I was glad to do them, to be asked to do them, pieces about a lobsterman in Maine and a man who grew the largest pumpkin on record for a Halloween piece. There were occasional celebrities like Alec Guinness, who Robin interviewed in a NY hotel room. There were always opportunities to meet interesting people. They ran the gamut from people like Ray Kurzweil and Jaron Lanier, both at the forefront of the coming digital revolution, to the aging yet extraordinary and luminous Talmudic scholar Rabbi Adin Steinsaltz.

On the other hand, our interview of Eudora Welty at her home in Jackson, MS, was different if for no reason other than it was part of the series of pieces that Nancy Nichols and I were doing together. I no longer remember if we decided to interview her or Robin asked us to do it. I think the occasion of the interview was her nomination for the National Book Award in 1983 for her book, *One Writer's Beginnings*. What made the interview truly rewarding was not the interview itself, interesting as it was. We wanted to take Eudora to dinner, and she took us to a diner where, she said, she usually ate. She was charming, gracious, and good-humored. Everyone seemed to know her, and we had a lovely evening.

On a Friday afternoon in early December 1983, I had lunch with Lee Blumer. We had met at a wedding and formed a friendship that lasted many years. She was working for Michael Lang, the original creator of the 1969 Woodstock Festival and, in fact, had worked on it back then. In her spare time, Lee promoted people and causes she believed in. She told me about a sculptor she had been introduced to by a Holocaust survivor. He was sculpting, she said, a monument to the American soldiers who had liberated the concentration camps during World War II.

A couple of weeks later, she took me to meet Nathan Rapaport, a man in his early seventies, with thinning gray hair and gold-rimmed spectacles. His eyes sparkled with enthusiasm and delight at being alive. He had been born in Warsaw and became a sculptor. During the war, he had escaped east to the Soviet Union and spent the remaining war years in Siberia, where he was allowed to continue his work. After the war, in 1948, he returned to Warsaw and amidst the rubble began to construct his thirty-six-foot high monument commemorating the uprising against the Nazis in the Warsaw Ghetto. The stone Nathan used for his memorial had been initially collected by the Nazis for a never-built monument celebrating Hitler's never achieved victory over Europe. After the war, he lived in Paris, Israel, and New York, becoming an American citizen in 1965.

In January 1984, I shot Nathan working on his sculpture in his studio/apartment on West 74th Street before it was enlarged to be cast in bronze and placed in Liberty Park, NJ, within sight of the Statue of Liberty. It was an American GI carrying the almost weightless body of a survivor in his arms. The final piece was a great success so far as the show was concerned. More important to me, though, was Nathan's opinion. He called after it aired to say how much he had liked it, how he felt it had communicated his true feelings. I couldn't have felt more gratified; it was what I always tried to do with people. I wanted them to be who they were, not what they thought they should pretend to be or what I wanted them to be.

Nathan was not only gifted, but he was an extraordinarily gentle, kind, and good man, a man who felt he never could give as much as he had received, though he would try.

My real life as a man and as an artist started really with the outbreak of World War II. I have spent 35 years now working. I am trying to communicate my feeling with all my heart really, to people, and the spoken word is not my medium of communication. I'm sorry. My works have been made of bronze, of stone; they are silent, heavy, and long-lasting.

World War II and the horrors inflicted on man, and the courage with which men fought to survive, has become the most powerful single force in my art. I don't know who said so, but it seems to me that Van Gogh said that there is something in the human eyes which the cathedrals doesn't have. Which means my vocabulary is the human being. Through this medium I can express myself. It's not only the hands, it's everything which must express my idea. If I need the hands playing a greater role, I make them bigger. I never am slave to nature. I'm only taking from nature what I need, and I manipulate it in a way that it should express what I want.

How do I have to make him? What does he want from me? How should he be? I made him tall, strong, noble. It's a fusion between this wonderful young man and the weightless and almost lifeless body of a concentration camp prisoner. He came from a land of plenty to save Europe from tyranny. He restored life, freedom, joy. It's really a tribute to the American liberators. So I can't make him an Apollo, but he's beautiful in my eyes. I didn't make him, you know, a victor coming with a gun. He doesn't have a gun. He's a human being. He came to save another human being. A gentleman came here, the moment he saw this country, he said, "It's me, it's me. They look like me, exactly like this. We should have gone to -- be dead in a few hours. In the last moment these -- the American soldiers saved me. We start to cry. It was me." You know?

So I think I had to do this. It was not a commission. Nobody asked me to do it. It just came out. I'm working for 35 years, and it is just a kind of apotheosis of the whole, you know -- in the beginning, of course, a man cries. We have to cry. Nobody can teach you how to cry. You are crying. It comes to you. And then little by little you don't have any more tears and you can see more clearly what was it all about. And that, my God, but we forgot those who liberated us. We are crying all the time about ourself, and it's about time to say thank you, and that's what I'm doing. It's a tribute to the American Army, to the American people.

After the piece aired, Lee (no, not Lee Blumer) and I would have dinner with Nathan and his girlfriend from time to time. Nathan divided his life between Israel and New York, and we made plans to visit Israel together. Unfortunately, before we got to make the trip, in June 1987, Nathan died in Israel. This is my small attempt to pay homage to a wonderful man and, more importantly, a friend.

A much more famous American artist, Robert Motherwell, said something similar when Nancy and I did a piece on him for his 70th birthday. I don't mean about the liberation of the Jews from the camps or the virtues of America but about the necessity of painting for the artist, for him.

A painter who saw this show wrote me a brief note saying that what struck him, having seen for the first time a big body of my work, is that all that grace and elegance that they talk about is really a counterbalance to real angst, real, almost unbearable anxiety and that people who talk about it as being suave or beautiful and so on, are people who don't see the death and angst and anxiety underneath it. I suppose that's one of the reasons that the problems of painting are as fresh and as difficult to me as the day I began. If I didn't [paint], I'd probably be devoured by my angst, and maybe to the degree of

> no longer being able to function as a human being at all. And
> it's in that sense that painting -- for all the artists I've known --
> not necessarily for exactly the same reasons, but in that sense,
> is a profound necessity and not a profession.

I learned something from Motherwell that day, nothing that he said, nothing that he intended, but something that I only understood while watching what I had shot in the editing room. I had asked him if we could shoot him painting, a request that I'm sure he understood the reasons for but which annoyed him because, I think, the act of picking up a brush and painting was so weighty for him. But he nonetheless acceded to our request. He leaned a blank canvas against a pile of other canvases, took a long stick — a broom handle, I think — with a two-inch brush taped to the end of it, dipped it in a can of orange paint, and slowly painted a horizontal line across the entire width of the canvass, right through the middle.

Sitting in the dark room, watching the line of orange gradually traveling across the white space in the monitor, I understood that the act, that line, changed everything, that it was magical. It was no longer the same canvas. Metaphorically, there were no longer an infinite number of possibilities of things one could do to that canvass. At most, there was now an infinity minus one, $\infty - 1$, a finite number of possibilities. In some indefinable way, the number of possibilities was reduced even further. It is almost as though that line insisted on the subsequent line in some equally ineffable and mysterious way. It was not/is not wholly arbitrary. And so I have found it to be true in everything I do, certainly creatively, and very possibly in life too. That realization, no matter if I had been unaware of its truth — its profundity — before, became the conscious bedrock of my work ever since. When working on decoding a script, the first decision about an image to accompany it somewhere, anywhere in the script, defines and limits every other possible choice that I might make. So, too, in writing. The mere writing of a word limits future possibilities. The writing of a sentence, an idea, forces the next idea through a logic all its own.

And so, the pieces rolled out through 1984.

Joe Akers, the 79-year-old editor, publisher, and owner of the weekly Randolph County Herald Tribune, in Chester, Illinois, was discovered by Nancy. He had taken over the newspaper from his brother after he retired. Joe despaired of the growing trend of syndicates taking over local newspapers, something that has gone on unabated until today and not only in newspapers but in banking, telecommunications, retailing, industry after industry in what is benignly called "consolidation." In the process, Joe felt then, and would undoubtedly feel even more so today, newspapers would lose touch with their readers' real lives.

> **Just this past summer, I hadn't been out of the house all day Saturday because I wasn't feeling well. In fact, I wasn't even dressed, wandering around in my pajamas, dressing gown. And about 6:15, the doorbell rang. I went to the door and here was a little boy, six years old. He looked up at me and he said, "Hi, Joe." And I said, "Well, hi, there, sonny. What can I do for you?" And it developed that he had caught the first fish he'd ever caught in his life. And it was about a seven-pounder, and he caught it right down here at the Chester waterfront. Very obvious that he'd like to have a picture. Well, I couldn't disappoint a little fella like that, so I tossed on some clothes and we came down here at the office, I got a camera and took a picture of him. That's the way you have to do it in a small town.**

It was a typically hot night in Tucson, AZ, when we watched 12-year-old Heather Conway pitch a shutout for her Little League team. It wasn't unusual; she was the best pitcher in Tucson, boy or girl. When we talked to her and her parents the next day, it was clear that Heather wanted to go on to the next level, to see just how far she could go. Her father thought she shouldn't, that girls couldn't/ shouldn't compete with boys as they got older; she was a girl and should do girl things. Her mother seemed to reluctantly agree with her husband. As for Heather, who would obey her parents in these pre-Title IX, pre-women's liberation days,

> **I'm sure I could have gone on if I was born as a boy, yeah.**

We ran across Katie Lee in Jerome, AZ, a small, one-time mining town alongside the Mingus River on Route 89 between Prescott and Sedona. Katie, then in her mid-60s, had been a popular performer during the beginnings of the folk music revival in the 40s and early 50s. She said she was the best-known female folk singer in America between the time of Burl Ives' greatest popularity and the Weavers. So, not surprisingly, I was interested in her recollections. I had seen Burl Ives as a kid, as I had Cisco Huston, a one-time boyfriend of Katie's. And I had at least a passing acquaintance with the Weavers' Pete Seeger, Lee Hayes, and Ronnie Gilbert, although I never met Fred Hellerman, the fourth member. But, inevitably, when talking about the folk scene of the 50s, the talk got around to politics.

> I came to Hollywood as a very young and -- not so young, maybe, but young to me. I mean, I was green. And I had never been involved in politics. And I found all of a sudden that folk singers were looked on as Communists. This was during the McCarthy era. And they seemed to be very hot to know all about Woody Guthrie and Cisco Houston and other people of that group, and these were people that I went to hootenannies with. I learned from them, and they learned from me. And this is where you get your education. It's imperative that you learn that way, firsthand. And the next thing I knew, I was being questioned by the Federal Bureau of Investigation. So I called them up one day and I said, "Hey, listen. This is where I'm from and this is where I'm coming from, and I don't know anything about labor and couldn't care less, and I'm not involved in that, and I sing with these people and that's it." And then they would call me periodically and ask me where these people were. They'd say, "I understand there's a party at such-and-such up in Topanga Canyon tonight. Would you tell us who's there?" And I said, "Why?" I said, "I already know who's going to be there, and so do you." Well, it got to the point where I just had to say, "Don't call me anymore. I'm not an informer. Leave me alone." And I don't -- I didn't behave in any way that I'm ashamed of, it's just that when I think back on that, even that slight contact with the Federal Bureau of Investigation kind of makes me cringe. I just -- I wonder what they thought, or if they had any feeling about it or if they even knew about it. I remember telling Woody Guthrie one time that somebody was trying to check up on him, and

> Will Geer, who was another one in Hollywood, I mentioned --
> I said, "They seem to be interested in your whereabouts." And
> he said, "Tell them to go to hell." And so I did.

I don't know that it was possible to remain neutral in the political maelstrom that engulfed the world of folk music performers during the '50s. There indeed were plenty of folk singers who were Communists and, if not actual party members, "fellow travelers" and sympathizers. But *everybody* wanted you to choose sides, even if some, like Katie, didn't really want to. The Left wanted you to pick a side, and so did the FBI and the Senate Internal Security Committee, and the House Un-American Activities Committee, not to mention organizations like Red Channels, one of the major propagators of the blacklist. Neutrality was not an option. Because she wasn't one of them, apparently, the Left disowned and shunned Katie even to that sunny day decades later sitting in front of her house.

> I kind of have to laugh at these people who don't seem
> to know when I leave my name at the box office or with their
> manager. That's one of the questions you asked me before.
> That's one of the things I never wanted to become or do. I
> never wanted to get so far out of line that I couldn't remember
> my old friends. Harry Belafonte does not call me back
> anymore when I leave a message. Even Judy Collins doesn't
> call me back when I leave a message. I know who'd call me
> back if I left a message. Josh White would, but he's dead.

Katie was not entirely happy with my portrayal of her, mostly because she felt she had too much life in her and thought she had left all that residual bitterness behind. But as we talked, she finally agreed that, yes, it really was all true, that she had never been able to really leave it behind.

Until her death in 2017, when in her 90s, Katie was still living in Jerome, still making records, writing, and working to preserve the rivers and canyons of Arizona she loved so much.

During the trip to Arizona, when we shot Katie, we stopped in Paulden to visit Jeff Cooper and his Gunsite Ranch. Even today, long after he died in 2006, Jeff is an icon of 2nd Amendment absolutists. He got his undergraduate degree from Stamford and then a Master's in history from the Univ. of California, Riverside. A combat veteran of World War 2 and Korea, he retired as a Marine Lt. Colonel. He was the founder of the American Pistol Institute in 1976, which was renamed the Gunsite Ranch and still exists as the Gunsite Academy.

Cooper's renown was in no small measure a result of his successful promotion of what he called the "Modern Handgun Technique," which is based on using a two-handed stance to hold the gun and the adoption of certain attitudes in life. When you see that stance in virtually every movie or TV show in which there are handguns, well, that's Jeff Cooper's influence. As for Gunsite, it probably was then, and for all I know still is, the foremost training center in small-arms use for law enforcement and military personnel along with civilians. I think if I wanted to be really well trained in the use of weapons for self-defense, Gunsite is where I'd choose to go.

Nancy and I spent the morning talking to him informally. Jeff was friendly, garrulous, good-humored — charming, even — after which we had lunch with him, his wife, and some of his staff. We shot various shooting classes in the afternoon, both in marksmanship and tactical simulations and a lecture.

I think we interviewed him the next day. The interview covered many topics, including his view about the rights of citizens to defend themselves if the state wouldn't do it or doesn't do it well enough, an issue that is still important. My guess is that he would have favored "stand your ground" and open-carry laws. Jeff also talked about the state of American cities and the presidential campaign of Jesse Jackson. He told us that he was considered *persona non grata* in several countries, particularly in West Africa and Central America. When asked if he had been a mercenary, he said he hadn't. So had he been in these countries at a time of upheaval and civil wars at the behest and employment of the US government? He wouldn't say, but the implications were clear.

When we got back to NY, we proceeded to edit the piece the way we usually did. That is to say, we got a transcript made, laid all the pages on the floor, marked, and literally cut up the transcript so that it made a coherent, linear interview. Nancy and I discussed whether we should leave his comments about Jesse Jackson in because they made Cooper seem like a racist. I decided to leave them in because taking them out would be misleading regarding what he was like as a human being.

As usual, I gave the piece to Les and Robin. I probably even screened it with them in Robin's office, as I usually did with everything I produced before Robin's retirement. They made no objection. A copy was sent to Jim. Les called me to say that Jim had asked that the remarks about Jackson be removed because it made Cooper appear to be a racist. I said I would not because that's, in fact, what he had revealed himself to be, even if we didn't know it before we went to Gunsite. And there matters stood. Jim never talked to me about the piece, and, in fact, I can't think of a time when he voluntarily spoke to me about anything I did. In the end, I said that I'd rather the piece didn't air rather than make the changes. Les agreed, so it's never been seen, though I may still have a copy somewhere or other. After all, it was a good piece.

In the years since, particularly as police killings of Blacks became a major political issue, I've wondered what Jeff Cooper would have thought. I thought he would have said they were a byproduct of poor training in most controversial cases in recent years. I don't know if he would have thought race was a determinative factor in these situations because I'm sure that he didn't see himself as a racist and, therefore, might be less likely to see others as such. But, on the other hand, I thought it probable that he would have thought George Zimmerman should never have been allowed to have a gun and that he had deliberately hunted down and, perhaps, provoked Trayvon Martin. I hope he would have not excused the three white men who hunted and killed Ahmaud Arbery. And I think he, too, would have found Derek Chauvin guilty of murder. But above all, I think a lack of proper training and self-discipline, not just initially but throughout one's policing career, would have been the critical factor for Cooper for all police shootings.

I don't think every piece I did served their subject as well as I hoped. For example, the piece I did about Frank Herbert, author of *Dune,* one of the great science fiction novels, was probably the most personally disappointing. Maybe that was because pieces about writers can be challenging in the form I was using, as it was heavily dependent on visual imagery. After all, what is it that writers do when they are writing? When Roger Rosenblatt's very young grandchild brought him to school one day and introduced him to her class, she said, using her nickname for Roger, "This is Beppo. He sits in the basement all day and does nothing." Not the most visually compelling scene you can imagine. But I wanted the piece to be better because of how I felt about Frank.

I have no idea why or how I knew that Frank had a house on Whidbey Island in Puget Sound, about 30 miles north of Seattle. Nancy and I had decided to go there to do a piece on Dale Chihuly, thought by many at the time, and still to this day, to be the most significant glass artist in post-War America and maybe the world, at his Pilchuk School in Stanwood, WA and thought that while there we would talk to Frank as well.

Meeting Frank was one of the eeriest experiences I've ever had. It felt like we had known each other for eons, as if he knew everything I thought before I said it, and I knew everything he was thinking.

"What name should I call you," he said.

"Whatever you'd like," I said. Then I thought for a moment longer. "Actually, people at work call me Mike. My family and wife call me Michael."

And then the three of us talked for two or three hours. Later that night, Nancy and I went over what he had told us, as was our usual practice, and drew up a long list of questions, mainly about *Dune* and what he had intended readers to learn from it. Then, the following morning, we went back to his house and interviewed him at his writing desk on the second floor of his A-frame house overlooking Puget Sound. We talked about the book and its themes, particularly the danger of religious messiahs and the necessity of skepticism toward anybody in power or who wants power.

> **In creating the characters for *Dune*, I went to the messiah story that's so strong in our mythology. But I wasn't going to do the Jesus story. I went to the Arthurian legend, and I was trying to create a mythology that would give people a different**

> view of how we give over our lives to leaders, not just to messiahs but to people who pose as our leaders, or who make themselves our leaders, or who entice us into following them. The religious commentary statement in *Dune* is the one we've discussed earlier that messiahs should come with a label on the forehead "may be dangerous to your health.

Perhaps the most important single thing he said when we talked never made it into the final piece was this:

> I don't believe absolute power corrupts absolutely. I think the real problem with power is that power attracts the corruptible.

Sitting in the editing room, I wondered if Frank had known L. Ron Hubbard in the early days when Hubbard was creating the always controversial Dianetics and Scientology, thinking that he probably had because so many science fiction writers of the '40s and '50s knew each other and because of Hubbard's talk of genetic memory in *Dianetics*. Was Hubbard someone he had in mind when writing *Dune?* I thought I'd be sure to ask him the next time we met, for I was sure we would meet again. When we left, he wrote an inscription in one of his books.

> **To Michael, who is not Mike to me**

We never did meet again. Frank died in February 1986.

In looking back over these pieces, things that, personally, were among the most important things that I ever did or experienced, I am struck by how attached each of these people are to the past, whether it was Frank Herbert as a Jungian or Jay Dusard's yearning to participate in a way of life that was a century in the past, or Katie Lee's youthful exuberance being painfully pummeled in the Red scare of the 50s forcing her to retreat to the Arizona desert.

I, too, am tied to the past and by more than my long-time scatter-shot interest in history. I never gave it much thought until sometime in the late '80s or very early '90s when the Vietnam War had emerged as a campaign issue. I had a young assistant (well, they were all young), and one day I said something to her about Vietnam's ongoing importance in our political life. She shrugged. "I was only 9 or 10 then. It doesn't mean a thing to me."

It was then that I thought for the first time, "I have lived through history." At what point in our lives do we see that the things we experienced have become part of a larger story, a story we call "History?" It also occurred to me then that I had lived through approximately ¼ of our nation's history. That was an extraordinary realization to me at the time, as it still is today. To be aware of that is to be aware of how truly young this country is, how much we are still being formed even as there are things about us that seem somewhat intractable: our preference for optimism, our inclination towards messianism, our lack of interest in the realities of the past, the idea that we can recreate ourselves in infinite variety even as we know its impossibility. But more importantly to me, it is to be aware of how meaningful our lives and the way we lead our lives are to creating our future as a nation. Just as in Motherwell's brushstroke, everything we do becomes a brick in the foundation of our future, both personally and as a nation, a brushstroke that both limits and helps define what is possible.

Speaking of living through history, sometime during the winter of 1988 or '89, I got another call from Lee Blumer. She had someone else she thought I should meet. Susan Morris and I met for lunch one day at the Metropolitan Museum of Art. She was working for the Museum's film department, and after lunch, she took me to see Karl Katz, the department director. We chatted about this and that, about what I was doing and had done for *M/L* and my background before PBS. It felt more like a job interview than anything else, more of a job interview than the one I had at that lunch with Les or with Don Sussman when he'd hired me in 1974. During the meeting, he got a phone call. After he was on the call for a couple of minutes, he said to whoever he was talking to, "I might have someone sitting in the office who would be right for this."

After the call ended, he told me that he was helping the Simon Wiesenthal Center in LA on a project. The SWC's Museum of Tolerance would soon be opening and was looking for someone to create some videos and other exhibits. Might I be interested? Sure I would. I cooked up some ideas, I had lunch with Al Franken (still with SNL at the time) and asked if he'd be interested in one or two of the concepts I had (maybe he was, let's see how things progress), and I talked to a couple of other people as well. I met with the Wiesenthal folks in LA and was told their real interest in me was for a short film about genocide. Why don't I come up with a specific proposal?

After a couple of days back home, I decided that rather than tell them my idea, I'd present the idea to them on video. For a few days, after I got home from work, I'd scour my collection of music, looking for the right track, the right sound. I even bought some CDs. Finally, I found what I was looking for. It was a Peter Gabriel song, a vaguely Middle Eastern thing with a soulful, sorrowful sound. The lyrics for this purpose were irrelevant. In fact, I had no idea what they were then or now. I asked my PA to dig up whatever Holocaust footage we had in the house, walked into my editing room, handed the tapes to Ruth Pohl, who had been my primary editor for a few years, and said, "Here's what we're doing." This was all footage I'd seen before, and I knew what I wanted to do with it, cutting the horrific scenes of the concentration camps with its dead and dying bodies against the Gabriel track.

The next time I was in LA (I probably was in LA at least once a month), I met with the Wiesenthal people again. Rabbi Marvin Hier, the Dean and founder of the Center, was there, as was Associate Dean Rabbi Abe Cooper. Also present were Dr. Gerry Margolis, the Museum of Tolerance's Executive Director, James Gardner, the museum's British exhibition designer, and Frances Belzberg, the wife of the museum's principal funder. Rabbi Hier asked me what my idea was.

"I want to make a music video."

I'm sure I heard more than one sharp intake of breath.

"Let me show you what I mean."

Before the meeting, I had asked Gerry Margolis if he could make sure there was a monitor and a tape playback machine available in the room. So I got up and walked to the tape deck and played the tape. The sound of Peter Gabriel's moan filled the room as images of boxcars stuffed with people, the haunted faces of starving children, the emaciated bodies of still living survivors scattered on the ground, dead bodies in piles, crematorium oven doors being slammed shut, all these images filled the screen.

The video only lasted three minutes. At its conclusion, Hier said, "We'd like you to make a film about genocide." What should be in that film was left undecided.

Not long after, many of the same people met with me in NY at the Marriott Hotel's Broadway location. The video, although about genocide, should not include the Holocaust. I was surprised and objected. Why shouldn't the Holocaust be seen as, in essence, not so different than other genocides? The simplest explanation had to do with the design of the museum. There was a Tolerance section — ½ of the museum — and a Holocaust section — the other half — and they wanted to separate them. Even if they saw the Holocaust as an event that differed in scope and magnitude, as well as being intrinsically different from other genocides, they wanted to make sure that those other genocides were not left out of the public's understanding of the world they lived in.

Although we didn't really agree, I could understand their viewpoint. The Holocaust was not, at that time, without controversy — not only between Jews and non-Jews in America but within the larger American Jewish community. It's not that there was disagreement about the fact of the Holocaust itself (well, you can still find people who are Holocaust deniers). Still, there was considerable disagreement about how the Holocaust should be understood, what was the meaning of the Holocaust, how it should be or could be used as a metaphor or as a cudgel to bash opponents, how it could be or should be used as motivation or excuse, and last but not least, how it should be taught in schools, even should it be taught in schools. As those events become ever more distant, as we feel more distanced from it in time, as the last survivors die out, will we Americans come to think of it as an event increasingly irrelevant to our lives? All good questions, don't you think?

In the end, we agreed my video would deal with three instances of genocide in the 20th century: the Armenian genocide by the Turks during World War 1, the Cambodian genocide perpetrated by the Khmer Rouge in the late 1970s, and the present-day killing of Indians in Latin America, particularly Brazil.

Although I wanted the video to be unaccompanied by narration, Gerry Margolis insisted that there had to be some narration to give context to the video. I agreed as long as it could be brief. Accordingly, I wrote a script with four highly condensed sections: a definition of genocide and its geographic universality in 150 words and then three separate introductions for each example of genocide averaging 75 words each.

I went to Anne Twomey for a narrator. I'd met Anne many years earlier when she was dating John Getz after he and Amy had returned from California. Amy had been the artistic director for a theater company for several years in Napa Valley, and John had been a member of the acting company. So I met them when they visited Amy at our parents' house in Copake. I also had seen Anne in her extraordinary performance as the lead in *Nuts*'s original 1980 Broadway production. She'd won a Theater World Award and a Tony nomination for Best Actress. I thought her low-pitched velvet voice could both be understated and compelling.

I tried to get Peter Gabriel to write the music. I didn't want lyrics but just a melodic line. He turned me down. I went to Lee Blumer and asked if she had any suggestions since she had spent a lifetime in the music business. In fact, she did. Willie DeVille, she thought, could do the job. I had never heard of him. Because Lee seemed to think so highly of him, I went and bought a couple of tapes of his and his one-time band, Mink DeVille. Why should I believe this rocker, who thought rock 'n roll really belonged in bars, could give me what I wanted? Lee was sure of him, so I agreed to listen to a demo if he was willing to write something. And he did. It was magnificent. It was slow, bluesy, and soulful, with a beautiful hymnal quality. Willie came to NY to record it. After laying down the instrumental tracks, he unexpectedly went into the sound booth and laid down a vocal track. There were no words, just him humming in contrast to the synthesizer melody for the last minute or so of the film — adding a human mourning feel to match the narrative phrase at the beginning and end of the final section, "The Indians are dying."

I hired one of my *M/L* PAs to hunt for stills after negotiating with several photo agencies I did a lot of business with. Then, with all the production elements in hand, I set about creating a video that I hoped would educate and move people.

Thirty years earlier, Bill Zimmerman had encouraged me to learn how to edit. He was convinced that films were made or broken in their editing; it was where every virtue and every flaw had to be maximized or repaired. I've never found a reason to think he was wrong. Editing sports films at Winik had given me a sense of timing and storytelling that had been incalculably important throughout my career. Over the years, there were many occasions when everything came together in a free-flowing continuum, things naturally flowing from one inevitable image to the next, from one idea to the next like a river. Such was the experience editing this Genocide video.

The week before the edit, I took photos to a studio and shot them on an animation stand. I had already pretty much decided what images would be used and how they would appear, how many seconds long pans and zooms should last, what should *happen* in the film, how to tell the story. In effect, I locked myself into decisions that I made before we even started to edit, leaving only a few options if things didn't work as I thought they would.

The video was to be shown in a small theater that would hold not more than 20 or 30 people at a time. No one was to be let in until the video was over. There were three screens in front of the audience, their combined width covering the entire curved front of the theater to roughly encompass the viewers' peripheral vision. Loudspeakers would be placed around the room so that the audience was surrounded by sound.

While writing this book, I asked Gerry Margolis, who became a close personal friend after my work for the Wiesenthal Center was completed, "Do you know how I thought of those three screens?" It was something we had never talked about. No, he had no idea.

"I thought of them as a cross."

He was, I think, surprised. I mean, there was a Jewish institution; everyone involved was Jewish. I was Jewish. "A Christian cross?" he asked.

"Yes. There was the middle screen, the center of everything, the core of the video's meaning, and there were the two other screens, the wings, the images supporting the core."

I was aware of the irony of the analogy, both in the current context and also historically. Unless one is an orthodox Jew, most of the reading in one's life has been of non-Jewish writers. At least that's been my experience, and we've become used to thinking of images and metaphors in religious terms, Christian terms at that, even if we don't mean something religious by their use. Although, we might intend something vaguely spiritual.

When the audience entered the theater, there would be a low-pitched drone, an almost ominous sound. The doors would close. The loud sound of a cell door slamming shut traveled from one side of the theater to the other behind the audience. And then a voice, Anne's voice — almost a whisper — would begin in the dark.

> **Bigotry, prejudice, racism, religious intolerance, tribal rivalry and jealousy, class conflict, the fear and hatred of others who are not us — they have all played and still play their part in the lives of nations.**
>
> **But on rare occasions, they escalate to an inconceivable level. A level of viciousness and brutality in which the leaders of a nation deliberately try to physically annihilate, eradicate, exterminate, massacre, murder a particular group of fellow human beings.**
>
> **There is a name for this evil. We call it Genocide.**

And we were off, music and images flooding the screen, sometimes the same on all the screens, sometimes different on each of them, sometimes the same on the two outside screens, sometimes different.

Turkish soldiers gloating over decapitated heads of Armenians displayed on racks.

Piles of bare-boned skulls in Cambodia.

A mass of dead bodies floating in the swirling eddies of a South American river.

Ruth Pohl and I used an editing room outside of WNET. Like

most editors, she liked to take part in decisions. She, too, after all, was a creator, a contributor in what is, at the very least, a somewhat collaborative process. But there I was standing behind her with the music playing, waving my arms like an orchestra conductor, knowing exactly where each image should be placed on which screen, where each dissolve should happen, and for how long, what should move and what shouldn't, where each image should go in which screen. She looked at me once.

"What?" I asked.

"Nothing. Just keep doing what you're doing."

She turned back to her monitors and keyboard, as intent on what she was doing as I was, trying her best to keep up with what I was asking of her. I don't know how long it took us, but I don't recall that it took all that long (whatever that means). Finally, when it was over, the last sounds of Willie disappearing into the distance, the final images fading out, I sat down, exhausted.

Ruth said, "Well, that was something. I don't think I've ever seen that." Me either.

Gerry loved it. Rabbi Hier loved it. James Gardner thought it was too different from everything else in the Tolerance section of the museum and should be discarded. Hier said, "It stays."

In the years since, thousands upon thousands of people, celebrities, politicians, tourists, and school children have seen it and a successor, "In Our Time" that I made in 1995. We all came to sadly discover that if we hadn't known it before, genocide is a continual occurrence among earth people.

Today, a film called "In Our Time" is still being presented in that theater, still using Willie's music (I think), but it has been reedited, changed. I had nothing to do with its current iteration and have never seen it. But those two pieces are among the things I am most proud of in my career.

And by the way, although I had gotten the agreement of *MacNeil/ Lehrer* to make the videos, as far as I know, no one who worked for the show other than my PA's ever saw it.

Some thirty years after I'd begun working on the genocide film for the Museum of Tolerance, Gerry Margolis told me that it might never have existed at all if it wasn't for George Deukmejian,

California's sitting governor. His parents were born in Armenia and had escaped the fate of 1,000,000 fellow Armenians, although his father's sister did not. In asking the state for a $5,000,000 grant, the museum promised to examine examples of genocide other than the Holocaust. Gerry said his understanding was that the inclusion of the Armenian Genocide was a necessary precursor for the grant. My film apparently solved that problem.

Is it possible that no genocide other than the Holocaust would have been mentioned in the museum without that financial cudgel? That's not something I'm willing to speculate about so long after the event.

There was one other episode involving the Wiesenthal Center, this having nothing to do with death and genocide and everything to do with money and politics. The Center was going to have a dinner in honor of Arnold Schwarzenegger — before his run for governor — and they asked me to make a video to introduce him to an audience of entertainment industry people. So when I was in LA for the *NewsHour*, I went to see Maria Shriver, his then-wife, who was the protector and promoter of the way she, and presumably he, wanted to be seen. She told me what she had in mind.

I wrote a script that everyone approved, and Tom Brokaw recorded it for me. I wanted to shoot Schwarzenegger in the museum, and he met me there with his entourage, all seemingly with cigars tightly clenched in their jaws, just a bunch of alpha male jocks accompanying the Big Guy who had his cigar, too. None of them, of course, was anywhere near as big as Arnie. While his guys waited patiently while we worked, he was the total professional. I knew what I wanted, and he was willing to do it. He was charming and fun in a jocular way. So far, so good.

Maria had sent a carton of all his films and other material to NY, which Ruth and I screened. We made our decisions and cut the video. It was pretty good. However, it wasn't what Maria had in mind. The Arnold I saw in these movies, the self-deprecating movie star as actor, with a winking self-awareness and good-humored, was the Arnold I put in the video. I sent it to the Wiesenthal Center; they liked it well enough to send it to Maria. She did not like it. She wanted a heroic Arnold, the golden hero of the Golden state.

She wanted Reagan's Morning in America with Arnold and her walking hand-in-hand atop the world. That was something I could not give her. For me, that was not Arnold, at least an Arnold I liked, even though there were lots of people for whom that might have been true.

Maria recut the video more to her liking, and the dinner was a big success, meaning that every studio bought a table. It was filled with the Hollywood elite, at least those who didn't object to him personally or his politics (and/or, perhaps, the politics of Rabbi Hier as well). Arnie was, after all, a STAR. Whatever the quality of the video, both Maria and the Wiesenthal Center got what they wanted. Arnold raised a lot of money for the Center; the Center bestowed a sheen of respectability, approval, and insulation from charges of anti-Semitism, along with Orthodox Jewish support when he needed it for his political future. As for me, I was happy to be out of it.

The interesting thing, at least in terms of making films, is that Maria's version of Arnold used the same script that I had written. She may have changed the images, but Tom Brokaw's narration stayed the same. Yet the two films were completely different. My Schwarznegger was a fallible, self-deprecating man, capable of mocking himself, of winking at the audience, while at the same time being deadly serious. But, at least as I recall, Maria's version had Schwarzenegger as a god for whom all that self-deprecation and humanness would have been impossible. I don't know if either image of him was accurate, although I liked my image of him. Regardless, it demonstrates the power of image in making movies, the fact that two different images can present different realities no matter what the words are. Or, to put it another way, images can have extraordinary power and shape the way we view the world. That's why directors are the most powerful figure when making movies despite the absolutely essential roles of writers and actors. And maybe that's why the essays were so successful and why TV is such a powerful medium.

Chapter 14
THE HEART OF THE MATTER

◆

1984 — 1995 (more or less)

I'd like to offer Roger Rosenblatt an apology in advance.

In my calendar, Roger's name first appeared on Friday, December 30th, 1983, but I don't know why. Perhaps it involved his book, *Children of War*. And then, on January 5th, 1984, I did something else involving him, maybe having to do with George Orwell and the year. But, from my perspective, the most important event of that day was that I finished editing the piece about Nathan Rapaport and his liberation sculpture.

What I *do* remember is this: On Thursday afternoon, January 19th, 1984, at 5:00 in the afternoon, Roger strode — sort of bounced is more like it — into my office, with his sandy hair, receding hairline, a grin, and one sarcastic wisecrack after another, an out-front persona that masked a deeply feeling, soul searching man who would only offer glimpses into that soul through his writing. Perhaps that's why we became friends; we kept so much that was most important to each of us inside, allowing — offering — a reflection, a glimpse of ourselves only through the prism of our work, even to each other.

A few days earlier, Les Crystal had given me an essay of Roger's published in *Time*, Roger's regular venue. It was titled "What Should We Lead With," and it was the beginning of an intimate working relationship that lasted 22 years. I remember the piece in great detail because it was — it is — the most significant essay that I worked on with Roger or with anyone else. Yes, there were others that I know were equally good, maybe even better, by Roger and others. But this was the most important.

Some would ask if anything could possibly have been more extraordinary or terrifying or painful than the essay Roger and I did about an exhibition of photographs of lynchings in the American South between the World Wars. We tend to think of lynchings as the acts of bigots and cowards done in the dark of night, acts to be hidden from seeing eyes. But no, these lynchings were witnessed by *thousands* of people, Americans all, all dressed in their Sunday best in the bright light of day. They were published as postcards and sent to friends and relatives all over the country. They are stark reminders that we Americans are not better than other people but the same, fully capable of the most dreadful and ignominious acts just as we are capable of the noblest and most generous.

Or, perhaps, this essay of Phyllis Theroux's ostensibly about a traveling art show at the New Orleans Museum of Art, but that was really about something else. It was about the kind of thing that Robert Motherwell had talked to us about a few years earlier, the same thing Nathan Rapaport spoke about, and that most of my road series of features were about. The same thing that saved me from being in the zipper business.

PASSIONATE VISIONS
Phyllis Theroux

Anybody who has gone to a museum lately realizes that many of today's artists have effectively buried the meaning of their own work, which is often unintelligible to most of us. This may or may not be because the artists lack something to say. But in any event, they're certainly saying it to a much smaller group of people who have to have the same educated taste and credentials as the artist to understand it.

That is why a new traveling exhibition of Southern folk artists at the New Orleans Museum of Art is such a sight for sore eyes. The museum has assembled over 80 artists who have produced their work over the past 50 years. All of it is museum quality, on a par with some of this century's acknowledged masters. Yet this is the first time that a major museum has provided such a comprehensive glimpse at a genre that, until recently, has not gotten much respect. Why? Because it exists outside the cultural mainstream. None of these artists ever received an art lesson, took a class in art history, or had even stepped into a museum until their own work drew them in.

Howard Finster, the most well-known artist in the show, only had six years of school --which is about average for the contributors. He happened upon his career while painting a bicycle.

HOWARD FINSTER: WELL, I WAS WORKING ON A BICYCLE ONE DAY AND I LEARNED THAT I COULD TAKE MY FINGER AND — AND PATCH ON THAT BICYCLE — I COULD DO IT BETTER WITH MY FINGER THAN I COULD WITH A BRUSH. AND ONE DAY I PUT SOME WHITE PAINT ON MY FINGER TO — TO PATCH A FENDER, I BELIEVE IT WAS, AND I LOOKED AT THAT FACE AND THERE'S A — THERE'S A HUMAN FACE IN THAT FINGER, IN THAT PAINT, THE EYES AND EVERYTHING, AND IT JUST SPOKE TO ME TO PAINT SACRED ART. AND I SAID TO IT I CAN'T DO THAT. A PROFESSIONAL CAN BUT NOT ME. AND IT COME TO ME, HOW DO YOU KNOW, HOW DO YOU KNOW, HOW DO YOU KNOW. AND I THINKS TO MYSELF, HOW DO I KNOW? AND SO, I JUST TOOK A DOLLAR BILL OUT OF MY BILLFOLD, TAPED IT ON A PIECE OF PLYWOOD AND WENT OUT IN FRONT OF MY BICYCLE SHOP, I STARTED GEORGE — DOING GEORGE WASHINGTON OFF OF THAT, OFF OF THAT DOLLAR BILL.

This may be the most "artless" group of American artists a museum has ever assembled. Although most of them don't think of themselves primarily as artists. Art is what they do, not what they are. And a high percentage of them are inspired by visions, dreams, and messages from God who came through with a saving grace, or talent to help them survive.

CHARLES LUCAS: WHEN I GOT DOWN REAL SICK THAT I COULDN'T TAKE CARE OF MY KIDS, I WENT TO GOD BECAUSE HE WAS THE ONLY PERSON THAT I KNOW THAT I COULD TALK TO, THAT WOULD GIVE ME THE ANSWERS THAT I NEEDED. AND SO, I ASKED HIM TO GIVE ME A TALENT THAT NO ONE HAD. AND I TOLD HIM I WOULD BE — I WOULD BE HONEST IN IT, I WOULD BE DISCIPLINED IN IT, I WOULD GO AS FAR AS I COULD GO WITH IT, AND I WOULDN'T PLAY NO GAMES IN IT FOR NOBODY. AND THAT NEXT MORNING I WOKE UP, I HAD — TEN DOLLARS IN MY POCKET, AND THAT WAS THE GIFT FROM GOD TO ME. AND THAT'S WHERE I SAID I'M THE TIN MAN, AND THAT WAS A NEW NAME FOR ME. THE WHOLE THING WAS JUST SOLID. I MEAN, I COULDN'T OVERRIDE IT. I SAID — OH, AIN'T NO WAY FOR ME TO OVERRIDE THIS. AND I'S STUCK WITH THAT, AND MY BELIEF IS STILL IN IT.

Most of them became artists at the end of their lives. Before that, they had to earn a living as farmers, housemaids, utility linemen, porters. A few were committed to mental institutions or homes for the retarded. Purvis Young, a street painter in Miami, was first introduced to painting by a prison guard when he went to jail.

PURVIS YOUNG: I DON'T LISTEN TO NO PREACHER BECAUSE I DON'T GET NO SUPPORT, SO I'M NOT INTERESTED IN HEARING HIM TELLING ME ABOUT THE BIBLE. I MUST LOOK UP THERE IN THE SKIES, SAY HEY MAN—IT'S A ROUGH DAY TODAY. YOU KNOW, I'M TRYING TO SURVIVE. I'M PAINTING THE PROBLEM OF THE WORLD. I'M THE PAINTER,

AND I KNOW   THE JAILHOUSES FILLED UP AND I PAINT THERE SOMETIMES. YOU KNOW, PEOPLE ARE — SOMETIME PEOPLE DON'T HAVE JOBS. AND I LOOK AND WATCH DC ON TV, WATCH OTHER PLACES JUST AS WORSE AS MIAMI. I SEE MORE CHURCHES BEING BUILT AND THE WORLD IS GETTING WORSE. SO YOU KNOW — AND THIS IS WHAT I SEE. I'M THE PAINTER. I GO LISTEN TO WHAT THE PEOPLE SAY. IF THEY'RE ANGRY — I FORGET HATE...WHAT COLOR ME. I PAINT WHITE PEOPLE, BLACK PEOPLE, WHITE ANGELS. IT'S THE, IT'S THE — IT'S THE WAY I FEEL. I'M, I'M LIKE THIS IN LIFE. IF I SIT HERE AND TELL YOU HOW I FEEL TOWARDS YOU, I'M GOING TO TELL A BLACK PERSON HOW I FEEL TOWARDS THEM; YOU KNOW, I AIN'T GOING TO BEAT AROUND NO BUSH. I DON'T CARE IF YOU LIKE ME OR NOT. SOMETIME I SEE THINGS — AS DON'T — DON'T — GET — GETTING BETTER. I JUST—I'M JUST A ARTIST. I'M JUST A PAINTER.

Many were born of slave backgrounds, which their work addresses -- a history that somehow seems even more terrible when seen through gentle eyes. But art has always been a purifier of the spirit. Many of the contributors in this show might, under other, artistically impoverished circumstances, become a problem as opposed to an illuminator of society.

JIMMY LEE SUDDATH: WHEN I FIRST STARTED — I — I WAS THREE YEARS OLD, AND I'M A — 83 YEARS OLD, AND STILL PAINTING! AND I ENJOY IT, I LOVE IT AND EVERYTHING! AND I PAINT EVERY NIGHT. I GOT SOMETHING IN, IN ONE OF THE BIG BUILDINGS HERE IN TOWN, I GOT SOME OF THE OLDER BUILDINGS IN THE WORLD THERE ON THE — IN THERE — AND I GOT SOME PICTURES OF THERE — OOH, AND I BELIEVE I DRAWED 'EM. MY NAME'S ON THERE TOO. I COULDN'T STAND IT IF I COULDN'T PAINT, I'D BE

— I'D JUST BE LOST. I WOULDN'T BE ABLE TO LIVE LONG. I BELIEVE I WOULD JUST DIE.

The materials in the work are what the artists found closest and most affordably at hand: chewing gum, mud, plastic pop bottles, turnip greens. Pictures are painted on old window shades, discarded television sets, asbestos shingles, coal scuttle buckets. Most have lived below or near the poverty line but they have found plenty of material for plenty to say. Perhaps that is what distinguishes these artists. They gush with plenty to say about everything — religion, family life, the world around them — what art has always tried to see — so that human beings can better see who, and where, we really are.

To see anything, we need light. And right now, the New Orleans Museum of Art is unusually full of it. Light streams from these canvases and sculptures. Our imaginations are quickened into understanding that we, too, could be artists if we are only willing to look within and around ourselves in a different way. Which is what the artist does. And if the look is true and pure enough, it shines back -- upon the artist as well.

BESSIE HARVEY: I TALK TO THE TREES, TO THE GRASS, AND THEN TALK TO GOD BECAUSE TO ME NATURE IS GOD. AND — THEN I BEGIN TO SEE FACES IN THE WOODS, SO THAT'S WHERE ALL THESE LITTLE PEOPLE WAS COMING FROM. THE CREATOR — DONE THE BIG ART. HE SAID ALL THINGS WERE MADE OF HIM. WITHOUT HIM THERE'S NOTHING MADE. THESE ARE HIS HANDS. HIS EYES. AND WHEN HE SHOWS ME SOMETHING, IT'S HIM THAT'S SEES, NOT ME. BUT HE USES MY HANDS TO BRING IT OUT WHERE YOU CAN SEE IT AND ALL OF US CAN SEE IT. THEY SAY SO MANY THINGS ABOUT RELIGION YOU DON'T HEAR THE SAME THING WHEN YOU READ THE BOOK THAT THEY HEAR. BUT WHAT I HEARD HIM SAY THERE, WHEN HE TOLD THE DISCIPLES

TO PRAY, OUR FATHER WHO A ... R ... T. A..R..T. IN
HEAVEN. THE ART OF HEAVEN. SEE?
I'm Phyllis Theroux.

Or Jim Fisher's after the bombing of the Federal building in
Oklahoma City. Back then, all the talk of the innocence of Middle
America in the media bothered me because it so ignored the past,
intentionally or not. We are not helped by the mythologizing of
our history because it makes it virtually impossible to deal with the
present.

THE INNOCENT HEARTLAND
Jim Fisher

The Oklahoma City Federal building -- target on April
19 for some surely touched with insanity, tomb for some (a
sign now burned into our consciousness) and backdrop for
countless news anchors and correspondents, more than a few
of whom intoned that now Middle America had been touched
by terror, formerly the exclusive phenomenon -- in this country
at least -- of the East or West Coasts. And which begat headlines. "Terror in the Heartland" was overused, bolstering the
attitude that out here in so-called flyover country with its long
vistas and small-town ways, we've somehow been shielded
from the evil some men do. No longer were we virgins.

Yet one wondered: Did those anchors or headline writers
ever study history? Has the dark past of this part of the country
been forgotten?

Begin with the killing of paramilitary Mormons by paramilitary gentiles and vice versa in Missouri, then Nauvoo,
Illinois.

Skip to the massacres of assorted Indians whose tribal
ways -- meaning the loose, free-roaming ways in which they
governed themselves -- got in the way of American settlers on
the move.

Then came old John Brown shunning society's shades of gray and whose followers hacked pro-slavery settlers to death over a slight.

Or this, the Beecher Bible and Rifle Church in Wabaunsee, Kansas, where the flock was bold enough to incise in stone for all to see those two instruments they favored in smiting what they saw as an oppressive federal government.

The list goes on: the outlaw James's, the Youngers, and the Daltons, anti-government to the core; Carrie Nation whose followers included dynamiters who leveled saloons in lieu of legislated prohibition; populists whose creed is now resurgent in its opposition to government; bomb-throwing Wobblies; and gaunt Depression-era farmers who stopped foreclosure sales by threatening, quite simply, to kill sheriffs. Add in Pretty Boy Floyd, Bonnie and Clyde, Creepy Karpis. Plus untold lynchings, including the last victim so dispatched in Kansas, a white man whose noose in 1934 was a strand of barbed wire. Plus assorted mass or serial murderers -- the Clutter killers and Charley Starkweather come to mind.

Middle America is hardly chaste.

Yet all that is mostly hidden, rarely talked about, or even remembered by those who followed the smoke and dust, bloodshed, and death to settle the country. They were too busy building the towns, establishing the churches, and turning what some called a desert into what most years is a garden.

They — the Okies, the hillbillies, the sodbusters — were, in the main, too busy to hate with those old passions. Leisure and easy money have resurrected those, they'll say. And that fertilizer is growing, not tearing down.

Still, there are reminders. Like here at 1425 Grand Avenue in Kansas City. In 1863 there was a frame structure here called the Women's Prison which held female sympathizers of Confederate guerrillas then infesting western Missouri. August 13th of that year, the building fell in -- apparently because of botched alterations to the structure next door. Four women, all under 4o, were killed, others injured.

The tragedy, due surely in part to the military's cramming

inmates into a dilapidated building, became analogous — at least in retrospect — to what happened almost 130 years later outside Waco, Texas. To the guerrillas, led by William Clark Quantrill, innocents had died. The government had hatched a conspiracy. Someone would pay.

It all sounds familiar. Eight days later, Quantrill and his men burned and looted nearby Lawrence, Kansas, killing 140 men and boys leaving 80 women widows.

The government itself reacted, imposing General Order No. 11, which depopulated Kansas-Missouri border country and turned it into a free-fire zone, not unlike another place where a future insurgent war would be fought. Order No. 11 was the most draconian measure ever levied by the government against its citizens until the forced internment of Japanese-Americans in the early days of World War II.

Tit for tat. Lawrence for the women's prison in Kansas City.

And Oklahoma City, at least from early indications, for Waco.

Flyover country? The bucolic Plains states? Virginal?

Not now. Not ever.

I'm Jim Fisher.

Is it even possible to pick a single essay of Richard Rodriguez and say, "This is his best?" I re-read many of them preparing for this book and still find many extraordinary. How can there be a "best?" Take the following essay, the most controversial piece Richard ever wrote for us, one which many viewers took to mean that he was saying that Osama bin Laden was a hero to him and should be a hero to the rest of us. That, of course, is not what Richard was saying, as you will understand after reading the essay. But television is a linear medium. It goes by, and you can't go back and say, "Wait for a second, what did he say?" At least that was true before the days when DVRs were common. Whatever else Richard was and still is, he was provocative. He wanted to think the unthought-of thought. He wanted us to take that thought and dream on it.

VILLAINS AND HEROES
Richard Rodriquez

For months, America has been searching for Osama bin Laden — dropping bombs on Afghan caves, offering a sultan's treasure to peasants in exchange for leads as to his whereabouts. But no one from this crowd of faces has claimed the reward, and I am reminded of a 19th-century Mexican cowboy in California named Joaquin Murrieta and the way some persons in history survive their own death.

Depictions of Joaquin Murrieta sometimes imagine a man who is light-skinned, sometimes dark. He has green eyes; he is tall. He is short; he has brown eyes. According to cowboy pulp fiction and Mexican legend and the memory of frail, old men, Joaquin Murrieta came to California in the 1850s, during the California gold rush. Like many other Latin American miners, Joaquin Murrieta got chased off his claim by Americans. Later, his wife or his mistress was raped by American miners. Then the good man turned bad, depending on your point of view. Joaquin became a Robin Hood or a cutthroat villain. So uncertain were sheriffs of the man they were looking for, posters around California merely shouted, "wanted: The bandit Joaquin."

PRESIDENT GEORGE W. BUSH: I don't care, dead or alive, either way.

According to "Bush at War," Bob Woodward's book about life in the White House after September 11, counterterrorist agents promised President Bush the head of Osama bin Laden in a box, a bellicose promise that reverts to fairy tale or to nightmare. All these months later, we are taunted by videotaped images of this tall, elegant man in his white robes, his serene gaze, his dark, fathomless eyes. A hauntingly refined voice was recently broadcast by the Al-Jazeera Arabic network. Technicians in Washington with their earphones and knobs were 90 percent certain that the voice was Osama's. Technicians in Switzerland were 90 percent certain that it was not.

More important than whether or not the tape was authentic was the way the voice attached itself to bombings in Yemen and Bali and Moscow and taunted the Israelis and their allies. Clearly, the man on the tape wants to cast himself as more than himself, as more than a rich, petulant Saudi in conflict with the royals of Riyadh. Think of the moment in the movie "Spartacus." Roman authorities are searching for a gladiator-turned-rebel. Then one man after another assumes the rebel's identity.

ACTOR: I'm Spartacus.

ACTOR: I'm Spartacus.

ACTOR: I'm Spartacus.

ACTOR: I'm Spartacus.

The crowd becomes Spartacus. Today there are children named for Osama, and his life is sung, and his face is hoisted on placards, on billboards — a figure of high romance for millions of people, even while we Americans see only the villain. Villain or hero? A historical figure ascends to myth when his life matches some common pride or grievance or sorrow. Then history is subsumed into myth. Spartacus, Joaquin, Che, Gandhi, Osama. America's search for Osama bin Laden in these mountain passes and crowded bazaars may be necessary militarily and for reasons of vengeance and justice and national pride, but it may also be beside the point. Dead or alive, Osama bin Laden already is mythic. The grievances of millions of people in the Middle East are joined to his name, and his name surely will outlast his death.

Some will think I dishonor the memory of a Mexican cowboy in California named Joaquin Murrieta by remembering him in the same sentence with Osama bin Laden. But my subject is myth, the way history turns into myth. In California, there are Mexican restaurants and bars named for Joaquin Murrieta. There are rock formations and caves and ridges named in his honor. There are probably children. The long resentments of Mexicans in America have invoked his myth. And look behind me. Here, on the edge of the Berkeley campus of the University of California: A building named in honor of a Mexican cowboy about whom almost nothing exactly is known.

I'm Richard Rodriguez.

In retrospect, it is interesting to note that President Obama was afraid of precisely this problem. If he allowed Osama's dead body to be displayed, he might be helping the martyring and mythologizing of America's great villain.

Years ago, before Barack Obama entered the national consciousness, Clarence Page looked into the Black community and found ...

INTO THE PROMISED LAND
Clarence Page
(A Black History Month Essay on the future of leadership)

Parents tell their kids: Be a leader, not a follower.

Kids want to be part of the crowd. It takes courage and confidence to be a maverick, to break out of that herd and say to the rest, Hey, let's do it this way, you guys!

Martin Luther King. He was my kind of leader. A good leader is a good persuader. The key to leadership is to have a good idea, then persuade other people that it was really THEIR idea all along.

Dr. King was a very good persuader. One of the best. For our generation of kids, King was a black Moses. Even when he seemed too patient through the eyes of our impatience, he had our respect. He defied Jim-crow segregation. He exposed injustice. He was leading us to the Promised Land.

All of which raises another age-old question: Do the times make a leader? Or does a good leader re-make the times?

Archbishop Desmond Tutu called himself "a leader by default" in the fight against apartheid, "only because nature does not allow a vacuum."

Dr. King's death left a vacuum. No one looked more

desperately than the media did for a new black Moses to finish the job. Leaders save media the trouble of trying to understand all of the rest of us.

Jesse Jackson won the audition. If he did not quite fill Dr. King's shoes, he came closer than anyone else did. He flashed rock-star charisma and rhymed like Muhammad Ali.

"Our time has come," he said when he ran for president twice. Sometimes these days, his time seems to have passed. His agenda seems adrift. His stature has been wounded by scandalous tabloid headlines. With questions surrounding his financial dealings and his out-of-wedlock child, he keeps his friends close—and the Rev. Al Sharpton even closer.

Sharpton wants to be the next premier black leader. But, if Jackson is burdened with political baggage, Sharpton has a steamer trunk of his own. From the Tawana Brawley affair to the New York mayor's race, Sharpton seems to divide as much as he unites....or multiplies.

Some look at that evolution — from King to Jackson to Sharpton — and wonder whether Darwin was wrong. Maybe we're moving backwards. Maybe there really is a crisis in black leadership.

Or maybe the times have changed. The America I see actually has more leaders than ever before. There they are, just beyond the civil rights arena, and they are not just leading blacks.

They are government leaders like Colin Powell and Condoleezza Rice leading the nation's foreign policy and national security. They are corporate leaders like Dick Parsons, now CEO at the world's largest media corporation, AOL Time Warner. They are superstar entrepreneurs like Oprah Winfrey, an industry in her own right. If Reverend Al is a go-to guy for New York Democrats, Oprah is a go-to woman for just about everyone else in the universe.

But most of today's black leaders are not on TV. They live in the real world, in troubled communities across America, wherever neighbors come together to fight crime, to provide role models for kids, to help out neighbors in need. They are ordinary neighborhood leaders — teachers, church ministers, police, firemen and factory workers rising up to fill the vacuum, as Archbishop Tutu said, whether by design or by default.

It's hard to imagine a single black Moses rising up again. The doors of opportunity are opening up, and so is the diversity of our choices. We can shop around. And we are. What makes a leader today? Don't ask.

Just look in the mirror.

I'm Clarence Page.

We know at least one person who, years later, looked in the mirror and found himself looking back and said, "Why not?" That was Barack Obama.

And here was Anne Taylor Fleming, ever aware of the precarious lives of boys and girls, speaking in 1993 of that year's California angel. If it seemed a fearful time then in so many places to so many people, perhaps it was one of the reasons that 20 plus years later, Donald Trump found an audience for his fear-mongering. Maybe fear is always bubbling away, just waiting for the heat to be turned up.

THE CALIFORNIA
CHRISTMAS ANGEL
Anne Taylor Fleming

If you had seen the face just once, you probably would have remembered it, so generically sweetly adolescent, head slightly atilt, dimples, radiant closed mouth smile, and long wavy hair -- the very essence of girldom.

But by the time it was over, and the small body of 12-year-old Polly Klass had been found, most of us had seen the face dozens of times, beseeching us in its innocence to keep the faith, keep up the search.

The poster seemed to be everywhere you turned, certainly up here in Northern California: in big towns and small hamlets, in post offices and bookstores, in cafes and coffee houses -- the face of a stolen child carried away by a bearded stranger the night of October first.

She was taken out of her very own bedroom here in the small town of Petaluma, an hour north of San Francisco. not to be seen or heard from since. We held our breaths, hoping that she would somehow miraculously be returned before the holidays, knowing -- pushing the knowledge away but knowing that should she find her way home, she would never be the same untouched girl who could slide back into her bedroom or behind her school desk as if she'd never been away.

Petaluma is as close to safe, mainstream America as you get in California, maybe as you get anywhere anymore, a spot of rural suburbia once known as "the World's Egg Basket" and used as the locale of some of Ronald Reagan's "Morning in America" 1984 campaign commercials. And even here, evil tiptoed in and tiptoed out with a child.

Her town, which so rallied itself to the search, setting up a foundation to blanket the state with her likeness, is subdued, its Christmas celebrations all tied up with mourning for its lost daughter, whose face now smiles from Christmas trees that have been turned into shrines.

Polly Klass is the poster girl of California this Christmas season, hanging over the state like a shiny-faced angel, reminding us that there is no safety anywhere anymore.

Not in the streets of big-city America,
not in the suburban malls a-twinkle with gilt and goodies,
and not in the Petalumas of the country either.

Turn on a local news show any place in the country now, from New York to Nashville, from LA to Omaha, and you will hear the same kinds of stories, the same unnerving litany of violence.

We are all linked by these stories. In this sprawling, multi-cultural country of ours, the one new thing that joins us now is fear. It cuts across ages and colors and races and religions. If we can agree on nothing else, we can agree on that: that we do not feel safe anymore.

Violence is the number one issue, the number one priority, our President says, on his next year's to-do list, and the fear of crime hums along under the holiday hubbub like a dark refrain. What has happened to us? What happened to Polly?

Is it a testament to her storybook prettiness that she haunts us this holiday? Or a testament to her parents and the grief-struck town that refused to let go of her?

After all, there are hundreds, thousands of other small faces caught in the deadly crossfire of our nation's life that might just as easily remind us of what we've become.

But that singular distinction belongs, at least for the moment, at least here in California, to Polly Klass, whose girlish laughter, you swear, if you stare at the still ever-present posters long enough, you can actually hear burst forth into the cold Christmas air.

I'm Anne Taylor Fleming.

There were *so* many essays over the years, over one thousand five hundred. How can I say which one was absolutely the best or which one someone else should remember? Each of us sees each essay, each everything from our own particular vantage point, our own specific perspective at our own unique time. Even I don't remember each one, though I remember many of them. A glance at the title of most of them, and I can probably still tell you of the important images in each, the style in which it was edited, and where it was shot. But when all is said and done, Roger's "What Should We Lead With," the essay we shot on January 19th, 1984, is still the one that stays with me, that had the most resonance for me, the one script that I kept with me in my briefcase until the day I retired from the *NewsHour*. Nothing else so completely expressed my deepest feelings about us pathetic and glorious humans, we earth people.

WHAT SHOULD WE LEAD WITH
Roger Rosenblatt

Newsmen put the question in practical terms. What should we lead with? The rest of us ask it more generally. What matters most? It comes to the same puzzle. Survey events in a given period of time and try to come up with a single moment, the headline by which the world may be characterized, stopped in its spin.

In the past couple of weeks, we have stood chest-high in choices. In Lebanon, one more last battle for Beirut, the collapse of the Gemayel government, the pullout of the U.S. Marines. In the Soviet Union, the death of Yuri Andropov and the succession of Konstantin Chernenko, a funeral in red. In Iowa, the small beginnings of an American presidential election, the first funny hats, and toots of the horns. In Sarajevo, one more winter Olympics done; memories on videotape. The ice dancers Torvill and Dean synchronized as if accidentally like birds in a wind. Four major acts then: war, ceremony, process, grace.

What should we lead with? What matters most? Let's concede from the start that the problem is subjective, that whatever choice we settle on, it is bound to be formed more by habit than by a command of history. We're not in control of history.

Getting bored with Beirut? It's not unheard of if you don't live there. Every few weeks, another upheaval, another onslaught, the familiar pictures of crushed Mercedes, balconies split open like stale cake, here a distraught mother, there a distraught maniac. Polls show that the American people are growing tired of Lebanon, of the Middle East as a whole. Too bad. The region matters. It's a lead. Boring or not, Beirut may be the center of the world, the place where everything comes together or apart.

So, too, for Moscow these past two weeks. After the obsequies and the miles of citizen mourners, after the visiting dignitaries have filed past a dead man's medals, half the world closes rank behind another mystery. Who is this Chernenko? Brezhnev's former water boy turned master of the house?

After Iowa, who is Mondale? Walter, we thought we knew you, but now we'd a better look a bit closer at him, who may become the leader of the other half of the world.

Which leaves us with Sarajevo, the least important place on our current events map. Perhaps. But before we say so definitely, play it again, that ice dance performed by the two Brits. I don't think that I caught it all the first time. I think I missed one of the turns of her head or an extension of his arm, the way they came together or apart.

Here is what one would like to say: That Torvill and Dean's routine was more important in its sublimity than all the shootings and elections time can muster, that life is short, and art is long and that the skating dance, brief and evanescent as it is, represents a perfection in which the entire universe may be encompassed.

Theodore Roethke described such an effect in a poem. "A ripple widening from a single stone, winding around the waters of the world." Nice. May even be true. Yet, we have no sure way of making such a judgment. It is just as likely that Beirut is the widening ripple by which everything is framed. What we confront in making such choices is not the events alone but ourselves, and it is ourselves we are not able to place in order. The mind, fickle as a southern belle, swishes rapidly from battles to dances, enthralled equally with every suitor, enthralled with itself.

Tell me a story about my mind, Mister News. Did I overturn a government this week? Did I come to power? Did I win an election? Did I skate flawlessly again? Was I murderous, decorous, triumphant? Beautiful? And if I was all those things, how should I order my priorities so as to know what is truly human? The essential prevailing act. The question is us. What should we lead with? What matters most?

In another poem, Roethke suggested that the widening

ripple is ourselves. "I lose and find myself in the long water. I am gathered together once more. I embrace the world." We do that every week, cursing and awestruck at all we are.

I'm still awestruck.

Almost forty years later, I still hear Ravel's *Bolero*. I still see Torvill and Dean. I remember watching them on television during the Winter Olympics. I don't need to see it again to remember it, though you can find it without any problem on the internet. I still remember sitting in the editing room watching the dancers dance and thinking the answer to Roger's question was obvious: Torvill and Dean mattered most. Or perhaps it is just that I yearned for it to be true. Robin once said that he thought I was not interested in hard news. He was right, at least in the way he meant, otherwise I might not have the same answer to Roger's question today as I did then. And I suppose that is one explanation of the career I had on the *NewsHour*. I'm not a journalist, or at least the kind of journalist that Robin had in mind, but I played one on TV. Sort of.

Much as I loved the essay, both what Roger wrote and what finally went on air, I can't say that I was entirely enthusiastic about doing it or the other essays I was asked to do that year. I was doing an enormous amount of work, particularly the features that I felt were of great personal importance. I was also doing a book review every week with a rotating group of reviewers (originally AC Greene, Richard Locke, John Aldridge, and Doris Grumbach). The books we reviewed were chosen either by me or me in combination with the reviewer. So not only was I reading the book we reviewed each week but at the very least skimming through dozens of books sent by publishers weekly. As soon as the presidential campaign got underway, I was asked to do a short segment every Friday night of political cartoons. Every Wednesday night or Thursday morning, in those pre-internet days, if you can imagine such a time, I would get something like 200 of the cartoons that had or would appear in that week's newspapers from which I'd pick about six. I had a group of improvisational actors come into the office early on Friday morning who would do their best to imitate the voices of Reagan, Mondale, and others as necessary. Then I'd shoot the cartoons with a video camera and an easel in these days before computerized editing systems, guessing at the kind of moves I might want to make, head to the editing room, and cut the cartoons adding voices and sound effects and somehow make Friday night's air. It was not a pace that I could keep up for very long.

Linda Winslow, the Deputy Executive Producer, asked if I would consider using a correspondent with the features on at least two occasions. I either said, "no," or said something like "I'll think about it," knowing that I would never do it if I could help it because I thought it would change their whole character or, even worse, come to be seen by whoever that correspondent was as their own. I didn't want them to become anyone else's; I'd rather see them disappear. And so they did.

The show was suffering that year. I don't think that Robin and Jim were entirely happy with it but what I do know is that many of the PBS affiliates were unhappy. It may have had to do with the program's structure in which news headlines were scattered in different sections of the show, which was different from the usual or expected practice of headlines coming at the beginning of a show. Or it might have simply been jealousy on the part of some of the larger stations that we had all that long-term corporate funding, which they might otherwise have had a shot at grabbing a piece of. Jealousy and envy are hardly unknown among the PBS brethren, human beings all. The competition for foundation and corporate underwriting, as well as grants from PBS and CPB, can be fierce, however polite it might all seem, particularly amongst the big stations, the stations in New York, Boston, Washington, DC, Dallas, Miami, Chicago, Los Angeles, and San Francisco.

For the next fiscal year, which began in July 1984, several changes were made in the *NewsHour*. The show moved to a more traditional form in which the audience was told what was going to be on the show at the top, followed by the news summary, and then would come clearly labeled segments (*everything* now had to have a label), and every segment had to have recognizable correspondent.

The postcards were discarded. Apparently, too many station managers didn't like them and, besides, they really were an unnecessary cost. The book reviews ended over time because Robin and

Jim felt compelled to read the books they were interviewing the reviewers about. So they were reading a book every other week that they may not have had any personal interest in reading or, even more, the time given all their other responsibilities. Curiously, neither of them (not even Les) ever asked how the reviewers and I chose the books we wanted to review, although I certainly could have told them. The cartoons lasted for another year or so, but they too were obviously doomed. Without a political campaign to create parallel targets, a cartoonist's inevitable inclination was to pop the biggest balloon, which tended to be the President of the United States. For a show that tried for political balance, it was untenable.

The essays, though, had been very well received. They were different than anything that was on television. They tried to be intellectually provocative without being politically partisan. They had the essayists who could (and would) become faces and personalities with whom our audience could establish an ongoing relationship (positive or not). The segments had a name by which they could be known: Essays. By the time 1985 rolled around, I was asked to devote my time exclusively to them, and, not so gradually, all the other things I was doing disappeared from the show.

In fact, the essays were so well received that Les asked if I could provide one every night of the week. But unfortunately, I was never able to accomplish that. At the most, I averaged between two and three a week while being assisted by two associate producers and about ten writers at a time working on essays. But even if I had been able to generate that many pieces, Robin and Jim would have ended it pretty quickly. They would have found the time left to the rest of the show too constricting. Even later, when I wanted them to designate either one or two specific nights to the essays, they refused because, they said, it was a matter of the tail wagging the dog. In other words, my tail and their dog.

The extent of the essays' conceptual originality, at least as a television form, was quickly evidenced in the industry by "The Roger Rosenblatt Essays," winning a Peabody Award, perhaps the most distinguished award to those in the industry, in 1984.

Aside from however wonderful "What Should We Lead With" was as an individual work or Roger as its writer, that essay became the hidden standard by which I measured every essay and writer against in the years after.

In 2007 when writing of the origins of the essays for a grant proposal, I said it as well as I ever have.

> **Thus was born the long run of the Essays on the *NewsHour*. In the ensuing twenty-three years, Roger and many other writers have asked similar questions over 1,500 times. What matters to our lives? How should we live, love, think? How should we understand the world around us? How should we understand others? How should we understand ourselves?**
>
> **The kind of essay the *NewsHour* presents, this amalgam of short literary work combined with the use of visual images as art, was unique in TV in 1984. Even today, it is rarely attempted and, if we may be so bold as to say, even more rarely successful. The rarity of the form is easily attested to by the fact that it is almost impossible to find a news and/or public affairs award category into which the Essays can fit.**

But awards, we did win or almost win.

Another Peabody in 1997 for "The Richard Rodriguez Essays."

It seemed that I might never win an Emmy because I always seemed to be competing in the same category as Charles Kuralt and, too often, his "On the Road" series. Finally, in 1991, an Emmy for "Historical Programming," a series of essays by different essayists about the meaning of Pearl Harbor 50 years after the surprise attack. In words his then CBS colleague, Dan Rather, might have said, Kuralt didn't have a dog in that hunt. By the way, I was so surprised that I won (not that I thought I shouldn't win, mind you) that I never prepared an acceptance speech. I managed to thank everybody except Robin and Jim, without whose support and backing nothing I ever did would have been on the air. Sorry, guys.

Finally, as far as awards go, a Gracie Allen Award in 2006, at long last, for Anne Taylor Fleming's essays from American Women in Radio & Television.

There were numerous times I tried to get an award for Clarence Page but failed in the attempt. Fortunately, he's won plenty on his own, including a Pulitzer for commentary in 1989. There's no way I could top that.

If I may continue this interlude of self-congratulation for a moment, Howard Rosenberg, then the *Los Angeles Times* television critic, wrote about the essays on May 26th, 1993.

ART OF THE ESSAY LIVES AT "NEWSHOUR"

Howard Rosenberg

At once fleeting and forgettable, television moments usually whooshhhhh by in a blur, making screeching pit stops in your brain and then zooming off again, out of sight, out of memory.

One that still lingers though – an inspired confluence of sounds and sights as indelible as anything can be – aired on "The MacNeil/Lehrer NewsHour" on Oct. 16, 1990. The familiar, sentimental music was from the Ken Burns documentary series "The Civil War," its background melody haunting the words that a young Rhode Island officer wrote to his wife shortly before dying in the Battle of Bull Run.

"Never forget how much I love you...," wrote Sullivan Balleu.

Yet on the screen were not the faded black-and-white scrapbook snapshots of young soldiers who fought for the Union or Confederacy at Manassas or Shiloh or Antietam, but the images of U.S. soldiers in the Persian Gulf, freeze-framed for history in their desert-camouflage fatigues while beaming their "Hi, moms" to the folks back home.

And the accompanying voice-over came not from "The Civil War" narrator David McCullough but from Roger Rosenblatt, who, in a few remarkable, era-hurdling minutes of overlapped realities, somehow compressed two distinctly different wars, separated by some 130 years, into a single emotional experience whose common denominator was the human factor.

Those televised messages from the Gulf, Rosenblatt concluded, were no less meaningful than Sullivan Balleu's letter, personifying "all the histories of soldiers who have known what permanent darkness they face, who pray to survive the terrible business of killing, to return to their homes where words go without saying."

Wow!

Although running a mere four to seven minutes and airing an average of only once a week, the personal essays concluding some installments of the "NewsHour" on PBS often resonate infinitely, the best of them compelling you to enter the 3-D universe of history's virtual reality and follow the cross-patterns of the entire human experience. Rarely on television are words so esteemed and so artfully and memorably intersected with pictures.

Recently on the "NewsHour," that process included wallpapering the screen with female faces for Anne Taylor Fleming's moving essay connecting the rape of women in Bosnia ("some of them over...and over...and over") to the United States ("where a woman is raped every six minutes").

To emphasize what the assaulted women had lost, "NewsHour" showed the faces of Bosnian females who hadn't been victimized, looking young and vibrant. In contrast, the women brutalized by the occupation forces bore a deep impenetrable sadness, their faces road-maps of misery that marked them as living dead.

"Looking at them," Fleming said, "I cannot imagine how they will heal."

Instead of experiencing the tragedy that Fleming was describing as an abstraction – how many of TV's horrors can be absorbed without desensitization setting in? – you felt enclosed by her vision, drawn by those words and pictures into an alien, befuddling chaos where sorrow was routine.

Among the "NewsHour essayists, none is more passionate or eloquent than Richard Rodriguez, an editor at the Pacific News Service in San Francisco. We "romanticize the Indian who no longer exists," he said in a beautifully crafted essay on

Columbus Day, "and ignore the Indian who does. The Indian who is forced to chop down his rain forests, for example. Or the Indian who refuses to practice birth control."

How textured yet seamless are these gems of graceful commentary – a cobbling of many components, yet giving the impression of a single, guiding hand. A *mis*impression, actually, for the process that begins with the 10 essayists (others are Timothy Ferris, Amei Wallach, Jim Fisher, Clarence Page, Jack Perkins, Phyllis Theroux, and Robert Maynard) ends with Mike Saltz.

Senior Producer for the "NewsHour" essays since their inception a decade ago, it's Saltz who gives them body and shape. He likens what he does to making music videos: "They give me the lyrics, and I provide the melody." In other words, it's the essayists' words, his production.

"We try to keep the responsibility for the pictures away from the essayists," Saltz said from New York. "None of them have been picked because they write scripts. For the most part, we have stayed away from people who have had extensive television experience. We're interested in the essay as a literary style as opposed to a video style. We're more interested in ideas than in pictures."

Even though they appear to coexist amiably on the "NewsHour," the words-versus-pictures battle is usually a mismatch on TV. "No matter what happens, the image overtakes the words," Rosenblatt said from New York, where he's a contributing editor for Vanity Fair magazine and the only "NewsHour" essayist on staff.

Like all nightly newscasts, moreover, "NewsHour" is a factory, Saltz notes. And to a writer, surrendering words to an assembly line for someone else to visually package is like relinquishing children for adoption. "They trust us to understand what they are trying to communicate," said Saltz.

"The guy [Saltz] is fabulous," says Fleming, who lives in Los Angeles. "I'm always pleasantly surprised by something he invents on top of the words," said Rosenblatt, a charter essayist along with Kansas City Star Columnist Fisher.

> In a recent piece for "NewsHour," *Newsday* art critic Wallach defined great art as something in which "an idea has found its perfect visual form." On television, nothing comes closer to that ideal than these essays.

Essays for the *NewsHour*, at least in the way I came to think of them, are a very personal form. For me, a good essay must start with the writer having some personal relationship to the subject, an emotional, visceral connection to it. It's not something that should be written with complete dispassion as though one feels nothing, feels disconnected from it. Not that there should be "feelings" splattered all over the page or the screen, but there has to be some kind of emotional subtext or thread that is felt rather than told. The subject or topic must *matter* to the writer and, hopefully, to me. And God knows, neither the show nor I were interested in polemics, in rants and diatribes. There's more than enough of that in our political life. That said, what was most important in these essays was what an essayist thinks and not what he feels. It is a distinction that our educational system seems to have lost somewhere along the way. What I mean is that when I read an essay, I first looked at the external idea or argument and its intellectual coherence (i.e., a series of facts leading to an understandable conclusion based on those facts).

But when imagining how to produce an essay, it is something else that I am looking for. In some, perhaps indefinable way, it must be written from inside the subject, not from outside. Another way to put it is this: The essayist stands outside a subject, looks at it, examines it, and then writes about what they see from inside themselves. And that is what I am really looking for, hoping for, *listening* for most of all; it is that *music*, the writer's soul, that will lead me to imagine the essay. It isn't for nothing that the word "image" and "imagine" have the same etymology. Somehow, both image and feeling must be inherent in the text and in harmony with the external intellectual argument for an essay to be really good, at least for my purposes. Maybe that's true in general for any essay regardless of form. If that doesn't make sense to you, try this: A woman with whom I collaborated on a couple of non-*NewsHour* screenplays would sometimes say after we had discussed something, some aspect of a character or plot, "Let me dream on that." Does that help? Probably not.

In the early days of the essays, I clearly remember questioning the cliché, "A picture is worth a thousand words." I thought then and still do that it is only worth a thousand words if you already know the thousand words. A picture only has real meaning if you know the context or have a context into which to put it, and contexts are composed of ideas, words, and experience. During the early days of the post11/9- war in Afghanistan, I saw a picture of women or girls in *chadors* in a classroom, a photograph by Lynsey Addario. "Aha," I thought, a group of Afghan Muslim women being educated in a school for the first time. How wonderful! As it turned out, the women were being instructed in the fine art of becoming suicide bombers. Maybe not so wonderful. Unless that is, I was a member of Al Qaeda. Context is all.

One might well ask where those thousand words that help us understand an image come from? It's not hard to find the answer if we think of ourselves as children or adults. However, at its most basic, it is not a simple question at all. For example, it seems that the immediate information about the world that we receive starts pouring into our minds primarily in the form of visual images as soon as we are born and can open our eyes and see (along with the data that we receive through our other senses), long before we have a language in which to understand or to formulate ideas. Yet, that is not necessarily wholly true since no baby is born as a completely blank slate. If all babies are different and each identifiable as singular beings, they already have unique dispositions and personalities that affect how they see and interpret images. Where, you ask yourself, do those dispositions and characters come from, how are they formed? Is it through their genes, their DNA? Is it through the constant communication between a mother and the fetus in her womb? Is it because they have a soul that has existed through time and therefore comes with a preexisting awareness even if the mechanism of their understanding is invisible to them? I don't know the answer.

For my part, for entirely pragmatic reasons, I'll stick with my original thesis until something more useful comes along. Context is all.

I owe David McMullen a debt of gratitude for encouraging me to think about the decisions I was making in those early days without asking myself why I was making them. When I met him in the 70s, he had recently completed a 12-week tryout as a science correspondent for NBC News, then coincidentally under the leadership of Les Crystal. We became friends and ate many breakfasts together through the years, during which we would discuss each other's work. It was clear to him from watching my work that there were aesthetic decisions I was making about images, about stills and video, about color and black & white, about normal and slow motion, about all sorts of things, and he kept asking why I was doing this or that. I discovered that there actually were reasons that I could articulate for all of my choices. One result was that as time went by, I rarely had to think very hard about how to go about producing an essay. Armed with that knowledge and the awareness of how choices limit and define possibilities, all I had to do was find the right image to start at any place in the script. All the rest would pretty much follow according to whatever principles I had stored in my head.

Similarly, I'm indebted to Roger Rosenblatt for encouraging me to seriously consider the idea that one thing that makes humans unique is our understanding of everything through storytelling. It seems obvious once it is said, but I had never really thought about it before, and ever since, I haven't been able to think of a circumstance in which it isn't true. I once proposed the idea to Professor Janna Levin, a friend. She deals in the most abstract of abstractions as an advanced mathematician and theoretical physicist and also writes lucid novels. She disagreed, saying that mathematics can be so abstract that no story can be told. I'm not entirely convinced since it seems to me that there must be some logical progression — a beginning, middle, and end — by which one must understand any formula, series of formulas, or mathematical construction, no matter how abstract. I'm willing to be wrong. Willing, but not convinced. There are things in math, she says, that we have no language for and thus cannot understand through a story, only through math, which might be said to be a language of its own and maybe, even, a universe of its own. Now that is really interesting to me. But as far as the idea of story goes, it might mean that only mathematicians have the language, a language that contains no words but only numbers and symbols, to tell the story because the words don't exist. On the other hand, she also says that there are things that math may not have the language to describe. Also interesting, don't you think?

Janna is filled with ideas that I always find intriguing to contemplate, letting them roll around my brain, whether it's for minutes or hours at a time. She has been teasing my mind for years. One of Janna's specialties is the topography of the universe. It had never occurred to me that the universe had a topography. It just was. It obviously has geography; just look at the stars. We can map them, which is one thing that astronomy does. And astrology is based on the presumed characters based on lines drawn around groups of stars as though they were on a two-dimensional plane. But an actual shape, a finite shape, to the universe? Are we living inside some sort of globular thing, a globe-like thing, and looking out towards the interior of its exterior surfaces? And what exactly is that shape? Who said it had to be globular? What twists and turns might it take? Could it be shaped like a pretzel? What bumps are there in the road?

Then there is this: Given Einstein's notion that space is curved, we could see our own backs if we were able to see far enough. No matter in what direction we look, no matter how many millions, billions, or trillions of light-years we traveled, at the end of the road, we'd find ourselves endlessly. Let that one roll around in your head a bit. Dream on it.

Artists have played with a variation of that idea for centuries, even if they were unaware they were doing it. Think of Socrates. When he said, "The unexamined life is not worth living," is he not saying something similar, at least in personal rather than scientific terms? If you look at a mirror, what do you see?

In *Makepeace's Blackouts*, when Mary "Peaches" Honeypiece says, "Really look. Don't make up. Don't invent. Don't ... juggle words while looking in a mirror. *Only* look," is she not saying something similar?

And then there is T.S. Eliot in *The Four Quartets*, who perhaps said it best.

> We shall not cease from exploration
> And the end of all our exploring
> Will be to arrive at where we started
> And know the place for the first time.

A legitimate question would be, is any of this self-examination, mirror-gazing, and personal exploration possible for most of us? How many of us can strip away all pretense and pretension, strip away all our biases and prejudices, all the things we have done to others and suffered at the hand of others? Could Eliot actually achieve that clear-eyed, pure view of himself? Could he recognize his anti-Semitism as the prejudice and bigotry it is, rather than think it was simply a part of the natural order of things, the way things were and should be? And if he couldn't, could he really see anything, be able to recognize where and who he truly was "for the first time?" Could I? Could you?

But getting back to Janna, if the universe has a definable shape, then what lies outside that shape? Is it nothing? Is there literally nothing, no thing, no mass, energy, space, or time outside the universe? Is there no there there? It is a hard idea to get my head around (so to speak). And if the universe is continually expanding, what is it expanding into? Into nothing and thereby creating something? Or is that simply putting something where nothing previously existed?

And what do we actually see when we are seeing? While reading her wonderful novel, *A Madman Dreams of Turing Machines*, I wondered what people see or imagine when looking at something like, say, a human body. What does a hematologist see when he looks at or imagines somebody? Does he see red and white corpuscles coursing through narrow pathways? What does a physicist see? Does she see millions, no, billions of atoms all frantically buzzing about yet clinging together in the shape of a human body with no apparent reason? And why only those atoms; why not every atom in the universe? I like that one myself. There is so much to learn about, think about, and engage the mind if we are willing to let our minds run free. Dream on.

Unfortunately, Janna and I never figured out a way to get her onto the *NewsHour*. They (don't ask me who "they" were; I don't know) always found her pieces too abstract even though I said I could translate them into something visually meaningful, compelling, and they should trust me. They just didn't want to take a chance. They were wrong. We all lost out (and that includes you, dear reader.)

On the other hand, we brought many other writers onto the show, some many times over. They all had one characteristic aside from being fine writers: I enjoyed being with and talking with them. Part of that is what I said before about essays having a personal dimension for them. It means that with rare exceptions, I had to find a way to relate to these writers on a personal level. It doesn't mean that we had to agree on everything, only that we had to be able to understand each other's point of view and have some understanding of the logic by which they presented their case. In other words, as I said to some of them, there can't be too many "buts," as in "but what about this" or "but what about that." I discovered a surprising amount of agreement with most writers if they (and I) could get underneath all the political surfaces, the dogmas, and ideological posturing that so many people cling to. Maybe most of all, I thought it had to be fun for all of us. To be sure, there was plenty of work involved, but there had to be some reward for the process because it sure wasn't the money involved. No essayist for the show ever made their living writing essays for the *NewsHour*. Maybe Nancy Gibbs, who had taken over Roger's column at *Time Magazine* when he left before she became the magazine's managing editor, said it best. Whenever I'd ask her if she'd like to write an essay, she always said, "Oh, goody, let's play!" And so we did, and I like to think so did all our repeat essayists over the years.

It shouldn't surprise you that I wanted to try my own hand at this form. Brandon, my son, was due to graduate from Culver City High School in the spring of 1984. So I wrote him a graduation present.

Here's a brief description for those too young to know who the people in the essay are. Angela Davis was the candidate for Vice President of the United States on the Communist Party ticket. Kathy Boudin was a member of the Weather Underground and was part of a group that murdered a Brink's truck guard during a robbery. Eliot

Abrams was a Republican neo-con and a member of the Reagan, Bush 41, and Trump administrations and involved in some of the most reprehensible acts in Central and South America undertaken by America during those years.

GRADUATION DAY
For air 6/13/84

Tonight, another class will graduate from my old high school. Fourteen children – barely adults – will rise from the hard wooden pews of that converted church, walk up onto the stage, and receive validation for their past achievements – a charter to sail in future uncharted seas. They will celebrate a rite of passage whose dimensions will not be clear to them for many years – any more than it was for me 27 years ago.

Who knows what will become of them? Who knew what would become of us?

In 1961, for example, Angela Davis stood on that stage. You know her. She's running again for Vice President of the United States on the Communist Party ticket. Still on stage. She has been ever since she was fired from the University of California because she was a Communist. Angela Davis. The very vocal advocate of a revolution who, so far as I know, has never committed a revolutionary act. Even the one act she was accused of (and of which she was found *not* guilty) — namely, supplying the guns to break the Soledad brothers out of jail, was rumored to have been born more of love than of politics.

In 1961, Kathy Boudin stood on that same stage and was sent forth into her future — our present.

You remember Kathy, don't you? She's the one in the plaid skirt and white blouse. The one with the penny loafers, the firm stride, the determined gaze. The most popular girl in school. The Leader.

You remember Kathy. She's the one who pleaded guilty.

One count of murder and one of robbery. Acts to feed and nurture the revolution. Acts of revolutionary necessity.

At least we know where we can find her for the next 20 years. For the longest time, we wondered where she was — ever since the townhouse on Tenth Street blew up, and she was seen running naked down the street. Years on the FBI's most-wanted list. "I wonder where Kathy is," we'd ask, our curiosity and memory jogged by the sudden reappearances of Bernadette Dohrn, Mark Rudd, Abbie Hoffman. Maybe she's in Moscow. How about Cuba? No. She was right here all along. Our next-door neighbor.

I remember Kathy. She's in my sister's bedroom. The two of them talking, laughing, arguing, pulling at each other's ideas. They're writing a paper on *Moby Dick*. The Great White Whale. The Pequod as metaphor for an America driven by a mad Ahab willing to sacrifice everything – everyone – to satisfy his own lust ... his own dreams ... his greed, hatred, and despair.

Who knew that she'd become her own Ahab, as tightly lashed to that Brink's truck by her ideals as the harpoon's rope that clutched Ahab to the White Whale's bosom?

Who knew that she'd turn out to be a bomber? A terrorist? Who knew that she'd come to believe in the cleansing quality of blood and anarchy – the destruction of the state by any means so that something else – some unimaginable, yearned for perfection – could be created, washed in the blood of the lamb.

In 1961, little Elliott Abrams stood in the wings, preparing to make his entrance. You know Elliott. He's all grown up now. Assistant Secretary of State for Human Rights. He's made sure we know that he, too, once made that same walk, even if it was four years later. He still basks in the afterglow of his predecessors. He's *known* the enemy. Is that where he learned to reason with all the hair-splitting logic of a medieval Talmudic scholar? Is that where he learned that the man who places the electrodes on my testicles, who beats my head with a truncheon in Afghanistan, Nicaragua, and Poland is quintessentially different than the man who does those same things to me in Chile, the Philippines, and El Salvador? Is that where he learned that there are classes of evil? That his evil is intrinsically better than mine? That I should welcome it with open arms? A mind capable of such fine discrimination could count the angels on the head of a pin.

The three of them then. Kathy Boudin, Angela Davis, Elliott Abrams. So different, so similar. Somewhere, somehow, they all learned the same old tired thing – that the end *does* justify the means.

But perhaps Kathy, at least, has begun to learn something else — something far more profound — something far more pedestrian — that it is the means that ultimately determines the end.

So tonight, 14 children — officially adults — will graduate from my old high school. Later this week, my own son will graduate from *his* high school. And they will all step forward into their future — our present.

What have they learned?

What have we learned?

Pretty good, don't you think?

For weeks the essay sat in the hands of Les Crystal and whoever he had decided to give it to, presumably Robin, Jim, and maybe Linda. Finally, after some prodding, he came back with a response: Whatever the virtues of the piece, they had decided that no one on staff (including the other anchors and correspondents) would be allowed to write essays. It was a policy decision that I understood even if I wasn't happy about it, and it is one that I enforced when others on the staff asked if they could write one.

Fortunately, there were other writers in America, 57 of them, who weren't subject to the same policy. So if I couldn't use my own voice to speak directly, I would find a way to speak with and through others.

Jim Fisher, who died in 2012, had initially been a columnist for the *Kansas City Times* and then the *Kansas City Star*. He wrote the first actual essay for the *NewsHour*, though I don't know if it was labeled as that. Either Robin or Jim thought we should do something about the Olympic torch being run across the country on its way to LA for the 1984 summer Olympics. After scouring through Midwest newspapers, someone in the Denver office suggested Jim Fisher, and he wrote the piece (I was not the producer). After we officially started the essays as a regular feature of the show sometime after Roger Rosenblatt's "What Shall We Lead With," Jim became a constant presence until his retirement.

Jim spent his life traveling the roads of Kansas and Missouri, writing about the life of the people in small towns along the way. We spent many long hours driving and talking, Jim with a wad of tobacco in his cheek, a Burger King cup in the cup holder in the console between the front seats that he'd use as a spittoon. Not the most appetizing sight or smell. At the beginning or end of most trips, we'd stop at Jim's ranch on the outskirts of Kansas City on the Kansas side of the river where his one-time airline stewardess wife raised about 45 head of Arabian horses. There were essays about farm auctions in the years of farm foreclosures and wheat harvests, missile silos on the plains and country Christmas's, the rich farmland in the boot heel of Missouri, and a trip to Scottsdale, AZ, for the Arabian horse auction during the days when they were a hefty tax deduction for multi-millionaires. There was an excellent series about the Lewis & Clark expedition (produced by our Denver office) and one about the archaeological remnants of black farming communities in Kansas. All sorts of things. And seemingly most of all, essays about the dying towns of the rural American heartland.

To be sure, the show tired of what seemed like the continual stream of depressing stories. Several years later, when looking for another midwestern essayist after Jim's retirement, I talked to a wonderfully talented young writer from the mid-west, Bonnie Rough, and told her of Jim's essays about dying towns. She said, "Guess what, they're still dying." Maybe today, when commodity prices are booming (well, that was yesterday now that I'm rereading this — it's hard to keep up with this stuff, isn't it?), things have begun to change. But that will change too. It always does. Regardless, I suspect that the most adventurous and ambitious young people in America's "heartland" are still heading off to the big city. Not just New York anymore, maybe, but, as the country has grown, to LA, San Francisco, Chicago, Dallas, Atlanta, Denver, Seattle. Even Kansas City.

AC Greene was a longtime friend and colleague of Jim Lehrer's. I've always assumed that Jim and AC met while Jim was a journalist and editor at both Dallas newspapers. When Jim moved to KERA, the Dallas public television station, to start a single story per program show, much as *The Robert MacNeil Report* and *The MacNeil/Lehrer Report* was later, AC was a frequent guest. In addition, he wrote a history column for the Dallas Morning News, along with short stories and history books. He seemingly knew everything worth knowing about Texas and was happy to share it. We did book reviews (while they lasted) and essays together for many years, essays about everything from the Alamo to toy talking parrots for Christmas, one of which lived on its perch in my office for as long as I had one.

After Jim moved to Washington, he and AC didn't see or talk together as much as AC would have liked, but when he needed a heart transplant, Jim moved heaven and earth to get him one. I don't know if Jim's efforts were of help, but AC got his heart. He credited Jim for prolonging his life by several years.

That was one thing that was characteristic of Jim, one of his most admirable virtues: if you were part of what he considered his extended family, and that included the *NewsHour* staff, he would do everything he possibly could to help you if you were in trouble. Many people benefited from his unadvertised efforts. I know of at least two people who had severe medical issues, and Jim used every resource, every contact he had to help them. No sooner had I gotten home from the hospital after my heart attack in 1999 than Jim was on the phone asking if he could do anything to help. I had no doubt that whatever I needed, Jim would try to find a way to help. Fortunately, I didn't need anything from him but time and that I got. But I knew what AC missed, something I'll get to in due time.

AC died in 2002, not from a failed heart but from brain cancer.

In 1983, Bob Maynard bought the *Oakland Tribune* becoming the only Black owner of a major urban daily newspaper. In the spring of 1984, I called him and asked if he'd consider writing essays for us. He would, and he did steadily through the next four years when he was first diagnosed with prostate cancer. We had a connection that neither of us knew about at the time of my phone call. His first wife, Liz Flynn, was the older sister of Judy Flynn, who had been a classmate of mine from the 7th grade until we graduated from high school. We talked about it briefly and then never mentioned it again, acknowledging a mutual connection but not necessarily a mutual or desirable tie.

When Bob was a reporter for the New York Post, having recently attended Harvard on a Nieman Fellowship, he was a neighbor of Herman and Peggy Shonbrun when they lived in Brooklyn Heights, not far from Liz's family. Herman asked Bob if he would read *Makepeace's Blackouts*. After reading it, they had a heated argument while sitting over coffee at the kitchen table and never spoke to each other again. On Herman's advice, I never mentioned my association with the Shonbruns or *Makepeace* to Bob, and I enjoyed our time together.

After a five-year absence and a couple of remissions and recurrences of his cancer, Bob agreed to do another essay in May 1993. But, unfortunately, it was his last; he died five months later.

Once I began to produce the essays full-time, I wanted to find someone who could write knowingly and entertainingly about pop culture. This was not a topic high on Robin, Jim, or Les's agenda, but they allowed me to look for someone. So I called Lee Blumer, who had introduced me to Nathan Rapaport, in the early winter of 1986 and asked if she knew anyone she thought might be right. She suggested Penny Stallings, with whom she had worked at the Woodstock Festival.

Sure enough, Penny lived up to Lee's recommendation. She was a pretty, blue-eyed Texas blond and, when a student at the University of Texas (naturally, a Tri Δ), had been an occasional runway model in Dallas. Now, she was a freelance writer about pop culture and had married a short, dark-haired Jewish guy from Brooklyn who was in the "rag" business when they met in Dallas. He was now a talent manager representing many current and/or former writers at *Saturday Night Live* and lived in Greenwich Village when we met.

Penny was a total fan while simultaneously having a clear-eyed and cynical view of the pop culture world she so loved. We did essays about Bob Dylan and Joan Baez. We went to the New Orleans Jazz Festival and the Texas State Fair. We spent a long night at Graceland watching the unending line of now gray-haired fans, candles in hand at 2 am as they slowly passed by the grave, paying homage to the King on the 10th anniversary of his death despite Robin not being sure anyone cared about him anymore. Maybe our greatest high was when we went somewhere (Nashville?) to meet with the Neville Brothers. That was fun. We would hang out together in New York, sometimes joined by her husband and Lee (my wife). We had a wonderful time together.

It all came to an end in 1992. Our essay production had been significantly cut back after the first Gulf War and, in fact, never fully recovered. Robin and Jim decided they didn't want Penny to do more essays. They had urged me to consider not using her before, but I had always been able to convince Robin otherwise. This time I knew there was no point in trying. Penny was devastated. Perhaps it was because her father had once told her that writing for the *NewsHour* was the only thing she had ever done that he respected. Whatever the reason, Penny refused to talk to me after that. She said she hoped I would understand why she couldn't. I didn't, but there was nothing I could say that changed her mind. From time to time, Lee Blumer would tell me the latest news, but, to this day, I miss her.

Penny was the last person I fired from the show. There had been too many, and I didn't have the stomach for it anymore. Too many were people I had brought into the show and didn't want to terminate. To Les's credit, he never insisted that I be the one to pass on the bad news. I felt, though, that since I had brought them on, I should be the one to show them the door on the way out. But I couldn't do it anymore after Penny. The price, the loss of Penny's friendship, was too much. So from then on, I let Les bear the burden.

Fortunately, I never had to miss Anne Taylor Fleming or her friendship. Les handed me a sheaf of her "My Turn" pieces from *Newsweek* in early 1984. He clearly wanted us to try to do something with her, so we did. Once we started, we never stopped, and Anne became one of the backbones of the essays ever after. Some of her pieces were not only among the finest we have done but have provided me with experiences that I have never forgotten.

I particularly remember our meeting with teenage single mothers in a South Central LA school and the earnestness with which they wanted to do well by their children while trying to continue their education;

the day we spent with the still tormented victims of torture from all over the world in the years before 9/11, places like Argentina, Chile, and Egypt, all countries with authoritarian governments, our steadfast allies in the Cold War with the Soviet Union;

the time spent with Claudia Bernardi, both an extraordinary artist and woman from Argentina, who spent every moment she could unearthing the graves of the *Desaparecidos*, the "disappeared" in Latin America's political civil wars regardless on whose side they were on (if, indeed, it had ever mattered to their murderers what side they were on) and whose remains insisted on inhabiting her very moving paintings;

an hour spent in a writer's workshop with a group of AIDs patients for whom the writing of their personal stories had become as vital and necessary to their lives as the taking of their daily regimen of pills if not more so;

a day spent with Dikla Bezheevi, a 38-year-old stage four breast cancer survivor, a woman of great heart, great bravery, and an enormous zest for life despite the severity of her illness. All these years later, she is, miraculously, still alive, still fighting, still trying to live her life to its fullest, and we are still in touch with each other.

These are just a few, among many others, experiences through which Anne and I continually learned as we saw, which, if you think about it, is precisely what being a journalist really is. In the process, we became close friends, a friendship that clearly transcended our working relationship, and we both knew would survive even the kind of trauma that Penny suffered.

Anne was born into a Hollywood family, with an actress mother, Phyllis Avery, and an actor/director father, Don Taylor, who divorced when Anne and her sister were young girls. Despite her industry connections, Anne was never interested in a Hollywood, a show business life but was, instead, drawn to journalism. A baby boomer to the core, she is also a pure California girl in the best sense of the word, or at least that's the way I think of her. She has blond hair, a naturally slim body that is reluctant to put on weight despite her love of food, and loves the beach. Having the sunniest disposition of anyone I know and an apparently carefree attitude, she is also one of the most serious, sanest, down-to-earth people and realists I know aside from Lee. A feminist to the core, she loves men, including her late husband, an alpha male of the first order. She found no contradiction between the two. They both clearly enjoyed each other's independence and total commitment to each other as long as he lived. There's no one, aside from Lee, who I enjoy spending time with more than Anne. And there's no one I feel more comfortable or safer talking to about anything, no matter what it is.

On the other hand, if I were to be asked would I prefer to spend a single evening with Anne or Richard Rodriguez, I would feel hard-pressed to decide, they are so different from each other — one light, the other dark.

There were only one or two occasions after I began producing the essays that I discussed them or their direction with Les, Robin, and Jim at one time. 1991 was one such occasion. Robin and Jim said they'd like me to add another minority essayist. I asked if it could be a Latino, and after some hesitancy, they agreed. As for most Americans in those pre-anti-immigration fervor days, "minority" automatically meant someone who was Black. To me, though, it was evident that Latinos were an ever-growing part of America that should not be ignored. So after a couple of weeks of looking and not finding anyone whose work I thought was right, I called Karl Fleming, Anne's husband, and asked if he could think of anyone.

Karl was a longtime journalist who, when the Atlanta bureau chief of *Newsweek,* chronicled the civil rights movement witnessing the worst and best of it from Birmingham to the photo that hung in his office of him walking alongside Martin Luther King, Jr.'s casket. After moving to LA, he was almost killed covering the Watts Riots. If you're interested (and I certainly was), you can read his autobiography, *Son of the Rough South.*

A couple of weeks later, Karl called back, suggesting I read an op-ed piece by Richard Rodriguez in that weekend's *LA Times.* I did and immediately knew that Richard was the person I was looking for. Just reading that column, I knew exactly how to deal with it visually. It had all the characteristics I was looking for. It was thoughtful, insightful, original, innately (if unintentionally) visual, empathetic, and had the kind of emotional subtext that was my ideal, always looked for, and not so often found.

Richard, however, was not so easily convinced. It was not so much that he had to be coaxed or pressured, neither of which would have been productive, but that he had to be courted without feeling overtly pressed. And so, for most of the following year, we would talk every so often. He came to New York to be interviewed by Bill Moyers, and we met in person for the first time. He left, and we continued to talk. Finally, he agreed to try an essay and found that it was not the worst experience in the world, though close to it, and would do another and then another and kept on until the Essays died. His first piece, in December 1991, was part of the Pearl Harbor Anniversary series that won an Emmy. I still remember his point in those days, when Americans were concerned about Japanese buying American businesses and real estate. We shouldn't forget, Richard said, that if the Japanese were buying, it was Americans who were selling. There were pieces from the Tijuana/San Diego border about those twin cities, from Sacramento, San Francisco, and Seattle.

We talked about how wars never end anything,

     how the Indians managed to survive and, in a way, triumph through intermarriage, about the battle between Catholicism and evangelical Protestantism in Latin America,

about the image of Osama bin Laden in Third World countries,

about the casting of the War on Terror in religious terms by America just as our foes did.

He, too, became part of the backbone of the essays.

We shared no experience more meaningful to me personally than a visit we made to the Apostolic Assembly Church in East Palo Alto. It was a small church, a painting of a blue lake partially hidden by the curtains behind the altar. There was a small band, a keyboard, a guitar, drums, and little more. The service was primarily, maybe entirely, in Spanish, the congregants raising their hands and voices to Jesus in Spanish too. Though predominantly working class, the congregation included everything from a dean at Stanford University to an old, stocky, peasant woman recently arrived from Nicaragua who I remember dancing, twirling her way joyfully down the aisle. What most impressed me was the congregants' enthusiastic devotion. There was the unmistakable feeling that they thought that their lives meant something to Jesus, that they had a personal relationship with Him, and that He cared about them as individuals and their lives.

After the service, I thought I understood something important about the evangelical movement in America and Latin America and why it was so powerfully attractive for working-class people. It wasn't that God or Jesus would make them rich or make their lives better. It wasn't that their suffering, hard work, and poverty would be rewarded in some future life. It was that their lives, the lives they were leading, the *fact* of their lives now, were meaningful to Jesus. It was that His love for them raised them in their own eyes. I thought then, as now, that it was a powerful experience, one that I would never have had without Richard.

In 2021 I asked Richard if he knew what had happened to that congregation in today's era when so many evangelical churches have become politicized. Unfortunately, he didn't. Looking at their website, it still appears a working-class congregation, involved in its primary missions of "exalt Christ," "equip the Church" (I'm not sure what that means other than raising money), and "evangelize the world." Since all the recorded videos of sermons on their Facebook page are in Spanish, I can't tell if they've taken a stance in national domestic politics.

In Richard, we had a writer who tried hard to be original, to consciously think thoughts that others had not or, if they had, had not expressed them in public or in the same way he did. In fact, whenever I proposed subjects for essays, he typically turned them down because he hadn't thought of them first. On the other hand, he often initiated long conversations about various matters, and I would find that things I had said had found their way into an essay. On the occasions that he did agree to do a subject, he insisted on his own take on it. I wouldn't have had it any other way; his originality, willingness to challenge orthodoxy, and "conventional wisdom" (whatever that is) are his coins.

Long ago, Richard reinvented himself several times, first as a scholar, then as an ad man, then as a public intellectual. The independent public intellectual, a person who makes a living solely on the quality of his ideas and their public presentation, not to mention their usefulness, is a dying breed in America. We have never thought all that much of intellectuals in the first place and perhaps less so as mass media has steadily increased its reach and variety. Political and social thought has become ever more institutionalized, polarized, dogmatic, sclerotic, and pedestrian. Richard would not cater to the political certitudes and strictures of the minority communities he most obviously belonged to, whether Latino, Mexican-American, Indian (Mexican version), church-going Catholic, or LGBTQ, not to mention any of the other communities to which every American belongs. It's not simply that America is a nation of immigrants, which is obvious. We are a nation built of thousands of subsets out of which we make generalities that are sometimes germane and sometimes not. We are an extraordinarily varied country and, yes, it is one of our greatest strengths that despite our differences, most of us seem able to get along with each other most of the time. However, these days extremists on both the left and right seem to be challenging that notion. Richard would insist on his Catholicism but not accept its politicization in an increasingly politicized religious America. He would insist on his Catholicism despite any Pope or bishop's abhorrence of his homosexuality. He would not cave into the imprecations of either major political party or ideological faction to align himself with their causes but was willing to contribute his ideas to anyone who wanted to hear them. There were and still are many who wanted to listen to them, and he created a lucrative career by writing and delivering lectures around the world. He once said that the *NewsHour* had helped tripled his lecture fees. I, for one, was delighted.

I learned an enormous amount from Richard, if for no other reason than he approaches everything from a different vantage point than mine. I like to think that he's learned from me as well. Regardless, he, too, is a friend, a real friend.

And, if I may be so bold as to say, our audience had much to learn from him. In particular, Richard had been at the forefront of the argument that America was changing. The old black/white construction of race relations was as dated as the dodo bird. He insisted for well over ten years that we were becoming an increasingly "brown" country, a country that was not post-racial when Barack Obama was elected in 2008 but, rather, multi-racial. It was a view that seemed alien to the *NewsHour*'s audience as it was to the *NewsHour* and its principals, which for an overly long time insisted that race be seen only in the context of the Black/white dialectic. As late as the 2008 election, it was not altogether clear that they agreed with Richard, at least if one was to judge by the show's coverage of the election. Maybe by the 2012 election that had changed, but I wouldn't know since I was long gone and no longer watched the show. Counter-intuitively perhaps, the Obama presidency demonstrated that the old racism — i.e., anti-Black racism — had hardly disappeared. The reality of a Black president didn't prove the absence of racism but seemingly gave license to more outward verbalization and too easily seen manifestations of it.

I've wondered, from time to time, how much of Richard's perceptions were because he was born and raised on the West Coast and northern California in particular, an area of the country in which Blacks were a minority of the minority. We once did an essay, for example, about San Franciso as an Asian city. It's another cliché to note that the media establishment, whether journalism or publishing, is dominated by the East Coast, and what the East Coast sees it assumes is true of the country as a whole. It is, of course, untrue. America can look very different from the West Coast, as I found out many years ago when I lived in LA. We on the East Coast have much to learn from the West Coast, just as we all have much to learn from the Southwest and the High Plains states. We all have much to learn from each other if we could just stop insisting that what we are personally familiar with is what is universally true for everyone forever and always.

Maybe what I'm saying is as simple as this: We all live within paradigms, sets of ideas that define the limits of what we are comfortably able to think, the boundaries of what we can see and understand. They are most obviously influenced by our family's milieu and background and the general region and culture in which we grow up. But they are also affected and modified or changed by our own life experiences. Those of my generation have influenced those ideas and paradigms by the second half of the 20th century. The end of the Second World War, Jim Crow, the Civil Rights Movement, political assassinations, Feminism, the Sexual Revolution, Vietnam, the Evangelical revival, the War on Terror, and the Cold War, and whatever we have understood from them, have defined what we have seen as being possible.

If the 2008 election was about anything, perhaps it was about this: That the paradigms by which we have lived our lives and defined our conception of possibility are more than a bit shopworn, that they increasingly don't fit the world in which we find ourselves. If Bill Clinton was trying to build a "bridge to the 21st century," the election of Bush 43 was, hopefully, the last gasp of the twentieth century, and the election of 2008 pitted the last Cold Warrior against the first candidate of the 21st century.

What Obama promised, when you really come down to it, is that the paradigm can shift, can change. I hoped he was right, and he would be successful in helping us navigate the journey and that it would lead to a better America and world. But, judging by his successor, that was hardly the case as Trump took us back to the campaigns of George Wallace. Trump, the self-declared builder and deal-maker, turned out to be the breaker of things, a creator of and master of chaos. Even more, Trump seemed to be supporting an idea of a colonial era, Anglo-Saxon, America. A pre-democratic America. An America where the ideals of freedom and liberty were at best hierarchical and class-structured. With Joe Biden succeeding Trump as president, the Democrats have an uneasy majority. Who knows how long he and they can hold off the Visigoths storming the capital.

Speaking of paradigms and viewpoints, points from which to view things, I mustn't forget Clarence Page, another essayist. Our association dates back to the mid-80s when he started writing for the *NewsHour* while still living in Chicago. The first essay we did together was about the Black middle-class. I'm not sure how many people were aware of how large the group had grown in the decade and a half after the assassination of Martin Luther King, Jr. I'm pretty sure I wasn't. But he also wrote about the plight of poor Blacks in the Cabrini Housing Project and the homeless, about Black History Month and gospel music, about poetry slams and rap music, about new Black leaders and relationships between Blacks and Jews. Clarence didn't only write essays about Black America, nor did we want him to, but he did plenty of them.

As one of the few nationally syndicated black newspaper columnists in the 80s, I often wondered if Clarence felt that one of his obligations, whether he wanted it or not, was to try to explain Black America to white folks. That is a large, maybe too large a burden for anyone, and I'm not sure it was always comfortable for him, even if it benefited his career. But the *NewsHour*'s audience benefited greatly from it. I know I did. As time has passed, Clarence has been less and less alone in carrying that burden as a viewer of any cable news channel knows. I always loved our long phone conversations and the occasional dinners with him and his wife, Lisa (herself a fine writer and teacher), that were always lively and much too infrequent.

There are many other writers with whom I worked over the years. Some of them wrote many essays for the *NewsHour*, others as few as one. But, almost without exception, the experiences were memorable for me.

Amei Wallach, an art critic with *Newsday* at the time, wrote many essays for us over several years on artists like Anselm Keifer, Kiki Smith, and Ilya Kabakov, all of whose work I knew nothing about. On the other hand, there were pieces on people like Merce Cunningham with whose work I was long familiar. We were friends for all those years. However, after she left the show, we drifted apart mainly because I began spending so much time in Washington.

Susan Shreve, primarily a novelist, was a member of the once small band of fiction writers living in Washington. She wrote essays for a couple years of in the 80s. Beneath the typical Victorian garb that she wore with its high lace collars, sleeves reaching down to the wrists, and long skirts beat a quite un-Victorian heart, which might make her a true Victorian after all.

Molly Ivins wrote for us over a few years, and we were all were sorry when she decided it took up too much of her time. Her devastating wit and sarcasm, her dislike for political posturing and corruption, not to mention the pretensions of the wealthy, kept us waiting for the next laugh, the next hot air balloon to be popped. As I remember it, Molly's first essay for us was about the seemingly unending corruption by the leadership of both Democrats and Republicans in the state legislature in Austin. For her, the place was infested by roaches. So I was delighted, as she suggested, to place a cockroach atop the Texas state capital's dome for her. In recent years, many who've witnessed the goings-on in recent years in, as we journalists say for some reason, the "*great* state of Texas" might easily conclude that the cockroach still belongs on its perch.

N. Scott Momaday, the great Kiowa Indian writer, wrote one essay for us many years ago, and I was always sorry that we never managed to do another.

Phyllis Theroux wrote many essays for us, and she did me the honor of excerpting the eulogy I wrote for my father's funeral in her excellent *The Book of Eulogies*.

Elie Wiesel wrote an essay for us in 1985 on the 40th anniversary of the liberation of Buchenwald. While we were shooting, he said that he wanted to begin writing about things other than the Holocaust. A few years later, I called and asked if he would do just that. In the fall of 1988, the 50th anniversary of *Kristallnacht* was approaching, another in the all too frequent anniversaries of the awful things that the Germans had done to the Jews over the years with no response from the rest of the world other than a blink at best. I thought it would help us all if Elie would write about the terrible things that were being done to other people in the world who *weren't* Jews, others that the world seemed as unable, unwilling, to aid just as they had failed to respond to that Night of Broken Glass fifty years earlier. He thought it a good idea, and a few weeks later, I received his essay. It was about the Holocaust. I called him. "Elie," I said, "I thought you were going to write about something else." "I tried," he said. "I just couldn't do it." It saddened me to think that Elie, this extraordinary man, a gifted writer and moralist with a sensitive, if troubled soul, might be as trapped in the memory of Auschwitz and Buchenwald as if he was still behind barbed wire fences.

Tom Pew, the Tucson editor who introduced me to Jay Dusard and told me of Katie Lee, wrote essays too for a while, primarily about the West. I am indebted to him for letting me walk down the street in Winslow, AZ (remember the Eagles', "Standing on the corner in Winslow, Arizona") just after it had been cut off from meaningful vehicle traffic by the coming of the Interstate, a slow death thus assured. It was the final end of the legendary Route 66 as a major cross-country route.

> There is a highway from coast to the coast,
> New York to Los Angeles
> I'm going down the road with troubles on my mind.
> I've got the 66 Highway Blues.
> —Woody Guthrie

Somewhere in the *NewsHour* tape archives (if they still exist), you can still see me sauntering down the main street in the midday sun, my back to the camera, the only person on the otherwise deserted street. There was no "girl in a flatbed Ford slowing down to take a look at me."

A fine carpenter, Richard Clark, who lived in Galena, IL, wrote essays for us for a year or two. Lee still has the jewelry box that I commissioned him to make for her one Christmas. In the end, he couldn't escape the "but what about this or that" test, the apparent exceptions to his argument.

And all the others: Jack Perkins, Bill Barol, Roger Mudd, Arthur Schlesinger, Jr., Roger Wilkens, Studs Terkle, Aaron Freeman, Isaac Asimov, Vern Smith, Paul Hoffman, Tim Ferris, John Edgar Wideman, Mike Lupica, Juan Williams, Roger Angel, Chet Raymo, Nancy Gibbs, Julia Keller. Altogether, fifty-seven different writers, mostly journalists and columnists, wrote one or more essays for the *NewsHour*.

Not every writer who we tried worked out. I remember coming across Charles Bowden for the first time. It was an article about a bat cave that I read in the mid or late 80s. The prose seemed as lush, as opulent as anything I'd ever read, so intense that it seemed almost hyperbolic. My mother would have called it "purple prose," a phrase I'd first heard her use in describing Lawrence Durell's *Alexandria Quartet*, which she read after I'd recommended it to her. She didn't mean it as a compliment.

After talking to Charles, he agreed to try something, and he sent me an essay about a sacred Indian site in the Arizona desert near Tucson. The place he described as a circle of stones, seemingly Stonehenge-like in size and significance. It was a wonderful piece. I ordered up a crew and a cherry picker to enable us to see the rocks from any height in all their magnificent glory. We all met up and drove out to the site with Charles. And there were the stones, all laid out in a circle, just as he'd described. But this was no Stonehenge, at least in scale. The rocks seemed ordinary, maybe two or three inches high at the most, some nearly flat like pieces of shale. We shot the piece, on and off the cherry picker, shot the stand-ups, recorded the voice-over track, wondering why we were even bothering. Since we were there already, it didn't cost any more to shoot it than not to, and maybe I could salvage something once I got into the editing room back in NY. I couldn't. There was no way to match the images to the words, each seeming to diminish the reality of the other.

Those failures didn't happen often, but they happened.

Unnamed by me in this book are all the staff and freelance people who helped along the way. All the reporters, associate producers, production assistants, graphic artists, editors, camera crews, and other producers without whom none of what I did could have been possible. If you are one of those people, rest assured that many of your names are acknowledged at the end of this book.

Before leaving the essays and the *NewsHour*, at least for this memoir's purposes, it feels right and proper that I return to Roger Rosenblatt. When Roger turned 60, Ginny, his wife, asked his friends to write him letters instead of giving him presents. And so, I did:

Dear Roger:

I like to think that we met in 1954, or was it '55? It was one of those glumly gray New York winter days, the slush on the streets as gray as the overcast sky, the air damp, the cold penetrating. Yuck.

It was in the gym of EI that we met, wasn't it? That small basketball court where the walls of the gym and the out-of-bounds sideline were one, guaranteeing a fair number of black and blue marks if you dared try to stop a ball from going out of bounds. But it was big in the aroma that always seems to fill so many gyms ... stale sweat. Yuck.

The trouble is, I don't think it ever happened. Not that it couldn't have. After all, we were born barely four months apart (yes, I know, you're the young one), we were both from middle-class Jewish families, we were both intent on demonstrating to our parents and our teachers that we weren't as bright and smart and talented as they thought we were (you gave that one up much earlier than I did), we liked to read, we liked poetry, we both went to small, progressive (in my case "progressive" should probably be in quotation marks) schools, we both played on the basketball team ... God, we should have gotten married!

Isn't that what our parents told us? When searching for a lifetime companion, we should look for someone similar to us?

But I guess if we never met, we couldn't have married, could we?

Besides, there was that other thing that was similar: we wanted romantic companions who were different from us, like girls. God knows it's impossible to be more different than a girl. Confusing objects of desire.

If we were similar in that, then we were different as well. After all, how could we get married when you met Ginny at about the same time that we either did or didn't meet? Good friend I may be, but I'm not in the same league as Ginny. There is that photo of her that I used to see in NY of Ginny and one of her babies (Carl, I think), and whenever I saw it, I would think that maybe you did marry the most beautiful girl in the world.

Thirty years later, in 1984, we met (again?). It was one of those glumly gray New York winter days ... actually, I think it was sunny. But it was winter, and it was cold, of that I'm sure, and if it wasn't, so what? And you had written this essay called "What Should We Lead With," which I was assigned to produce. You remember it, don't you? It presented two contemporaneous events: the civil war in Lebanon and the ice dancing in the Olympics (I'm tempted to say Sarajevo, but I don't remember if that was it—that would have been too perfect in terms of later events in that sad city). The essay asked the question: Which was more important, the world ending or the world in love, death, or hope. It was a toss-up, except that it wasn't, really. I remember sitting in the dark of the editing room as Torvill and Dean danced to Bolero, counterpoint to the insanity in Beirut, tears in my eyes, knowing that there was an answer. Torvill and Dean, hands down.

The creation of "What Should We Lead With" was an important moment for me. In terms of my life, it was the real beginning of a friendship that has lasted for many years. If it hadn't happened, I wouldn't know Anne or Richard. There are few people as important to me as the three of you in my life.

In terms of my career, it determined the path I would take for the next 16 years. But, more importantly, as I sat in the editing room that day, with Bolero throbbing through the speakers, with Torvill and Dean skating with their long and sinuous lines, I understood what the essays were about: The way that they were identical to the things I had been trying to create for the NewsHour. I understood how extraordinary a medium television is, unlike any other, one which is capable of communicating grace, beauty, death, hope, love, and above all, a kind of emotional and intellectual complexity in a very personal way. What I had been trying to say in my features and what we really said in your essay is that there is rationality, there is understanding, there is beauty, there is hope, there is salvation even amidst death and destruction and insanity. Of course, it's pretty hard to find it sometimes.

The tape of "What Should We Lead With" has long since disappeared, but for many years I carried the script with me. It's still in the briefcase that I carried down to Washington when the *NewsHour* deserted New York.

One of the things that most confused me about your reputation among *NewsHour* staffers was their thinking that you were a prophet of doom and gloom. They didn't understand then, they don't really understand now (though you have no idea how your stock improved with them after the roast of Jim Lehrer).

That understanding of what we were creating, you and I (and Richard and Anne after), has remained constant through the years we have worked together. You and I have probably done something over 300 pieces together. We have both gotten better at what we do, and we both take what we do for granted more than at least I did at the beginning. But in all that time, through all those pieces, that essential understanding of what essays should be and what the medium is capable of has never changed.

Although I am writing this at the beginning of August 2000, I know what will be happening on the day that you receive this letter. We will be in the midst of a presidential campaign that few are excited about; in Africa, there will be people being killed in some Civil War, others will be starving to death largely because of the killing; the Balkans will still be a tinder box; so will the middle east; there will still be poor people, there will be homeless people; there will have been a murder or two or three somewhere. The new American century still has some dark spots.

And you will be in Quogue.

Perhaps there is a fall chill in the evening air and a fire in the fireplace. You are surrounded by your family, by Ginny, Carl and Wendy, Amy and Harris, John, and, of course, Hector. You are looking back at 60 years spent doing pretty much what you wanted to do, having achieved most of what you tried for without quite knowing how you managed to pull it off. You are looking forward to a future with hopeful expectations, a future that, at the end of the day, will find you very much as you are now, surrounded by the people you love most and who feel equally strongly about you.

I know what I would call this essay. "What Should We Lead With."

Not so long ago, I was talking to Gerry Margolis about the essays. By now, Gerry, the former Director of the Museum of Tolerance, had been one of my closest friends for many years. He said that he'd always thought the essays were the best part of the *NewsHour*. Of course, I've heard that from quite a few people over the years, directly or indirectly. But, whatever I might think of them, I know for sure that they were unlike anything else on the show then or now. I'm sure that's true of almost everything I did for Robin and Jim.

Then Gerry, thinking of the rest of the show, asked, "If Robin and Jim were the cool, dispassionate, questioning brains of the show, what were the essays?"

I thought for a moment, hyperbole overflowing,

"The beating heart."

Chapter 15

THE GHOST OF ELIAKUM

◆

1985 — 2009

Lest you think I have forgotten about Eliakum, my great grandfather, I assure you he's never gone away. I may not have thought of him often, but he resided quietly in my mind. Or maybe he was just a tiny fragment of my DNA. There's no better reason why I became a *badchen* of the Saltz/Zunser family, a performer at weddings and funerals. Of course, I say this with a bit of tongue in cheek, with a wink and a nod, but still ...

In 1985, Jesse Zunser died. He was the son of Grandpa Zunser's brother and my godfather, a role he took seriously. A college dropout, he became one of the founders and editors of Cue Magazine, a publication that devoted itself to the cultural life of New York City long before magazines like *New York* and *Time Out*. He was also its movie and TV critic. He once said he had seen and reviewed something like 12,000 movies. Upon occasion, he would take Amy and me to see premiers of films like *The Red Pony*, which had children as its primary audience. When I was 13, he gave me a Civil War-era cap and ball rifle that still sits in my closet. Also, a Japanese samurai sword, now disappeared.

After his death, for some reason never explained, his daughter, Sheila Rogoff — the same Sheila who had eulogized my father by talking about the summer of 1939 — Sheila asked if I would deliver a eulogy on behalf of the family at his memorial. Sheila knew my work at the *NewsHour*, of course, but she had never read anything I'd written or heard me speak in public. Nevertheless, there I stood in front of the assembled mourners at the opulent Moorish-styled Central Synagogue on Lexington Avenue in NYC, delivering the kind of remarks that I hoped she had in mind. Jesse, of course, was a writer, and I saved his own words, written the year before his death, for last.

> **Life has had its many surprises. I am certain Death has some, too. For who knows what is beyond the grave: Now, *that is* a mystery – but not for long. All of us – each in his way and time – will find out – and it may be a happy surprise. For all of our fears, a *welcome* surprise...**
>
> **Dreams can and *do* become realities. Many times in our life, we have seen it...We may see it again...Nothing – not even Death – is forever! In that sense, let us all look forward – and with Hope, always Hope, welcome the inevitable...**
>
> **And not forget that we *can* recall the Dead by remembering them – as *I* believe they remember us.**

On Memorial Day weekend in 1990, Lee and I went to my parents' house on Lake Copake. We'd decided to buy a house and were looking in the area. Lee asked how long I thought it would take to find one.

"Maybe the whole summer."

"Not a chance," Lee said.

She was right, as she usually is. We bought a house the next day. Not only that, but we decided to get married there in September. My parents were thrilled. We not only bought a place only a mile or so away from them, but it meant that they would continue to see my children, Brandon and Michelle, who had spent at least part of every summer with them ever since Lynne and I had our final separation. It also meant they would see more of Alicia, Lee's daughter, who by now was 12.

As for the forthcoming marriage, they were happy about that too. Mom and Dad liked Lee and thought their son was in good hands. In August, they bought us a dozen fruit trees that we planted together on a hill to the side of the house. Michelle came from the West Coast to help. Trees had much meaning to my mother. They were a sign of permanence and increased one's ties to the land, a reminder, perhaps, of her father's planting vegetables when she was a child in Ardsley, a reminder, perhaps, of the urging of her grandfather, Eliakum, that Jews should not forget their ties to the land and agriculture in Russia both before and after he arrived in America.

Mom had a long-standing tradition of planting trees in the back of her own house in the name of family members, a practice that we have carried on. With my mother, we planted a dogwood for Alicia and much later on planted trees for her daughter, Karas, and my son Brandon and Sallie's twin daughters, Jane and Cleo. Penny Stallings gave us a Blue Spruce as a wedding present, as I had suggested because Lee loved them so much. Jesse Zunser's sister gave us a tree as well, a tri-colored beech, as did a cousin of Lee's who brought us a fir the first time she visited. And my mother planted flowers in our garden that she brought from hers, including some that had gotten their start in her sister's garden in Shelter Island and from Mary and Jesse Zunser's garden in Saratoga Springs: lilies, peonies, and poppies, lilac and forsythia bushes among many, many others. So, in a way, our landscape is filled with our family and friends. And, of course, Mom.

We didn't want a complicated, fancy wedding. I don't know what Lee's first wedding was like, but I certainly didn't want anything resembling my wedding ceremony to Lynne with its drunken minister and a herd of strangers. This was to be our wedding, a wedding for us. So on a cool, drizzly day in September with the leaves on the trees already on their way to their full fall outburst, Lee and I were wed. We pitched a large tent in the driveway and only invited family and friends. Michelle, who had come in August to help plant the fruit trees, stayed for the wedding. Of course, Alicia was there, as were my parents and Rosie, Lee's mother. Brandon, traveling in Europe with his girlfriend, couldn't make it back in time. Lee's sister was there along with her oldest brother and his wife, as was Amy. Various other relatives and friends came, including Herman Shonbrun and Virginia, his second wife. Some of my essayists came too: Roger, Anne, Penny, and Amei, Julie Klapper (my assistant at the time), and Les and his wife. Kids played and rolled around in the wet grass. The local Justice of the Peace, a former New York

City mounted policeman, conducted the ceremony, something plain and simple. Lee looked beautiful in a suit (the kind with a skirt), I looked handsome in a suit (the kind without). We both changed back into jeans as soon as the ceremony was over. There was great food (home-cooked over the previous few days), good wine, and enthusiastic dancing. Everybody seemed to have a good time, and so did we. So life continued, not exactly as before but not entirely different either.

The day before Thanksgiving, 1992, Les Crystal asked me to accompany Charlayne Hunter-Gault and a crew to Somalia. We were to leave right after the Thanksgiving break, camp out on the beach, shoot whatever Charlayne wanted us to shoot, and get out of there ASAP. The country was amidst a civil war between the military dictatorship and other military officers. Individual warlords had joined in, and although a cease-fire had been declared, the fighting between various factions hadn't stopped.

I could already feel the adrenaline start to kick in. I may not have been a hard-news journalist in Robin's eyes, but I knew what it meant and felt like to cover a breaking story. It was all about adrenaline, the rush when covering a breaking story, particularly a dangerous one. But my life was not the same since my single days when I was free to rush off to hot spots around the world. So I told Les that I'd have to discuss it with my wife.

Lee's reaction was predictably Lee. "You mean you'll go camp out on a beach in the middle of a war, but you won't go camping with me?"

Well, maybe yes. I'll think about it over the weekend.

The next day, Thanksgiving, we went to my parents' apartment, the same place that I'd grown up in, for the traditional meal: Turkey with cornbread and sausage stuffing, along with all the trimmings. It's basically the meal I still make all these years later. The usual crowd was there, the 20 or so relatives I'd known all my life.

When we were leaving, my mother said, "We have to have a family meeting," the first and only time I can remember her saying that. The next day, Amy and I met Mom for her meeting. She said that she had lung cancer.

As far as the show went, I told Les that I couldn't go to Somalia.

On the other hand, I continued traveling the country, looking for America. But the year was not easy, certainly not for Mom or Dad. She had small cell lung cancer. Stage 4. Inoperable. Despite the poor prognosis, she decided to undergo chemotherapy. Her concern was not so much for her own survival but for Dad, whose health was increasingly precarious. His continually increasing deafness and blindness combined with congestive heart failure and creeping dementia made her try to survive long enough to outlive him.

"What's going to happen to Jerry?" she would ask. No one had an answer. She lost her hair and became steadily weaker. Despite the chemo, by the summer of 1993, her cancer had metastasized to her brain. Her doctors recommended radiation treatments but held out no hope for a cure, only the possibility of forestalling the inevitable for a few more months. She asked Lee's opinion.

Clear-headed as usual, Lee said, "Only if you have things that you have left unsaid."

She did, indeed, have things left unsaid, and so she underwent the treatments, making sure she talked to everyone about the things she had left unsaid, things unsaid to Brandon, to Amy, to Lee, to Alicia, to anyone who was left of her friends and relatives.

I was sitting in her hospital room one night in September, and she said, "I love you. I haven't told you that often enough." After a while, she added, "I want to tell you that I admire you. I respect you for what you have accomplished; you have made me very proud." I thanked her. She said, "I don't know why I haven't said that before."

"You probably thought if you told me that, I would stop working so hard."

She laughed and laughed. "Probably," she said.

Before she came home from the hospital the last time after the treatments were finished and we knew her end was just a matter of waiting, I was sitting in the semi-dark room by the side of the bed, my father in an easy chair against the far wall; it was hard to tell how aware he was of what was going on. Then, finally, she turned her bald head towards him.

"Jerry," she said in as loud a voice as she could muster. "Jerry," she said, "do you want to go with me?"

"No."

She sighed, looked at him for a long moment, turned her face to the ceiling, and closed her eyes.

Amy, by the way, says she was in the room during this scene and remembers it a little differently. It doesn't matter. It's as true, as factual, as it needs to be.

Ever since I was a teenager, my mother spoke freely of death. She had no fear of death, she'd say. What she did fear, which she said she would never allow, was losing her mind. To her, her mind was everything. It was through her mind that she had created her life, a life of thinking and doing. It was her mind that tried to guide her husband through his life, to protect him, that guided the path through hers. It was her mind that made it possible, acceptable, to compromise her ambition when she thought it best for my father, for them both as a couple. It was her mind that allowed her to write, to indulge her passion for gardens, the feeling of soil running through her fingers, the destruction of weeds so that beauty might flower. It was through her mind that she understood the world. It was through her mind that she could impose or try to impose her will on those around her, including her children, for their own good, whatever they may have thought of the effort. She would not allow her mind to fade without her life disappearing first.

My mother came from a line of strong-willed women, including her sister, Helen, and her mother, Miriam. Each of them had cancer. I was told that they each had taken their lives before their cancers could. So would my mother. Not right away, but when she thought the time was right.

So Mom went home, home to 61 Pierrepont Street where she and Dad had lived since 1943, home to where Amy had come home as a baby, home to where I had silently watched Benny watching me, home to what was, in a way, still home to Amy and me despite our having other homes.

Ever so gradually, her days and nights were filled with sleeping, with slipping in and out of consciousness, and still, she lived.

On Thanksgiving Day, 1993, one year after her call for a family meeting, we gathered for one last celebratory meal. This time, the first time in all those years — all the years of my life — there were no more relatives or friends of long-standing. There was no hilarity, no jokes and puns whipping across the table, no children getting bored and restless, no twenty-odd pound turkey with cornbread, chestnut and sausage stuffing, and gravy, and sweet potatoes, and cranberry sauce, all the things that made for our traditional Thanksgiving meal. Instead, we brought a roast chicken and maybe some chicken soup for this last gathering of the family (except for Michelle, who was in Alaska): Amy, Brandon, Lee, Alicia, and me.

We sat around her bed, a hospital bed that had been placed between the dining room and the room where I had seen her 50 years before, her hair spread out on the pillow, after walking on Love Lane in the blazing sun the day she and Amy came home from the hospital. We talked with her, laughed, and made jokes. Amy says, "I remember a room filled with love." And then, while she slept, the rest of us ate dinner.

When dinner was over, it was time to say our goodbyes.

To Amy and me: "I want you to come tomorrow."

And then, one by one, she called the others over to say goodbye — Lee, Alicia, Brandon. I have no more substantial recollection of the event, perhaps because I knew Amy and I would come again, more probably because I didn't want to.

The next day Amy and I arrived around noon. Mother sat in the orange armchair in the living room, dressed in her pink bathrobe, rousing herself from her deep sleep with the force of her extraordinary will, knowing somehow that we were there. She was very tired, and we helped her to her bed.

"It's time," she said.

And so it was.

In writing a eulogy for her funeral, I discovered something. Sitting at the computer, tears streaming down my face as I pecked at the keyboard, I also felt joy.

Are you surprised? Shocked, even? I was. Why this combination of sorrow and happiness? They seemed such a contradiction. In the years since, I've come to think that, in a way, the death of my mother and my father, too, a few months later, liberated me in some mysterious way. Perhaps that's because, for the first time, I was free to define her life without interference. And by doing so, I could see my own in a way that I had never been able to do before, a definition without the possibility of her contradiction. Maybe by some alchemic process, the death of our parents, all our parents, frees us to be adults, if we are only willing to be, able to be adults in a way we never were before. I have never seen a child — a child now an adult —who, when in the presence of their parents, doesn't revert to childhood in some way, the way they behaved as a child. Rebellious or loving, giving or taking, angry or joyful, smiling or sad, it all repeats. Maybe not precisely, but recognizably. Once our parents have died, who is there left to rebel against, to separate from? Who can comfort us as they did when we were children? No one.

Dad died nine months after Mom, in the early morning hours of August 30th, 1994. His death was much, much too slow in coming. He went into the hospital during the last week of August and didn't come out. Both Amy and I wanted to make sure he was given his due in planning his funeral. Our mother, sparkling as she was, was not the anchor that held everything together. That was Dad. Yet his decline had been so tortuous and lasted so many years that I thought it was easy for people to forget who he really was. So I sought to remind them in my eulogy.

> Thinking about Dad over the past few years, it has occurred to me that it is possible to outlive your life.
>
> Lee, my wife, with whom I've been for eleven years, used to say about my mother that she deserved a purple heart for putting up with my father. That may be true, but then she never really had a chance to know Dad. By the time she came into my life, Dad was well on the way out of his.
>
> How would she know that this is the man who made herring salad for Emily's wedding?
>
> How would she know that this man would take me to the baseball fields along the Belt Parkway when I was six or seven to watch the ball games and play catch with me?
>
> Or take me on his shopping trips to Washington Market, which contained a world of strange and exotic tastes and flavors and aromas?

How would she know that this is the man who on Sunday morning would sit in his chair, eyes closed, enraptured by the sounds of Berlioz?

How would she remember his every-morning ritual of swimming in Copake Lake instead of taking a shower?

How would she know of his love of working with carpenter's tools? And the pleasure he got from building the dock, from making a cabinet?

How would she know of his sense of humor? His love of puns? She could not know the man who named the metal sculptures hanging in Avery Fisher Hall "Distrait and Distraught."

How would she know that if you told this man that you loved him, he would cry?

Mom and Dad are buried next to each other in a cemetery in Westchester County, where many of their relatives are also buried. They are, as I said, "where they were for 60 years, side by side, where they wanted to be — 'For better or for worse, in sickness or in health, 'til death do us part.'"

There was one more remembrance to write and to deliver. But, this time, it wasn't for a relative. Herman Shonbrun died in 2008, and Virginia and their children asked if I would speak at his memorial. How could I not? And so, on a sunny, chilly Saturday in October on a hilltop in South Westerlo, NY, amidst the seasonal spectacle of fall, I talked about Herman, his life, and his place in my life.

... Before ending, let me return to 1959.

On that Wednesday in 1959, I was 19 years old and lost. The previous night I had told my parents that I was dropping out of college. I didn't know what I was doing there, didn't know what I was doing with my life, didn't know what I was doing, period.

That evening changed my life. I don't know how many of you remember moments that clearly defined your lives, became the basis, the rock upon which you built your future, but that was *the* moment for me. It was only after that moment that my life began to — was able to — coalesce. And it was all Herman's doing. Even now, 49 years after the event, after a lifetime of other events big and small, I cannot imagine what my life would have been like if it weren't for Herman and what he allowed me, caused me to see and experience that evening.

So, Herman, if you're hanging around and listening to this, the fact that I'm here, the fact that Virginia and your children have asked me to speak this afternoon and dared me to bore all of you — well, it's all your fault.

As our master, Shakespeare emphatically did *not* say, I've come to praise Herman, not to bury him.

I don't know if Eliakum actually did funerals. But he certainly did weddings, and so did I. To my surprise, at least initially, each of my children has asked me to perform at their weddings. Brandon and Sallie got married in Copake with the marriage ceremony at my parents' house that now belongs to my sister. Alicia, Lee's daughter and my step-daughter (or semi-daughter or daughter — I've been known to call her all three at one time or another) was married to her first husband on the deck of our house in Copake. Michelle and Jim were married on a beach in Jamaica (the Caribbean island, not Queens), and Alicia's marriage to Daniel was in Alba, Italy, because it was ... well, truffle season. Each speech was different because each couple was different. But all were clever, all were true, all were heartfelt. All were wonderful. If you want to read them, send a self-addressed stamped envelope.

I think I'll show you a bit of one because it's part of what this book tries to do, as does each chapter and story within each chapter. After all, this book is a road story, isn't it? This is the beginning of Alicia and Daniel's wedding in Italy in 2009, an event that took place seven months after I left the *NewsHour*. So the end of one story and the beginning of another, you might say.

Alicia and Daniel asked that I tell, as Alicia put it, "Our Story." A daunting task, not least because there are so many ways, genres, viewpoints through which to tell it. It might be told as a fairy tale — a contemporary one in which everything is, "I'm OK, you're OK." Or it might be an old-fashioned one, something out of those color-coded books of my childhood — stories filled with witches and hobgoblins and things that go bump in the night — stories telling us that we were innocents and unsafe in a very dangerous world. It might be a "road story" or a "coming of age" story. It might be a comedy or ... well, we wouldn't be here if it was a tragedy, would we?

Regardless of the genre, all stories begin the same way, no matter if they are sweet dreams or nightmares, if they reflect harsh reality or the most divine fantasy. It doesn't matter if they are fact or fiction. It doesn't even matter if the actual words are used or not; they are *always* understood because that is how we – we human beings – understand everything. That is true for this story, for Alicia and Daniel's "Our Story" as well, which, like all stories, begins with a magical incantation:

Once upon a time ...

Finally, there was the last one. It may have been the last but hardly the least. Amy asked me to speak at her wedding on the lawn of our house in Copake. So, I sang.

What is this thing called love ...

Let me know when you find the answer.

Chapter 16

GOODBYE YELLOW
BRICK ROAD

◆

1995 — 2009

No natural pond is a perfect circle. It has nooks and crannies, inlets and outlets. Taking the pond metaphor at this book's beginning, it's safe to say that by now, some of the ripples in the water are brushing the shore.

In the winter of 1995, Robin announced he was leaving the *NewsHour*. He was retiring. After 20 years, he was tired of it; there were other things he wanted to do with his life. It might have been later in the year that he made the announcement, but it makes sense. Call it the winter of our — my — discontent. Not only that, but WNET was closing its studio, and most of the technical staff would be released, some of whom I'd known for almost 30 years. Soon the building housing its offices would be sold to become a hotel.

Yes, the show would continue, now under Jim's leadership. There would be no NY office, and those who wanted to stay with the show were guaranteed a job in Washington.

Of course, I was upset. Twenty years of my life had been devoted to that show. Twenty years dedicated to Robin and, by extension at least, to Jim. It was the most permanent home I'd had as an adult. Besides, what else could I do? Where else could I go? Was there anywhere else that I could do what I did? Was there any producing job at a network that wouldn't have me at the age of 55 competing with people who were, maybe, younger, hungrier, more ambitious, and who had more energy? Would I even want to do the kinds of things they might want? At least at the *NewsHour,* I didn't think I had to

389

prove anything about my ability. Not that I didn't feel somewhat stressed when producing a piece. As much as I liked the volume of the work, the sheer number of individual pieces, every one of them always held the possibility of failure.

Besides, how could I easily surrender the intimate working relationships and genuine friendships that I had with Roger, Anne, Richard, and all the others, the work we had created together, the ability to hold and see the world reflected and refracted through our eyes? What other organization would or could give me the kind of freedom and airtime that I'd achieved at the *NewsHour* where I'd been given the freedom to look for America, to think about America, to present to America what I'd found, even if it was through other voices? And all with very little interference. Yes, there were a few things that I had wanted to do that Robin or Jim vetoed but not much. Do you have any idea how rare that is in the television news industry? Maybe in any industry?

What to do?

I talked to people. Tom Brokaw said, "I don't think you'll be happy anywhere else." To agents. They told me the same thing. "Yes," one agent said, "I'm sure I can get you onto one of the network magazine shows. Are you sure you really want to do that?" He named one he had in mind. I didn't like the show. I didn't like their story selection or how they shot and edited pieces. So, no.

I talked to Lee. No, she wouldn't move to Washington under any circumstances. Her business was in NY. Even when she worked for other companies based in other states, she was located in NYC, the buying center for her industry, and traveled to trade shows and vendors all over the country. She loved her work, the buying and selling, the negotiating. Considered a tough negotiator by her vendors, she was also regarded as an eminently fair and honest one. Her reputation was enviable. To top it off, her industry simply didn't exist in DC, at least not as a buying center; to find a job there, she'd have to take a significant salary cut and give up the considerable professional success she'd achieved through her career. How could I ask her to do that? But, she said, if I wanted to continue with the show and commute to Washington, she was okay with that.

All through the spring, Dan Werner would come up to the city from Washington. He had moved from being a reporter in NY to a senior producer in DC. Aside from producing, he'd been running the Washington office on a day-to-day basis. He was in charge of moving the NY staff to the reconfigured old offices in the WETA studio building, located across the Potomac just south of the Pentagon, and new offices in another building a ten-minute walk away. Whenever Dan was in NY, he'd come to my office to tell me how important I was to the show and how much he wanted me to stay with it. I could only presume he meant it because he was a supporter through my years at *M/L*. Although in retrospect, I don't think I ever heard him say that Jim felt similarly, I just assumed that his views represented Jim's as well. I have no idea if that was true.

Finally, after a few months of this, I sat down to talk to Les. He was, after all, both the show's executive producer and my direct boss. I told him that I'd like to stay with the show. However, I couldn't simply move to Washington. I would get an apartment there to be there as much as I needed to be. After thinking about it for a few minutes, leaning back in his chair, his elbows resting on its arms, his two index fingers holding up his chin as he tilted his head back, figuring out whatever he was figuring out, he said, "Okay."

I found an apartment in Arlington, just blocks from the studio, and bought another car so I could get around. Lee came down for a weekend, and we bought furniture. It was a studio and, as I would describe it, was like a motel without room or maid service, an apartment (at best) somewhere between a Holiday Inn and a Motel 6. In all the years I worked in Washington, Lee came down only one other time for the wedding of one of Sheila Rogoff's daughters. I emphatically did not want Washington to be my home; home was wherever Lee was, not where I was.

I had no concerns about the arrangement. The work was the work, and I loved what I did. I was confident working with those I thought of as "my" writers, secure and comfortable in the editing room, and knowing what I was doing when shooting in the field. I loved seeing pieces come together as I had imagined them, and sometimes it felt almost magical. Even if I didn't know WETA's editors, I was sure I could work with them; I always was willing to believe the people assigned to work with me were at least competent until or unless they proved to be otherwise. I never had reason to find fault with any of the camera crews I worked with out of our Denver office or the many freelance crews I used around the country.

As for Jim, I had no concerns about him either. After all, I knew Jim. Aside from when I was the ½ hour show's production supervisor and seeing him regularly, I'd worked with him on several specific projects. I had, with Duke, staved off disaster for him in La Grange, TX, even if he later reamed us out for daring to suggest that the producer didn't know what she was doing. And, yes, we'd disagreed about the Jeff Cooper piece, but really. If those were the only real problems that existed between us out of the hundreds of things I'd produced up until then, I saw no reason for concern. Besides, the Ruth Lo show had been an enormous success, not simply for me and the show generally, but for Jim personally. He successfully put his friend AC Greene in my hands and other friends in Texas and Washington, such as Doris Grumbach, Roger Mudd, and Larry McMurtry.

More than that, when we were in Denver for the Ruth Lo show, the two of us had dinner together in the Brown Palace Hotel. It was a long and warm dinner during which we mostly talked about our families, our wives, and our children. Then, when we were in Kansas City together for something and on the bus from the airport terminal to the rental car agency, we talked about his ill mother. So there was a relationship, right?

Wrong, maybe. People are so confusing sometimes, aren't they?

In all the time I was based in Washington, from 1995 until I left in 2009, 14 years, I only had one face-to-face discussion with Jim, and that was the morning of the day I left the show, and that was no discussion at all. From time to time, we'd see each other outside his office in the studio building and exchange a polite, "Hi, how are ya?" as we passed by each other, and that's all.

Every year Jim would have a Christmas party for the staff at his house. I went to a couple in the first years I was there, and once after my heart attack. From what I saw, Jim would talk to his friends, to those he considered his peers or near peers, and to no one else. Maybe since he saw most of the editorial staff every day, he didn't feel any need to chat them up at a party. Being the sort of reclusive guy I'm inclined to be and being uncomfortable in large gatherings, I didn't make any effort to change that and simply stopped going to them. Did others see these parties the same way? I know a couple of people did, but I don't know that they particularly cared. After all, Jim was Jim, and they expected nothing other than that.

The same was true of the annual Washington Correspondents Association dinners. I went to a couple before Robin retired and one after the show moved to DC, but I didn't enjoy them for similar reasons and turned down the yearly invitations.

Perhaps my reactions to Jim while I was in DC were a bit petty and self-defeating, but I am who I am, for better or for worse, just as Jim was who he was. I never could get past the multiple sides of his personality. To me, he was like a southern belle. He could be totally charming, friendly, warm, outgoing, and inviting while seemingly simultaneously seem not to mean a word of it. Or maybe he meant it at that moment, but there was always the next moment. To me, too much of the public Jim came to seem like a performance. In all my years in Washington, I never again saw the man I had seen in Denver or Kansas City. Frankly, it ... I was going to say I was hurt, but that's not quite right. I was, I don't know, insulted by it? Irked? Pissed off? Annoyed? Any of them will do.

If it wasn't for AC Greene, I'd chalk this up to my particular sensitivities and quirks. AC and Jim had been friends when they worked on newspapers in Dallas. After Jim moved to KERA, AC was a guest on his show every week. He was part of Jim's social circle, and they'd often talk, not as work colleagues but as friends, a relationship far closer than anything I ever thought I had with Jim. And then, once Jim moved to DC, they'd hardly ever talked again except when it came to work-related things, like when Jim would interview AC during a book review segment. It was as if Jim had moved into a newer, higher social circle and left his old friends behind. AC never understood the wall that seemed to have gone up between them and was hurt by it.

This is not to say that AC wasn't grateful for Jim's effort to get him a new heart. He was. Enormously so, but he never got over the hurt from what he felt was Jim's rejection for as long as I knew him.

This is not a matter of speculation on my part; it's something AC talked about on more than one occasion.

I had two telephone conversations with Jim during all those years. One was after he rejected a script of Roger's, a message conveyed by Les, who couldn't clearly explain what Jim thought was problematic. So I asked if I could talk to Jim about it. Weird, huh? That I'd have to ask permission to speak to Jim? Yet that seemed to be one of Les's jobs: to be the gatekeeper, to keep people away from Jim unless they were directly involved with that night's show, at least when it came to me. But, yes, I could call Jim, which I did, and the issue was resolved in less than a minute to our mutual satisfaction (and to Roger's).

The other phone call was after my heart attack in 1999. Again, as with AC, Jim called to ask if he could do anything for me or if there was anything I needed. Again, I never doubted his sincerity. But, at the same time, I was glad that I could tell him that I didn't need a thing from him, at least not medically.

Isn't that strange? That ability or willingness to be all-in when there's an emergency, as with AC and the others I know about who he helped, and then the complete withdrawal. Maybe you can explain it. I can't, and I'm not really interested in trying. But, at the same time, I know this is not how most people saw Jim. All I know is that those I know of who've talked publicly about him are those he considered to be his peers or almost peers. I've never spoken about this to anyone else on the show, either when writing this book or when I was still there, so I don't know what they would say.

It wasn't until the first week of the show, now all in Washington (except for our Denver bureau), I began to realize how much things were changing. I asked Les if I should be going to the morning planning meeting. No. The meetings in DC would be different from when Robin was running things and welcomed anyone who wanted to join the discussion. Jim apparently wanted to see the fewest people necessary to plan that night's show. Since I was disconnected from the daily broadcast, my presence was neither needed nor wanted. Whatever presence I had on any night's show was determined by a row of edited master tapes sitting on a shelf waiting to be aired whenever the executive or deputy executive producers decided.

I was of two minds about this. On the one hand, I had liked the morning meetings in NY; I liked knowing what was on Robin and Jim's minds and what others were thinking about. I even liked saying what was on my mind. Now, I would be dependent on Les to tell me if anything I should know had happened in the meetings. But, on the other hand, if I didn't have things that I had to specifically do in DC, I would have the ability to do everything my job required from home. Having long equipped myself to do my job from anywhere in the country after buying my first computers in 1984, working from home was easily done.

Interestingly (or not), I read in an interview of Jim that he described his planning meetings as collegial. I think he even used the word "democratic" to describe them. Was he oblivious that there was a pre-planning meeting gathering every morning between Les and some of those same people to preplan what Jim would be told? All I can say is that Jim's and Robin's definitions of collegial were different.

If Robin's impulses were egalitarian despite his reserved manner, Jim's were the opposite despite his southern folksiness and charm. For all their differences, and they were almost completely opposite in terms of personalities, they were extraordinarily close and placed enormous faith and trust in each other. They each envied the personal qualities in the other that they felt they lacked in themselves. Back in the early days of the show, I'd established a tie-line between the two of them. All they had to do was pick up the telephone, and the other would be on the line. They talked to each other throughout each day. It worked as a perfect and frictionless partnership as long as both anchored the show. There may have been disagreements, but they were never on public display as far as I knew.

It's not that they saw the world or the show's mission identically. Robin tended to be interested in a broader variety of subjects, a more eclectic view of the world. Perhaps this was because he was a Canadian by birth and had only come to the States as an adult. He, too, had been a foreign correspondent, including in America, and had spent time at the BBC and was well-traveled in the world as a journalist and not as a tourist. Jim, on the other hand, seemed to have more parochial interests. Before he was a TV journalist, he had been the city editor of a Dallas paper. His TV journalism experience was in Dallas, at PBS in Washington, and then at WETA. I don't think he'd ever been to Europe before our show because he was afraid of flying, something he worked hard to cure himself of. After Robin's retirement, the show seemed to primarily reflect Jim's interests as a city editor. That city was Washington, the Federal city, not so much the city where people lived.

It's my impression that Robin and Jim were inclined to think of news differently. Robin, I think, was more interested in problems and policy and Jim in politics and the process of government. And those differences were reflected in the show before and after Robin's retirement. I don't want to make too much of this because I'm not sure I'm right, but it fits the difference in their working backgrounds, the foreign correspondent vs. the city editor.

Regardless, Robin was the ship's captain — the unquestioned leader — until he retired and Jim assumed that role. After Robin's retirement, Jim was in absolute control of the show. A few years after his retirement, I asked Robin if he ever spoke to Jim about the show. He said he never did.

I use the "captain" term intentionally for two reasons. One is the naval background of Robin's family, which I've mentioned before. Robin knew what being a captain meant. As for Jim, he knew what it meant as well. He voluntarily joined the Marines as a 2nd Lieutenant between the Korean and Vietnam Wars and served for three years. His father and brother were also ex-Marines. So, Jim knew what a captain was, and his leadership style reflected that experience. The captain was the captain, and captains are meant to lead and be followed without question. So, it is not surprising that he was a top-down manager, very different from Robin.

Even more, Jim never stopped being a Marine. The values that were inculcated in him during his service became lifelong values. He believed in honor, in acting honorably. He had learned how to be apolitical during his service, and he carried that attitude into the show. He never voted in an election because that might indicate his preference for one political side or another or for one political party over another or one politician over another because of a policy position they held. Of course, this was true on the air, but it was also true within every staff meeting I ever attended. Yes, he might have something to say about an individual's personal qualities (never on the air) but never about their politics.

Finally, Jim thought there was a bright line that separated news reporting from commentary, and that was a line that he tried to maintain, although that sometimes seemed to be fuzzy. But he, himself, would not be a commentator or analyst. No correspondent would be a commentator, nor any staff member, and that included my attempt to write an essay. That would be left to guests.

And where did the Essays fit into that? They were clearly commentary, although they sought to be non-political in a partisan sense. Except for Roger Rosenblatt, no essayist was ever under contract to the *NewsHour*. I think Jim found he had to defend the presence of the essays to his friends and acquaintances in Washington, which included lobbyists, politicians, and Supreme Court justices far more often than he liked as partisan fervor increasingly took hold in the nation's capital, starting, in particular, with the Bush 43 election.

As for Robin, he fully subscribed to Jim's code. Their partnership and the show were based on their mutual convictions about how to conduct themselves and the show. Robin never voted if for no reason other than that he wasn't a citizen. He didn't become a citizen until 2 years after he retired. I never heard him express an opinion about either political party. Like Jim, he might talk in staff meetings about the personal qualities of individual politicians but never expressed views about their politics that I can remember.

Although they were sometimes attacked for being "liberals," whatever that meant, I have no idea about their real politics. If I were to guess, I'd say that Robin was more of a liberal than Jim and that Jim was more of a centrist Democrat or, maybe, a right-of-center Republican. Regardless, I never gave it a first, much less a second thought.

You will have noticed, I'm sure, that I've heaped a bunch of praise on both Robin and Jim, and I mean to praise them both. I had some criticisms of the show and thought some of the decisions made were wrong, but I never thought they were dishonest or made without some reason, usually understandable. Of all the pieces I produced for the show — over two thousand — none were rejected outright over my objections. There were two we disagreed about that I asked not to be aired, and there were a couple that just weren't good enough. And there was one (not an essay) that aired despite my objections, but that is a separate story altogether and had nothing to do with either anchor.

Perhaps a minor thing, but over time I came to believe that they were too generous in assessing our audience, thinking that it was better informed than was justified. Most people don't read a major newspaper every day, no matter how well educated or intelligent. They don't even watch the network news shows every night. After cable news shows debuted, comparatively few people watched their actual news broadcasts during the day. In the evenings, there was little pretense that they were anything other than commentary and evolved into pure propaganda. Not that they weren't useful, but still …

In moving from the ½ hour show to the hour, we had the ironic result of a single topic with three or four guests being reduced to 6 to 10-minute segments devoted to a topic with two guests. More time = less time. Huh? Was the entire premise of the ½ show wrong? I didn't think so.

Increasingly, as politicians clung to their talking points, discussions became less valuable, particularly since there weren't other voices to challenge them. And even if there were conflicting points, they'd just stick to those bullet points in their briefing books. And neither Robin nor Jim was willing to challenge their guests. Robin always said that he thought our audience was well-informed enough to know when guests were dissembling, avoiding, or lying, and he didn't need to point it out. I thought he was giving the audience a bit too much credit.

I found this particularly galling after the events of 9/11 when we seemed far too accepting of the Bush administration's view of the world. In the lead-up to the wars in Afghanistan and Iraq, we never seemed to challenge administration spokesmen. Nor did we during the course of those wars. In the early days of the Iraq war, I wanted questions to be asked that never were. Not that I expected forthright answers or honesty from government officials, but asking the questions mattered. I sent a couple of memos regarding war-related questions, but they disappeared into a black hole. But, of course, Jim was running things by then, and I have no idea if things would have been different if Robin was still there. Could it be that Jim, the ex-Marine, found it difficult to challenge the commander-in-chief, his subordinates, or his military officers? On the other hand, with Robin at the helm, I would have been in the planning meetings and had the opportunity to suggest the questions directly, and he would have responded to them one way or another.

Sour grapes? Maybe. But it does illustrate the difference for me between the pre and post-1995 *NewsHour.*

The move to typically two guests in the hour show had the ironic result of helping nudge political discussion in Washington to two sides without room for divergent points of view when politics were becoming ever more partisan, binary, and unpleasantly adversarial. I never thought that was a goal of the show nor useful to our viewers.

Robin had often said of the ½ hour show that people should watch the network news shows and then turn to us for a fuller explanation of the day's top news story. With the move to the hour, the premise of the show changed. One didn't need to watch the network news broadcasts and should just turn to us because we usually covered the same stories but with more depth. But the depth was too often an illusion. For example, if you read the first three paragraphs about the same story in the *NY Times*, you'd probably get as much information as in the five to ten-minute discussion with two people. Too often, it was not enough.

Whatever flaws I saw in the show were outweighed by both Robin and Jim's strict adherence to their abiding principle of what the real meaning of "fair and balanced" was and the insistence on draining passionate advocacy from the show. No heat but light. And no covering a subject just because our audience might want to see our take on it. We didn't, for example, cover the OJ Simpson trial, which America and the TV media were obsessed with. Maybe we did one show at the beginning, one in the middle, and one at the end, but that was it. On the other hand, at least some of the staff (including me) watched every minute of the trial we could. Somewhere, I thought, there could be something of a balance between what I thought and what they thought. If, however, it was a choice between the way I would have run things and the way they did, theirs was probably the better, or at least safer, option.

Perhaps, even more, it was a way to preserve the show's longevity, which really meant keeping the staff's jobs. Jim often referred to his employees as "family." Of course, like many families, it had its dysfunctional aspects, but he (and Robin, too) were always concerned about the welfare of their employees. Salaries were always fair within the public television context. They instituted a pension plan, and health insurance was first-rate (even if increasingly costly to employees). The people they hired were universally excellent, and if someone didn't work out, they were slow to fire them. And the show has certainly lasted. It might have long since been canceled if I had been running it in line with my thinking.

On the other hand, there are always stories that deserve coverage that don't get it. A news program, after all, has a limited amount of time and resources; it has to make choices. After either 9/11 or the second Iraq war, when we had been devoting the entire program for days on end to those events and were doing no essays, the program finally started covering other stories. Roger and I did an essay about all the important stories we had missed during the interim. There were a lot of them.

I don't know what the *PBS NewsHour* did during the Trump years because I wasn't watching. But the news cable networks seemed to devote all their time to Trump and his carryings-on. With all the seeming time in the world, it was all Trump all the time. Most of what his administration and regulatory agencies were doing were barely mentioned. I don't think they had many choices because of how Trump governed. If one network — Fox — became a propaganda outlet for the president, MSNBC was almost forced to become the opposite. Neither was healthy for the country. I have no idea how they will evolve in the future, but I'm not optimistic. Once you become a propaganda machine, it can be hard to find your way back to real, responsible journalism.

If you think Jim's principles and the show's principles under both Robin and Jim were ignored by the Washington political establishment, you'd be wrong. Just consider the following: There isn't a network or cable news anchor, all of whom were far better known and had far more press than Jim, who moderated more presidential debates than Jim. He was so highly regarded for his integrity, fairness, and even-handedness that he was asked to moderate thirteen of them. No one else came close.

Jim's non-confrontational style may have been part of the reason he was so acceptable to both political parties. Debate moderators are in at least one unfortunate position. Virtually no matter how they act, someone will fault their performance. Sometimes they will deserve the criticism. But sometimes, it is just someone trying to make political hay out of their own poor performance.

In the context of the show's entire existence, my criticisms are pretty minor. Unless one reads at least one major newspaper a day (and these days I only include the *NY Times* and the *Washington Post)*, at least for national news, and a local paper regardless of the size, the *NewsHour* in any of its iterations, was the most reliable single source of news available to anyone in this country. Of course, it's no trick to find opinions and commentary that either differ or agree with your own beliefs. That's what the cable news networks and most digital news outlets have decided to provide. But straight news in the evening that is fair, reliable, at least somewhat expansive, and generally non-political or ideological in its presentation is much harder to find. And the *NewsHour* was the most reliable place to find it while I was there, certainly on TV. Under Judy Woodruff's direction, I'm sure that's still the case.

During my final years at the *NewsHour*, many things happened, some pleasant, some less so. There were occasional periods when there were no essays whatsoever, particularly in the immediate aftermath of 9/11. I was at home in NY working at the computer when I got a phone call from Alicia, Lee's daughter. "You have to turn on the TV. Right now!" And so I rushed to the TV just in time to see a plane crash into the second tower of the World Trade Center. Alicia, as it happened, was going to work on the last subway train to stop at the station beneath the towers and had made it out just in time. I called Les and said that I was in NYC and ready to help in any way they needed. He said they didn't need my help. Eventually, they asked me to oversee a couple of interconnects with the new headquarters of WNET, but that's all.

Like everyone else in America, I was stunned by the tragedy at the World Trade Center, and I tried to figure out a way to deal with that odd combination of feelings that I think many Americans felt. The push and pull of it. Being pulled toward the horror and being repelled by it simultaneously. I had seen some of the photos taken of the event, some of them taken by the best photojournalists in America, some by ordinary people. A couple of people I knew were collecting all the photos they could and putting together an exhibition in a storefront in Soho. It was called "Here is New York."

There were thousands of pictures, many hung on wires like a clothesline and others piled in cartons. Many were extraordinary, and I wanted to do something with them for the *NewsHour*. I thought back to the Armenian earthquake in 1987. I had managed to convince Les to let me try something, a series of still photos to be shown with no narration but a classical musical background by an Armenian composer that conveyed the breadth of the disaster and the profound personal loss. He agreed, and I created a visual/non-verbal essay that did what I thought it would. It was highly effective. I took what I learned from that experience and carried it into the films I made for the Wiesenthal Center's Museum of Tolerance.

And then, after 9/11, I asked to try it again. Les agreed. Still images of the towers falling, firemen digging in the rubble with smoke and dust still rising, of the American flag atop the Brooklyn Bridge still flying, people fleeing and the terror in their eyes, the candlelit nighttime vigils in Union Square, the posters on the walls of people still missing, a cemetery with the smoke rising from the towers in the far distance, of a rose on a smashed car. And I searched for music that would say what I felt when looking at all this, at the images, at the smell of the burning wreckage still permeating the air, of that push and pull that I felt. Finally, I found it in an unexpected place. A song by the Irish singer, Enya. The song was "Evening Falls."

> **When the evening falls**
> **And the daylight is fading**
> **From within me calls**
> **Could it be I am sleeping?**

> For a moment I stray
> Then it holds me completely
> Close to home, I cannot say
> Close to home, feeling so far away

"Close to home, feeling so far away." The line encapsulated what I was feeling and what I thought others — those who lived in NY and those who did not — might be feeling as well. I thought then and now that this was one of the finest things ever produced by the *NewsHour*. In a way, I saw it as a gift to our viewers, at least for those who felt the same way I did, and found it articulated, though unspoken other than through the images along with Enya's voice, lyrics, and melody. It is one of the few pieces produced for the *NewsHour* that had more than one airing.

Les decided that it could not run labeled as an essay and had Ray Suarez, one of the show's correspondents, introduce the piece saying that it was about the exhibit, which, of course, it was but was not. As in the 1987 Armenian earthquake piece, I had found a way to sidestep the prohibition against staff members writing essays. Although I tried, it was not a device I was ever allowed to use again.

As the years went on, essayists came and went. Phyllis Theroux, Amei Wallach, and Jim Fisher dropped away as the essays became scarcer.

On the other hand, starting in 2005, I was finally given permission to bring on other essayists.

Chris Rose was the first. The New Orleans newspaper columnist whose extraordinary columns about the horrors, tragedies, and absurdities of Hurricane Katrina were memorably collected and published as *One Dead in the Attic*, wrote a string of exceptional essays for us about The Big Easy in the hurricane's aftermath. Not many writers can pack so much fact and feeling, so much punch into so few words.

Julia Keller, at the time a Pulitzer Prize-winning feature writer for the *Chicago Tribune*, came on board as an essayist in 2006 and stayed until the essays died. She's since left the newspaper business and is now a full-time writer of crime fiction set in the Appalachians where she was born.

Nancy Gibbs, who had taken over Roger Rosenblatt's old essay writing spot for *Time,* also joined us in 2006. One of her essays, "Miracle Workers," is still one of my all-time favorite pieces. We went into the elementary school classroom of Marguerite Izzo, who had won New York's Teacher of the Year Award.

Marguerite said, "I can remember being on the steps in my elementary school, thinking about the incredible power that a teacher has. And I wanted to be that powerful person. I wanted to make children's lives better. I wanted to make children think beyond what they had; thought they were capable of."

Watching her in action with her fifth graders, I thought she, indeed, might be a miracle worker and couldn't help but wonder if even she would have been able to break through whatever barriers I had had as a student.

Today, Nancy is Director of the Shorenstein Center on Media, Politics, and Public Policy at Harvard.

Scott McMillion was a newspaper reporter for Montana's *Bozeman Daily Chronicle.* We met because my son and his family were living in Bozeman. I was always interested in finding essayists in the west, a place far different than my more usual haunts of the east and west coasts, as I had discovered over the years, beginning with my ex-wife's Las Vegas family. So why not Montana? Described by writer William Kitteridge as "The Last Best Place," the question Scott was trying to answer was, "Is The Last Best Place still the last best place." If we're not careful, he said, "The last best place might become just another place."

Scott is now the editor of *Montana Quarterly.*

John Edgar Wideman, the PEN/Faulkner award-winning novelist, took us to Homewood, the neighborhood in Pittsburgh where he grew up, a place he'd left 40 years before. "Pittsburgh, [is] balkanized by three rivers and abrupt, steep hills, an abundance of tunnels and bridges divided as much as connected the city's diverse inhabitants. Detente, rather than interpenetration, except in the still of the night, characterized relationships among its cultures."

Pittsburgh, of course, is famously the hometown of August Wilson, one of America's greatest playwrights, and the setting of his "Pittsburgh Cycle" of plays. He was a friend of my sister, and she had directed a couple of early versions of his plays when she was spending summers at the National Playwrights Conference at the Eugene O'Neill Theater in Connecticut. I had met Wilson at a Passover seder of Amy's and used that as a way to get in touch with him later. So, with the agreement of MacNeil/Lehrer Productions, Amy and I flew to Pittsburgh to see a production of *Jitney* and then to talk to August. We told him that M/LP would get him 2 hours of airtime on PBS to do almost anything he'd like. After thinking about it for a while, he turned us down, not because he wasn't intrigued but because we weren't Black. Too bad. Though we understood and even sympathized with the reasons for his rejection, I think we all missed out on something that had the potential to be pretty special.

Jeff Brown, *NewsHour* correspondent for the arts, and I visited novelist Philip Roth for an interview in 2004 after the publication of *The Plot Against America.* The interview was substantial and interesting enough that it ran in two parts. Although there was no indication from Roth that he foresaw a Trump-like figure in our future, the dangers of a Charles Lindbergh-like politician couldn't have been that far from his imagination, could it? It hadn't been beyond Sinclair Lewis to imagine it in *It Can't Happen Here* and *Elmer Gantry* decades earlier.

Jeff and I also did an award-winning and lovely piece about John Patrick Shanley's Broadway play, *Doubt.* It was fun to shoot the performance and interview the actors and Shanley. However, what I found totally unexpected was Shanley's apartment in Brooklyn Heights. It was the same building that my elementary and high school friend Judy Flynn had lived in fifty years before, as had her sister, who later became Bob Maynard's first wife. Not only that, but it felt like the same apartment. Weird, yes?

In June 2007, I produced a couple of stories about mental health with Susan Dentzer, the *NewsHour's* medical correspondent, that had gone very well. Then, in October, Les asked me to produce a series of panel interviews concerning the views of prospective presidential candidates about health care. These were live-streamed on the internet leading up to the presidential nominating conventions and broadcast remotely from downtown DC. Susan and a panel of medical journalists from the Wall Street Journal, Washington Post, and ABC interviewed one candidate per broadcast. We talked to Hillary Clinton, Joe Biden, John McCain, Dennis Kucinich, and John Edwards. Barack Obama was the only major candidate to turn us down. But, of course, he became the Democratic nominee and president.

Those broadcasts were fun for me. Sure, there was a bit of anxiety, as there always is in a live production, and it is you who is on the line. But then again, everyone is on the line, from the moderator to the grip. You either get it done, or you don't. So it felt good to be back in a live control room with a clock counting down the seconds, a group of journalists who put their trust in me, a group of funders who had taken Les's word that I could be relied on, technicians and, in particular, a technical supervisor who would do all they could to help me do my job.

If ever I needed one, it was a reminder of how many people and pieces of electronic equipment have to mesh to get something on the air. Whether that something is good or bad is irrelevant. Live productions have so many moving parts, so many things that can go wrong, that it's kind of amazing that they happen at all. Yet, we all take them for granted as viewers, don't we? As producers, I think most of us take them for granted, too, but only up to a point. No matter the kind of production, no matter how small or large, no matter how well it seems to be going at the back of our minds, we are waiting for disaster to befall us at any moment and game planning what the response might be to any emergency. And sometimes, disaster does strike, whether it is as consequential as losing an audio feed in the 1976 Ford/Carter presidential debate or losing a program feed to an internet provider at the beginning of one of those 2007 health care live-streaming broadcasts. Don't be in the TV business if you're not willing to have stress in your working life.

For me and the essays, the stresses were of a different sort. The process of getting a writer to trust you enough to put his babies, his words, in your hands, trusting that you will understand what he is trying to say and that you will elevate rather than diminish what he is trying to communicate, that he will not look or sound like a fool, is only the beginning. Then, after working on the script with the writer (and each writer had to be handled differently because each writer is a different human being), it had to be submitted to Les, Robin, and Jim for their approval, which was almost always forthcoming. Although they might ask for changes from time to time, they were usually modest. Then, after shooting, after the PAs gathered the visual and audio elements I'd requested, it was time for the editing. And that, for me, was where the magic happened, where words and images came alive, where they became more than they were as individual things. That was where the lyrics and melody became a song.

And then there was something else, something I have yet to talk about. The audience. In particular, my responsibility to it. The morning after I won the Emmy, I walked through the plaza at 10 Columbus Circle on my way from the subway to our offices on 58th Street. The bright sunlight cut through the frosty morning air, bouncing off the hard concrete beneath my feet. I remember thinking that I wield enormous power, the power to make people — *millions* of people — feel something, to make them think something, to change their viewpoint or see something from another point of view, even if only for a few seconds. The feeling was visceral. Unthinkingly, I stopped in the middle of the plaza, my hand rising up in front of me, palm outstretched, holding ... Two million people (more or less) saw every piece I made. Sometimes the same people, sometimes different ones. Millions of people over the course of the years! What an extraordinary opportunity. An awesome responsibility! And I thought how important it was to use it wisely and with restraint. And then not to think of the audience when making something but to think only of the piece itself, making it as good as I could with the tools, time, and money available. Doing that was what I owed the writer, the audience, Robin and Jim, the rest of the *NewsHour* staff, and myself.

When I had to edit my first essay in Washington, my editor used a computerized editing system that I was unfamiliar with. I didn't know what it could or couldn't do. All I knew was that it was supposed to be able to do anything I wanted it to. I didn't realize at first that the equipment was pretty new to my editor as well. I was asking him to do things that he had never done before with the Avid editing system, and he was struggling. Rather than say he couldn't do it and ask me to simplify my requests, he asked me to let him figure it out.

It took him a week, but he eventually got it all to come out the way I wanted. There was another editor who I didn't initially get along with, mostly because he didn't like to admit there was something he didn't know how to do. Eventually, he figured it out too and became comfortable operating the tools we both needed, and we edited many complex pieces together.

Most of the editors who worked on my pieces gradually learned my ticks, my sense of timing, the way I liked to do my audio mixes and visual effects. Some usually cut the last-minute news packages for the show where speed was of the essence, and they found cutting my pieces hard because I was doing things in the editing room that most of our other producers weren't doing. I couldn't blame them for not knowing or feeling uncomfortable doing what I wanted. This is all a collaborative process. Like everybody else, from cameramen to production assistants, editors want to contribute whatever they can to the final product, not only because they have a job to do but because they love what they do and take pride in it. After all, that's why they do what they do, why they want to be in this business. If they couldn't hold up their end, they would feel embarrassed about their lack of skill.

After the editing was done, the final product would have to be approved before it aired. In NY, Robin, Les, and I screened most of my pieces together in Robin's office, and I would immediately know if they were approved or had to be fixed in some way (believe it or not, I don't think everything that I do is perfect). In Washington, things were different. I'd drop a screening copy of the essay off on Les's desk, and I'd hear whether it was approved or needed tweaking within a couple of days. Only on occasion would he say something to me about an essay after he approved it and before it aired. I once asked him why that was. He said that what I did was so excellent that the excellent had become normal, and there was no point in saying anything about it. About things that were even better than that, well, he would say something. Otherwise, no.

Or maybe he preferred not to say something until Jim saw the essay. Since Jim rarely screened any of the essays before he saw them on the air, it would be in the following morning's meeting if he had anything to say. I rarely heard anything about the essays from

Jim, even indirectly. If I heard anything, it would be via Les after the morning planning meeting, and then it was only if Jim had said something particularly critical, something that was very rare, or, only a bit less rarely, complimentary. He may have said other things, but Les would rarely repeat them. One day, Elizabeth Farnsworth, a San Francisco-based documentary maker who had been brought into the show, in part to be a substitute anchor for Jim, told me that Jim had said something particularly nice about one of my essays. I told her I hadn't heard about it.

"Doesn't anybody fill you in about what gets said in those meetings?"

"No. I never have any idea what's said about much of anything."

"Les never tells you?"

"No."

"I'll try to keep you in the loop."

And she did for a while, but that wasn't her job. It was Les's, and apparently, he didn't think it was necessary. Within weeks, Elizabeth's post-meeting phone calls became less and less frequent. Aside from this small event, we did one piece together, a lovely piece about a Cambodian sculpture exhibition. A beautiful script, beautiful camera shots, and a beautiful editing job. The rest didn't really matter. It was this that mattered. It's why we did what we did.

I once ran across Howard Weinberg, one of the two original producers on the *Robert MacNeil Report*, who had left the show many years before. He was now working as a producer for CBS News' *Sunday Morning*. I asked him if he ever heard about his pieces from Shad Northshield, the show's notoriously mercurial and ill-tempered executive producer. Howard said, "No, and, believe me, you hope not to." Maybe I should have been glad that I never heard from Jim. After all, he, too, could be notoriously short-tempered. Oh, you didn't know that about southern, genial gentleman Jim?

In all the years I was with the show, there was only one person I had a falling out with. The economics correspondent for many years was Paul Solman. Coincidentally, he, too, was a graduate of EI, my old high school. During the 2008 Great Recession and market crash, Les asked me to produce a couple of pieces with Paul explaining various aspects of the collapse, particularly the billions and billions worth of bonds largely based on sub-prime mortgages and other risky bets. They were good pieces in that they explained what had occurred no matter how irrational it all was. Supposedly highly sophisticated investors, Tom Wolfe's "Masters of the Universe," had made investments in bonds that made no sense. They got caught and dragged the rest of us down with them.

No matter. Paul and I had gotten along, so I was asked to do a couple of other pieces with him. We did one about a charter high school in California specializing in engineering. The school was inspiring.

Then there was another piece, this about the LA County school system. I set up several interviews, including one with someone from the county Board of Education. Paul arranged for us to shoot in a school where a relative of his was a teacher. The interview with his relative took place in a classroom filled with Latino students, all of whom were failing or had failed in math. With his students in front of him, the relative explained that they were really incapable of learning. We then interviewed the county's representative. He was a Mexican-American. Paul kept trying to get him to admit that Latino students could not learn, which might explain why county school performance was so poor. Paul pushed and pushed, increasingly confrontational, and the interviewee refused to go where Paul clearly wanted.

Paul ran out of the building to have dinner with someone as soon as the interview was over. The cameraman turned to me and said, "What was that?" I was aghast. I had no inkling that Paul was planning on conducting a hostile interview. I was also furious because I had arranged the interview and discussed what we would be asking about without having been told by Paul that the interview would really be about something else. When I got back to my hotel, I emailed Les, relating what had happened as I understood it, saying that it had violated every principle I had learned from Robin and that I felt Paul had not only sandbagged the interviewee but me as well. I sent a copy to Paul. The next day, Paul was furious. I should have talked to him and not sent an email to Les. "I'll conduct an interview any way I damn well like." We agreed he'd shoot the rest of the piece without me, and I returned to DC.

Les asked to see a transcript. He thought the interview seemed okay to him. I asked him to watch the interview, the actual version of what had happened. He said it wasn't necessary. Then he asked me to edit the piece. I said that I wouldn't, that I thought it was a deliberate distortion of reality, that it had as a thesis that Latino kids couldn't learn. He said that I didn't have a choice about editing it. In effect, I was being told to either edit it or resign. I said I'd edit it long as my name did not appear on it as the producer or anything else. He agreed, and I edited it as Paul wanted. It aired. Neither Paul nor I were willing to work with each other again.

To this day, I think that Les didn't want to screen the original tapes because he might feel compelled to agree with me. And if that happened, it was sure to be escalated to Jim to adjudicate, and Paul had long seemed to be a favorite of Jim's. Besides, by then, Les knew my days at the show were numbered, partly because of age, partly because Jim had decided that the essays had to go.

The first Iraq War, that of George H.W. Bush, provided the initial impetus to decrease the number of essays we were airing. The second Iraq War, that of George W. Bush, provided another. Increasing budget pressures on the show provided still another. As the number of essays decreased, I was pressed to reduce their length. Roger Rosenblatt's "What Should We Lead With," the first real essay for me, was seven minutes long. By the time I left the show, I was told their ideal length was three to four minutes. It is hard to make any complex, nuanced argument in that short time. Perhaps that was the point.

When Bush 43 was elected, and increasingly radical right-wing politicians came to Washington, PBS's federal funding was constantly threatened, just as it is today when any Republican is elected president. As partisan politics increasingly engulfed the capital, more and more issues, particularly cultural ones, became nationalized. It seemed that there gradually came to be more and more subject areas that the essayists and I weren't allowed to deal with or, at best, had to tiptoe around, issues that Jim felt had to be reserved for the rest of the show. They were now *Washington* issues. During the Bush and Obama years, I asked if the show, and the essays, in particular, were being pressured by the right-wing. I was told that wasn't the case; I didn't believe it. It was right and proper for Jim and Les to try and protect us from feeling political pressure, and I'm sure it was there.

The essays were artfully and powerfully made commentaries and the only segment of the show for which there wasn't a built-in counter-argument. However, since the foundational premise of the show was that there are at least two sides to every story, I couldn't help but wonder if Jim didn't feel that defending the essays was worth it.

In 2005 Linda Winslow became the show's Executive Producer, and Les became the President of MacNeil/Lehrer Productions. I think she was the one who told me in 2007 or maybe early 2008 that Jim wanted to end the essays at the end of the broadcast year (the broadcast year running from September through August). The reason, she said, was budgetary constraints. It was a plausible reason. After all, salaries had already been frozen, the show's contribution to the employee retirement plan had been eliminated, and the employees' share of medical insurance costs were continually rising, particularly for those who had families. Add to that my salary and the salaries of my assistant, staff camera crews and editors, visual and audio elements, etc., amounted to a considerable amount of money. But, for what it's worth, Jim never thought it necessary to explain to me why he thought the essays should be abandoned. Nor did Linda. The decision was the decision.

I asked if they could continue if I could raise the money. Linda agreed, and I contacted Roger Rosenblatt, who had left the show the previous year, and asked if he had any suggestions. It turned out that he did; he knew someone who had a foundation that was liquidating. After we met with the potential funder, he agreed to give us $100,000 towards producing the essays. The money could be used for the outside expenses, that is, the fees for the essayists, freelance camera crews, the purchasing of visual and audio elements, along with travel expenses. The show would pick up the rest of the costs, meaning the salaries of my assistant and me and the technical staff and facilities of WETA. Through various savings in the way I was shooting things and purchasing visual elements, I managed to stretch the money to cover the costs of an additional twenty-seven pieces.

In 2008, Linda asked if I had given any thought to retirement since the essays were being eliminated. Of course, I had. After all,

I was 68. Driving every week between DC and Copake (I was typically driving between 800 and 1,000 miles most weekends regardless of the weather), and spending four nights a week in the DC apartment unless I was in LA, San Francisco, or somewhere else was no fun. I might have actually said that I'd retire immediately if the stock market hadn't crashed, something that put a big dent in my retirement savings. So, I told her that I'd thought about it but hadn't made any plans.

Once in a rare while, she'd urge me to seriously consider retirement. She wanted to know when the money from the grant would run out, which would force the end of the essays. However, she had made no proposal herself about what retirement would mean by this point. Even more, she never offered a specific role in the show if I wasn't going to retire. The next time it was brought up, I said, "What are you offering?" She had no answer and said she'd get back to me. To this day, I wonder if she had expected me to simply disappear, but I've never asked. Finally, she got back to me with a package of retirement benefits that seemed fair, and I gave her a date, March 18th, 2009.

On March 17th, I finished editing my final essay, one by Julia Keller. It ran 3:56. Of all the essayists, Julia's pieces almost always managed to stay within the three to four-minute mark that the show preferred. That evening Linda and Les took me to a farewell dinner with the other senior producers, my production assistant, and others who had worked closely with me. At the end of the meal, Linda said that Jim would like to see me the following morning before I left.

And so, at 11 am the following day, I arrived at Jim's office for what was one of the most bizarre and surprising conversations I'd ever had. I'm sorry I can't quote our dialog verbatim but what follows comes close in length and substance.

> **Jim: Uh, I guess at the beginning of the show, you had something to do with money.**
>
> **Me: Yes, that's right.**
>
> **Jim: Well, if we need a free-lance producer, you'll be at the top of the list.**
>
> **Me: I'd like that.**

Jim: Well, Good luck.
Me: Thanks.

And that was it. No mention of the Emmy, two Peabody Awards, the Cine Award for Jeff's piece about *Doubt*, the Gracie Award for Anne's essays, not to mention other nominations. No mention of Ruth Lo, La Grange, or our first Presidential Debate coverage. No mention of the hundreds upon hundreds of essays I'd produced and the role they'd played in the show, of the way they'd enhanced the show and its reputation. No word about the William Morris agent I'd introduced him to who represented the show and M/LP for many years. No mention of the effort I'd made to get the staff to vote against unionization, which he had adamantly opposed. No mention of the thirty-four years I'd dedicated to his and Robin's interests. No mention of anything. The past was a blank slate aside from the fact I once had something to do with money.

Do you suppose it was a momentary lapse of his memory, a moment of senioritis? I thought Jim's on-screen performance had been slipping for several years, his mind not as quick or agile as it once was, and he really had forgotten the past at that moment. Were there other reasons? Perhaps.

Perhaps Jim felt that I had slighted him somehow, just as Howard Weinberg had been accused of doing long ago by Jim's wife. Still living in NY despite my apartment a few minutes away from the *NewsHour's* offices, not going to his Christmas parties or the White House Correspondents dinners, or something else. Who knows? Thin-skinned people can be ... well, pretty thin-skinned.

Or perhaps it was the purest reflection of his opinion about the value of producers — that they really didn't matter all that much — and that my role as the initial production supervisor (including budget management) had been far more significant.

All pointless speculation, don't you think? The bottom line is Jim had asked for this meeting, and it had served no purpose other than to piss me off and confirm I no longer belonged on this show or with Jim. By 11:15, I'd said goodbye to everyone I wanted to and left the building and Washington for the last time.

The road was leading me home.

Chapter 17

THE WATER'S EDGE

◆

2009 – 2021

On May 16, 1987, Penny Stallings, Lee, and I went to see the live broadcast of *Saturday Night Live*. Gary Shandling was the host. The cold opening sketch was fabulous: Robert McFarlane testifying in front of the Senate committee investigating the Iran/Contra affair, the same McFarlane who Roger Rosenblatt once noted tried to kill himself for his reasons and not ours.

Most extraordinary, though, was not Shandling or any of the now legendary comics who first entered our homes during the heyday of *SNL*. No, it was that guitar riff, the one that gave me goosebumps, and still does, the opening of Los Lobos' "One Time, One Night," a song about the tragic immigrant experience in America as only they could write and sing it.

A wise man was telling stories to me
About the places he had been to and the
things that he had seen
A quiet voice is singing something to me
An age-old song 'bout the home of the brave
in this land here of the free
One time one night in America

In August, just three months later, Penny and I went to Graceland for the 10th anniversary of Elvis Presley's death. We stood and watched the long lines of now blue-haired old ladies — old ladies who had once been teenage girls screaming at his mere presence, old ladies who had once been middle-aged women clutching at the scarves he tossed into the audience in a Las Vegas showroom — old

415

ladies we now watched as they silently, slowly filed past his grave at two in the morning. Robin had asked, "Does anyone even care about him anymore?" Oh, yes, Robin, they do, they do, as I heard the sound of Paul Simon's "Graceland" playing in my head.

> **The Mississippi Delta**
> **Was shining like a national guitar**
> **I am following the river**
> **Down the highway**
> **Through the cradle of the Civil War**
>
> **I'm going to Graceland, Graceland**
> **Memphis, Tennessee**
> **I'm going to Graceland**
> **Poor boys and pilgrims with families**
> **And we are going to Graceland**

The Magical Mystery Tour along the winding road may have ended for me, but it lives on in my memory if nowhere else. No matter what else I might say about Robin and Jim, they gave me extraordinary freedom. They may never have known quite what to do with me because I never fit into an easily defined and recognizable journalistic role for them, at least not one that matched their definition of what the show and a journalist should be. I was always something of a square peg in a round hole, being inside the show but outside it as well, both literally and figuratively. Despite this, they allowed me to discover what I could do within the show's confines and discover what I was capable of. That accrued to their benefit as well as mine.

What Robin and Jim did most of all, the gift they gave me, even if they didn't know what a gift it was, was to allow me to look at America, to look for America. With their support, I traveled wide ...

> **From the dying remains of the Kansas City Stockyards to the glittering Arabian horse auction in Scottsdale.**
> **From a young woman playing the massive organ in the dim loft of New York's Cathedral of St. John the Divine to a retired nun playing the piano in the spare, sunlit auditorium of a Sisters of Mercy convent in California.**

From the flood-ravaged 9th Ward in New Orleans to the moisture-starved Black Hills of South Dakota.

From the craggy island off the coast of Maine where Jack Perkins lived to the rocky promontory above Big Sur where Robinson Jeffers once wrote his muscular poetry.

From the playground for the wealthy and celebrities in Montana's Big Sky country to students of the working poor in a school just around the corner.

From the glittering Frank Gehry-designed Walt Disney Music Hall in downtown LA to the still reeking wreckage of the World Trade Center in downtown Manhattan.

From a thriving working-class Hispanic evangelical church in East Palo Alto to the shuttering of a Catholic church in San Francisco to a wooden orthodox synagogue in the Bay area, a replica of a once-prominent synagogue in Poland before the Holocaust.

From sleeping one afternoon in a luxurious bed of the Georges V hotel on the way to Tehran to sleeping in a chair in the lobby of a rural Mississippi motel while a hurricane howled outside as Robin and I made our way to the torna-do-torn Mississippi coast.

And a street corner on Manhattan's Upper West Side where a homeless man had set up his living room with a rug, an easy chair, and a lamp hooked up to a street light as he waited to welcome visitors.

So many things, so many *more* things left unmentioned. Hundreds of stories could still be told. Too many for any one book. They filled my life with room to spare.

Here's a question you might ask. With all that looking, seeing, experiencing, did you ever find America? No, not really. America is not one thing. It is everything, ever-changing, ever-becoming. There's too much I still don't know, still discovering. But I'm still looking, still trying to understand all I saw, all that I am still seeing. And I still know that you will never find it sitting in Washington, DC, or New York City. No matter where you stand in the country, no matter what city, what cornfield, what mountain top, America will look different than it does from the news desks in those two cities.

Here's another question. Did you ever make a perfect piece? No, I did not. I remember the story I did about the aging Katie Lee. It was nine minutes long because she sang such a lovely song for us about time and age as a river that I couldn't bear to cut it as I intercut it with her talking about the long stream of her life. Les had suggested I shorten it but was willing to let it air as is. I watched it again some twenty-five years later and walked into Les's office. "You know, you were right about Katie. It was too long." He smiled. But he still remembered it.

I wince if I ever look at something I made long after its completion. It's almost painful. This silent space isn't long enough, or it's too long. This cut happens too fast. The scene should have been longer or shorter. This picture should be better. Why didn't I shoot this or that? The lighting's wrong. The audio track is too muddy. This word isn't right; that sentence should be easier to understand; maybe we should have just rewritten the whole damned thing.

Perfection is not possible. We reach for it but never find it. But we always reach.

After retiring in 2009, I didn't do much of anything for many years; I just wanted to stop. In 2018, the publisher of the Hudson Register-Star, a paper in the biggest town nearest our house in Copake, where I spend most of my time these days, said that if I ever wanted to send him something, he would like to see it. Timing is everything, isn't it? A couple of months later, I sent him something. An essay. And I kept sending them, not every day or every week or even every month, but I send them, and the paper publishes them. After the January 6th insurrection at the capital, I wrote a series of eight essays for the paper, trying to understand how we got to that tragic event. I published them in a booklet; it's still for sale through Amazon. Some people actually bought it.

The point of this is simple or complicated depending on how you look at it (isn't that true of most things?). I recently searched through the *NewsHour*'s online database and discovered three things.

1) There are no texts for the essays or anything else I did available before 2000. So nothing I did before then can be read.

2) No essays (or anything else) can be viewed the way they were meant to be seen and so are incomplete, only the beginning of the creation; they are the words without the music; there is no song. You cannot *see* any of my work.

3) How's this for irony: You can search for my name on Amazon and find my short booklet of eight essays. However, when I searched the *NewsHour* database, there was no mention of me despite everything I did. I'm a ghost.

> *I am sitting at the computer in my office in Copake, looking out the wide bay window. It is early morning, the sun creeping above the trees in the east, gradually spilling its light across the hills and the pond that is spread out before me. The light first touches the tips of the trees at the top of the hill and then gradually flows down the hillside. It glides over the grasses along the shore, then floats across the pond ever-so-slowly. A white-tailed doe meanders across the lawn followed by her two fawns, all nibbling on the grass before quietly slipping into the brush at the side of the field. A rabbit sits quietly, its nose twitching, hoping not to be noticed. Two red-tailed hawks swoop through the blue sky. A heron stands on one foot as still as a statue at the near edge of the pond. The leaves of the trees and shrubs flutter in the breeze that also stirs the water ever so slightly. A flock of honking geese crashes down onto the pond, sudden ripples fanning out. A buck stands in the water at the far side, drinking, water rippling as his nose ducks beneath the surface.*
>
> *The ripples move across the wide water. They intersect with each other, conflict with each other, meld with each other, reach for the rushes along the shore.*
>
> *I watch all this, the muted horn of Gil Evans' "Where Flamingos Fly" murmuring in the background. There are ghosts, all the ghosts of my life. Eliakum and Shomer. Grandma and Grandpa. Mom and Dad. Herman and*

Peggy, and so many more. They are all there, some-where. If I listen hard enough, I can hear their whispers, all singing the same song.

Say something real, true, heartfelt.

ACKNOWLEDGMENTS

◆

No book, no television show, no life exists entirely independently, no matter how many of us like to think it does. This book, in particular, could not have been written, my professional life could not have been lived without the help of an enormous number of people along the way. I've not wanted to burden you, the reader, with keeping track of the plethora of names of people without whom I never could have achieved anything.

That said, there are particular individuals aside from Robin and Jim (do you think I'm still trying to make up for forgetting to thank them when I won an Emmy?) who I'd like to specifically mention. And if I haven't mentioned your name, I apologize in advance. But that doesn't mean I don't know what you did for me.

Nancy Nichols was the reporter who helped me find the people that inhabited many of those early features. Though never seen or heard on camera, she conducted the interviews with people like Frank Herbert, Robert Motherwell, Eudora Welty, and Jeff Cooper. We would have long discussions about what questions to ask. She would stay with me in the office at night while editing the transcripts and, in so doing, helped me find my voice.

Meagan Crowley was my first production assistant for the features and essays. She was followed by Carolyn Goldman, Michelle Acevedo, Demetria Galleagos, Mike Million, Dave Coles, Nicole Vinnola, Hillary LeBon, Beth Summers, Jessica Biggs, Emily Birr, Adela Maskova, and Stephen Fee. Julie Klapper was first a PA and then an associate producer along with Kate Olson during the essays' most prolific period. There is not a single one of them who wasn't extraordinary. They were all different, all singularly dedicated, and I could not possibly have done what I did without them.

There were the video editors in New York who worked on most of my pieces. In particular, there was Ruth Pohl, along with Lewis Erskine and Marcie Turman. In Washington, there was Dan Knapp and John Morgan, among others. And though he left not long after the move to DC, there was Ben Howard with whom I first began to discover what digital software could do.

There were the camera crews at WNET, WETA, the M/L Denver office, and all the free-lancers over the years. I think of names like Bill McMillan and Bill Ruth, who worked on almost all my early features and essays. And Johnny and Patty Sharaf, who shot dozens of pieces for me in LA. But also Jim van Vranken out of Denver and Bobby Long and Greg Barna in New York, and Charlie Ide and Jeff Rathner in Washington. Then, out of San Francisco, Bob Goldsborough and his group along with Al Lopez and Larry Warner. There are so many people all over the country. They all tried to accomplish whatever I asked of them.

The graphic artists Cathe Ishino, Calvin Soloman, and the other artists in their departments in NY and DC helped with the look and feel of the essays (and helped watch over Alicia when, as a young child, she'd come to work with me).

And, of course, there was Duke Struck and Judi Elterman along with all the studio technicians and video engineers, the directors and assistant directors, lighting designers, stage managers, makeup artists, and all the others, particularly at WNET. All of them played a role in my career.

And then there are the writers, all 57 of them, "my" essayists, who wrote for the *NewsHour.* And the others who didn't work out because, perhaps, I wasn't skillful or clever enough to properly present them to Robin and/or Jim.

In particular, though, Roger Rosenblatt, Anne Taylor Fleming, Richard Rodriguez, Jim Fisher, and Clarence Page deserve all the accolades I can shower on them. They formed the backbone of the essays. They were a true band of brothers even as they were scattered all over this big country and barely knew each other. But, even more than their wisdom, curiosity, and skill, their friendship meant the world to me then and now.

Finally, we get to the book itself as a thing. It would not exist were it not for Amy, my sister, who said at precisely the right moment, "Why don't you write a book about *MacNeil/Lehrer*?" Since she'd suggested it once or twice over the years, suggestions that I ignored, I have no idea why this time was the right time, but it was.

Gerry Margolis read every word of every draft, asked particularly useful questions, and made helpful suggestions. But, more importantly, he was willing to talk about what I was doing almost endlessly.

My very long-time friend, Terry McKay, read a late draft with her usual intelligence and taste and made some particularly astute observations.

Michelle, my daughter, cast her unusually sensitive and discerning eye over every word in the manuscript. The fact that she is my daughter did not prevent her from pointing out things that needed to be considered. And I'm glad to say that as her father, I happily considered all of them.

And then there is Glen Edelstein, the book's designer — its cover and interior formatting. His enthusiasm for the project and the *NewsHour* made him the perfect choice for this task. It was the first step in putting this accumulation of 0s and 1s residing in some mysterious cloud into the physical universe. Believe me, that's a giant leap.

Last but never least and always first, there is Lee Garro, my wife. We joined our individual roads just weeks before the *NewsHour*'s birth and have been traveling together ever since.

And I cannot leave out Max, our great big bullmastiff, who patiently lay down or snored by my side through all the months it took to create this book.

Finally, there's you, the reader. What is a TV producer or a writer — any artist, really — without an audience? Knowingly or not, you have always been a part of what I have done.

ABOUT THE AUTHOR

MICHAEL SALTZ, the winner of an Emmy, among other awards, was a senior producer with PBS's *The MacNeil/Lehrer NewsHour*. Beginning with *The Robert MacNeil Report* in 1974, he retired in 2009 as a senior producer for *The NewsHour with Jim Lehrer*, the show's final iteration before becoming *The PBS NewsHour*. With over 40 years of experience in the television industry, Saltz has been involved in practically every facet of television public affairs production as producer, director, writer, editor, and production manager. In recent years, he has spent much of his time writing, reading, and doing whatever retired people do at his home in upstate New York, accompanied by his wife and dog. He intermittently contributes op-ed columns to his local paper, *The Hudson Register-Star*. A collection of some of those columns, *Down the Rabbit Hole: How We Got to the January 6th Insurrection*, is available on Amazon.com. In addition, he is on the board of directors of School Life Media, an organization that teaches journalism — its practice and ethics — to children in the public school system.